From Many, One

From Many, One

Readings in American
Political and Social Thought

EDITED BY

RICHARD C. SINOPOLI

GEORGETOWN UNIVERSITY PRESS / WASHINGTON, D.C.

Georgetown University Press, Washington, D.C. 20007
© 1997 by Georgetown University Press. All rights reserved.

10 9 8 7 6 5 4 3 2 1   1997

THIS VOLUME IS PRINTED ON ACID-FREE ⊗ OFFSET BOOK PAPER

Library of Congress Cataloging-in-Publication Data

From many, one : readings in American political and social
thought /
    edited by Richard C. Sinopoli.
        p.   cm.
     1. Political science—United States—History. 2. Civil rights—
United States—History. 3. Religion and politics—United States—
History.   I. Sinopoli, Richard C.
JA84.U5F76   1997
320'.01'1—dc20   96-11854
ISBN 0-87840-626-3 (pbk.)

Contents

Acknowledgments

While always grateful to those who have contributed to my publications, I have never been more so than regarding this book. Putting together a volume of this sort is a more daunting task than I had realized, despite the advice and warnings of knowledgeable colleagues and friends. It could not have been completed without the support of the following people and institutions. Thanks go to the Institute of Governmental Affairs of UC–Davis, through which I was able to hire three very able undergraduate research assistants. Petra Lurie, Sonia Chavez, and Tracy Walling performed a variety of tasks, including entering texts on disks, proofreading, and bibliographic research. Perhaps most important, they were "guinea pigs" on whom I could test my intuitions about what undergraduates could and might enjoy to read. Thanks also go to the UC–Davis Humanities Institute, which provided me a leave, more of which went to work on this project than they may know. They also supported a graduate research assistant during the 1994–95 academic year, about whom more must be said in a moment. Numerous colleagues and graduate students at UC–Davis have provided useful advice, comments on various parts of the text, and information. Of these, Larry Peterman, Ed Costantini, Clarence Walker, John Bubba Gates, Jimmy Spriggs, Jeanette Money, Monte Freidig, and Heather Allen deserve mention. It was very helpful to have an editor, John Samples, with a background in and talent for political theory. Thanks go to him for asking me to do this project, and for his advice and patience along the way. Finally, my deepest appreciation goes to my graduate research assistant, coauthor of the last chapter, and friend, Teena Gabrielson. Teena has been involved in every aspect of this project from reviewing texts for selection, to assisting on and writing several introductions to the excerpts, to managing the numerous technical details that arose. Teena's keen insight, determination to see this through, and good cheer were truly indispensable to completing this project.

In the interest of making the readings in this volume as accessible as possible, archaic spelling, punctuation and capitalization of letters have been modernized in some documents. We have taken care, however, to see that the original meanings of the texts have not been altered.

Introductory Essay: From Many, One

There are many windows through which one can look at a subject as complex as the social and political thought found in the United States. The view we choose for this collection of readings looks upon a central question of American public life, a question that has taken many different forms throughout our history. How do we think about and act in politics upon the problem of the many and the one? So central to American politics is this question that it is expressed in what may well be the only bit of Latin most Americans know: *e pluribus unum*. From many, one.

Thinking About Diversity in America

Today the word "diversity," when used in a political context, is largely conceived in terms of difference in ethnicity, gender, and sexual orientations. It is worth remembering, however, that the United States has always been diverse in its diversities. We are a country made up of different peoples not only in terms of racial and ethnic origin, but of religious affiliation, state and regional identification and interests, urban versus rural upbringings, and occupational and class groupings. A key question for Americans long has been how—or whether—we seek to reconcile our many partial, communal identities with a single identity as Americans.

Does the African-American, for example, seek to live a life that is, as Dr. Martin Luther King, Jr. said, "deeply rooted in the American dream"? Does she, that is, seek the path of integration and full participation in the American political system, accepting its liberal, democratic, and capitalist norms? Or does she follow Marcus Garvey and his successors like Malcolm X, who preached black nationalism and separatism in rejecting these norms or, at least, the possibility of blacks and whites living under them as free, equal citizens? Does the immigrant to these shores seek to become what Theodore Roosevelt called, in an excerpt reprinted here, a "true American" by adopting the English language and American customs at the expense of those of her land of origin? Or does she seek somehow to maintain her status as what came to be called in the early part of this century a "Hyphenated American," i.e., one who maintains a cultural even if not a political allegiance to her former homeland?[1] Do nineteenth and early twentieth century women seek the vote so as to become equal to men in this important regard? Or is political

1

equality, in some sense, not enough—even perhaps a sham, because equality can obscure important differences? The latter view of gender relations and politics is adopted by contemporary radical feminists, represented here by Catharine MacKinnon and bell hooks. As a last example, how does the deeply religious person reconcile the duties generated from his faith with his obligations as a citizen when these conflict? We will see in Part Five a series of attempts from colonial times through the present to explore the tensions between church and state and the loyalties Americans owe to both.

This collection includes many texts that are often not included in readers on American political thought. Yet the questions raised by them are central to understanding the American political tradition. So much of that tradition has revolved around considerations of *inclusion* and *exclusion*, of whether and/or how the American conception of democracy could be expanded to allow in the previously excluded. And each time this question arises, whether having to do with the end of slavery and the Civil War Amendments to the Constitution, the struggle over the vote for women, or responses to immigration throughout our history, it invites a reconsideration of what it means to be a democratic citizen of the United States. Further, each time an excluded group considers whether to *assimilate*, *accommodate*, or *separate*, they too must reflect upon what their particular identity means and how it relates to their role in the broader public.[2]

Inclusion, and its antonym *exclusion*, form a key pair of concepts for framing the readings to follow. Another key concept to keep in mind while reading this collection is *identity*. Many of our authors ask directly what it means to be an American. This question often has had a direct political relevance, as it did during the American Revolution when revolutionaries sought to identify themselves as something other than British subjects. One way this was done is witnessed in the Declaration of Independence, where Jefferson suggests that an aspect of American uniqueness is a commitment to universal principle. Americans are such not by ties to blood and soil, sources of identification in the old world, but by attachment to a set of political ideas and ideals. "All men," Jefferson writes, "are endowed by their Creator with certain unalienable rights, that among these are life, liberty and the pursuit of happiness." The American Revolution, he suggests, is being fought to uphold these principles that apply to "all men" but have special resonance for those once-British subjects, the Americans.

Jefferson points to one answer of what it means to be an American, but there are others that have been posed to address somewhat different questions. How are Americans different not only from Europeans but from any people that has come before? Did the passage across the Atlantic that early Americans took—some voluntarily and others not—"strip off the garments of civilization," as the historian Frederick Jackson Turner once argued, and form us into a unique breed of human? Does an American, as French emigre Hector St. John de Crevecoeur put it in the late eighteenth century, leave "behind him all his ancient prejudices and manners, [and] receive new ones from the new mode of life he embraces"? If Crevecoeur and Turner are correct, what are the defining attributes of this odd species known as the American?

Relating to this cultural question of American identity have always been other more directly political ones. For instance, how alike must we be in order to share in the same political institutions and to accord to each other the degree of civility and mutual respect that is necessary for the daily operations of a democratic republic? We will see, for example, that the debate over the ratification of the 1787 Constitution hinged to a considerable degree on the weight to be given to the competing claims of cultural homogeneity versus diversity. In these debates, opponents of the Constitution, who came to be known as the Anti-Federalists, generally believed that democracies could only flourish in small territories where citizens were very much alike in terms of national origin, customs, language, and religious beliefs. The Federalists, who urged adopting the Constitution, were more open to accommodating differences within a political framework. This was not so much because diversity was to be "celebrated," as some might say today, as a good in itself. It was rather because a variety of interests and identifications tend to balance each other out, seeing that none becomes so dominant as to threaten the liberty of others. This debate between Federalists and Anti-Federalists on the importance of cultural homogeneity has deeper roots in the **liberal** and **republican** traditions in American thought, and we will explore these frameworks of ideas as well.

Political thought revolving around American identity has focused historically not only on the vast powers promoting assimilation toward an American character type, but also on how one could (or should) resist this assimilation to remain true to whatever else one is. The debates today about multiculturalism, for example, however ironically, resemble in some ways earlier concerns of proud Virginians, or New Yorkers, as to how one combines an American national identity with another affiliation which is as or more vital to one's sense of self. How, in other words, do we harmonize the many that we are, with the one nation that we also are or aspire to be?

What, however, of those who either do not share this aspiration or, more common, those to whom it has been denied? One common way of writing American history is in what we might call its "Whig version." This term derives from an approach to British history especially common in the nineteenth century, in which history was viewed as a steady progress toward ever greater liberty. In a similar vein, one often finds American history presented as a march toward ever greater inclusiveness and political equality. American "Whig historians" would claim that the system is sound and that the our great challenge has been to let previously excluded groups into the game. Hence, slavery ends and African-Americans are, however slowly and painfully, extended the full rights of American citizenship. The same can be said for women, to whom the franchise is not extended until this century. Immigrants too have faced the struggle for inclusion, a struggle that is won in time.

Not only historians but major political personages have "clamored at the gates" seeking nothing more—nor less—than to be treated as any other American, which has most often meant like white male Americans. We see some of this in the "Declaration of Sentiments and Resolutions," reprinted here, of the first women's convention in this country held at Seneca Falls in 1848. The document is based quite directly on the Declaration of Independence, and the resolutions it contains—most radically that demanding the right to vote—ask little more than that women be granted the rights of citizenship that men already possess. We hear echoes of this theme as well in Dr. Martin Luther King, Jr.'s famous remark that his dream is "deeply rooted in the American dream," a dream grounded in the proposition that all men are created equal and endowed by their Creator with unalienable rights to life, liberty, and the pursuit of happiness. The women of Seneca Falls, Dr. King, and countless others ask that those Americans privileged by race or gender be true to the principles found in revered texts like the Declaration of Independence, principles that they loudly and proudly espouse. Indeed, Americans calling for inclusion, from the former slave and great abolitionist orator Frederick Douglass (whose optimism regarding the possibilities of racial harmony in the United States rose and fell several times through his life) to the suffragists, often saw themselves as the conscience of America. We as a nation would judge ourselves—and would be judged—regarding the consistency of our practices with our ideals by how we treat the least powerful among us. The subtext of this call is that those ideals are good, are worth preserving and extending to all persons regardless of race, class, or ethnic origin.

However, the political and social thought of Americans has long exhibited a pessimistic side regarding the prospects and desirability of inclusion as well. I refer here not only to the resistance of power holders to extending equal citizenship to previously excluded groups, a sentiment we see expressed in this collection by an 1855 piece from the "Know-Nothing" party regarding their perception of the dangers of immigration. I refer also to the self-perception of members of groups denied full citizenship, for whom entry into the mainstream of American society has not held great promise. Two main options have been open to those with the latter view. Either separate oneself and one's group from the mainstream, geographically and/or culturally, or seek to transform the mainstream itself through radical and/or revolutionary political action. Minority religious communities, such as the Mennonites or Amish, have followed this separatist path fearing that their religious and cultural norms could not survive without some distance from the dominant culture. Revolutionaries and radicals such as Emma Goldman have urged the transformative path. If these paths are less followed than are those seeking inclusion, they are still rather frequent in American political history. Moreover, they are instructive as a means of pointing to the limitations and inadequacies of American life as it is experienced by those shut off from and doubtful of its benefits.

American political and social thought is a reflection of American life. Its occasional abstraction should not obscure the fact that every reading contained in this text starts with a story. It may be the story of Frederick Douglass, an escaped slave, who considers in the selection here the role of blacks in the political community and their relation to the man sometimes referred to as the "Great Emancipator." Or it may be the story of Abraham Lincoln himself, viewing America during the bloodiest war of the nineteenth century. It may be the story of an heroic woman, Elizabeth Cady Stanton, struggling with all her might to win for women the vote, or that of a chicana daughter of undocumented immigrants who wishes to attend public school in Texas. Or it may be the story of a Christian Scientist mother facing manslaughter charges for failing to seek medical aid for her ailing daughter, believing instead that she could be cured by prayer.

Stories such as these have meaning beyond themselves. The lessons they teach apply to other people in other circumstances. One task of political and social thought is to draw out these lessons in a way that causes us to reflect more deeply on who we are as Americans, as members of particular communities and as individuals. They also lead us to reflect more deeply on the *principles* we believe in or, at least, espouse. For example, the idea that we as Americans should believe in religious freedom comes easily—perhaps too easily—to the lips of most Americans. For example, most of us have grown up with the story—far too simplistic to be the whole truth—that the Pilgrims came to the New World largely to worship as they saw fit. Yet, what does this high-toned principle of religious toleration mean in practice when, as in the case cited, it conflicts with other values we hold dear? Surely, most Americans would agree that the protection of innocent life, as that of the ailing child of Christian Scientist parents, is a legitimate function of the state. Moreover, we think that anyone who takes this life, whether by negligence or by direct action, ought to be punished. What, however, if the failure to do all possible to preserve the life is grounded in religious belief? Where does the interest of the state to preserve life and that of the parent to act on faith begin or end?

These are not easy questions, and individual stories alone do not tell us the answers. The answers lie, if they are to be found at all, in setting the particular case in a broader context of the political and social ideas that guide our common lives. This is one thing that political theory tries to do. American political thought exists on the intersection between thought and action, and at its best leads to actions guided by thought. The United States has not produced political or moral philosophers of the stature of a Plato, Aristotle, Confucius, or Hobbes, who reflect on politics and society at the deepest and purest level. Many of the great thinkers in the American political tradition were also politicians in one form or the other (and, no, this is not a dirty word!). Roger Williams, James Madison, Thomas Jefferson, Abraham Lincoln, Frederick Douglass, Susan B. Anthony, Marcus Garvey, Martin Luther King, Jr., and the list goes on, both thought and led. Moreover, in part they led so well because they thought so deeply. Our task in this book is to track the political and social thought of such figures not so much out of historical curiosity as to gain a deeper understanding into ourselves. This understanding must be guided by some background knowledge of the main liberal and republican ideas that have shaped American life from the very beginning, and we turn to these now.

The Liberal Tradition in America

Liberalism is a political philosophy that stresses the importance of individual rights, government by consent of the people, and private property. American political thought is not exclusively liberal, but it is fair to say that liberalism is the "first language" of American politics.[3] We tend to think about political issues most readily in terms of rights, whether it be the right of the pregnant woman or of the fetus in the abortion debate, the right of the defendant to a fair trial, the right, or lack of it, of the child to pray in public schools, or of the individual to be compensated for property taken by the state for public uses. This reliance—some would say overreliance—on "rights talk" today is a legacy of a liberal political culture which has changed over our history but which retains a set of core beliefs and convictions that, despite all the changes, would be intelligible to our founders. Liberalism is a source of continuity in American politics, but what exactly does it mean to be a liberal?

"Every man, and every body of men on earth," writes Thomas Jefferson, "possess the right of self-government. They receive it with their being from the hand of nature. Individuals exercise it by their single wills;

collections of men by that of their majority."[4] In this remark, Jefferson is using the phrase "self-government" in two distinct senses—one pertaining to individuals, the other to societies—each of which forms a key element of classical or "Lockean" liberalism. When he says that men (and, yes, as we will discuss later, it is worth noting that he refers to *men)* receive a right of self-governance "from the hand of nature," he suggests that governing oneself as an individual is a fundamental right of human beings. Each person, Jefferson believes, should be conceived of as a purposive moral being, capable of choosing and acting upon a path of life or, in the language of moral philosophy, upon a "conception of the good life." Moreover, each is entitled to the respect and toleration of others as long as he does not interfere with their rights to do the same. This "right to liberty" is, in the language of the Declaration of Independence, an "unalienable right." It cannot be denied a human being without treating him as something less than a person.

Like all political theories, liberalism is built upon basic ideas defining *human nature, society, and government.* Liberals like Jefferson believe that individuals are best conceived as free, equal, rational beings, capable of determining their own fate by their choices and actions—whether this means a particular form of religious worship, the choice of a career, of marriage partner, etc. Liberalism involves a certain degree of faith, even if it is a tempered faith. It is a faith that people, when left to their own devices, will *generally* use their freedoms wisely. Thus, they do not need an all-powerful government to tell them the best way to live, worship, or produce and exchange material goods. Indeed, they are wise and virtuous enough to choose their political leaders and, thus, to be governed through their *consent* rather than by force.

To put this view in terminology familiar to Jefferson himself, they will exercise "liberty," not "license." License is simply doing whatever one pleases, regardless of its effects on others. Liberty, or what Jefferson calls "self-government" in the passage quoted, entails, as his term suggests, self-restraint. In the words of British philosopher John Locke (1632–1704), an important originator of liberal thought, there is a "Law of Nature" "which obliges every one: And Reason which is that Law, teaches all Mankind, who will but consult it, that being all equal and independent, no one ought to harm another in his Life, Health, Liberty, or Possessions."[5] To exercise liberty as opposed to license is to act on this law of nature, thereby respecting the freedom and dignity of other moral persons.

This liberal faith in the capacity of individuals to direct their own lives without harming others is tempered, however, by the recognition that human beings do not always act as their morality dictates. Indeed, this recognition forms, for liberals, a prime motive for forming government. "If men were angels," James Madison writes in *The Federalist Papers*, "no government would be necessary."[6] We would not need laws to punish wrongdoers, enforce contracts, and the like, if people never were inclined to unfairly take advantage of their neighbors. Sadly, this is not to be expected. So government is instituted first and foremost to preserve those rights to life, liberty, and property that are the birthrights of all persons. Government, however, is meant to be limited in its powers. To paraphrase Madison, it must be strong enough to control the governed yet not so powerful as to become a threat to the very liberties it is designed to protect. Indeed, the task of constitution-building in the United States was largely one of devising a government that meets these two conditions and does so in ways consistent with rule by consent of the governed. This last point returns us to Jefferson's second sense of self-government—government under majority rule. Thus, *liberal democracies* combine (as many of the readings in this collection will show) the rights of individuals with the will of the majority in often-uneasy harmony.

We have said a bit about liberal understandings of human nature and government. Let us now take a closer look at the middle term in our triad—society. Liberals believe that if people are left free to choose their own ways of life—as they should be—then society is bound to be made up of a great diversity of social groups. These groups will be characterized by different beliefs, passions, and interests. For example, if people are free to choose the forms of worship they believe to be most pleasing to God, we should expect that a plurality of religious communities will form. These sects and denominations may share some basic tenets of faith, as was the case in overwhelmingly Christian early America, but they may also differ over matters of practice and doctrine that are of great importance to their members.

Liberalism as a political philosophy was born largely out of religious conflict in seventeenth century England. Philosophers like John Locke came to believe that, within certain limits, religious diversity is a fact to which politics should be accommodated. That is, it should not be the role of the state to dictate one form of worship, thereby eliminating freedom of worship, but to provide a framework of law within which people could worship as they chose so long as they respected the rights of others to do the same.[7] It should be added that, from all indications, Locke believed this not because he was skeptical about religion generally or because he thought all religions equally true and valuable. Liberalism is quite compatible with strong convictions on matters of faith, as well as on other convictions regarding the best way to live. Rather, Locke's defense of *tolerance*, an eminent liberal virtue, is grounded in a combination of moral belief and political pragmatism. On the latter, it is simply not possible to *persuade* everyone to accept a single form of worship as the right one. We can dictate practice but not conscience. This means that the only way out of religious pluralism is to *coerce* faith as was tried, for example, in the Spanish Inquisition. Locke and fellow liberals believed that such efforts were doomed to failure, and bloody failure at that, as many people are willing to die—and to kill—for their faiths. It is also simply a moral wrong, however, to attempt to force people to practice faith in a way their own reason leads them to reject. To do so is to show a profound disrespect for persons.[8] Far better for both moral and pragmatic reasons to agree to disagree on matters of faith—that is, to allow individuals and communities within the state to act on their beliefs as they see most pleasing to their Creator, so long as they respect the like right of others.

Religion does not, of course, exhaust the full range of issues about which people are likely to differ and to be brought into conflict. In Federalist #10, Madison notes that a "zeal for different opinion" extends to such issues as those "concerning government, . . . an attachment to different leaders ambitiously contending for pre-eminence and power," and to what he calls the "most common and durable source" of conflict, that over the division of property. We cannot—it would be morally wrong—do away with the conflict that liberty gives rise to, as the only way to do so would be to do away with liberty itself. This cure, Madison argues, would be far worse than the disease. Therefore, we must try instead to ameliorate its effects. This is the task of government. It is a task built on the assumption that society is and likely always will be made up of diverse groups with differing and often competing interests. Insofar as liberals recognize this, it is fair to say that diversity and difference—of the sorts we explore in the American context in this book—are central notions of liberal political thought.

It is a demanding task to be a good citizen in a liberal state. This political philosophy asks us, in essence, to wear two hats. Under one we have particular loyalties, whether they be to our faith, our family, or other private associations we may join to pursue ends we consider valuable. Under the other, we are asked as *citizens* to interact with and tolerate in the public sphere those whose basic values and beliefs in the private sphere may be greatly different from our own. It is not surprising, therefore, that discussions of the relation of public to private morality becomes a running theme in American political history. It is important to add here that "private" as I am using it does not mean simply personal or individual, but rather those spheres of belief and action, whether on the part of individuals or particular communities or sects, that are shielded from interference by government. We see this relation raised in this collection in a 1960 campaign speech by President Kennedy, in which he addresses public concerns that perhaps he could not be both a loyal Catholic and a good leader of the American people as a whole. We see it also in the speech by Ralph Reed, executive director of the Christian Coalition, in which he argues for a greater degree of overlap between the two moralities than President Kennedy endorses.

Liberalism is not a feasible form of politics in all countries or at all times. Think of Iran under Ayatollah Khomeini, or the former Yugoslavia today. Some types of religious beliefs and/or nationalist fervors are so strong and their partisans so single-minded that it is simply impossible for them to tolerate those different from themselves. If this is the case, no liberal solution to the conflicts arising from problems of pluralism is likely to succeed. And this is not a situation we find only in far parts of the world. Intolerance has long been a fact of American life, as the professed liberalism of most Americans is periodically overcome by racial prejudice, nativist enmity, or religious and political rivalries. Any realistic story of diversity in America must take into account the intolerance and hatreds we find acted upon and defended in various ways, as well as the liberal creed by which this intolerance is so justly derided. One question posed by our readings on race, gender, immigration, and religion is whether the answer to intolerance is a recommitment to the core liberal values that tell us it is wrong or whether, as radicals from Marcus Garvey to Catharine MacKinnon suggest, the very intolerance and mistreatment of minorities is a deeper symptom of something wrong with the whole liberal enterprise.

Missing Persons: Who Is Left Out of Classical Liberalism?

I noted that it was significant that Jefferson said in the Declaration of Independence that "all men" were created equal. Inevitably, when the Declaration is discussed in a classroom setting, students will note this passage and quickly list exceptions. For example, where do women fit in Jefferson's picture? What about slaves, Native Americans, and even, though this applies more to other early Americans than to Jefferson, non-property-owning whites? Property restrictions on voting were common in American states in the Revolutionary and early Constitutional era.[9]

While it is true that early Americans believed that all "persons" were created equal and thereby entitled to equal protection of basic rights, it is quite clear that not all human beings counted as having the moral and legal status of personhood. This is less confusing than it sounds. In one sense of the term dating back to the ancient Romans, to be a person is to have legal status, a right to sue and be sued in courts of law. Even today this sense of personhood remains, as when we hear in the abortion debate the contention that the fetus is a "person." Antiabortionists who claim this are saying that the fetus has legal and moral status and is thereby entitled to full protection under law. Specifically, it cannot be denied "life, liberty, or property without due process of law," a right ascribed to all "persons" under the Fourteenth Amendment to the Constitution. This is, of course, a contentious claim. Prochoicers disagree. Whoever is right, we see that whether someone counts as a person with full protection of law can be contested and can, in fact, change over time.

Early American law and politics denied the status of personhood most absolutely to slaves and Native Americans, but also to varying degrees to women and to poor white males. Moreover, this distinction between persons and nonpersons fed into and even encouraged an American style of racism. The only way to maintain the universality of liberal language as used in the Declaration of Independence is to consider those to whom rights are denied as less than persons, as less than fully human. In the self-serving ideology of the antebellum South, for example, slaves were discussed and portrayed quite frequently as uncivilized and childlike, or in need of "adult" supervision that was provided by their owners. Such views regarding Africans and different but equally demeaning views of Native Americans were certainly commonplace in early America, and this explains the brutality exhibited toward these peoples. The legacy of this racism is a running sore that persists through our history.

As real as this legacy is, it is also true that the *justice* of the denial of the status of personhood to women and to Africans bound in slavery was contested by whites from colonial times and first days of our republic. Note the selections from the early republican period by Benjamin Rush on slavery and by both Abigail Adams and Judith Sargent Murray on the status of women in this collection. Rush is adamant in his claim that the freedoms Americans conceive of as "natural rights" ought—indeed, must—be extended to African-Americans and that slavery is an abomination of the very precepts of "justice and morality."[10] Moreover, he was far from alone among the founding generation in these views. Neither Abigail Adams nor Murray are so bold as to ask outright for women to be allowed to vote, but each asserts the basic principle that the moral personality of women should be recognized in law and custom. You might also note John Adams' rather brief and flip remark in response to Abigail's request that he "remember the women."

It should be clear that attaining the status of personhood, in the sense we are understanding it, is often the result of political struggle. An important theme of American political history has been the expansion of the class of persons under the law and opposition to this expansion. Let's take an example. During the Civil Rights movement in the 1960s there took place a strike of garbage men in Memphis, Tennessee. As these black men picketed during the strike, several held signs that read simply, "I Am A Man." What did this sign mean? Clearly it was not meant just to call attention to the gender of the strikers. Rather, it was meant to send a *moral* message. Read more fully, it was saying, "I am a man, that is a *person,* like you are. I am entitled to the same dignity and respect that you are and should not be discriminated against under law."

Many of the readings in this book center on struggles to expand the definition of personhood, i.e., to expand the class of persons to whom rights and privileges under the Constitution and ordinary law should apply. This is not the only story of diversity in America, but it is an important one. It is not the only one because American political thought is more complex than can be captured by understanding liberalism alone. Further, liberalism is a political philosophy that itself maintains a tension between particular personal and communal identities and the universal one of American citizenship. Let's explore these complexities a bit further.

Republican Influences: How Alike Must We Be to Live Together?

I have suggested that liberal states are those in which citizens share some basic beliefs but disagree about others. They agree to a conception of justice, which is essentially an agreement to disagree about other deep-seated moral issues and interests that separate them. But just how deep must this moral and political consensus be? Must we, for example, share a common language if we are to act together as citizens? What about a common ethnic identity? We may think today that the case for sameness in some or all of these regards is a sign of narrow-mindedness or prejudice—and, indeed, the failure to incorporate those who are different into American politics has been grounded all too frequently in such dispositions. However, we surely must have *some* traits in common if we are to think of ourselves in any meaningful sense as one nation. Even liberals see this need, even as they also see dangers in the demands for too much consensus, dangers that these demands generate in terms of intolerance for those who are different. In other schools of political thought, also influential in shaping American political ideas, the demand for sameness across a number of dimensions is even more essential.

Early American political thought was profoundly influenced by a tradition of political discourse often referred to as "classical republicanism." If the British thinker John Locke was a main bearer of liberal ideas to the United States, a major republican influence came through the works of an eighteenth century Frenchman, Baron de Montesquieu (1689–1755). This important writer communicated a number of vital principles to early Americans. Among them is the idea that republics—i.e., political communities where the "many," as opposed to the "one" or "few," rule—require a much higher level of "civic virtue" than do other forms of government. Despotic governments, Montesquieu wrote, require little more of the common man than that he *fear* the ruler. Monarchies at their best rely upon *honor,* whereas aristocracies require that the nobility practice *moderation* among themselves and concerning the lower social orders, over whom they have great power. Republics, however, require *virtue* on the part of citizens because this form of government asks so much more of them. The very definition of a republican citizen is, to paraphrase Aristotle, to take part in ruling and being ruled. Republican citizens make the laws under which they are expected to live; they are lawmakers and subjects at the same time. And to both make laws and be bound by them demands a willingness to act upon the common good, as opposed to narrow self-interest. Indeed, it requires that acting on the common good is seen *as* self-interest, because I think of myself first and foremost as a *citizen*.

Civic virtue, for Montesquieu, "may be defined as the love of laws and of our country." Fostering civic virtue then becomes one of the principle objectives of republican government, and how this is best accomplished is a question that Montesquieu also considered in ways relevant to early Americans. Certainly, education was critical. People must be *taught* to be virtuous, and communicating love of country in a manner that inspires republican loyalties that last a lifetime "ought to be the principal business of education."[11] Montesquieu believed that the most virtuous republics would likely be small in size, on the scale of ancient Athens, which had no more than 40,000 or so citizens.[12] This was so as a willingness to sacrifice for the whole depended upon knowing who the other citizens were and that they were disposed to share common burdens as well. In small republics, fellow citizens would be neighbors and friends, not just anonymous others. Further, civic virtue was most likely to flourish in a community that was relatively homogeneous, where people were neither too rich nor too poor, and similar in language, religion, and "manners."

It is fair to say that prior to the drafting of the Constitution, Montesquieu's views on the link between republican virtue and small, culturally homogeneous, republics represented the conventional wisdom of early America. Indeed, the Constitution and its defense in *The Federalist Papers* represented a radical break with the conventional view and, in a sense, legitimized large size and diversity in a way that had not been done before. This comes through most clearly in Federalist #10, reprinted in this text. The Constitution's opponents remained in the camp of traditionalists on this score, as is indicated by the following remark of Montesquieu which is quoted by Brutus, an Anti-Federalist from New York, in the selection in this volume.

> In a large republic, the public good is sacrificed to a thousand views; it is subordinate to exceptions, and depends on accidents. In a small one, the interest of the public is easier perceived, better understood

and more within the reach of every citizen; abuses are of less extent, and of course are less protected.

Brutus adds in his own words that in "a republic, the manners, sentiments, and interests of the people should be similar. If this be not the case, there will be a constant clashing of opinions; and the representatives of one part will be continually striving against those of the other." Small size, which encouraged ties of acquaintance and a sense of sharing a common fate, as well as similar customs and interests, are vital to a well-functioning republic. If a republic gets too large, as other Anti-Federalists suggested, it would degenerate into either a tyranny where one ruled through fear, or anarchy where there was no legitimate authority at all.

It is worth contemplating that Brutus makes these remarks at a time when the nonslave population of the United States is little more than three million, and "is capable of containing much more than ten times that number." Much more is correct! Yet already Brutus and other Anti-Federalists are worried about the diversity of American society and about our ability to identify with fellow citizens over such a vast territory and thereby maintain "free institutions." Although his prediction about the eventual size of the United States is not so accurate, the concern he raises is still with us, if in a rather amended form.

To be sure, American society today is far more diverse than Brutus could have imagined. It is also true that American citizenship means something rather different to most of us today than it did to Brutus. To be a citizen for Brutus and others influenced by classical republican ways of thinking is to *actively* take part in the life of the political community, to rule and be ruled. Only by doing so, moreover, do we develop the best aspects of human personality. To think of oneself as a citizen in this strong sense, where public affairs play so large a role in one's life, is still among the ideals of American life, but an increasingly distant one. We live in an era when only about half of Americans vote in presidential elections and only about a third can name their congressperson, much less aspire to such a role. Our very notion of citizenship has taken on a more passive character, in which being a citizen is conceived by many as simply being protected by the state and eligible for the benefits it provides such as student loans, unemployment insurance, and old age pensions.

Moreover, as the demands of citizenship have weakened, it seems less pressing than it did to Montesquieu, Brutus, and others inspired by classical republicanism that our society be as culturally homogeneous as these political thinkers argued. It comes more readily to most of us, as it did to Madison, to think of the American public not as one people but as many, or, more accurately, as many and one at the same time. Cultural pluralism is correspondingly not seen as threatening to us as it was to Brutus. Brutus's strong notion of citizenship demands an affection for fellow citizens that can only be grounded in a common identity. This identity, moreover, includes the sorts of similarities in custom, religion, and interests that republicans tend to stress as vital to free government. In one sense, "Madisonian" liberal citizenship asks something less of us, though it too has its challenges.

It is easier to simply tolerate fellow citizens than to be asked to love them. The former asks that we simply let them be, whereas the latter demands an affection that comes from personal knowledge and shared values. Nonetheless, it is still important that Americans feel some common bond, some sense of shared enterprise. Without this, such necessary qualities as respect for law and a willingness to abide by it (as discussed by Abraham Lincoln in his speech to Springfield's Young Men's Lyceum), and even tolerance itself for fellow citizens who do not look or think as we do inevitably will be eroded. How thick this set of shared values must be to keep us going as a nation and to prevent the kind of fragmentation we see in the former Yugoslavia and all too many other parts of the world is an ongoing question of our public life. It is a question that has been given a new urgency by what has come to be called by some "identity politics."

Identity Politics: How Different Can We Be and Still Live Together?

At the end of the nineteenth century, a young W. E. B. Du Bois posed a troubling question about the African-American in the United States.

> No Negro who has given earnest thought to the situation of his people in America has failed . . . to ask himself at some time: What, after all, am I? Am I an American or am I a Negro? Can I be both? Or is it my duty to cease to be a Negro as soon as possible and be an American? If I strive as a Negro, am I not perpetuating the very cleft that threatens and separates Black and White America? Is not my only possible practical aim the subduction of all that is Negro in me to the American? Does my black blood place upon me any more obligation to assert my nationality than German, or Irish or Italian blood would?

Du Bois' dilemma is particularly poignant given the harsh history of African-Americans in the United States, where it would not be unreasonable for him to think that identifying as an "American" is to the disadvantage of his race.

One's identity is one's most fundamental sense of self. It is our deepest sense of who we are. For example, the devout person may not be able to even imagine herself without her faith, which may be so deeply rooted that she does not see it as a matter of choice but simply as an expression of who she is. National or ethnic identity, or that of sexual orientation, can take the same form. Not all personal characteristics cut this deeply. I can imagine myself being a bit heavier, or driving a different type of car, or preferring chocolate to vanilla ice cream without thinking that any of these facts about myself really define to any great degree who I am. These seem peripheral to my sense of self, while my race, religion, national origin, gender, or sexual orientation may not.

Identity politics is concerned with public questions where people's most profound senses of self enter into the public sphere. We see it expressed, for example, in debates about education and whether school districts should adopt "multicultural" or "Afrocentric" textbooks. We see it in the activities of gay political activists, such as those in the organization "Act Up," who protest what they see as a lack of recognition by government of the specific concerns of gays and lesbians, whether these are support for AIDS research or rights to marry or to serve in the military. We see it in higher education, where it is debated whether or not it is good for different ethnic groups to have separate dormitories and even, in some institutions, separate graduation ceremonies, or whether campuses should adopt speech codes to punish those who engage in hateful speech directed at minorities. We see it also in one of our most vexing public debates, that over abortion. This issue does not lend itself to ready compromise and brings to the fore people's most deeply experienced religious and moral commitments.

It is not surprising that identity politics is often intensely emotional and divisive. Many political issues can be resolved by splitting the difference, especially where money is involved. For example, we can spend a bit more for defense and a bit less for social programs, or decide to build a museum in our city as opposed to a public swimming pool. One's identity, however, is not so easily compromised. If, for example, I am a gay activist and I see government spending too little for AIDS research, I may well take that to be not just another budget decision but a fundamental attack on me and people like me. Identity politics lies at the intersection of the personal and the political, and it is therefore not surprising that it can be taken very personally indeed.

Identity politics presents serious challenges to pluralistic liberal democracies such as ours. On the one hand, liberal societies recognize diversity and in fact seek to foster it by promoting a legal and moral climate in which people are free to act with others on their own self-chosen conceptions of the good life. Liberals do not seek a state that tells people what is good for them, but one in which individuals and communities make choices for themselves so long as they extend the same rights to others. Yet no liberal polity could survive if its citizens did not recognize that they have certain things in common. Otherwise, how would we prevent our disagreements from degenerating into hostility, as happens all too often in our society as it is? I am alluding again to the "two hat" theory of liberalism I already discussed. As a liberal citizen I am asked to practice tolerance and show mutual respect for fellow citizens, though I may disagree vehemently with them on what is truly important in life. The challenge is to be true to myself while recognizing at the same time that people unlike me in their most basic identifications are still entitled to my concern and respect.

Du Bois believed in 1897 that this was possible, that he could be both an American and, in his words, "a Negro." "We are Americans," he writes, "not only by birth and by citizenship, but by our political ideals, our language, our religion. Further than that Americanism does not go." He goes on to note the tremendous contribution those of African origin have made to American culture and concludes that "race solidarity" is a vital and legitimate way to continue that contribution as well as being true to oneself. Racial solidarity becomes for him not a bellicose expression of superiority nor, of course, an acceptance of inferiority. Rather it is the "realization of that broader humanity which freely recognizes differences in men, but sternly deprecates inequality in their opportunities for development."

As noble as Du Bois' sentiment is, is it practical? Can the cacophony of voices in American society be brought into harmony along the lines he suggests—i.e., respecting diversity while still recognizing a shared humanity? There are reasons for Americans to be both optimistic and pessimistic on this score. Many of us, this author included, think it good that America has never attained the degree of cultural homogeneity that some Americans from Brutus to Theodore Roosevelt thought good and observers from Crevecoeur to Frederick Jackson Turner thought inevitable. America, we believe, is enriched by its diversity and has done about as well as any nation in dealing with it. As the historian of immigration, Lawrence Fuchs, argued, "No nation before had ever made diversity itself a source of national identity and unity."[13]

Yet it is also quite possible to make the pessimistic case from two different standpoints. It is easy enough to point to the many instances of race and ethnic hatred, from the slaughter of Native Americans to hostility to immigrants and religious minorities that have checkered our past. To paraphrase Michael Walzer, tar and feathering is every bit as much an American tradition as freedom of speech. And often the targets of this abuse and worse have been such merely because they are different from the majority population. Although Americans have done as well as or better than other countries in recognizing the value of diversity, our record is still very far from perfect. Moreover, we cannot rely on some simple faith in progress to convince us that we will outgrow these problems. Backsliding is always a live option.

Our second ground for pessimism is that there is reason to fear "identity politics" if it leads, as Arthur Schlesinger, Jr. among others has suggested, to too much emphasis on the "pluribus" and too little on the "unum." If Americans see themselves first and foremost as members of groups with similar identifications in terms of race, sexual orientation, ethnicity, etc., and only peripherally as citizens of one nation as a whole, the society runs a deep risk of fragmentation and declines in norms of civility and mutual respect. We will return to these concerns in the last chapter. Let us conclude this introduction by noting that the tension between the one and the many, the unum and the pluribus, is one that we are destined to live with as Americans. It can be a creative or a destructive tension, depending upon how we choose to address it. The readings in this collection give some sense of the ways it has been addressed in our past. But the true goal of this book is to offer students the tools for thinking about their own identities as Americans, as individuals, and as members of particular communities as, together, we make our future.

ENDNOTES

1. For further discussion of these terms and for their sources, see the introduction to Part 3 as well as the readings by Theodore Roosevelt, Horace Kallen, and John Dewey. The rule followed for citations in this book is as follows. For authors whose writings are included in this collection, a bibliographic citation is provided at the beginning of the excerpt. Works by all other authors are cited in standard endnotes.

2. I will be using these three terms in different contexts throughout the book. To *assimilate* means literally to make similar. The term often arises in discussions of immigration where assimilated immigrants become like other Americans by adopting local customs and abandoning those of their native lands. *Accommodation* suggests some recognition of group difference and actions by governments, corporations, or individuals to take those differences into account. For example, an airline might accommodate an orthodox Jewish passenger by providing a kosher meal. To *separate* means to isolate one's particular group, whether based on religious, racial, or other affinities, from the mainstream of society. The Amish in Pennsylvania are a community that has separated itself from the broader society in order to maintain its religious identity.

3. I borrow this phrase from Robert N. Bellah et al., *Habits of the Heart: Individualism and Commitment in American Life* (Berkeley: University of California Press, 1985), p. 20.

4. *The Life and Selected Writings of Thomas Jefferson.* Edited by Adrienne Koch and William Peden. (New York: The Modern Library, 1972), p. 316.

5. John Locke, *Two Treatises of Government*, edited by Peter Laslett (New York: New American Library, 1963), p. 311.

6. James Madison, Alexander Hamilton, and John Jay, *The Federalist Papers*, edited by Isaac Kramnick (New York: Penguin Books, 1987), p. 319.

7. We should not overstate, however, the extent of tolerance as it emerged from British religious controversies of that time. John Locke did as much as anyone to articulate and defend a principle of toleration, but even he did not extend it to atheists. Locke wrote that "neither Pagan, Mahometan, nor Jew, ought to be excluded from the civil rights of the commonwealth because of his religion." But, "those are not all to be tolerated who deny the being of God." See Locke's "Letter Concerning Toleration," in *Treatise of Civil Government and Letter Concerning Toleration.* Edited by Charles L. Sherman (New York: Irvington Publishers, Inc., 1965), pp. 212, 218.

8. We see such moral arguments in Madison's "Memorial and Remonstrance" in this collection.

9. It has been estimated that by 1789, the year the Constitution was adopted, between 70% and 90% of white males were eligible to vote. (Kramnick introduction to *The Federalist Papers*, p. 23.)

10. See Rush's "Address to the Inhabitants of the British Settlements in America Upon Slave-keeping," in Part 4.

11. Baron de Montesquieu. *The Spirit of the Laws.* Translated by Thomas Nugent. (New York: Hafner Publishing Company, 1949), p. 34.

12. The total population of the Athenian city-state including the families of citizens, aliens, and slaves was much larger, of course, in the range of 350,000.

13. Quoted in Arthur M. Schlesinger, *The Disuniting of America: Reflections on a Multicultural Society* (New York: W.W. Norton & Co., 1992), p. 131.

PART I

American Unity and Diversity: Political Principles and National Identity

PART I

American Unity and Diversity:
Political Principles and National Identity

I think it fortunate for the United States to have become the asylum for so many virtuous patriots of different denominations: but their [e.g., the states'] circumstances . . . enabled them to be but a bare asylum, & to offer nothing for [these people] but an entire freedom to use their own means & faculties as they please. There is no such thing in this country as what would be called wealth in Europe. The richest are but a little at ease, & obliged to pay the most rigorous attention to their affairs to keep them together . . . In our private pursuits it is a great advantage that every honest employment is deemed honorable.

—Thomas Jefferson, 1795[1]

The readings in this part are meant to introduce you to several important dimensions of the interplay of unity and diversity in American political and social history. Reconciling unity and diversity is a recurrent theme of American politics and these readings are essential to understanding the terms of debate for doing so, terms that originate in the founding but recur throughout our history. They can be divided into two types. The first deals with central liberal and republican political principles and how they have come to be reflected in our political intitutions. The second deals with what we might call American character or the "American way of life."

Unity and diversity interact in a number of paradoxical ways in American politics. We are a nation that has defined itself historically by a commitment to a set of political ideas. These ideas are found first and foremost in the Declaration of Independence and embodied institutionally in the Constitution. The ideas set out by Jefferson in the Declaration were meant both as a political creed to apply to "all men" in all places and as a statement of American national identity. Both themes are evoked by Jefferson's phrase, "We hold these truths to be self-evident . . .". The "we"

---

[1] The quote is from a letter to M. de Meusnier. See *The Life and Selected Writings of Thomas Jefferson*, p. 533.

are Americans who are holding certain unifying truths in common as part of forging a national identity. However, the truths themselves—about the moral equality of persons and their natural rights to life, liberty, and the pursuit of happiness—are universal ones.

So, Americans are united by a set of political "truths." Yet, central to the truths Americans hold as self-evident has been a commitment in one form or another to political institutions that allow for considerable diversity in how individuals and communities lead their lives. Our unity is forged, however ironically, in large measure by a commitment to difference. We get some sense of this in the remark from Jefferson that heads this Part. This quote comes from a letter Jefferson wrote to a Frenchman interested in learning more about the United States. In referring to the United States as a "bare asylum" within which settlers could use their abilities to pursue their happiness as they saw fit, he points to an ideal of freedom that has been central to the American experience.

In the United States people can make their own lives, unconstrained by the oppressive states and social structures found in Europe. And it is inevitable that as people exercise their liberty, they will differentiate themselves in all sorts of ways. Madison gives us some sense of this as well when he writes in *Federalist #10* that "liberty is to faction what air is to fire." Free peoples will form themselves into all sorts of groups based on everything from religious affiliation, or attachment to charismatic political leaders, to economic interests. And though there are dangers of instability and conflict associated with the exercise of liberty, to do away with liberty would be a cure worse than the disease. Freedom and diversity are joined at the hip, and both are goods a liberal democratic republic must seek to preserve and promote.

There is one more wrinkle. Jefferson's letter suggests that Americans have certain traits in common, traits that extend beyond a commitment to shared political principles. The United States takes in "patriots of diverse origins" but the very natural, social, and economic climate of this colonial settler nation tends to generate a certain uniformity of character among them. Americans—excluding slaves, who are clearly omitted from Jefferson's considerations in the letter—are more alike than members of European nations are like each other. When Jefferson says, for example, that there is not wealth in the United States, he is not suggesting that the American states are or should be absolutely egalitarian societies with no difference between rich and poor. Rather, he is making a point about social structure and history. The America of his day, or so he claims, does not have aristocratic families like those found in Europe, families whose members are freed from the necessity of labor and contemptuous of those who labor for them. Even the "rich" in America must tend to their businesses and farms and learn to honor the dignity of labor. Moreover, for Jefferson, the widespread availability of land, the largely agricultural economy, and the history of self-governance in American localities encourages the emergence of such virtues as diligence, frugality, self-discipline, and fraternity—the sorts of virtues Benjamin Franklin catalogues in *Poor Richard's Almanac*—as defining traits of an American character type. James Bryce and Frederick Jackson Turner, both excerpted here and both writing around the dawn of the twentieth century, also note a certain uniformity in American character, a character that Turner both admires and finds threatened by the closing of the American frontier.

The question of what it means to be an American becomes more problematic over time, particularly as tensions between the slave economy of the south and the capitalist one of the north grow more pronounced, and as the flow and diversity of immigrants to American shores increases. We return to political concerns raised by the increased saliency of issues related to race, immigration, and gender in later parts. The question, however, was never *un*problematic and arises in many different forms, as the writings in this section show. As we have suggested in the introduction, the issue of how much cultural homogeneity was necessary to sustain free political institutions is hotly contested in the debates over ratification of the Constitution. We give witness to this issue with excerpts from the *Federalist Papers* and from two major Anti-Federalist pamphlets. Further, Washington's Farewell Address is aimed largely at maintaining a sense of national unity in response to an increasingly partisan political atmosphere, in which he is worried both by sectional strife in the United States and about America's role in the world. Lincoln is represented twice in this Part, first by a speech on the "perpetuation" of our institutions, in which he addresses the threats of increasing lawlessness precipitated by increasing tensions over slavery. Lincoln's Gettysburg Address is aimed at reforging a commitment to American national unity at a time when it had collapsed altogether, during the Civil War. The excerpt from John C. Calhoun, a prominent Southerner writing before the Civil War, offers an institutional scheme for dealing with regions in the United States that have conflicting economic interests and social mores.

Finally, the writings of the great Native American leader, Tecumseh, remind us that the "bare asylum(s)" Jefferson refers to were not so bare after all. America is a colonial settler nation, and European settlers carved out a space for themselves at the expense of the natives of the land. Tecumseh's powerful words do not allow us to forget this truth of the American political experience.

These writings taken as a whole, and those that follow in latter Parts, show just how complex—but also how central—the dance of unity, diversity, and American identity are to understanding American politics and society in past and present.

The Declaration of Independence:
The Unanimous Declaration of the Thirteen United States of America In Congress, July 4, 1776

Editor's Introduction: The Declaration of Independence is perhaps the best short introduction to the political thought of early Americans. By July 1776, armed conflict had broken out in several colonies and sentiment in favor of independence was on the rise. The Continental Congress formally accepted the Declaration on July 4 by a twelve to nothing vote, with New York abstaining. New York approved the measure on July 9, making the vote unanimous. The Declaration was drafted by Thomas Jefferson except for a few amendments. Commenting on the Declaration some fifty years after its adoption, Jefferson noted that it was "(n)either aiming at originality of principle or sentiment, nor yet copied from any particular and previous writing." Rather, "it was intended to be an expression of the American mind, and to give to that expression the proper tone and spirit called by the occasion." Jefferson was, he claimed, doing little more than expressing the "common sense" of his age in his affirmation of unalienable rights to life, liberty, and the pursuit of happiness and the duty of government to protect these rights.[1]

The Declaration does not say all there is to say about politics. It was written for the specific purpose of justifying rebellion and national independence, after all. Nonetheless, it is as clear and concise a statement of political principles put into action as one is likely to find at any place or time. It consists of three basic sections. The first is a statement of philosophical principles addressing such fundamentals as the natural rights of persons, the purpose of government, and the right to rebel against illegitimate government. These principles then become the basis for a list of grievances against the British government and, finally, give rise to a pledge of honor on the part of the former colonies to unite and establish themselves as united independent states.

*   *   *

When in the Course of human events, it becomes necessary for one people to dissolve the political bands which have connected them with

---

[1] From a letter to Henry Lee, May 8, 1825. In *The Life and Selected Writings of Thomas Jefferson*, ed. by Adrienne Koch and William Peden (New York: The Modern Library, 1972), p. 719.

another, and to assume among the Powers of the earth, the separate and equal station to which the Laws of Nature and of Nature's God entitle them, a decent respect to the opinions of mankind requires that they should declare the causes which impel them to the separation.

We hold these truths to be self-evident, that all men are created equal, that they are endowed by their Creator with certain unalienable Rights, that among these are Life, Liberty, and the pursuit of Happiness. That to secure these rights, Governments are instituted among Men, deriving their just powers from the consent of the governed. That whenever any Form of Government becomes destructive of these ends, it is the Right of the People to alter or to abolish it, and to institute new Government, laying its foundation on such principles and organizing its powers in such form, as to them shall seem most likely to effect their Safety and Happiness. Prudence, indeed, will dictate that Governments long established should not be changed for light and transient causes; and accordingly all experience hath shown, that mankind are more disposed to suffer, while evils are sufferable, than to right themselves by abolishing the forms to which they are accustomed. But when a long train of abuses and usurpations, pursuing invariably the same Object evinces a design to reduce them under absolute Despotism, it is their right, it is their duty, to throw off such Government, and to provide new Guards for their future security.

—Such has been the patient sufferance of these Colonies; and such is now the necessity which constrains them to alter their former Systems of Government. The history of the present King of Great Britain is a history of repeated injuries and usurpations, all having in direct object the establishment of an absolute Tyranny over these States. To prove this, let Facts be submitted to a candid world.—He has refused his Assent to Laws, the most wholesome and necessary for the public good. He has forbidden his Governors to pass Laws of immediate and pressing importance, unless suspended in their operation till his Assent should be obtained; and when so suspended, he has utterly neglected to attend to them.—He has refused to pass other Laws for the accommodation of large districts of people, unless those people would relinquish the right of Representation in the Legislature, a right inestimable to them and formidable to tyrants only.—He has called together legislative bodies at places unusual, uncomfortable, and distant from the depository of their public Records, for the sole purpose of fatiguing them into compliance with his measures.—He has dissolved Representative Houses repeatedly, for opposing with manly firmness his invasions on the rights of the people.—He has refused for a long time, after such dissolutions, to cause others to be elected whereby the Legislative powers, incapable of Annihilation, have returned to the People at large for their exercise; the State remaining in the meantime exposed to all the dangers of invasion from without, and convulsions within.—He has endeavoured to prevent the population of these States; for that purpose obstructing the Laws of Naturalization of Foreigners; refusing to pass others to encourage their migrations hither, and raising the conditions of new Appropriations of Lands.— He has obstructed the Administration of Justice, by refusing his Assent to Laws for establishing Judiciary powers.—He has made Judges dependent on his Will alone, for the tenure of their offices, and the amount and payment of their salaries.

He has erected a multitude of New Offices, and sent hither swarms of Officers to harass our people, and eat out their substance.—He has kept among us, in times of peace, Standing Armies without the Consent of our legislatures.—He has affected to render the Military independent of and superior to the Civil power.

He has combined with others to subject us to a jurisdiction foreign to our constitution, and unacknowledged by our laws; giving his Assent to their Acts of pretended Legislation.—

For quartering large bodies of armed troops among us:—

For protecting them, by a mock Trial, from Punishment for any Murders which they should commit on the Inhabitants of these States:

For cutting off our Trade with all parts of the world:

For imposing Taxes on us without our Consent:

For depriving us in many cases, of the benefits of Trial by Jury:

For transporting us beyond Seas to be tried for pretended offences:

For abolishing the free System of English Laws in a neighbouring Province, establishing therein an Arbitrary government, and enlarging its Boundaries so as to render it at once an example and fit instrument for introducing the same absolute rule into these Colonies:

For taking away our Charters, abolishing our most valuable Laws, and altering fundamentally the Forms of our Governments:

For suspending our own Legislatures, and declaring themselves invested with power to legislate for us in all cases whatsoever.—

He has abdicated Government here, by declaring us out of his Protection and waging War against us.—

He has plundered our seas, ravaged our Coasts, burnt our towns, and destroyed the Lives of our people.—

He is at this time transporting large armies of foreign mercenaries to compleat the works of death, desolation and tyranny, already begun with circumstances of Cruelty & perfidy scarcely paralleled in the most barbarous ages, and totally unworthy the Head of a civilized nation.

He has constrained our fellow Citizens taken Captive on the high Seas to bear Arms against their Country, to become the executioners of their friends and Brethren, or to fall themselves by their Hands.

He has excited domestic insurrections amongst us, and has endeavoured to bring on the inhabitants of our frontiers, the merciless Indian Savages, whose known rule of warfare, is an undistinguished destruction of all ages, sexes and conditions.

In every stage of these Oppressions We have Petitioned for Redress in the most humble terms: Our repeated Petitions have been answered only by repeated injury. A Prince, whose character is thus marked by every act which may define a Tyrant, is unfit to be the ruler of a free people.

Nor have We been wanting in attention to our British brethren. We have warned them from time to time of attempts by their legislature to extend an unwarrantable jurisdiction over us. We have reminded them of the circumstances of our emigration and settlement here. We have appealed to their native justice and magnanimity, and we have conjured them by the ties of our common kindred to disavow these usurpations, which would inevitably interrupt our connections and correspondence. They too have been deaf to the voice of justice and of consanguinity. We must, therefore, acquiesce in the necessity, which denounces our Separation, and hold them, as we hold the rest of mankind, Enemies in War, in Peace Friends.—

We, therefore, the Representatives of the United States of America, in General Congress, Assembled, appealing to the Supreme Judge of the world for the rectitude of our intentions, do, in the Name, and by Authority of the good People of these Colonies, solemnly publish and declare, That these United Colonies are, and of Right ought to be Free and Independent States; that they are Absolved from all Allegiance to the British Crown, and that all political connection between them and the State of Great Britain, is and ought to be totally dissolved; and that as Free and Independent States, they have full Power to levy War, conclude Peace, contract Alliances, establish Commerce, and to do all other Acts and Things which Independent States may of right do. And for the support of this Declaration, with a firm reliance on the Protection of Divine Providence, we mutually pledge to each other our Lives, our Fortunes and our sacred Honor.

JOHN HANCOCK, *President*
Attested, CHARLES THOMSON, *Secretary*

New Hampshire

JOSIAH BARTLETT
WILLIAM WHIPPLE
MATTHEW THORNTON

Massachusetts-Bay

SAMUEL ADAMS
JOHN ADAMS
ROBERT TREAT PAINE
ELBRIDGE GERRY

Rhode Island

STEPHEN HOPKINS
WILLIAM ELLERY

Connecticut

ROGER SHERMAN
SAMUEL HUNTINGTON
WILLIAM WILLIAMS
OLIVER WOLCOTT

Georgia

BUTTON WINNETT
LYMAN HALL
GEO. WALTON

Maryland

SAMUEL CHASE
WILLIAM PACA
THOMAS STONE
CHARLES CARROLL
of Carrollton

Virginia

GEORGE WYTHE
RICHARD HENRY LEE
THOMAS JEFFERSON
BENJAMIN HARRISON
THOMAS NELSON, JR.
FRANCIS LIGHTFOOT LEE
CARTER BRAXTON

New York

WILLIAM FLOYD
PHILIP LIVINGSTON
FRANCIS LEWIS
LEWIS MORRIS

Pennsylvania

ROBERT MORRIS
BENJAMIN RUSH
BENJAMIN FRANKLIN
JOHN MORTON
GEORGE CLYMER
JAMES SMITH
GEORGE TAYLOR
JAMES WILSON
GEORGE ROSS

Delaware

CAESAR RODNEY
GEORGE READ
THOMAS M' KEAN

North Carolina

WILLIAM HOOPER
JOSEPH HEWES
JOHN PENN

South Carolina

EDWARD RUTLEDGE
THOMAS HEYWARD, JR.
THOMAS LYNCH, JR.
ARTHUR MIDDLETON

New Jersey

RICHARD STOCKTON
JOHN WITHERSPOON
FRANCIS HOPKINS
JOHN HART
ABRAHAM CLARK

The Anti-Federalists:
Brutus and Cato

Editor's Introduction: The debates over the ratification of the 1787 Constitution produced some of the best writings in American political history. This applies most obviously to the *Federalist Papers* but also to some of the works of the Constitution's opponents, e.g., the "Anti-Federalists." People opposed the Constitution for a variety of reasons, but some common points of principle tended to unite the Anti-Federalist camp. Among these was the view expressed by both Brutus and Cato that democratic government could not survive on as large a scale as that envisioned by the Constitution's supporters.[1] The Anti-Federalists expressed in this conviction views inspired by "classical republican" writers including Montesquieu (see introduction). Montesquieu and others argued that republics required a "virtuous citizenry" to flourish and that civic virtue was best promoted in small states where citizens had face-to-face contact with one another, where public service was a realistic possibility for many if not all, and where there was a similarity in beliefs, interests, and customs. The Anti-Federalists described what the Constitution proposed as "consolidated government" and did not believe that the states would be preserved as important political entities under it. Moreover, they feared that power taken from the states and consolidated in the national capital would lead to the emergence of a political class that would lose touch with the interests of ordinary Americans and that these ordinary citizens in turn would lose their sense of allegiance toward government. The worst-case scenarios were that government would degenerate into the extremes of tyranny or anarchy, i.e., political order produced only by the threat of force or no political order at all.

Anti-Federalist themes, as you see, are not entirely alien to contemporary American politics. At the same time, the republican vision of the Anti-Federalists, relying as it does on cultural and social homogeneity and uniformity of interests within small republics, points back to an idyllic past of social harmony and similitude that never existed in the United

---

Source: *New York Journal,* October 18, 1787.

[1] The names Brutus and Cato are, of course, pseudonyms. Like the authors of the *Federalist Papers,* who adopted the pen name of Publius, Anti-Federalists often took on the names of Roman republican heroes. There is some doubt among scholars as to who the actual authors are, so we will not attempt further identification here.

States in as pure a form as their writings suggest. Nonetheless, though the theory of government held by the Anti-Federalists was defeated with the passage of the Constitution, they are still important contributors to the American political tradition. It was largely at Anti-Federalist insistence that a bill of rights was included in the Constitution. Fearing as they did the proposed powers of the new national government, it was particularly important to them that the Constitution also explicitly limited those powers. It should contain, they argued, specific protections of our fundamental freedoms in the form of a list of rights, including those to freedom of speech, press, and worship, with which the national government could not interfere. Though the Constitution was adopted without a bill of rights attached, there was a tacit promise that one would be considered in the first congressional session under the new Constitution. This promise was kept and the Bill of Rights, thanks largely to the promptings of the Anti-Federalists, was formally adopted in 1791. The unique and fascinating combination of liberal and republican themes, as well as their enormous practical contribution to our politics through the Bill of Rights, assure that Anti-Federalist political thought will remain of continued interest to politically aware Americans citizens.

*   *   *

ESSAYS OF BRUTUS (1787–1788)

To the Citizens of the State of New-York,
18 October 1787.

When the public is called to investigate and decide upon a question in which not only the present members of the community are deeply interested, but upon which the happiness and misery of generations yet unborn is in great measure suspended, the benevolent mind cannot help feeling itself peculiarly interested in the result.

In this situation, I trust the feeble efforts of an individual, to lead the minds of the people to a wise and prudent determination, cannot fail of being acceptable to the candid and dispassionate part of the community. Encouraged by this consideration, I have been induced to offer my thoughts upon the present important crisis of our public affairs.

Perhaps this country never saw so critical a period in their political concerns. We have felt the feebleness of the ties by which these United-States are held together, and the want of sufficient energy in our present confederation, to manage, in some instances, our general concerns. Various expedients have been proposed to remedy these evils, but none have succeeded. At length a Convention of the states has been assembled, they have formed a constitution which will now, probably, be submitted to the people to ratify or reject, who are the fountain of all power, to whom alone it of right belongs to make or unmake constitutions, or forms of government, at their pleasure. The most important question that was ever proposed to your decision, or the decision of any people under heaven, is before you, and you are to decide upon it by men of your election, chosen specially for this purpose. If the constitution, offered to your acceptance, be a wise one, calculated to preserve the invaluable blessings of liberty, to secure the inestimable rights of mankind, and promote human happiness, then, if you accept it, you will lay a lasting foundation of happiness for millions yet unborn; generations to come will rise up and call you blessed. You may rejoice in the prospects of this vast extended continent becoming filled with freemen, who will assert the dignity of human nature. You may solace yourselves with the idea, that society, in this favoured land, will fast advance to the highest point of perfection; the human mind will expand in knowledge and virtue, and the golden age be, in some measure, realized. But if, on the other hand, this form of government contains principles that will lead to the subversion of liberty—if it tends to establish a despotism, or, what is worse, a tyrannic aristocracy; then, if you adopt it, this only remaining assylum for liberty will be shut up, and posterity will execrate your memory.

[Text omitted]

With these few introductory remarks, I shall proceed to a consideration of this constitution:

The first question that presents itself on the subject is, whether a confederated government be the best for the United States or not? Or in other words, whether the thirteen United States should be reduced to one great republic, governed by one legislature, and under the direction of one executive and judicial; or whether they should continue thirteen confederated republics, under the direction and controul of a supreme federal head for certain defined national purposes only?

This enquiry is important, because, although the government reported by the convention does not go to a perfect and entire consolidation, yet it approaches so near to it, that it must, if executed, certainly and infallibly terminate in it.

This government is to possess absolute and uncontroulable power, legislative, executive and judicial, with respect to every object to which it extends, for by the last clause of section 8th, article 1st, it is declared "that the Congress shall have power to make all laws which shall be necessary and proper for carrying into execution the foregoing powers, and all other powers vested by this constitution, in the government of the United States; or in any department or office thereof." And by the 6th article, it is declared "that this constitution, and the laws of the United States, which shall be made in pursuance thereof, and the treaties made, or which shall be made, under the authority of the United States, shall be the supreme law of the land; and the judges in every state shall be bound thereby, any thing in the constitution or law of any state to the contrary notwithstanding." It appears from these articles that there is no need of any intervention of the state governments, between the Congress and the people, to execute any one power vested in the general government, and that the constitution and laws of every state are nullified and declared void, so far as they are or shall be inconsistent with this constitution, or the laws made in pursuance of it, or with treaties made under the authority of the United States.—The government then, so far as it extends, is a complete one, and not a confederation. . . . It is true this government is limited to certain objects, or to speak more properly, some small degree of power is still left to the states, but a little attention to the powers vested in the general government, will convince every candid man, that if it is capable of being executed, all that is reserved for the individual states must very soon be annihilated, except so far as they are barely necessary to the organization of the general government. The powers of the general legislature extend to every case that is of the least importance—there is nothing valuable to human nature, nothing dear to freemen, but what is within its power. It has authority to make laws which will affect the lives, the liberty, and property of every man in the United States; nor can the constitution or laws of any state, in any way prevent or impede the full and complete execution of every power given. The legislative power is competent to lay taxes, duties, imposts, and excises; . . . It is proper here to remark, that the authority to lay and collect taxes is the most important of any power that can be granted; it connects with it almost all other powers, or at least will in process of time draw all other after it; it is the great mean of protection, security, and defence, in a good government, and the great engine of oppression and tyranny in a bad one. . . .

It might be here shewn, that the power in the federal legislative, to raise and support armies at pleasure, as well in peace as in war, and their controul over the militia, tend, not only to consolidation of the government, but the destruction of liberty. . . .

[Text omitted]

How far the clause in the 8th section of the 1st article [i.e., the "necessary and proper clause"] may operate to do away all idea of confederated states, and to effect an entire consolidation of the whole into one general government, it is impossible to say. The powers given by this article are very general and comprehensive, and it may receive a construction to justify the passing almost any law. A power to make all laws, which shall be *necessary and proper*, for carrying into execution, all powers vested by the constitution in the government of the United States, or any department or officer thereof, is a power very comprehensive and definite [indefinite?], and may, for ought I know, be exercised in a such manner as entirely to abolish the state legislatures. . . .

It is not meant, by stating this case, to insinuate that the constitution would warrant a law of this kind; or unnecessarily to alarm the fears of the people, by suggesting, that the federal legislature would be more likely to pass the limits assigned them by the constitution, than that of an individual state, further than they are less responsible to the people. But what is meant is, that the legislature of the United States are vested with the great and uncontroulable powers, of laying and collecting taxes, duties, imposts, and excises; of regulating trade, raising and supporting armies, organizing, arming, and disciplining the militia, instituting courts, and other general powers. And are by this clause invested with the power of making all laws, *proper and necessary*, for carrying all these into execution; and they may so exercise this power as entirely to annihilate all the state governments, and reduce this country to one single government. And if they may do it, it is pretty certain they will; for it will be found that the power retained by individual states, small as it is, will be a clog upon the wheels of the government of the United States; the latter therefore will be naturally inclined to remove it out of the way. Besides, it is a truth confirmed by the unerring experience of ages, that every man, and every body of men, invested with power, are ever disposed to increase it and to acquire a superiority over every thing that stands in their way. This disposition, which is implanted in human nature, will operate in the federal legislature to lessen and ultimately to subvert the state authority, and having such advantages, will most certainly succeed, if the federal government succeeds at all. It must be very evident then, that what this constitution wants of being a complete consolidation of the several parts of the union into one complete government, possessed of perfect legislative, judicial, and executive powers, to all intents and purposes, it will necessarily acquire in its exercise and operation.

Let us now proceed to enquire, as I at first proposed, whether it be best the thirteen United States should be reduced to one great republic, or not? It is here taken for granted, that all agree in this, that whatever government we adopt, it ought to be a free one; that it should be so framed as to secure the liberty of the citizens of America, and such an one as to admit of a full, fair, and equal representation of the people. The question then will be, whether a government thus constituted, and founded on such principles, is practicable, and can be exercised over the whole United States, reduced into one state?

If respect is to be paid to the opinion of the greatest and wisest men who have ever thought or wrote on the science of government, we shall be constrained to conclude, that a free republic cannot succeed over a country of such immense extent, containing such a number of inhabitants, and these increasing in such rapid progression as that of the whole United States. Among the many illustrious authorities which might be produced to this point, I shall content myself with quoting only two. The one is the baron de Montesquieu, spirit of laws, chap. *xvi.* vol. I [book VIII]. "It is natural to a republic to have only a small territory, otherwise it cannot long subsist. In a large republic there are men of large fortunes, and consequently of less moderation; there are trusts too great to be placed in any single subject; he has interest of his own; he soon begins to think that he may be happy, great and glorious, by oppressing his fellow citizens; and that he may raise himself to grandeur on the ruins of his country. In a large republic, the public good is sacrificed to a thousand views; it is subordinate to exceptions, and depends on accidents. In a small one, the interest of the public is easier perceived, better understood, and more within the reach of every citizen; abuses are of less extent, and of course are less protected." . . .

History furnishes no example of a free republic, any thing like the extent of the United States. The Grecian republics were of small extent; so also was that of the Romans. Both of these, it is true, in process of time, extended their conquests over large territories of country; and the consequence was, that their governments were changed from that of free governments to those of the most tyrannical that ever existed in the world.

Not only the opinion of the greatest men, and the experience of mankind, are against the idea of an extensive republic, but a variety of reasons may be drawn from the reason and nature of things, against it. In every government, the will of the sovereign is the law. In despotic governments, the supreme authority being lodged in one, his will is law, and can be as easily expressed to a large extensive territory as to a small one. In a pure democracy the people are the sovereign, and their will is declared by themselves; for this purpose they must all come together to deliberate, and decide. This kind of government cannot be exercised, therefore, over a country of any considerable extent; it must be confined to a single city, or at least limited to such bounds as that the people can conveniently assemble, be able to debate, understand the subject submitted to them, and declare their opinion concerning it.

In a free republic, although all laws are derived from the consent of the people, yet the people do not declare their consent by themselves in person, but by representatives, chosen by them, who are supposed to know the minds of their constituents, and to be possessed of integrity to declare this mind.

In every free government, the people must give their assent to the laws by which they are governed. This is the true criterion between a free government and an arbitrary one. The former are ruled by the will of the whole, expressed in any manner they may agree upon; the latter by the will of one, or a few. If the people are to give their assent to the laws, by persons chosen and appointed by them, the manner of the choice and the number chosen, must be such, as to possess, be disposed, and consequently qualified to declare the sentiments of the people; for if they do not know, or are not disposed to speak the sentiments of the people, the people do not govern, but the sovereignty is in a few. Now, in a large extended country, it is impossible to have a representation, possessing the sentiments, and of integrity, to declare the minds of the people, without having it so numerous and unwieldly, as to be subject in a great measure to the inconveniency of a democratic government.

The territory of the United States is of vast extent; it now contains near three millions of souls, and is capable of containing much more than ten times that number. Is it practicable for a country, so large and so numerous as they will soon become, to elect a representation, that will speak their sentiments, without their becoming so numerous as to be incapable of transacting public business? It certainly is not.

In a republic, the manners, sentiments, and interests of the people should be similar. If this be not the case, there will be a constant clashing of opinions; and the representatives of one part will be continually striving against those of the other. This will retard the operations of government, and prevent such conclusions as will promote the public good. If we apply this remark to the condition of the United States, we shall be convinced that it forbids that we should be one government. The United States includes a variety of climates. The productions of the different parts of the union are very variant, and their interests, of consequence, diverse. Their manners and habits differ as much as their climates and productions; and their sentiments are by no means coincident. The laws and customs of the several states are, in many respects, very diverse, and in some opposite; each would be in favor of its own interests and customs, and, of consequence, a legislature, formed of representatives from the respective parts, would not be too numerous to act with any care or decision, but would be composed of such heterogenous and discordant principles, as would constantly be contending with each other.

The laws cannot be executed in a republic, of an extent equal to that of the United States, with promptitude.

The magistrates in every government must be supported in the execution of the laws, either by an armed force, maintained at the public expence for that purpose; or by the people turning out to aid the magistrate upon his command, in case of resistance.

In despotic governments, as well as in all the monarchies of Europe, standing armies are kept up to execute the commands of the prince or the magistrate, and are employed for this purpose when occasion requires: But they have always proved the destruction of liberty, and [are] abhorrent to the spirit of a free republic. In England, where they depend upon the parliament for their annual support, they have always been complained of as oppressive and unconstitutional, and are seldom employed in executing of the laws; never except on extraordinary occasions, and then under the direction of a civil magistrate.

A free republic will never keep a standing army to execute its laws. It must depend upon the support of its citizens. But when a government is to receive its support from the aid of the citizens, it must be so constructed as to have the confidence, respect, and affection of the people. Men who, upon the call of the magistrate, offer themselves to execute the laws, are influenced to do it either by affection to the government, or from fear; where a standing army is at hand to punish offenders, every man is actuated by the latter principle, and therefore, when the magistrate calls, will obey: but, where this is not the case, the government must rest for its support upon the confidence and respect which the people have for their government and laws. The body of the people being attached, the government will always be sufficient to support and execute its laws, and to operate upon the fears of any faction which may be opposed to it, not only to prevent an opposition to the execution of the laws themselves, but also to compel the most of them to aid the magistrate; but the people will not be likely to have such confidence in their rulers, in a republic so extensive as the United States, as necessary for these purposes. The confidence which the people have in their rulers, in a free republic, arises from their knowing them, from their being responsible to them for their conduct, and from the power they have of displacing them when they misbehave: but in a republic of the extent of this continent, the people in general would be acquainted with very few of their rulers: the people at large would know little of their proceedings, and it would be extremely difficult to change them. The people in Georgia and New Hampshire would not know one another's mind, and therefore could not act in concert to enable them to effect a general change of representatives. The different parts of so extensive a country could not possibly be made acquainted with the conduct of their representatives, nor be informed of the reasons upon which measures were founded. The consequence will be, they will have no confidence in their legislature, suspect them of ambitious views, be jealous of every measure they adopt, and will not support the laws they pass. Hence the government will be nerveless and inefficient, and no way will be left to render it otherwise, but by establishing an armed force to execute the laws at the point of the bayonet—a government of all others the most to be dreaded.

In a republic of such vast extent as the United-States, the legislature cannot attend to the various concerns and wants of its different parts. It cannot be sufficiently numerous to be acquainted with the local condition and wants of the different districts, and if it could, it is impossible it should have sufficient time to attend to and provide for all the variety of cases of this nature, that would be continually arising.

In so extensive a republic, the great officers of government would soon become above the controul of the people, and abuse their power to the purpose of aggrandizing themselves, and oppressing them. The trust committed to the executive offices, in a country of the extent of the United-States, must be various and of magnitude. The command of all the troops and navy of the republic, the appointment of officers, the power of pardoning offences, the collecting of all the public revenues, and the power of expending them, with a number of other powers, must be lodged and exercised in every state, in the hands of a few. When these are attended with great honor and emolument, as they always will be in large states, so as greatly to interest men to pursue them, and to be proper objects for ambitious and designing men, such men will be ever restless in their pursuit after them. They will use the power, when they have acquired it, to the purposes of gratifying their own interest and ambition, and it is scarcely possible, in a very large republic, to call them to account for their misconduct, or to prevent their abuse of power.

These are some of the reasons by which it appears, that a free republic cannot long subsist over a country of the great extent of these states. If then this new constitution is calculated to consolidate the thirteen states into one, as it evidently is, it ought not to be adopted.

Though I am of opinion, that it is a sufficient objection to this government, to reject it, that it creates the whole union into one government, under the form of a republic, yet if this objection was obviated, there are exceptions to it, which are so material and fundamental, that they ought to determine every man, who is a friend to the liberty and happiness of mankind, not to adopt it. I beg the candid and dispassionate attention of my countrymen while I state these objections—they are such as have obtruded themselves upon my mind upon a careful attention to the matter, and such as I sincerely believe are well founded. . . .

Brutus.

LETTERS OF CATO (1787–1788)

To the Citizens of the State of New–York.
In the close of my last introductory address, I told you, that my object in future would be to take up this new form of national government, to compare it with the experience and opinions of the most sensible and approved political authors, and to show you that its principles, and the exercise of them [,] will be dangerous to your liberty and happiness.

[Text omitted]

The freedom, equality, and independence which you enjoyed by nature, induced you to consent to a political power. The same principles led you to examine the errors and vices of a British superintendence, to divest yourselves of it, and to reassume a new political shape. It is acknowledged that there are defects in this, and another is tendered to you for acceptance; the great question then, that arises on this new political principle, is, whether it will answer the ends for which it is said to be offered to you, and for which all men engage in political society, to wit, the mutual preservation of their lives, liberties, and estates.

The recital, or premises on which this new form of government is erected, declares a consolidation or union of all the thirteen parts, or states, into one great whole, under the firm [form?] of the United States, for all the various and important purposes therein set forth.—But whoever seriously considers the immense extent of territory comprehended within the limits of the United States, together with the variety of its climates, productions, and commerce, the difference of extent, and number of inhabitants in all; the dissimilitude of interest, morals, and policies, in almost every one, will receive it as an intuitive truth, that a consolidated republican form of government therein, can never *form a perfect union, establish justice, insure domestic tranquility, promote the general welfare, and secure the blessings of liberty to you and your posterity,* for to these objects it must be directed: this unkindred legislature therefore, composed of interests opposite and dissimilar in their nature, will in its exercise, emphatically be, like a house divided against itself.

[Text omitted]

... It is natural, says Montesquieu, *to a republic to have only a small territory, otherwise it cannot long subsist: in a large one, there are men of large fortunes, and consequently of less moderation; there are too great deposits to intrust in the hands of a single subject, an ambitious person soon becomes sensible that he may be happy, great, and glorious by oppressing his fellow citizens, and*

Source: *New York Journal.* October 25, 1787.

that he might raise himself to grandeur, on the ruins of his country. In large republics, the public good is sacrificed to a thousand views; in a small one the interest of the public is easily perceived, better understood, and more within the reach of every citizen; abuses have a less extent, and of course are less protected— he also shews you, that the duration of the republic of Sparta, was owing to its having continued with the same extent of territory after all its wars; and that the ambition of Athens and Lacedemon to command and direct the union, lost them their liberties, and gave them a monarchy.

From this picture, what can you promise yourselves, on the score of consolidation of the United States, into one government—impracticability in the just exercise of it—your freedom insecure—even this form of government limited in its continuance—the employments of your country disposed of to the opulent, to whose contumely you will continually be an object—you must risque much, by indispensably placing trusts of the greatest magnitude, into the hands of individuals, whose ambition for power, and aggrandizement, will oppress and grind you—where, from the vast extent of your territory, and the complication of interests, the science of government will become intricate and perplexed, and too mysterious for you to understand, and observe; and by which you are to be conducted into a monarchy, either limited or despotic; the latter, Mr. Locke remarks, *is a government derived from neither nature, nor compact.*

Political liberty, the great Montesquieu again observes, *consists in security, or at least in the opinion we have of security;* and this *security* therefore, or the *opinion,* is best obtained in moderate governments, where the mildness of the laws, and the equality of the manners, beget a confidence in the people, which produces this security, or the opinion. This moderation in governments, depends in a great measure on their limits, connected with their political distribution.

The extent of many of the states in the Union, is at this time, almost too great for the superintendence of a republican form of government, and must one day or other, revolve into more vigorous ones, or by separation be reduced into smaller, and more useful, as well as moderate ones. You have already observed the feeble efforts of Massachusetts against their insurgents; with what difficulty did they quell that insurrection; and is not the province of Main at this moment, on the eve of separation from her. The reason of these things is, that for the security of the *property* of the community, in which expressive term Mr. Lock makes life, liberty, and estate, to consist—the wheels of a free republic are necessarily slow in their operation; hence in large free republics, the evil sometimes is not only begun, but almost completed, before they are in a situation to turn the current into a contrary progression: the extremes are also too remote from the usual seat of government, and the laws therefore too feeble to afford protection to all its parts, and insure *domestic tranquility* without the aid of another principle. If, therefore, this state, and that of N. Carolina, had an army under their controul, they never would have lost Vermont, and Frankland, nor the state of Massachusetts suffer an insurrection, or the dismemberment of her fairest district, but the exercise of a principle which would have prevented these things, if we may believe the experience of ages, would have ended in the destruction of their liberties.

Will this consolidated republic, if established, in its exercise beget such confidence and compliance, among the citizens of these states, as to do without the aid of a standing army—I deny that it will.—The malcontents in each state, who will not be a few, nor the least important, will be exciting factions against it—the fear of dismemberment of some of its parts, and the necessity to enforce the execution of revenue laws (a fruitful source of oppression) on the extremes and in the other districts of the government, will incidentally, and necessarily require a permanent force, to be kept on foot—will not political security, and even the opinion of it, be extinguished? can mildness and moderation exist in a government, where the primary incident in its exercise must be force? will not violence destroy confidence, and can equality subsist, where the extent, policy, and practice of it, will naturally lead to make odious distinctions among citizens?

The people, who may compose this national legislature from the southern states, in which, from the mildness of the climate, the fertility of the soil, and the value of its productions, wealth is rapidly acquired, and where the same causes naturally lead to luxury, dissipation, and a passion for aristocratic distinctions; where slavery is encouraged, and liberty of course, less respected, and protected; who know not what it is to acquire property by their own toil, nor to oeconomise with the savings of industry—will these men therefore be as tenacious of the liberties and interests of the more northern states, where freedom, independence, industry, equality, and frugality, are natural to the climate and soil, as men who are your own citizens, legislating in your own state, under your inspection, and whose manners, and fortunes, bear a more equal resemblance to your own?

It may be suggested, in answer to this, that whoever is a citizen of one state, is a citizen of each, and that therefore he will be as interested in the happiness and interest of all, as the one he is delegated from; but the argument is fallacious, and, whoever has attended to the history of mankind, and the principles which bind them together as parents, citizens, or men, will readily perceive it. These principles are, in their exercise, like a pebble cast on the calm surface of a river, the circles begin in the center, and are small, active, and forcible, but as they depart from that point, they lose their force, and vanish into calmness.

The strongest principle of union resides within our domestic walls.

The ties of the parent exceed that of any other; as we depart from home, the next general principle of union is amongst citizens of the same state, where acquaintance, habits, and fortunes, nourish affection, and attachment; enlarge the circle still further, and, as citizens of different states, though we acknowledge the same national denomination, we lose the ties of acquaintance, habits, and fortunes, and thus, by degrees, we lessen in our attachments, till, at length, we no more than acknowledge a sameness of species. Is it therefore, from certainty like this, reasonable to believe, that inhabitants of Georgia, or New-Hampshire, will have the same obligations towards you as your own, and preside over your lives, liberties, and property, with the same care and attachment? Intuitive reason, answers in the negative.

In the course of my examination of the principals of consolidation of the states into one general government, many other reasons against it have occurred, but I flatter myself, from those herein offered to your consideration. I have convinced you that it is both presumptuous and impracticable consistent with your safety. . . .

Cato.

The Federalist Papers (1787)

Editor's Introduction: As revered as the Constitution is today by most Americans, it is worth remembering that it was the subject of heated controversy when first proposed in 1787. A convention was held in Philadelphia in the summer of 1787, made up of representatives of twelve of the thirteen states. Rhode Island did not attend. It had been authorized to revise the Articles of Confederation, the supreme law of the land from 1781 until the Constitution was adopted in 1789. The Articles were based on the notion that the American union was a confederation of states loosely linked by a central government with very limited powers to raise money or troops, or to pass laws of any sorts. Doing so required that nine of the thirteen states consented, and rarely were representatives of more than ten present at the national congress' deliberations. There was a general sense in the land that reform was in order, though how great a reform was much in question. The delegates to the Philadelphia Convention quickly abandoned the framework of the Articles altogether and proceeded to draft a new constitution, which was to be presented to conventions held in each of the thirteen states to vote on its adoption. Controversy over the proposed constitution gave rise to an enormous pamphlet literature, with friends and foes seeking to influence the vote at the ratifying conventions. The most highly regarded contribution to this literature is the *Federalist Papers*. This series of 85 essays appeared in New York City newspapers over a ten-month period, beginning in the summer of 1787. They were written under the pseudonym Publius by John Jay, James Madison, and Alexander Hamilton, with all but a handful written by the latter two. Madison, of course, also had played a critical role in the Constitutional Convention and took the best notes of its proceedings which are widely available today. If anyone deserves the title of father of the Constitution, it is he.

The *Federalist Papers* make a strong case for a "more energetic" government than existed under the Articles. Similar to ideas found in the Declaration of Independence, they ground this case in deep reflections on human nature, society, and government. *Federalist #1* sets out what Hamilton sees as the central question of the whole work: "whether societies of men are really capable or not of establishing good government from reflection or choice," or whether government will always be deter-

Source: Available in many editions and on the internet. One particularly useful edition is Isaac Kramnick, ed. *The Federalist Papers* (New York: Penguin Books, 1987).

mined by "accident and force." It expresses the view, long held by Americans, that we were engaged in an experiment in self-government unique in world history and one that would serve as an example, for better or ill, throughout the world. In *Federalist #10*, reproduced here in its entirety, Madison sets forth a rather dark view of human nature and defines the role of government as managing factional strife in the interests of preserving individual liberty. As long as people are free to live as they choose, Madison suggests, society will be rent by disagreements based on moral and/or religious conviction, political passions, and material interests. The only way to eliminate such conflicts is to eliminate liberty itself, and this is a cure worse than the disease. In developing this argument, Madison places himself squarely in the liberal tradition of political thought as discussed in the introduction to this volume. *Federalist #45* addresses fears of the Constitution's opponents that the document poses threats to the continued existence of state governments. It attempts to reassure people that the states will always hold a special place in the hearts of citizens. This foray into political psychology, consideration of conditions under which people feel a sense of allegiance to government(s), is an important and often overlooked aspect of these essays. The *Federalist Papers* represents one of the classic contributions to liberal democratic political thought and is generally regarded as the finest work in political theory that Americans have produced.

*   *   *

FEDERALIST NO. 1 (HAMILTON)

AFTER an unequivocal experience of the inefficiency of the subsisting federal government, you are called upon to deliberate on a new Constitution for the United States of America. The subject speaks its own importance; comprehending in its consequences nothing less than the existence of the UNION, the safety and welfare of the parts of which it is composed, the fate of an empire in many respects the most interesting in the world. It has been frequently remarked that it seems to have been reserved to the people of this country, by their conduct and example, to decide the important question, whether societies of men are really capable or not of establishing good government from reflection and choice, or whether they are forever destined to depend for their political constitutions on accident and force. If there be any truth in the remark, the crisis at which we are arrived may with propriety be regarded as the era in which that decision is to be made; and a wrong election of the part we shall act may, in this view, deserve to be considered as the general misfortune of mankind.

This idea will add the inducements of philanthropy to those of patriotism, to heighten the solicitude which all considerate and good men must feel for the event. Happy will it be if our choice should be directed by a judicious estimate of our true interests, unperplexed and unbiased by considerations not connected with the public good. But this is a thing more ardently to be wished than seriously to be expected. The plan offered to our deliberations affects too many particular interests, innovates upon too many local institutions, not to involve in its discussion a variety of objects foreign to its merits, and of views, passions and prejudices little favorable to the discovery of truth.

Among the most formidable of the obstacles which the new Constitution will have to encounter may readily be distinguished the obvious interest of a certain class of men in every State to resist all changes which may hazard a diminution of the power, emolument, and consequence of the offices they hold under the State establishments; and the perverted ambition of another class of men, who will either hope to aggrandize themselves by the confusions of their country, or will flatter themselves with fairer prospects of elevation from the subdivision of the empire into several partial confederacies than from its union under one government.

It is not, however, my design to dwell upon observations of this nature. I am well aware that it would be disingenuous to resolve indiscriminately the opposition of any set of men (merely because their situations might subject them to suspicion) into interested or ambitious views. Candor will oblige us to admit that even such men may be actuated by upright intentions; and it cannot be doubted that much of the opposition which has made its appearance, or may hereafter make its appearance, will spring from sources, blameless at least, if not respectable—the honest errors of minds led astray by preconceived jealousies and fears. So numerous indeed and so powerful are the causes which serve to give a false bias to the judgment, that we, upon many occasions, see wise and good men on the wrong as well as on the right side of questions of the first magnitude to society. This circumstance, if duly attended to, would furnish a lesson of moderation to those who are ever so thoroughly persuaded of their being in the right in any controversy. And a further reason for caution, in this respect, might be drawn from the reflection that we are not always sure that those who advocate the truth are influenced by purer principles than their antagonists. Ambition, avarice, personal animosity, party opposition, and many other motives not more laudable than these, are apt to operate as well upon those who support as those who oppose the right side of a question. Were there not even these inducements to moderation, nothing could be more ill-judged than that intolerant spirit which has, at all times, characterized political parties. For in politics, as in religion, it is equally absurd to aim at making proselytes by fire and sword. Heresies in either can rarely be cured by persecution.

And yet, however just these sentiments will be allowed to be, we have already sufficient indications that it will happen in this as in all former cases of great national discussion. A torrent of angry and malignant passions will be let loose. To judge from the conduct of the opposite parties, we shall be led to conclude that they will mutually hope to evince the justness of their opinions, and to increase the number of their converts by the loudness of their declamations and the bitterness of their invectives. An enlightened zeal for the energy and efficiency of government will be stigmatized as the offspring of a temper fond of despotic power and hostile to the principles of liberty. An over-scrupulous jealousy of danger to the rights of the people, which is more commonly the fault of the head than of the heart, will be represented as mere pretense and artifice, the stale bait for popularity at the expense of the public good. It will be forgotten, on the one hand, that jealousy is the usual concomitant of love, and that the noble enthusiasm of liberty is to apt to be infected with a spirit of narrow and illiberal distrust. On the other hand, it will be equally forgotten that the vigor of government is essential to the security of liberty; that, in the contemplation of a sound and well-informed judgment, their interest can never be separated; and that a dangerous ambition more often lurks behind the specious mask of zeal for the rights of the people than under the forbidding appearance of zeal for the firmness and efficiency of government. History will teach us that the former has been found a much more certain road to the introduction of despotism than the latter, and that of those men who have overturned the liberties of republics, the greatest number have begun their career by paying an obsequious court to the people, commencing demagogues and ending tyrants.

In the course of the preceding observations, I have had an eye, my fellow-citizens, to putting you upon your guard against all attempts, from whatever quarter, to influence your decision in a matter of the utmost moment to your welfare, by any impressions other than those which may result from the evidence of truth. You will, no doubt, at the same time have collected from the general scope of them that they proceed from a source not unfriendly to the new Constitution. Yes, my countrymen, I own to you that after having given it an attentive consideration, I am clearly of opinion it is your interest to adopt it. I am convinced that this is the safest course for your liberty, your dignity, and your happiness. I affect not reserves which I do not feel. I will not amuse you with an appearance of deliberation when I have decided. I frankly acknowledge to you my convictions, and I will freely lay before you the reasons on which they are founded. The consciousness of good intentions disdains ambiguity. I shall not, however, multiply professions on this head. My motives must remain in the depository of my own breast. My arguments will be open to all and may be judged of by all. They shall at least be offered in a spirit which will not disgrace the cause of truth.

I propose, in a series of papers, to discuss the following interesting particulars:
*The utility of the **union** to your political prosperity
*The insufficiency of the present confederation to preserve that union
*The necessity of a government at least equally energetic with the one proposed, to the attainment of this object
*The conformity of the proposed constitution to the true principles of republican government
*Its analogy to your own state constitution and lastly,
*The additional security which its adoption will afford to the preservation of that species of government, to liberty, and to property.

In the progress of this discussion I shall endeavor to give a satisfactory answer to all the objections which shall have made their appearance, that may seem to have any claim to your attention.

It may perhaps be thought superfluous to offer arguments to prove the utility of the UNION, a point, no doubt, deeply engraved on the hearts of the great body of the people in every State, and one which, it may be imagined, has no adversaries. But the fact is that we already hear it whispered in the private circles of those who oppose the new Constitution, that the thirteen States are of too great extent for any general system, and that we must of necessity resort to separate confederacies of distinct portions of the whole. This doctrine will, in all probability, be gradually propagated, till it has votaries enough to countenance an open avowal of it. For nothing can be more evident to those who are able to take an enlarged view of the subject than the alternative of an adoption of the new Constitution or a dismemberment of the Union. It will therefore be of use to begin by examining the advantages of that Union, the certain evils, and the probable dangers, to which every State will be exposed from its dissolution. . . . PUBLIUS

FEDERALIST NO. 10 (MADISON)
(THE UNION AS A SAFEGUARD AGAINST DOMESTIC
FACTION AND INSURRECTION)

AMONG the numerous advantages promised by a well constructed Union, none deserves to be more accurately developed than its tendency to break and control the violence of faction. The friend of popular governments never finds himself so much alarmed for their character and fate, as when he contemplates their propensity to this dangerous vice. He will not fail, therefore, to set a due value on any plan which, without violating the principles to which he is attached, provides a proper cure for it. The instability, injustice, and confusion introduced into the public councils, have, in truth, been the mortal diseases under which popular governments have everywhere perished, as they continue to be the favorite and fruitful topics from which the adversaries to liberty derive their most specious declamations. The valuable improvements made by the American constitutions on the popular models, both ancient and modern, cannot certainly be too much admired; but it would be an unwarrantable partiality to contend that they have as effectually obviated the danger on this side, as was wished and expected. Complaints are everywhere heard from our most considerate and virtuous citizens, equally the friends of public and private faith, and of public and personal liberty, that our governments are too unstable, that the public good is disregarded in the conflicts of rival parties, and that measures are too often decided, not according to the rules of justice and the rights of the minor party, but by the superior force of an interested and overbearing majority. However anxiously we may wish that these complaints had no foundation, the evidence of known facts will not permit us to deny that they are in some degree true. It will be found, indeed, on a candid review of our situation, that some of the distresses under which we labor have been erroneously charged on the operation of our governments; but it will be found, at the same time, that other causes will not alone account for many of our heaviest misfortunes; and, particularly, for that prevailing and increasing distrust of public engagements and alarm for private rights which are echoed from one end of the continent to the other. These must be chiefly, if not wholly, effects of the unsteadiness and injustice with which a factious spirit has tainted our public administrations.

By a faction I understand a number of citizens, whether amounting to a majority or a minority of the whole, who are united and actuated by some common impulse of passion, or of interest, adversed to the rights of other citizens, or to the permanent and aggregate interests of the community.

There are two methods of curing the mischiefs of faction: the one, by removing its causes; the other, by controlling its effects.

There are again two methods of removing the causes of faction: the one, by destroying the liberty which is essential to its existence; the other, by giving to every citizen the same opinions, the same passions, and the same interests.

It could never be more truly said than of the first remedy that it was worse than the disease. Liberty is to faction what air is to fire, an aliment without which it instantly expires. But it could not be a less folly to abolish liberty, which is essential to political life, because it nourishes faction than it would be to wish the annihilation of air, which is essential to animal life, because it imparts to fire its destructive agency.

The second expedient is as impracticable as the first would be unwise. As long as the reason of man continues fallible, and he is at liberty to exercise it, different opinions will be formed. As long as the connection subsists between his reason and his self-love, his opinions and his passions will have a reciprocal influence on each other; and the former will be objects to which the latter will attach themselves. The diversity in the faculties of men, from which the rights of property originate, is not less an insuperable obstacle to a uniformity of interests. The protection of these faculties is the first object of government. From the protection of different and unequal faculties of acquiring property, the possession of different degrees and kinds of property immediately results; and from the influence of these on the sentiments and views of the respective proprietors ensues a division of the society into different interests and parties.

The latent causes of faction are thus sown in the nature of man; and we see them everywhere brought into different degrees of activity, according to the different circumstances of civil society. A zeal for different opinions concerning religion, concerning government, and many other points, as well of speculation as of practice; an attachment to different leaders ambitiously contending for pre-eminence and power; or to persons of other descriptions whose fortunes have been interesting to the human passions, have, in turn, divided mankind into parties, inflamed them with mutual animosity, and rendered them much more disposed to vex and oppress each other than to co-operate for their common good. So strong is this propensity of mankind to fall into mutual animosities that where no substantial occasion presents itself the most frivolous and fanciful distinctions have been sufficient to kindle their unfriendly passions and excite their most violent conflicts. But the most common and durable source of factions has been the verious and unequal distribution of property. Those who hold and those who are without property have ever formed distinct interests in society. Those who are creditors, and those who are debtors, fall under a like discrimination. A landed interest, a manufacturing interest, a mercantile interest, a moneyed interest, with many lesser interests, grow up of necessity in civilized nations, and divide them into different classes, actuated by different sentiments and views. The regulation of these various and interfering interests forms the principal task of modern legislation and involves the spirit of party and faction in the necessary and ordinary operations of the government.

No man is allowed to be a judge in his own cause, because his interest would certainly bias his judgment, and, not improbably, corrupt his integrity. With equal, nay with greater reason, a body of men are unfit to be both judges and parties at the same time; yet what are many of the most important acts of legislation but so many judicial determinations, not indeed concerning the rights of single persons, but concerning the rights of large bodies of citizens? And what are the different classes of legislators but advocates and parties to the causes which they determine? Is a law proposed concerning private debts? It is a question to which the creditors are parties on one side and the debtors on the other. Justice ought to hold the balance between them. Yet the parties are, and must be, themselves the judges; and the most numerous party, or in other words, the most powerful faction must be expected to prevail. Shall domestic manufacturers be encouraged, and in what degree, by restrictions on foreign manufacturers? are questions which would be differently decided by the landed and the manufacturing classes, and probably by neither with a sole regard to justice and the public good. The apportionment of taxes on the various descriptions of property is an act which seems to require the most exact impartiality; yet there is, perhaps, no legislative act in which greater opportunity and temptation are given to a predominant party to trample on the rules of justice. Every shilling with which they overburden the inferior number is a shilling saved to their own pockets.

It is in vain to say that enlightened statesmen will be able to adjust these clashing interests and render them all subservient to the public good. Enlightened statesmen will not always be at the helm. Nor, in many cases, can such an adjustment be made at all without taking into view indirect and remote considerations, which will rarely prevail over the immediate interest which one party may find in disregarding the rights of another or the good of the whole.

The inference to which we are brought is that the *causes* of faction cannot be removed and that relief is only to be sought in the means of controlling its *effects*.

If a faction consists of less than a majority, relief is supplied by the republican principle, which enables the majority to defeat its sinister views by regular vote. It may clog the administration, it may convulse the society; but it will be unable to execute and mask its violence under the forms of the Constitution. When a majority is included in a faction, the form of popular government, on the other hand, enables it to sacrifice to its ruling passion or interest both the public good and the rights of other citizens. To secure the public good and private rights against the danger of such a faction, and at the same time to preserve the spirit and the form of popular government, is then the great object to which our inquiries are directed. Let me add that it is the great desideratum by which alone this form of government can be rescued from the opprobrium under which it has so long labored and be recommended to the esteem and adoption of mankind.

By what means is this object attainable? Evidently by one of two only. Either the existence of the same passion or interest in a majority at the same time must be prevented, or the majority, having such coexistent passion or interest, must be rendered, by their number and local situation, unable to concert and carry into effect schemes of oppression. If the impulse and the opportunity be suffered to coincide, we well know that neither moral nor religious motives can be relied on as an adequate control. They are not found to be such on the injustice and violence of individuals, and lose their efficacy in proportion to the number combined together, that is, in proportion as their efficacy becomes needful.

From this view of the subject it may be concluded that a pure democracy, by which I mean a society consisting of a small number of citizens, who assemble and administer the government in person, can admit of no cure for the mischiefs of faction. A common passion or interest will, in almost every case, be felt by a majority of the whole; a communication and concert results from the form of government itself; and there is nothing to check the inducements to sacrifice the weaker party or an obnoxious individual. Hence it is that such democracies have ever been spectacles of turbulence and contention; have ever been found incompatible with personal security or the rights of property; and have in general been as short in their lives as they have been violent in their deaths. Theoretic politicians, who have patronized this species of government, have erroneously supposed that by reducing mankind to a perfect equality in their political rights, they would at the same time be perfectly equalized and assimilated in their possessions, their opinions, and their passions.

A republic, by which I mean a government in which the scheme of representation takes place, opens a different prospect and promises the cure for which we are seeking. Let us examine the points in which it varies from pure democracy, and we shall comprehend both the nature of the cure and the efficacy which it must derive from the Union.

The two great points of difference between a democracy and a republic are: first, the delegation of the government, in the latter, to a small number of citizens elected by the rest; secondly, the greater number of citizens and greater sphere of country over which the latter may be extended.

The effect of the first difference is, on the one hand, to refine and enlarge the public views by passing them through the medium of a chosen body of citizens, whose wisdom may best discern the true interest of their country and whose patriotism and love of justice will be least likely to sacrifice it to temporary or partial considerations. Under such a regulation it may well happen that the public voice, pronounced by the representatives of the people, will be more consonant to the public good than if pronounced by the people themselves, convened for the purpose. On the other hand, the effect may be inverted. Men of factious tempers, of local prejudices, or of sinister designs, may, by intrigue, by corruption, or by other means, first obtain the suffrages, and then betray the interests of the people. The question resulting is, whether small or extensive republics are more favorable to the election of proper guardians of the public weal; and it is clearly decided in favor of the latter by two obvious considerations:

In the first place it is to be remarked that however small the republic may be the representatives must be raised to a certain number in order to guard against the cabals of a few; and that however large it may be they must be limited to a certain number in order to guard against the confusion of a multitude. Hence, the number of representatives in the two cases not being in proportion to that of the constituents, and being proportionally greater in the small republic, it follows that if the proportion of fit characters be not less in the large than in the small republic, the former will present a greater option, and consequently a greater probability of a fit choice.

In the next place, as each representative will be chosen by a greater number of citizens in the large than in the small republic, it will be more difficult for unworthy candidates to practice with success the vicious arts by which elections are too often carried; and the suffrages of the people being more free, will be more likely to center in men who possess the most attractive merit and the most diffusive and established characters.

It must be confessed that in this, as in most other cases, there is a mean, on both sides of which inconveniences will be found to lie. By enlarging too much the number of electors, you render the representative too little acquainted with all their local circumstances and lesser interests; as by reducing it too much, you render him unduly attached to these, and too little fit to comprehend and pursue great and national objects. The federal Constitution forms a happy combination in this respect; the great and aggregate interests being referred to the national, the local and particular to the State legislatures.

The other point of difference is the greater number of citizens and extent of territory which may be brought within the compass of republican than of democratic government; and it is this circumstance principally which renders factious combinations less to be dreaded in the former than in the latter. The smaller the society, the fewer probably will be the distinct parties and interests composing it; the fewer the distinct parties and interests, the more frequently will a majority be found of the same party; and the smaller the number of individuals composing a majority, and the smaller the compass within which they are placed, the more easily will they concert and execute their plans of oppression. Extend the sphere, and you take in a greater variety of parties and interests; you make it less probable that a majority of the whole will have a common motive to invade the rights of other citizens; or if such a common motive exists, it will be more difficult for all who feel it to discover their own strength and to act in unison with each other. Besides other impediments, it may be remarked that, where there is a consciousness of unjust or dishonorable purposes, communication is always checked by distrust in proportion to the number whose concurrence is necessary.

Hence, it clearly appears that the same advantage which a republic has over a democracy in controlling the effects of faction is enjoyed by a large over a small republic—is enjoyed by the Union over the States composing it. Does the advantage consist in the substitution of representatives whose enlightened views and virtuous sentiments render them superior to local prejudices and schemes of injustice? It will not be denied that the representation of the Union will be most likely to possess these requisite endowments. Does it consist in the greater security afforded by a greater variety of parties, against the event of any one party being able to outnumber and oppress the rest? In an equal degree does the increased variety of parties comprised within the Union increase this security. Does it, in fine, consist in the greater obstacles opposed to the concert and accomplishment of the secret wishes of an unjust and interested majority? Here again the extent of the Union gives it the most palpable advantage.

The influence of factious leaders may kindle a flame within their particular States but will be unable to spread a general conflagration through the other States. A religious sect may degenerate into a political faction in a part of the Confederacy; but the variety of sects dispersed over the entire face of it must secure the national councils against any danger from that source. A rage for paper money, for an abolition of debts, for an equal division of property, or for any other improper or wicked project, will be less apt to pervade the whole body of the Union than a particular member of it, in the same proportion as such a malady is more likely to taint a particular county or district than an entire State.

In the extent and proper structure of the Union, therefore, we behold a republican remedy for the diseases most incident to republican government. And according to the degree of pleasure and pride we feel in being republicans ought to be our zeal in cherishing the spirit and supporting the character of federalists. PUBLIUS.

FEDERALIST NO. 45 (MADISON)

HAVING shown that no one of the powers transferred to the federal government is unnecessary or improper, the next question to be considered is whether the whole mass of them will be dangerous to the portion of authority left in the several States. The adversaries to the plan of the convention, instead of considering in the first place what degree of power was absolutely necessary for the purposes of the federal government, have exhausted themselves in a secondary inquiry into the possible consequences of the proposed degree of power to the governments of the particular States. But if the Union, as has been shown, be essential to the security of the people of America against foreign danger; if it be essential to their security against contentions and wars among the different States; if it be essential to guard them against those violent and oppressive factions which embitter the blessings of liberty and against those military establishments which must gradually poison its very fountain; if, in a word, the Union be essential to the happiness of the people of America, is it not preposterous to urge as an objection to a government, without which the objects of the Union cannot be attained, that such a government may derogate from the importance of the governments of the individual States? Was, then, the American Revolution effected, was the American Confederacy formed, was the precious blood of thousands spilt, and the hard-earned substance of millions lavished, not that the people of America should enjoy peace, liberty, and safety, but that the government of the individual States, that particular municipal establishments, might enjoy a certain extent of power and be arrayed with certain dignities and attributes of sovereignty?

We have heard of the impious doctrine in the old world, that the people were made for kings, not kings for the people. Is the same doctrine to be revived in the new, in another shape—that the solid happiness of the people is to be sacrificed to the views of political institutions of a different form? It is too early for politicians to presume on our forgetting that the public good, the real welfare of the great body of the people, is the supreme object to be pursued; and that no form of government whatever has any other value than as it may be fitted for the attainment of this object. Were the plan of the convention adverse to the public happiness, my voice would be, Reject the plan. Were the Union itself inconsistent with the public happiness, it would be, Abolish the Union. In like manner, as far as the sovereignty of the States cannot be reconciled to the happiness of the people, the voice of every good citizen must be, Let the former be sacrificed to the latter. How far the sacrifice is necessary has been shown. How far the unsacrificed residue will be endangered is the question before us.

[Text omitted]

We have seen, in all the examples of ancient and modern confederacies, the strongest tendency continually betraying itself in the members to despoil the general government of its authorities, with a very ineffectual capacity in the latter to defend itself against the encroachments. Although, in most of these examples, the system has been so dissimilar from that under consideration as greatly to weaken any inference concerning the latter from the fate of the former, yet, as the States will retain under the proposed Constitution a very extensive portion of active sovereignty, the inference ought not to be wholly disregarded.

[Text omitted]

The State governments will have the advantage of the federal government, whether we compare them in respect to the immediate dependence of the one on the other; to the weight of personal influence which each side will possess; to the powers respectively vested in them; to the predilection and probable support of the people; to the disposition and faculty of resisting and frustrating the measures of each other.

The State governments may be regarded as constituent and essential parts of the federal government; whilst the latter is nowise essential to the operation or organization of the former. Without the intervention of the State legislatures, the President of the United States cannot be elected at all. They must in all cases have a great share in his appointment, and will, perhaps, in most cases, of themselves determine it. The Senate will be elected absolutely and exclusively by the State legislatures. Even the House of Representatives, though drawn immediately from the people, will be chosen very much under the influence of that class of men whose influence over the people obtains for themselves an election into the State legislatures. Thus, each of the principal branches of the federal government will owe its existence more or less to the favor of the State governments, and must consequently feel a dependence, which is much more likely to beget a disposition too obsequious than too overbearing towards them. On the other side, the component parts of the State governments will in no instance be indebted for their appointment to the direct agency of the federal government, and very little, if at all, to the local influence of its members.

The number of individuals employed under the Constitution of the United States will be much smaller than the number employed under the particular States. There will consequently be less of personal influence on the side of the former than of the latter. The members of the legislative, executive, and judiciary departments of thirteen and more States, the justices of peace, officers of militia, ministerial officers of justice, with all the county, corporation, and town officers, for three millions and more of people, intermixed, and having particular acquaintance with every class and circle of people, must exceed, beyond all proportion, both in number and influence, those of every description who will be employed in the administration of the federal system. Compare the members of the three great departments of the thirteen States, excluding from the judiciary department the justices of peace, with the members of the corresponding departments of the single government of the Union; compare the militia officers of three millions of people with the military and marine officers of any establishment which is within the compass of probability, or, I may add, of possibility, and in this view alone, we may pronounce the advantage of the States to be decisive. If the federal government is to have collectors of revenue, the State governments will have theirs also. And as those of the former will be principally on the seacoast, and not very numerous, whilst those of the latter will be spread over the face of the country, and will be very numerous, the advantage in this view also lies on the same side. It is true that the Confederacy is to possess, and may exercise, the power of collecting internal as well as external taxes throughout the States; but it is probable that this power will not be resorted to, except for supplemental purposes of revenue; that an option will then be given to the States to supply their quotas by previous collections of their own; and that the eventual collection, under the immediate authority of the Union, will generally be made by the officers, and according to the rules, appointed by the several States. Indeed it is extremely probable, that in other instances, particularly in the organization of the judicial power, the officers of the States will be clothed with the correspondent authority of the Union. Should it happen, however, that separate collectors of internal revenue should be appointed under the federal government, the influence of the whole number would not bear a comparison with that of the multitude of State officers in the opposite scale. . . .

The powers delegated by the proposed Constitution to the federal government are few and defined. Those which are to remain in the State governments are numerous and indefinite. The former will be exercised principally on external objects, as war, peace, negotiation, and foreign commerce; with which last the power of taxation will, for the most part, be connected. The powers reserved to the several States will extend to all the objects which, in the ordinary course of affairs, concern the lives, liberties, and properties of the people, and the internal order, improvement, and prosperity of the State.

The operations of the federal government will be most extensive and important in times of war and danger; those of the State governments in times of peace and security. As the former periods will probably bear a small proportion to the latter, the State governments will here enjoy another advantage over the federal government. The more adequate, indeed, the federal powers may be rendered to the national defense, the less frequent will be those scenes of danger which might favor their ascendancy over the governments of the particular States.

[Text omitted]

George Washington,
"Farewell Address" (1796)

Editor's Introduction: George Washington (1732–1799) occupies a unique place in American history. His leadership of the Continental Army during the Revolutionary War cemented his high status among his fellow Americans. He was later to serve as presiding officer of the Constitutional Convention in Philadelphia in 1787. In fact, much of the success of this convention in overcoming divisions among delegates was due to his unifying influence. Moreover, the widespread assumption that Washington would serve as the first president under the Constitution eased public fears about adopting the document and enhanced the powers and prestige of the office of the presidency. Washington determined in 1796 that he would not seek a third term as president, hence starting a tradition that presidents observed until Franklin Delano Roosevelt, who ran for and won four presidential elections.

The Farewell Address was Washington's attempt not so much to summarize his contributions as president as to offer advice to his country as he returned to private life. The Address was actually drafted by Alexander Hamilton, using ideas and statements from Washington but imparting his own views as well. It was never delivered in person but was published in newspapers throughout the country beginning in September 1796. The Address was written at a time when foreign policy was becoming subject to heated partisan conflict. War was raging in Europe as the British were fighting the revolutionary government in France. The emerging Democratic–Republican Party wished that America would support the French, whereas Washington's Federalist administration had proclaimed neutrality in the conflict. The Address is one of the most important statements of principle regarding U.S. foreign policy. It urges that the United States follow a neutral course among nations and avoid "entangling" foreign alliances. Washington also uses the Address to help forge a sense of national identity at home. He stresses the importance of national attachment and identity as a means to overcome the threats of partisan and sectional strife.

*　　　　　*　　　　　*

Friends, and Fellow-Citizens: The period for a new election of a Citizen, to Administer the Executive government of the United States, being not far distant, and the time actually arrived, when your thoughts must be employed in designating the person, who is to be cloathed with that important trust, it appears to me proper, especially as it may conduce to a more distinct expression of the public voice, that I should now apprise you of the resolution I have formed, to decline being considered among the number of those, out of whom a choice is to be made.

[Text omitted]

I rejoice, that the state of your concerns, external as well as internal, no longer renders the pursuit of inclination incompatible with the sentiment of duty or propriety; and am persuaded whatever partiality may be retained for my services, that in the present circumstances of our country, you will not disapprove my determination to retire.

[Text omitted]

But a solicitude for your welfare, which cannot end but with my life, and the apprehension of danger, natural to that solicitude, urge me on an occasion like the present, to offer to your solemn contemplation, and to recommend to your frequent review, some sentiments; which are the result of much reflection, of no inconsiderable observation, and which appear to me all important to the permanency of your felicity as a People. These will be offered to you with the more freedom, as you can only see in them the disinterested warnings of a parting friend, who can possibly have no personal motive to biass his counsel.

[Text omitted]

Interwoven as is the love of liberty with every ligament of your hearts, no recommendation of mine is necessary to fortify or confirm the attachment.

The Unity of Government which constitutes you one people is also now dear to you. It is justly so; for it is a main Pillar in the Edifice of your real independence, the support of your tranquility at home; your peace abroad; of your safety; of your prosperity; of that very Liberty which you so highly prize. But as it is easy to foresee, that from different causes and from different quarters, much pains will be taken, many artifices employed, to weaken in your minds the conviction of this truth; as this is the point in your political fortress against which the batteries of internal and external enemies will be most constantly and actively (though often covertly and insidiously) directed, it is of infinite moment, that you should properly estimate the immense value of your national Union to your collective and individual happiness; that you should cherish a cordial, habitual and immoveable attachment to it; accustoming yourselves to think and speak of it as the Palladium of your political safety and prosperity; watching for its preservation with jealous anxiety; discountenancing whatever may suggest even a suspicion that it can in any event be abandoned, and indignantly frowning upon the first dawning of every attempt to alienate any portion of our Country from the rest, or to enfeeble the sacred ties which now link together the various parts.

For this you have every inducement of sympathy and interest. Citizens by birth or choice, of a common country, that country has a right to concentrate your affections. The name of American, which belongs to you, in your national capacity, must always exalt the just pride of Patriotism, more than any appelation derived from local discriminations. With slight shades of difference, you have the same Religion, Manners, Habits and political Principles. You have in a common cause fought and triumphed together. The independence and liberty you possess are the work of joint councils, and joint efforts; of common dangers, sufferings and successes.

But these considerations, however powerfully they address themselves to your sensibility are greatly outweighed by those which apply more immediately to your Interest. Here every portion of our country finds the most commanding motives for carefully guarding and preserving the Union of the whole.

The *North*, in an unrestrained intercourse with the *South*, protected by the equal Laws of a common government, finds in the productions of the latter, great additional resources of Maritime and commercial enterprise and precious materials of manufacturing industry. The *South* in the same Intercourse, benefitting by the Agency of the *North*, sees its agriculture grow and its commerce expand. Turning partly into its own channels the seamen of the *North*, it finds its particular navigation envigorated; and while it contributes, in different ways, to nourish and increase the general mass of the National navigation, it looks forward to the protection of a Maritime strength, to which itself is unequally adapted. The *East*, in a like intercourse with the *West*, already finds, and in the progressive improvement of interior communications, by land and water, will more and more find a valuable vent for the commodities which it brings from abroad, or manufactures at home. The *West* derives from the *East* supplies requisite to its growth and comfort, and what is perhaps of still greater consequence, it must of necessity owe the *secure* enjoyment of indispensable *outlets* for its own productions to the weight, influence, and the future Maritime strength of the Atlantic side of the Union, directed by an indissoluble community of Interest as *one Nation*. . . .

While then every part of our country thus feels an immediate and particular Interest in Union, all the parts combined cannot fail to find in the united mass of means and efforts greater strength, greater resource, proportionably greater security from external danger, a less frequent interruption of their Peace by foreign Nations; and, what is of inestimable value! they must derive from Union an exemption from those broils and Wars between themselves, which so frequently afflict neighbouring countries, not tied together by the same government; which their own rivalships alone would be sufficient to produce, but which opposite foreign alliances, attachments and intriegues would stimulate and imbitter. Hence likewise they will avoid the necessity of those overgrown Military establishments, which under any form of Government, are inauspicious to liberty, and which are to be regarded as particularly hostile to Republican Liberty: In this sense it is, that your Union ought to be considered as a main prop of your liberty, and that the love of the one ought to endear you to the preservation of the other.

[Text omitted]

In contemplating the causes wch. may disturb our Union, it occurs as a matter of serious concern, that any ground should have been furnished for characterizing parties by *geographical* discriminations: *Northern* and *Southern*; *Atlantic* and *Western*; whence designing men may endeavor to excite a belief that there is a real difference of local interests and views. One of the expedients of Party to acquire influence, within particular districts, is to misrepresent the opinions and aims of other Districts. You cannot shield yourselves too much against the jealousies and heart burnings which spring from these misrepresentations. They tend to render Alien to each other those who ought to be bound together by fraternal affection.

[Text omitted]

To the efficacy and permanency of Your Union, a Government for the whole is indispensable. No Alliances however strict between the parts can be an adequate substitute. They must inevitably experience the infractions and interruptions which all Alliances in all times have experienced. Sensible of this momentous truth, you have improved upon your first essay, by the adoption of a Constitution of Government, better calculated than your former for an intimate Union, and for the efficacious management of your common concerns. This Government, the offspring of your own choice uninfluenced and unawed, adopted upon full investigation and mature deliberation, completely free in its principles, in the distribution of its powers, uniting security with energy, and containing within itself a provision for its own amendment, has a just claim to your confidence and your support. Respect for its authority, compliance with its Laws, acquiescence in its measures, are duties enjoined by the fundamental maxims of true Liberty. The basis of our political systems is the right of the people to make and to alter their Constitutions of Government. But the Constitution which at any time exists, 'till changed by an explicit and authentic act of the whole People, is sacredly obligatory upon all. The very idea of the power and the right of the People to establish

Government presupposes the duty of every Individual to obey the established Government.

[Text omitted]

In all the changes to which you may be invited, remember that time and habit are at least as necessary to fix the true character of Governments, as of other human institutions; that experience is the surest standard by which to test the real tendency of the existing Constitution of a country; that facility in changes upon the credit of mere hypothesis and opinion exposes to perpetual change, from the endless variety of hypothesis and opinion; and remember especially that for the efficient management of your common interests, in a country so extensive as ours, a Government of as much vigor as is consistent with the perfect security of Liberty is indispensable. Liberty itself will find in such a Government, with powers properly distributed and adjusted, its surest Guardian. It is indeed little else than a name, where the Government is too feeble to withstand the enterprises of faction, to confine each member of the Society within the limits prescribed by the laws, and to maintain all in the secure and tranquil enjoyment of the rights of person and property.

I have already intimated to you the danger of Parties in the State, with particular reference to the founding of them on Geographical discriminations. Let me now take a more comprehensive view, and warn you in the most solemn manner against the baneful effects of the Spirit of Party, generally.

This spirit, unfortunately, is inseparable from our nature, having its root in the strongest passions of the human Mind. It exists under different shapes in all Governments, more or less stifled, controulled, or repressed; but, in those of the popular form it is seen in its greatest rankness and is truly their worst enemy.

[Text omitted]

It serves always to distract the Public Councils and enfeeble the Public administration. It agitates the Community with ill founded jealousies and false alarms, kindles the animosity of one part against another, foments occasionally riot and insurrection. It opens the door to foreign influence and corruption, which find a facilitated access to the government itself through the channels of party passions. Thus the policy and the will of one country, are subjected to the policy and will of another.

[Text omitted]

Of all the dispositions and habits which lead to political prosperity, Religion and morality are indispensable supports. In vain would that man claim the tribute of Patriotism, who should labour to subvert these great Pillars of human happiness, these firmest props of the duties of Men and citizens. The mere Politician, equally with the pious man ought to respect and to cherish them. A volume could not trace all their connections with private and public felicity. Let it simply be asked where is the security for property, for reputation, for life, if the sense of religious obligation *desert* the oaths, which are the instruments of investigation in Courts of Justice? And let us with caution indulge the supposition that morality can be maintained without religion. Whatever may be conceded to the influence of refined education on minds of peculiar structure, reason and experience both forbid us to expect that National morality can prevail in exclusion of religious principle.

'Tis substantially true that virtue or morality is a necessary spring of popular government. The rule indeed extends with more or less force to every species of free Government. Who that is a sincere friend to it can look with indifference upon attempts to shake the foundation of the fabric?

Promote then as an object of primary importance, Institutions for the general diffusion of knowledge. In proportion as the structure of a government gives force to public opinion, it is essential that public opinion should be enlightened.

[Text omitted]

Observe good faith and justice towards all Nations. Cultivate peace and harmony with all. Religion and morality enjoin this conduct; and can it be that good policy does not equally enjoin it? It will be worthy of a free, enlightened, and, at no distant period, a great Nation, to give to mankind the magnanimous and too novel example of a People always guided by an exalted justice and benevolence. Who can doubt that in the course of time and things the fruits of such a plan would richly repay any temporary advantage which might be lost by a steady adherence to it? Can it be, that Providence has not connected the permanent felicity of a Nation with its virtue? The experiment, at least, is recommended by every sentiment which enobles human Nature. Alas! is it rendered impossible by its vices?

In the execution of such a plan nothing is more essential than that permanent, inveterate antipathies against particular Nations and passionate attachments for others should be excluded; and that in place of them just and amicable feelings towards all should be cultivated. The Nation, which indulges towards another an habitual hatred, or an habitual fondness, is in some degree a slave. It is a slave to its animosity or to its affection, either of which is sufficient to lead it astray from its duty and its interest. Antipathy in one Nation against another, disposes each more readily to offer insult and injury, to lay hold of slight causes of umbrage, and to be haughty and intractable, when accidental or trifling occasions of dispute occur. . . .

So likewise, a passionate attachment of one Nation for another produces a variety of evils. Sympathy for the favourite nation, facilitating the illusion of an imaginary common interest, in cases where no real common interest exists, and infusing into one the enmities of the other, betrays the former into a participation in the quarrels and Wars of the latter, without adequate inducement or justification. . . .

[Text omitted]

Against the insidious wiles of foreign influence, (I conjure you to believe me fellow citizens) the jealousy of a free people ought to be *constantly* awake; since history and experience prove that foreign influence is one of the most baneful foes of Republican Government. But that jealousy to be useful must be impartial; else it becomes the instrument of the very influence to be avoided, instead of a defense against it. Excessive partiality for one foreign nation and excessive dislike of another, cause those whom they actuate to see danger only on one side, and serve to veil and even second the arts of influence on the other. Real Patriots, who may resist the intriegues of the favourite, are liable to become suspected and odious; while its tools and dupes usurp the applause and confidence of the people, to surrender their interests.

[Text omitted]

Our detached and distant situation invites and enables us to pursue a different course. If we remain one People, under an efficient government, the period is not far off, when we may defy material injury from external annoyance; when we may take such an attitude as will cause the neutrality we may at any time resolve upon to be scrupulously respected; when belligerent nations, under the impossibility of making acquisitions upon us, will not lightly hazard the giving us provocation; when we may choose peace or war, as our interest guided by justice shall Counsel.

Why forego the advantages of so peculiar a situation? Why quit our own to stand upon foreign ground? Why, by interweaving our destiny with that of any part of Europe, entangle our peace and prosperity in the toils of European Ambition, Rivalship, Interest, Humor, or Caprice?

'Tis our true policy to steer clear of permanent Alliances, with any portion of the foreign world. So far, I mean, as we are now at liberty to do it, for let me not be understood as capable of patronising infidility to existing engagements (I hold the maxim no less applicable to public than to private affairs, that honesty is always the best policy). I repeat it therefore, let those engagements be observed in their genuine sense. But in my opinion, it is unnecessary and would be unwise to extend them.

Taking care always to keep ourselves, by suitable establishments, on a respectably defensive posture, we may safely trust to temporary alliances for extraordinary emergencies.

Harmony, liberal intercourse with all Nations, are recommended by policy, humanity and interest. But even our Commercial policy should hold an equal and impartial hand: neither seeking nor granting exclusive favours or preferences; consulting the natural course of things; diffusing and deversifying by gentle means the streams of Commerce, but forcing nothing; establishing with Powers so disposed; in order to give to trade a stable course, to define the rights of our Merchants, and to enable the Government to support them; conventional rules of intercourse, the best that present circumstances and mutual opinion will permit, but temporary, and liable to be from time to time abandoned or varied, as experience and circumstances shall dictate; constantly keeping in view, that 'tis folly in one Nation to look for disinterested favors from another; that it must pay with a portion of its Independence for whatever it may accept under that character; that by such acceptance, it may place itself in the condition of having given equivalents for nominal favours and yet of being reproached with ingratitude for not giving more. There can be no greater error than to expect, or calculate upon real favours from Nation to Nation. 'Tis an illusion which experience must cure, which a just pride ought to discard.

[Text omitted]

Relying on [my country's] kindness in this as in other things, and actuated by that fervent love towards it which is so natural to a Man, who views in it the native soil of himself and his progenitors for several Generations, I anticipate with pleasing expectation that retreat, in which I promise myself to realize, without alloy, the sweet enjoyment of partaking, in the midst of my fellow Citizens, the benign influence of good Laws under a free Government, the ever favourite object of my heart, and the happy reward, as I trust, of our mutual cares, labours and dangers.

Geo. Washington.

Tecumseh, "Sleep Not Longer, O Choctaws and Chickasaws" and "Father, Listen! The Americans Have Not Yet Defeated Us By Land"

Editor's Introduction: Tecumseh (1768–1813) was a famed warrior of the Shawnee tribe. Tecumseh's life was witness to the encroaching white man and a desperate attempt to thwart those forces that threatened Native American lands and ways of life. Tecumseh and his brother, The Prophet, maintained that their people must return to the ways of their forefathers in order to be pure and free of the white man's influence. The Prophet was especially concerned with the use of alcohol among tribe members, for The Prophet had suffered from alcoholism before his transformation into a religious leader.

In the continued struggles and conflicts between Native Americans, frontier settlers, and the United States military, the land of the Shawnee became increasingly threatened. Tecumseh realized that in order to protect their lands and present a credible threat to the United States forces, all tribes must set aside their rivalries and unite. In the end, Tecumseh could not attain his goal and settled for fighting against American troops with the British in the War of 1812, where he died a distinguished warrior.

The first of the speeches by Tecumseh is a rallying cry encouraging Native Americans to bond together against the whites. The second speech reveals Tecumseh's bewilderment with the British for retreating from the fight with Americans in the War of 1812 and his sense of betrayal after fighting with the British in both the Revolutionary War and the War of 1812.

*   *   *

"SLEEP NOT LONGER, O CHOCTAWS AND CHICKASAWS" (1811)

In view of questions of vast importance, have we met together in solemn council tonight. Nor should we here debate whether we have been wronged and injured, but by what measures we should avenge ourselves; for our merciless oppressors, having long since planned out their proceedings, are not about to make, but have and are still making attacks upon our race who have as yet come to no resolution. Nor are we ignorant by what steps, and by what gradual advances, the whites

---

Source: H. B. Cushman, *History of the Choctaw, Chicksaw and Natchez Indians* (Greenville, Texas: Headlight Printing House, 1899).

break in upon our neighbors. Imagining themselves to be still undiscovered, they show themselves the less audacious because you are insensible. The whites are already nearly a match for us all united, and too strong for any one tribe alone to resist; so that unless we support one another with our collective and united forces; unless every tribe unanimously combines to give check to the ambition and avarice of the whites, they will soon conquer us apart and disunited, and we will be driven away from our native country and scattered as autumnal leaves before the wind.

But have we not courage enough remaining to defend our country and maintain our ancient independence? Will we calmly suffer the white intruders and tyrants to enslave us? Shall it be said of our race that we knew not how to extricate ourselves from the three most dreadful calamities—folly, inactivity and cowardice? But what need is there to speak of the past? It speaks for itself and asks, Where today is the Pequod? Where the Narragansetts, the Mohawks, Pocanokets, and many other once powerful tribes of our race? They have vanished before the avarice and oppression of the white men, as snow before a summer sun. In the vain hope of alone defending their ancient possessions, they have fallen in the wars with the white men. Look abroad over their once beautiful country, and what see you now? Naught but the ravages of the pale face destroyers meet our eyes. So it will be with you Choctaws and Chickasaws! Soon your mighty forest trees, under the shade of whose wide spreading branches you have played in infancy, sported in boyhood, and now rest your wearied limbs after the fatigue of the chase, will be cut down to fence in the land which the white intruders dare to call their own. Soon their broad roads will pass over the grave of your fathers, and the place of their rest will be blotted out forever. The annihilation of our race is at hand unless we unite in one common cause against the common foe. Think not, brave Choctaws and Chickasaws, that you can remain passive and indifferent to the common danger, and thus escape the common fate. Your people, too, will soon be as falling leaves and scattering clouds before their blighting breath. You, too, will be driven away from your native land and ancient domains as leaves are driven before the wintry storms.

Sleep not longer, O Choctaws and Chickasaws, in false security and delusive hopes. Our broad domains are fast escaping from our grasp. Every year our white intruders become more greedy, exacting, oppressive and overbearing. Every year contentions spring up between them and our people and when blood is shed we have to make atonement whether right or wrong, at the cost of the lives of our greatest chiefs, and the yielding up of large tracts of our lands. Before the palefaces came among us, we enjoyed the happiness of unbounded freedom, and were acquainted with neither riches, wants nor oppression. How is it now? Wants and oppression are our lot; for are we not controlled in everything, and dare we move without asking, by your leave? Are we not being stripped day by day of the little that remains of our ancient liberty? Do they not even kick and strike us as they do their black-faces? How long will it be before they will tie us to a post and whip us, and make us work for them in their corn fields as they do them? Shall we wait for that moment or shall we die fighting before submitting to such ignominy?

Have we not for years had before our eyes a sample of their designs, and are they not sufficient harbingers of their future determinations? Will we not soon be driven from our respective countries and the graves of our ancestors? Will not the bones of our dead be plowed up, and their graves be turned into fields? Shall we calmly wait until they become so numerous that we will no longer be able to resist oppression? Will we wait to be destroyed in our turn, without making an effort worthy of our race? Shall we give up our homes, our country, bequeathed to us by the Great Spirit, the graves of our dead, and everything that is dear and sacred to us, without a struggle? I know you will cry with me: Never! Never! Then let us by unity of action destroy them all, which we now can do, or drive them back whence they came. War or extermination is now our only choice. Which do you choose? I know your answer. Therefore, I now call on you, brave Choctaws and Chickasaws, to assist in the just cause of liberating our race from the grasp of our faithless invaders and heartless oppressors. The white usurpation in our common country must be stopped, or we, its rightful owners, be forever destroyed and wiped out as a race of people. I am now at the head of many warriors backed by the strong arm of English soldiers. Choctaws and Chickasaws, you have too long borne with grievous usurpation inflicted by the arrogant Americans. Be no longer their dupes. If there be one here tonight who believes that his rights will not sooner or later be taken from him by the avaricious American pale faces, his ignorance ought to excite pity, for he knows little of the character of our common foe.

And if there be one among you mad enough to undervalue the growing power of the white race among us, let him tremble in considering the fearful woes he will bring down upon our entire race, if by his criminal indifference he assists the designs of our common enemy against our common country. Then listen to the voice of duty, of honor, of nature and of your endangered country. Let us form one body, one heart, and defend to the last warrior our country, our homes, our liberty, and the graves of our fathers.

Choctaws and Chickasaws, you are among the few of our race who sit indolently at ease. You have indeed enjoyed the reputation of being brave, but will you be indebted for it more from report than fact? Will you let whites encroach upon your domains even to your very door before you will assert your rights in resistance? Let no one in this council imagine that I speak more from malice against the pale face Americans than just grounds of complaint. Complaint is just toward friends who have failed in their duty; accusation is against enemies guilty of injustice. And surely, if any people ever had, we have good and just reasons to believe we have ample grounds to accuse the Americans of injustice; especially when such great acts of injustice have been committed by them upon our race, of which they seem to have no manner of regard, or even to reflect. They are a people fond of innovations, quick to contrive and quick to put their schemes into effectual execution no matter how great the wrong and injury to us; while we are content to preserve what we already have. Their designs are to enlarge their possessions by taking yours in turn; and will you, can you longer dally, O Choctaws and Chickasaws?

Do you imagine that that people will not continue longest in the enjoyment of peace who timely prepare to vindicate themselves, and manifest a determined resolution to do themselves right whenever they are wronged? Far otherwise. Then haste to the relief of our common cause, as by consanguinity of blood you are bound; lest the day be not far distant when you will be left single-handed and alone to the cruel mercy of our most inveterate foe.

"FATHER, LISTEN! THE AMERICANS HAVE NOT YET DEFEATED US BY LAND" (1813)

Father, listen to your children! You have them now all before you.

The war before this, our British father gave the hatchet to his red children, when our old chiefs were alive. They are now dead. In the war, our father was thrown on his back by the Americans, and our father took them by the hand without our knowledge; and we are afraid that our father will do so again this time.

Summer before last, when I came forward with my red brethren, and was ready to take up the hatchet in favor of our British father, we were told not to be in a hurry, that he had not yet determined to fight the Americans.

Listen! When war was declared, our father stood up and gave us the tomahawk and told us that he was then ready to strike the Americans; that he wanted our assistance; and that he would certainly get our lands back, which the Americans had taken from us.

Source: Wallace A. Brice, *History of Fort Wayne* (Fort Wayne, Ind.: D. W. Jones & Son, 1868).

Listen! You told us, at that time, to bring forward our families to this place; and we did so; and you promised to take care of them, and they should want for nothing, while the men would go out and fight the enemy; that we need not trouble ourselves about the enemy's garrisons; that we knew nothing about them, and that our father would attend to that part of the business. You also told your red children that you would take good care of your garrison here, which made our hearts glad.

Listen! When we were last at the Rapids it is true we gave you little assistance. It is hard to fight people who live like groundhogs.

Father, listen! Our fleet has gone out. We know they have fought. We have heard the great guns, but we know nothing of what has happened to our father with that arm. Our ships have gone one way, and we are much astonished to see our father tying up everything and preparing to run away the other, without letting his red children know what his intentions are. You always told us to remain here and take care of our lands. It made our hearts glad to hear that was your wish. Our great father, the king, is the head, and you represent him. You always told us that you would never draw your foot off British ground; but now, father, we see you are drawing back, and we are sorry to see our father doing so without seeing the enemy. We must compare our father's conduct to a fat dog, that carries its tail upon its back, but when afrighted, it drops it between its legs and runs off.

Father, listen! The Americans have not yet defeated us by land. Neither are we sure that they have done so by water. We therefore wish to remain here and fight our enemy, should they make their appearance. If they defeat us, we will then retreat with our father.

At the battle of the Rapids, last war, the Americans certainly defeated us, and when we retreated to our father's fort at that place the gates were shut against us. We were afraid that it would now be the case; but instead of that, we now see our British father preparing to march out of his garrison.

Father! You have got the arms and ammunition which our great father sent for his red children. If you have an idea of going away, give them to us, and you may go and welcome for us. Our lives are in the hands of the Great Spirit. We are determined to defend our lands, and if it be his will, we wish to leave our bones upon them.

John C. Calhoun,
"A Disquisition on Government" (1853)

Editor's Introduction: John C. Calhoun (1782–1850) was born in South Carolina, the son of Scott-Irish Calvinist parents. He was to become a leading Southern statesman before the Civil War and also a leading philosophical defender of slavery and the Southern cause. Calhoun was elected to Congress in 1811 and, in 1817, was appointed Secretary of War by President James Monroe. He served in this post for seven and a half years and then ran for Vice President, an office he held under John Quincy Adams and Andrew Jackson. As Vice President, Calhoun began to formulate his doctrines of states' rights and "nullification." He did so initially in response to the 1828 Tariff Act, which was opposed throughout the South but especially in South Carolina. Calhoun wrote a document, the "Exposition and Protest" for the South Carolina legislature, where he argued that states had the right to "nullify," or not enforce, federal laws and to secede from the union if they so chose. This document was met with little favor by President Jackson, who was prepared to enforce the tariff law by military means if necessary.

Calhoun became a Senator in 1832 and held that office until 1844, when he was named Secretary of State. He returned to the Senate in 1845 and remained there until his death. During his last Senate term, Calhoun wrote the *Disquisition on Government.* In this work, he further develops ideas that had been brewing at least since the tariff controversies of the late 1820s. His main concern is defending the interests of minorities (which for him means the South) against majority tyranny. He argues that the franchise and the other protections of minority rights built into the Constitution are not sufficient to do this and that some other "organism" in government is required. Thus, he develops the idea of "concurrent majority." The main point of concurrent majority is to grant a veto power to major interests in society that may be adversely affected by legislation. In developing this view, Calhoun is a proponent for a "group rights" approach to politics. That is, he would build into the Constitution the protection of certain groups (in his case defined by region, but the principle allows for other types of groups as well) rather than simply recognizing the rights of individuals.

*　　　*　　　*

Source: Richard K. Cralle, ed. *The Works of John C. Calhoun* (New York: D. Appleton & Co., 1883).

If the whole community had the same interests so that the interests of each and every portion would be so affected by the action of the government that the laws which oppressed or impoverished one portion would necessarily oppress and impoverish all others—or the reverse—then the right of suffrage, of itself, would be all-sufficient to counteract the tendency of the government to oppression and abuse of its powers, and, of course, would form, of itself, a perfect constitutional government. The interest of all being the same, by supposition, as far as the action of the government was concerned, all would have like interests as to what laws should be made and how they should be executed. All strife and struggle would cease as to who should be elected to make and execute them. The only question would be, who was most fit, who the wisest and most capable of understanding the common interest of the whole. This decided, the election would pass off quietly and without party discord, as no one portion could advance its own peculiar interest without regard to the rest by electing a favorite candidate.

But such is not the case. On the contrary, nothing is more difficult than to equalize the action of the government in reference to the various and diversified interests of the community; and nothing more easy than to pervert its powers into instruments to aggrandize and enrich one or more interests by oppressing and impoverishing the others; and this, too, under the operation of laws couched in general terms and which, on their face, appear fair and equal. Nor is this the case in some particular communities only. It is so in all—the small and the great, the poor and the rich—irrespective of pursuits, productions, or degrees of civilization; with, however, this difference, that the more extensive and populous the country, the more diversified the condition and pursuits of its population; and the richer, more luxurious, and dissimilar the people, the more difficult it is to equalize the action of the government, and the more easy for one portion of the community to pervert its powers to oppress and plunder the other.

Such being the case, it necessarily results that the right of suffrage, by placing the control of the government in the community, must, from the same constitution of our nature which makes government necessary to preserve society, lead to conflict among its different interests—each striving to obtain possession of its powers as the means of protecting itself against the others or of advancing its respective interests regardless of the interests of the others. For this purpose, a struggle will take place between various interests to obtain a majority in order to control the government. If no one interest be strong enough, of itself, to obtain it, a combination will be formed between those whose interests are most alike—each conceding something to the others until a sufficient number is obtained to make a majority. The process may be slow and much time may be required before a compact, organized majority can be thus formed, but formed it will be in time, even without preconcert or design, by the sure workings of that principle or constitution of our nature in which government itself originates. When once formed, the community will be divided into two great parties—a major and minor—between which there will be incessant struggles on the one side to retain, and on the other to obtain the majority and, thereby, the control of the government and the advantages it confers.

[Text omitted]

[The Concurrent Majority]

As, then, the right of suffrage, without some other provision, cannot counteract this tendency of government, the next question for consideration is, What is that other provision? This demands the most serious consideration, for of all the questions embraced in the science of government it involves a principle, the most important and the least understood, and when understood, the most difficult of application in practice. It is, indeed, emphatically that principle which *makes* the constitution, in its strict and limited sense.

From what has been said, it is manifest that this provision must be of a character calculated to prevent any one interest or combination of interests from using the powers of government to aggrandize itself at the expense of others. Here lies the evil: and just in proportion as it shall prevent, or fail to prevent it, in the same degree it will effect, or fail to effect, the end intended to be accomplished. There is but one certain mode in which this result can be secured, and that is by the adoption of some restriction or limitation which shall so effectually prevent any one interest or combination of interests from obtaining the exclusive control of the government as to render hopeless all attempts directed to that end. There is, again, but one mode in which this can be effected, and that is by taking the sense of each interest or portion of the community which may unequally and injuriously affected by the action of the government separately, through its own majority or in some other way by which its voice may be fairly expressed, and to require the consent of each interest either to put or to keep the government in action. This, too, can be accomplished only in one way, and that is by such an organism of the government—and, if necessary for the purpose, of the community also—as will, by dividing and distributing the powers of government, give to each division or interest, through its appropriate organ, either a concurrent voice in making and executing the laws or a veto on their execution. It is only by such an organism that the assent of each can be made necessary to put the government in motion, or the power made effectual to arrest its action when put in motion; and it is only by the one or the other that the different interests, orders, classes, or portions into which the community may be divided can be protected, and all conflict and struggle between them prevented—by rendering it impossible to put or keep it in action without the concurrent consent of all.

Such an organism as this, combined with the right of suffrage, constitutes, in fact, the elements of constitutional government. The one, by rendering those who make and execute the laws responsible to those on whom they operate, prevents the rulers from oppressing the ruled; and the other, by making it impossible for any one interest or combination of interests, or class, or order, or portion of the community to obtain exclusive control, prevents any one of them from oppressing the other. It is clear that oppression and abuse of power must come, if at all, from the one or the other quarter. From no other can they come. It follows that the two, suffrage and proper organism combined, are sufficient to counteract the tendency of government to oppression and abuse of power and to restrict it to the fulfillment of the great ends for which it is ordained.

[Text omitted]

The necessary consequence of taking the sense of the community by the concurrent majority is, as has been explained, to give each interest or portion of the community a negative on the others. It is the mutual negative among its various conflicting interests which invests each with the power of protecting itself, and places the rights and safety of each where only they can be securely placed, under its own guardianship. Without this there can be no systematic, peaceful, or effective resistance to the natural tendency of each to come into conflict with the others; and without this there can be no constitution. It is this negative power—the power of preventing or arresting the action of the government, be it called by what term it may, veto, interposition, nullification, check, or balance of power—which in fact forms the constitution. They are all but different names for the negative power. In all its forms, and under all its names, it results from the concurrent majority. Without this, there can be no negative, and without a negative, no constitution. The assertion is true in reference to all constitutional governments, be their forms what they may. It is, indeed, the *negative* power which makes the constitution, and the *positive* which makes the government. The one is the power of acting, and the other the power of preventing or arresting action. The two, combined, make constitutional governments.

Abraham Lincoln, "The Perpetuation of Our Political Institutions" Address Before the Springfield Young Men's Lyceum, January 27, 1838

Editor's Introduction: Abraham Lincoln's (1809–1865) speech before the Springfield Young Men's Lyceum is an important early statement of his political ideas. At the time of the speech, Lincoln was in his second term in the Illinois legislature and thus in the early stages of his political career.

Some three months before his address, an abolitionist editor, Elijah P. Lovejoy, had been murdered in Alton, Illinois. This was the immediate occasion for Lincoln's expression of concern about the dangers of mob violence and disrespect for law, which were on the rise as the national debate about slavery grew increasingly contentious. Lincoln urges that Americans do all they can in schools, pulpits, and legislative halls to foster a reverence for law until it becomes the "political religion" of the United States. This theme anticipates Lincoln's great concern with maintaining American union, which was his prime objective as our sixteenth President during the Civil War. It also shows his awareness of the importance of moral consensus, or what is sometimes called "civil religion," to preserving union.

Also of interest in the speech is Lincoln's curious attitude toward the American founders. "The field of glory is harvested," he contends, "in the act of founding a republic." Founders achieve an eternal fame that those who follow in their footsteps as ordinary politicians cannot hope to match. Lincoln warns against the dangers of the "towering genius" who refuses to accept this diminished role and seeks to build his own fame at the expense of the republic. Ironically, Lincoln's role in American history and iconography as the man who saved the union and paid for it with his own martyrdom has assured him a place in history on a par with, if not surpassing, the founders themselves.

*   *   *

As a subject for the remarks of the evening, *the perpetuation of our political institutions*, is selected.

In the great journal of things happening under the sun, we, the American People, find our account running, under date of the nineteenth

Source: Abraham Lincoln, *Early Speeches: 1832–1856*, Vol. 2 (New York: The Current Literature Publishing Co., 1907).

century of the Christian era. We find ourselves in the peaceful possession, of the fairest portion of the earth, as regards extent of territory, fertility of soil, and salubrity of climate. We find ourselves under the government of a system of political institutions, conducing more essentially to the ends of civil and religious liberty, than any of which the history of former times tells us. We, when mounting the stage of existence, found ourselves the legal inheritors of these fundamental blessings. We toiled not in the acquirement or establishment of them—they are a legacy bequeathed us, by a *once* hardy, brave, and patriotic, but *now* lamented and departed race of ancestors. Their's was the task (and nobly they performed it) to possess themselves, and through themselves, us, of this goodly land; and to uprear upon its hills and its valleys, a political edifice of liberty and equal rights; 'tis ours only, to transmit these, the former, unprofaned by the foot of an invader; the latter, undecayed by the lapse of time, and untorn by [usurpation—to the latest generation that fate shall permit the world to know. This task of gratitude to our fathers, justice to] ourselves, duty to posterity, and love for our species in general, all imperatively require us faithfully to perform.

How, then, shall we perform it? At what point shall we expect the approach of danger? By what means shall we fortify against it? Shall we expect some transatlantic military giant, to step the Ocean, and crush us at a blow? Never! All the armies of Europe, Asia and Africa combined, with all the treasure of the earth (our own excepted) in their military chest; with a Buonaparte for a commander, could not by force, take a drink from the Ohio, or make a track on the Blue Ridge, in a trial of a thousand years.

At what point then is the approach of danger to be expected? I answer, if it ever reach us, it must spring up amongst us. It cannot come from abroad. If destruction be our lot, we must ourselves be its author and finisher. As a nation of freemen, we must live through all time, or die by suicide.

I hope I am over wary; but if I am not, there is, even now, something of ill-omen amongst us. I mean the increasing disregard for law which pervades the country; the growing disposition to substitute the wild and furious passions, in lieu of the sober judgement of Courts; and the worse than savage mobs, for the executive ministers of justice. This disposition is awfully fearful in any community; and that it now exists in ours, though grating to our feelings to admit, it would be a violation of truth, and an insult to our intelligence, to deny. Accounts of outrages committed by mobs, form the every-day news of the times. They have pervaded the country, from New England to Louisiana;—they are neither peculiar to the eternal snows of the former, nor the burning suns of the latter;— they are not the creature of climate—neither are they confined to the slaveholding, or the non-slaveholding States. Alike, they spring up among the pleasure hunting masters of Southern slaves, and the order loving citizens of the land of steady habits. Whatever, then, their cause may be, it is common to the whole country.

It would be tedious, as well as useless, to recount the horrors of all of them. Those happening in the State of Mississippi, and at St. Louis, are, perhaps, the most dangerous in example, and revolting to humanity. In the Mississippi case, they first commenced by hanging the regular gamblers: a set of men, certainly not following for a livelihood, a very useful, or very honest occupation; but one which, so far from being forbidden by the laws, was actually licensed by an act of the Legislature, passed by a single year before. Next, negroes, suspected of conspiring to raise an insurrection, were caught up and hanged in all parts of the State: then, white men, supposed to be leagued with the negroes; and finally, strangers, from neighboring States, going thither on business, were, in many instances, subjected to the same fate. Thus went on this process of hanging, from gamblers to negroes, from negroes to white citizens, and from these to strangers; till, dead men were seen literally dangling from the boughs of trees upon every road side; and in numbers almost sufficient, to rival the native Spanish moss of the country, as a drapery of the forest.

Turn, then, to that horror-striking scene at St. Louis. A single victim was only sacrificed there. His story is very short; and is, perhaps, the most highly tragic, of any thing of its length, that has ever been witnessed in real life. A mulatto man, by the name of McIntosh, was seized in the street, dragged to the suburbs of the city, chained to a tree, and actually burned to death; and all within a single hour from the time he had been a freeman, attending to his own business, and at peace with the world.

Such are the effects of mob law; and such are the scenes becoming more and more frequent in this land so lately famed for love of law and order; and the stories of which, have even now grown too familiar, to attract any thing more, than an idle remark.

But you are, perhaps, ready to ask, "What has this to do with the perpetuation of our political institutions?" I answer, it has much to do with it. Its direct consequences are, comparatively speaking, but a small evil; and much of its danger consists, in the proneness of our minds, to regard its direct, as its only consequences. Abstractly considered, the hanging of the gamblers at Vicksburg, was of but little consequence. They constitute a portion of population, that is worse than useless in a[ny community; and their death, if no perni]cious example be set by it, is never matter of reasonable regret with any one. If they were annually swept, from the stage of existence, by the plague or small pox, honest men would, perhaps, be much profited, by the operation. Similar too, is the correct reasoning, in regard to the burning of the negro at St. Louis. He had forfeited his life, by the perpetration of an outrageous murder, upon one of the most worthy and respectable citizens of the city; and had he not died as he did, he must have died by the sentence of the law, in a very short time afterwards. As to him alone, it was as well the way it was, as it could otherwise have been. But the example in either case, was fearful. When men take it in their heads today, to hang gamblers, or burn murderers, they should recollect, that, in the confusion usually attending such transactions, they will be as likely to hang or burn some one, who is neither a gambler nor a murderer [as] one who is; and that, acting upon the [exam]ple they set, the mob of to-morrow, may, an[d] probably will, hang or burn some of them, [by th]e very same mistake. And not only so; the innocent, those who have ever set their faces against violations of law in every shape, alike with the guilty, fall victims to the ravages of mob law; and thus it goes on, step by step, till all the walls erected for the defence of the persons and property of individuals, are trodden down, and disregarded. But all this even, is not the full extent of the evil. By such examples, by instances of the perpetrators of such acts going unpunished, the lawless in spirit, are encouraged to become lawless in practice; and having been used to no restraint, but dread of punishment, they thus become, absolutely unrestrained. Having ever re-garded Government as their deadliest bane, they make a jubilee of the suspension of its operations; and pray for nothing so much, as its total annihilation. While, on the other hand, good men, men who love tranquil-ity, who desire to abide by the laws, and enjoy their benefits, who would gladly spill their blood in the defence of their country; seeing their prop-erty destroyed; their families insulted, and their lives endangered; their persons injured; and seeing nothing in prospect that forebodes a change for the better; become tired of, and disgusted with, a Government that offers them no protection; and are not much averse to a change in which they imagine they have nothing to lose. Thus, then, by the operation of this mobocratic spirit, which all must admit, is now abroad in the land, the strongest bulwark of any Government, and particularly of those consti-tuted like ours, may effectually be broken down and destroyed—I mean the *attachment* of the People. Whenever this effect shall be produced among us; whenever the vicious portion of population shall be permitted to gather in bands of hundreds and thousands, and burn churches, ravage and rob provision stores, throw printing presses into rivers, shoot editors, and hang and burn obnoxious persons at pleasure, and with impunity; depend on it, this Government cannot last. By such things, the feelings of the best citizens will become more or less alienated from it; and thus it will be left without friends, or with too few, and those few too weak, to make their friendship effectual. At such a time and under such circumstances, men of sufficient tal[ent and ambition will not be want]ing to seize [the opportunity, strike the blow, and overturn that fair fabric], which for the last half century, has been the fondest hope, of the lovers of freedom, throughout the world.

I know the American People are *much* attached to their Government;—I know they would suffer *much* for its sake;—I know they would endure evils long and patiently, before they would ever think of exchanging it for another. Yet, notwithstanding all this, if the laws be continually despised and disregarded, if their rights to be secure in their persons and property, are held by no better tenure than the caprice of a mob, the alienation of their affections from the Government is the natural consequence; and to that, sooner or later, it must come.

Here then, is one point at which danger may be expected.

The question recurs "how shall we fortify against it?" The answer is simple. Let every American, every lover of liberty, every well wisher to his posterity, swear by the blood of the Revolution, never to violate in the least particular, the laws of the country; and never to tolerate their violation by others. As the patriots of seventy-six did to the support of the Declaration of Independence, so to the support of the Constitution and Laws, let every American pledge his life, his property, and his sacred honor;—let every man remember that to violate the law, is to trample on the blood of his father, and to tear the character [charter?] of his own, and his children's liberty. Let reverence for the laws, be breathed by every American mother, to the lisping babe, that prattles on her lap—let it be taught in schools, in seminaries, and in colleges;—let it be written in Primmers, spelling books, and in Almanacs;—let it be preached from the pulpit, proclaimed in legislative halls, and enforced in courts of justice. And, in short, let it become the *political religion* of the nation; and let the old and the young, the rich and the poor, the grave and the gay, of all sexes and tongues, and colors and conditions, sacrifice unceasingly upon its altars.

While ever a state of feeling, such as this, shall universally, or even, very generally prevail throughout the nation, vain will be every effort, and fruitless every attempt, to subvert our national freedom.

When I so pressingly urge a strict observance of all the laws, let me not be understood as saying there are no bad laws, nor that grievances may not arise, for the redress of which, no legal provisions have been made. I mean to say no such thing. But I do mean to say, that, although bad laws, if they exist, should be repealed as soon as possible, still while they continue in force, for the sake of example, they should be religiously observed. So also in unprovided cases. If such arise, let proper legal provisions be made for them with the least possible delay; but, till then, let them if not too intolerable, be borne with.

There is no grievance that is a fit object of redress by mob law. In any case that arises, as for instance, the promulgation of abolitionism, one of two positions is necessarily true; that is, the thing is right within itself, and therefore deserves the protection of all law and all good citizens; or, it is wrong, and therefore proper to be prohibited by legal enactments; and in neither case, is the interposition of mob law, either necessary, justifiable, or excusable.

But, it may be asked, why suppose danger to our political institutions? Have we not preserved them for more than fifty years? And why may we not for fifty times as long?

We hope there is no *sufficient* reason. We hope all dangers may be overcome; but to conclude that no danger may ever arise, would itself be extremely dangerous. There are now, and will hereafter be, many causes, dangerous in their tendency, which have not existed heretofore; and which are not too insignificant to merit attention. That our government should have been maintained in its original form from its establishment until now, is not much to be wondered at. It had many props to support it through that period, which now are decayed, and crumbled away. Through that period, it was felt by all, to be an undecided experiment; now, it is understood to be a successful one. Then, all that sought celebrity and fame, and distinction, expected to find them in the success of that experiment. Their *all* was staked upon it;—their destiny was *insepa-rably* linked with it. Their ambition aspired to display before an admiring world, a practical demonstration of the truth of a proposition, which had hitherto been considered, at best no better, than problematical; namely, *the capability of a people to govern themselves*. If they succeeded, they were to be immortalized; their names were to be transferred to counties and cities, and rivers and mountains; and to be revered and sung, and toasted through all time. If they failed, they were to be called knaves and fools, and fanatics of a fleeting hour; then to sink and be forgotten. They succeeded. The experiment is successful; and thousands have won their deathless names in making it so. But the game is caught; and I believe it is true, that with the catching, end the pleasures of the chase. This field of glory is harvested, and the crop is already appropriated. But new reapers will arise, and *they*, too, will seek a field. It is to deny, what the history of the world tells us is true, to suppose that men of ambition and talents will not continue to spring up amongst us. And, when they do, they will as naturally seek the gratification of their ruling passion, as others have *so* done before them. The question then, is, can that gratification be found in supporting and maintaining an edifice that has been erected by others? Most certainly it cannot. Many great and good men sufficiently qualified for any task they should undertake, may ever be found, whose ambition would aspire to nothing beyond a seat in Congress, a gubernatorial or a presidential chair; *but such belong not to the family of the lion, or the tribe of the eagle* [.] What! think you these places would satisfy an Alexander, a Caesar, or a Napoleon? Never! Towering genius disdains a beaten path. It seeks regions hitherto unexplored. It sees *no distinction* in adding story to story, upon the monuments of fame, erected to the memory of others. It *denies* that it is glory enough to serve under any chief. It *scorns* to tread in the footsteps of *any* predecessor, however illustrious. It thirsts and burns for distinction; and, if possible, it will have it, whether at the expense of emancipating slaves, or enslaving freemen. Is it unreasonable then to expect, that some man possessed of the loftiest genius, coupled with ambition sufficient to push it to its utmost stretch, will at some time, spring up among us? And when such a one does, it will require the people to be united with each other, attached to the government and laws, and generally intelligent, to successfully frustrate his designs.

Distinction will be his paramount object; and although he would as willingly, perhaps more so, acquire it by doing good as harm; yet, that opportunity being past, and nothing left to be done in the way of building up, he would set boldly to the task of pulling down.

Here then, is a probable case, highly dangerous, and such a one as could not have well existed heretofore.

Another reason which *once was*; but which, to the same extent, is *now no more*, has done much in maintaining our institutions thus far. I mean the powerful influence which the interesting scenes of the revolution had upon the *passions* of the people as distinguished from their judgment. By this influence, the jealousy, envy, and avarice, incident to our nature, and so common to a state of peace, prosperity, and conscious strength, were, for the time, in a great measure smothered and rendered inactive; while the deep rooted principles of *hate*, and the powerful motive of *revenge*, instead of being turned against each other, were directed exclusively against the British nation. And thus, from the force of circumstances, the basest principles of our nature, were either made to lie dormant, or to become the active agents in the advancement of the noblest cause[s?]— that of establishing and maintaining civil and religious liberty.

But this state of feeling *must fade, is fading, has faded*, with the circumstances that produced it.

I do not mean to say, that the scenes of the revolution *are now* or *ever will be* entirely forgotten; but that like every thing else, they must fade upon the memory of the world, and grow more and more dim by the lapse of time. In history, we hope, they will be read of, and recounted, so long as the bible shall be read;—but even granting that they will, their influence *cannot be* what it heretofore has been. Even then, they *cannot be* so universally known, nor so vividly felt, as they were by the generation just gone to rest. At the close of that struggle, nearly every adult male had been a participator in some of its scenes. The consequence was, that of those scenes, in the form of a husband, a father, a son or a brother, a *living history was* to be found in every family—a history bearing the indubitable testimonies of its own authenticity, in the limbs mangled, in the scars of wounds received, in the midst of the very scenes related—a history, too, that could be read and understood alike by all, the wise and the ignorant, the learned and the unlearned. But *those* histories are gone. They *can* be read no more forever. They *were* a fortress of strength; but, what invading foemen could *never do*, the silent artillery of time *has done*; the levelling of its walls. They are gone. They *were* a forest of giant oaks; but the all-resistless hurricane has swept over them, and left only, here and there, a lonely trunk, despoiled of its verdure, shorn of its foliage; unshading and unshaded, to murmur in a few more gentle breezes, and to combat with its mutilated limbs, a few more ruder storms, then to sink, and be no more.

They *were* the pillars of the temple of liberty; and now that they have crumbled away, that temple must fall, unless we, their descendants, supply their places with other pillars, hewn from the solid quarry of sober reason. Passion has helped us; but can do so no more. It will in future be our enemy. Reason, cold, calculating, unimpassioned reason, must furnish all the materials for our future support and defence. Let those [materials] be moulded into *general intelligence*, [*sound*] *morality* and, in particular, *a reverence for the constitution and laws*; and, that we improved to the last; that we remained free to the last; that we revered his name to the last; [tha]t, during his long sleep, we permitted no hostile foot to pass over or desecrate [his] resting place; shall be that which to le[arn the last] trump shall awaken our WASH[INGTON.

Upon these] let the proud fabric of freedom r[est, as the] rock of its basis; and as truly as has been said of the only greater institution, *"the gates of hell shall not prevail against it."*

Abraham Lincoln,
"Gettysburg Address" (1863)

Editor's Introduction: Lincoln delivered this famous address at a ceremony to dedicate a national cemetery on the site of the great battle that was the turning point in the Civil War. Lincoln was asked to make a few remarks after the principal speaker, Edward Everett, had finished his address. The next day, Everett sent a note to the President: "I should be glad, if I could flatter myself that I came as near to the central idea of the occasion, in two hours, as you did in two minutes." In plain biblical language, Lincoln forged the theme of national unity at a time of crisis. He harks back to the act of founding, "four score and seven years" prior, and points to the promise of future greatness once the wounds of the present have healed.

*   *   *

Four score and seven years ago our fathers brought forth on this continent, a new nation, conceived in Liberty, and dedicated to the proposition that all men are created equal.

Now we are engaged in a great civil war, testing whether that nation, or any nation so conceived and so dedicated, can long endure. We are met on a great battle-field of that war. We have come to dedicate a portion of that field, as a final resting place for those who here gave their lives that that nation might live. It is altogether fitting and proper that we should do this.

But, in a larger sense, we cannot dedicate—we cannot consecrate—we cannot hallow—this ground. The brave men, living and dead, who struggled here have consecrated it, far above our poor power to add or detract. The world will little note nor long remember what we say here, but it can never forget what they did here. It is for us the living, rather, to be dedicated here to the unfinished work which they who fought here have thus far so nobly advanced. It is rather for us to be here dedicated to the great task remaining before us—that from these honored dead we take increased devotion to that cause for which they gave the last full measure of devotion—that we here highly resolve that this nation under God shall have a new birth of freedom—and that government of the people, by the people, for the people, shall not perish from the earth.

Frederick Jackson Turner,
"The Significance of the Frontier in American History" (1893)

Editor's Introduction: Frederick Jackson Turner (1861–1932) is on a very short list of academic historians whose ideas have achieved a life of their own in American folklore. Turner believed that the key to learning what made America unique was understanding its western frontier experience. The frontier for Turner is very much the edge of "civilization." It takes the European settler and "strips off the garments of civilization, and arrays him in the hunting shirt and the moccasin." The traits Americans have seen celebrated in countless Hollywood westerns—rugged individualism, a "can do" attitude, populist politics, a general distrust of authority, etc.—are the qualities Turner notes and, to a degree, celebrates.

Turner's "frontier thesis" has drawn extensive scholarly criticism. Indeed, he greatly overstates the degree to which Americans shed their past identities in settling the west, as attested by the ethnic and cultural diversity of frontier settlements. Nonetheless, Turner's work is instructive as much because it establishes an image of American identity which has found broad acceptance as for the truth it contains. It is worth pondering both this image and why it has such a strong hold in American popular culture.

*   *   *

IN A RECENT BULLETIN of the superintendent of the census for 1890 appear these significant words: "Up to and including 1880 the country had a frontier of settlement, but at present the unsettled area has been so broken into by isolated bodies or settlement that there can hardly be said to be a frontier line. In the discussion of its extent, its westward movement, etc., it cannot, therefore, any longer have a place in the census reports." This brief official statement marks the closing of a great historic movement. Up to our own day American history had been in a large degree the history of the colonization of the Great West. The existence of an area of free land, its continuous recession, and the advance of American settlement westward, explain American development. Behind institutions, behind constitutional forms and modifications, lie the vital forces that call these organs into life, and shape them to meet changing conditions. Now,

Source: Frederick Jackson Turner, *The Frontier in American History* (New York: Henry Holt and Co., 1920).

the peculiarity of American institutions is the fact that they have been compelled to adapt themselves to the changes of an expanding people—to the changes involved in crossing a continent, in winning a wilderness, and in developing at each area of this progress out of the primitive economic and political conditions of the frontier into the complexity of city life. Said Calhoun in 1817, "We are great, and rapidly—I was about to say fearfully—growing!" So saying, he touched the distinguishing feature of American life. All peoples show development: the germ theory of politics has been sufficiently emphasized. In the case of most nations, however, the development has occurred in a limited area; and if the nation has expanded, it has met other growing peoples whom it has conquered. But in the case of the United States we have a different phenomenon. Limiting our attention to the Atlantic coast, we have the familiar phenomenon of the evolution of institutions in a limited area, such as the rise of representative government; the differentiation of simple colonial governments into complex organs; the progress from primitive industrial society, without division of labor, up to manufacturing civilization. But we have in addition to this *a recurrence of the process of evolution in each western area reached in the process of expansion*. Thus American development has exhibited not merely advance along a single line, but a return to primitive conditions on a continually advancing frontier line, and a new development for that area. American social development has been continually beginning over again on the frontier. This perennial rebirth, this fluidity of American life, this expansion westward with its new opportunities, its continuous touch with the simplicity of primitive society, furnish the forces dominating American character. The true point of view in the history of this nation is not the Atlantic coast, it is the Great West. Even the slavery struggle, which is made so exclusive an object of attention by writers like Professor Von Holst, occupies its important place in American history because of its relation to westward expansion.

In this advance, the frontier is the outer edge of the wave—the meeting point between savagery and civilization. Much has been written about the frontier from the point of view of border warfare and the chase, but as a field for the serious study of the economist and the historian it has been neglected.

What is the frontier? It is not the European frontier—a fortified boundary line running through dense populations. The most significant thing about it is, that it lies at the hither edge of free land. In the census reports it is treated as the margin of that settlement which has a density of two or more to the square mile. The term is an elastic one, and for our purpose does not need sharp definition. We shall consider the whole frontier belt, including the Indian country and the outer margin of the "settled areas" of the census reports. . . .

In the settlement of America we have to observe how European life entered the continent, and how America modified and developed that life, and reacted to Europe. Our early history is the study of European germs developing in an American environment. Too exclusive attention has been paid by institutional students to the Germanic origins, too little to the American factors. Now, the frontier is the line of most rapid and effective Americanization. The wilderness masters the colonist. It finds him a European in dress, industries, tools, modes of travel, and thought. It takes him from the railroad car and puts him in the birch canoe. It strips off the garments of civilization, and arrays him in the hunting shirt and the moccasin. It puts him in the log cabin of the Cherokee and the Iroquois, and runs an Indian palisade around him. Before long he has gone to planting Indian corn and plowing with a sharp stick; he shouts the war cry and takes the scalp in orthodox Indian fashion. In short, at the frontier the environment is at first too strong for the man. He must accept the conditions which it furnishes, or perish, and so he fits himself into the Indian clearings and follows the Indian trails. Little by little he transforms the wilderness, but the outcome is not the old Europe, not simply the development of Germanic germs, any more than the first phenomenon was a case of reversion to the Germanic mark. The fact is, that here is a new product that is American. At first, the frontier was the Atlantic coast. It was the frontier of Europe in a very real sense. Moving westward, the frontier became more and more American. *As successive terminal moraines result from successive glaciations, so each frontier leaves its traces behind it, and when it becomes a settled area the region still partakes of the frontier characteristics.* Thus the advance of the frontier has meant a steady movement away from the influence of Europe, a steady growth of independence on American lines. And to study this advance, the men who grew up under these conditions, and the political, economic and social results of it, is to study the really American part of our history.

[Text omitted]

COMPOSITE NATIONALITY

First, we note that the frontier promoted the formation of a composite nationality for the American people. The coast was preponderantly English, but the later tides of continental immigration flowed across the free lands. This was the case from the early colonial days. The Scotch Irish and the Palatine Germans, or "Pennsylvania Dutch," furnished the stock of the colonial frontier. With these peoples were also the freed indented servants, or redemptioners, who at the expiration of their time of service passed to the frontier. Governor Spottswoood of Virginia writes in 1717, "The inhabitants of our frontiers are composed generally of such as have been transported hither as servants, and, being out of their time, settle themselves where land is to be taken up and that will produce the necessarys of life with little labor." Very generally these redemptioners were of non-English stock. In the crucible of the frontier the immigrants were Americanized, liberated and fused into a mixed race, English in neither nationality or characteristics. The process has gone on from the early days to our own. Burke and other writers in the middle of the eighteenth century believed that Pennsylvania was "threatened with the danger of being wholly foreign in language, manners, and perhaps even inclinations." The Germans and Scotch-Irish elements in the frontier of the South were only less great. In the middle of the present century the German element in Wisconsin was already so considerable that leading publicists looked to the creation of a German state out of the commonwealth by concentrating their colonization. Such examples teach us to beware of misinterpreting the fact that there is a common English speech in America into a belief that the stock is also English.

[Text omitted]

GROWTH OF DEMOCRACY

But the most important effect of the frontier has been in the promotion of democracy here and in Europe. As has been pointed out, the frontier is productive of individualism. Complex society is precipitated by the wilderness into a kind of primitive organization based on the family. The tendency is anti-social. It produces antipathy to control, and particularly to any direct control. The tax-gatherer is viewed as a representative of oppression. Professor Osgood, in an able article, has pointed out that the frontier conditions prevalent in the colonies are important factors in the explanation of the American revolution, where individual liberty was sometimes confused with absence of all effective government. The same conditions aid in explaining the difficulty of instituting a strong government in the period of the confederacy. The frontier individualism has from the beginning promoted democracy.

The frontier states that came into the Union in the first quarter of a century of its existence came in with democratic suffrage provisions, and had reactive effects of the highest importance upon the older states whose peoples were being attracted there. It was *western* New York that forced an extension of suffrage in the constitutional convention of that state in 1820; and it was *western* Virginia that compelled the tidewater region to put a more liberal suffrage provision in the constitution frame in 1830, and to give to the frontier region a more nearly proportionate representation with the tidewater aristocracy. The rise of democracy as an effective force in the nation came in with western preponderance under Jackson and

William Henry Harrison, and it meant the triumph of the frontier—with all of its good and with all of its evil elements. An interesting illustration of the tone of frontier democracy in 1830 comes from the same debates in the Virginia convention already referred to. A representative from western Virginia declared: "But, sir, it is not the increase of population in the West which this gentleman ought to fear. It is the energy which the mountain breeze and western habits impart to those emigrants. They are regenerated, politically I mean, sir. They soon become *working politicians*; and the difference, sir, between a *talking* and a *working* politician is immense. The Old Dominion has long been celebrated for producing great orators; the ablest metaphysicians in policy; men that can split hairs in all abstruse questions of political economy. But at home, or when they return from congress, they have negroes to fan them asleep. But a Pennsylvania, a New York, an Ohio, or a western Virginia statesman, though far inferior in logic, metaphysics and rhetoric to an old Virginia statesman, has this advantage, that when he returns home he takes off his coat and takes hold of the plough. This gives him bone and muscle, sir, and preserves his republican principles pure and uncontaminated."

So long as free land exists, the opportunity for a competency exists, and economic power secures political power. But the democracy born of free land, strong in selfishness and individualism, intolerant of administrative experience and education, and pressing individual liberty beyond its proper bounds, has its dangers as well as its benefits. Individualism in America has allowed a laxity in regard to governmental affairs which has rendered possible the spoils system, and all the manifest evils that follow from the lack of a highly developed civic spirit. In this connection may be noted also the influence of frontier conditions in permitting lax business honor, inflated paper currency and wild-cat banking. The colonial and revolutionary frontier was the region whence emanated many of the worst forms of an evil currency. The West in the War of 1812 repeated the phenomenon on the frontier of that day, while the speculation and wild-cat banking of the period of the crisis of 1837 occurred on the new frontier belt of the next tier of states. Thus each one of the periods of lax financial integrity coincides with periods when a new set of frontier communities had arisen, and coincides in area with these successive frontiers, for the most part. The recent Populist agitation is a case in point. Many a state that now declines any connection with the tenets of the Populists, itself adhered to such ideas in an earlier stage of the development of the state. A primitive society can hardly be expected to show the intelligent appreciation of the complexity of business interests in a developed society. . . .

[Text omitted]

INTELLECTUAL TRAITS

From the conditions of frontier life came intellectual traits of profound importance. The works of travellers along each frontier from colonial days onward describe for each certain traits, and these traits have, while softening down, still persisted as survivals in the place of their origin, even when a higher social organization succeeded. The result is that to the frontier the American intellect owes its striking characteristics. That coarseness and strength combined with acuteness and inquisitiveness, that practical, inventive turn of mind, quick to find expedients, that masterful grasp of material things, lacking in the artistic but powerful to effect great ends, that restless, nervous energy, that dominant individualism, working for good and for evil, and withal that buoyancy and exuberance which comes with freedom—these are traits of the frontier, or traits called out elsewhere because of the existence of the frontier. Since the days when the fleet of Columbus sailed into the waters of the New World, America has been another name for opportunity, and the people of the United States have taken their tone from the incessant expansion which has not only been open but has even been forced upon them. He would be a rash prophet who should assert that the expansive character of American life has now entirely ceased. Movement has been its dominant fact, and, unless this training has no effect upon a people, the American intellect will continually demand a wider field for its exercise. But never again will such gifts of free land offer themselves. For a moment at the frontier the bonds of custom are broken, and unrestraint is triumphant. There is not *tabula rasa*. The stubborn American environment is there with its imperious summons to accept its conditions; the inherited ways of doing things are also there; and yet, in spite of environment, and in spite of custom, each frontier did indeed furnish a new field of opportunity, a gate of escape from the bondage of the past; and freshness, and confidence, and scorn of older society, impatience of its restraints and its ideas, and indifference to its lessons, have accompanied the frontier. What the Mediterranean Sea was to the Greeks, breaking the bond of custom, offering new experiences, calling out new institutions and activities, that, and more, the ever retreating frontier has been to the United States directly, and to the nations of Europe more remotely. And now, four centuries from the discovery of America, at the end of a hundred years of life under the Constitution, the frontier has gone, and with its going has closed the first period of American history.

James Bryce, "The Uniformity of American Life" *from* The American Commonwealth *(1908)*

Editor's Introduction: James Bryce (1838–1922), was born in Belfast, Northern Ireland, to become a noted jurist, historian, politician, and ambassador. Bryce first came to the United States in 1870 and made several subsequent visits prior to being named British Ambassador to the United States, a post in which he served from 1907 to 1913. Bryce began his classic work regarding the United States, *The American Commonwealth*, in the 1880s and it appeared in four substantially revised editions, the last published in 1910. Bryce's book and Tocqueville's *Democracy in America* (1830) are probably the two greatest comprehensive works written on American politics in the nineteenth century.

Like Tocqueville, Bryce was a keen observer who traveled widely throughout the country, spoke to people from all walks of life, and sought to capture in the book "the whole political system of the country in its practice as well as its theory." Thus he studied national and state governments, courts, schools, and other institutions as well as the "the ideas, tempers [and] habits of the sovereign people." Also like Tocqueville, Bryce often compares American with European cultural and political experience, as he does explicitly in the following passage. Bryce observes in the United States a certain uniformity of tastes and opinions that he does not find in Europe. He attributes this to the newness of the institutions and political culture and to a rough "equality in material conditions."

*   *   *

To the pleasantness of American life there is one, and only one, serious drawback—its uniformity. Those who have been struck by the size of America, and by what they have heard of its restless excitement, may be surprised at the word. They would have guessed that an unquiet changefulness and turmoil were the disagreeables to be feared. But uniformity, which the European visitor begins to note when he has traveled for a month or two, is the feature of the country which Englishmen who have lived long there, and Americans who are familiar with Europe, most frequently revert to when asked to say what is the "crook in their lot."

It is felt in many ways. I will name a few.

Source: James Bryce, *The American Commonwealth*, Vol. 2, (New York, The Commonwealth Publishing Company, 1908).

[Text omitted]

Of the uniformity of political institutions over the whole United States I have spoken already. Everywhere the same system of State governments, everywhere the same municipal governments, and almost uniformly bad or good in proportion to the greater or smaller population of the city; the same party machinery organized on the same methods, "run" by the same wirepullers and "workers." In rural local government there are some diversities in the names, areas, and functions of the different bodies, yet differences slight in comparison with the points of likeness. The schools are practically identical in organization, in the subjects taught, in the methods of teaching, though the administration of them is as completely decentralized as can be imagined, even the State commissioner having no right to do more than suggest or report. So it is with the charitable institutions, with the libraries, the lecture-courses, the public amusements. All these are more aboundant and better of their kind in the richer and more cultivated parts of the country, generally better in the North Atlantic than in the inland States and in the West than in the South. But they are the same in type everywhere. It is the same with social habits and usages. There are still some differences between the South and the North; and in the Eastern cities the upper class is more Europeanized in its code of etiquette and its ways of daily life. But even these variations tend to disappear. Eastern customs begin to permeate the West, beginning with the richer families; the South is more like the North than it was before the war. Travel where you will, you will feel that what you have found in one place that you will find in another. The thing which hath been, will be: you can no more escape from it than you can quit the land to live in the sea.

Last of all we come to man himself—to man and to woman, not less important than man. The ideas of men and women, their fundamental beliefs and their superficial tastes, their methods of thinking and their fashions of talking, are what most concern their fellow-men; and if there be variety and freshness in these, the uniformity of nature and the monotony of cities signify but little. If I observe that in these respects also the similarity of type over the country is surprising, I shall be asked whether I am not making the old mistake of the man who fancied all Chinese were like one another, because, noticing the dress and the pigtail, he did not notice minor differences of feature. A scholar is apt to think that all business men write the same hand, and a business man thinks the same of all scholars. Perhaps Americans think all Englishmen alike. And I may also be asked with whom I am comparing the Americans. With Europe as a whole? If so, is it not absurd to expect that the differences between different sections in one people should be as marked as those between different peoples? The United States are larger than Europe, but Europe has many races and many languages, among whom contrasts far broader must be expected than between one people, even if it stretches over a continent.

It is most clearly not with Europe, but with each of the leading European peoples that we must compare the people of America. So comparing them with the people of Britain, France, Germany, Italy, Spain, one discovers more varieties between individuals in these European peoples than one finds in America. Scotchmen and Irishmen are more unlike Englishmen, the native of Normandy more unlike the native of Provence, the Pomeranian more unlike the Wurtemberger, the Piedmontese more unlike the Neapolitan, the Basque more unlike the Andalusian, than the American from any part of the country is to the American from any other. Differences of course there are between the human type as developed in different regions of the country,—differences moral and intellectual as well as physical. You can generally tell a Southerner by his look as well as by his speech. A native of Maine will probably differ from a native of Kentucky, a Georgian from an Oregonian. But these differences strike even an American observer much as the difference between a Yorkshireman and a Lancastrian strikes the English, and is slighter than the contrast between a middle-class southern Englishman and a middle-class Scotchman, slighter than the differences between a peasant from Northumberland and a peasant from Dorsetshire. Or, to take another way of putting it: If at some great gathering of a political party from all parts of the United Kingdom you were to go round and talk to, say, one hundred, taken at random, of the persons present, you would be struck by more diversity between the notions and the tastes and mental habits of the individuals comprising that one hundred than if you tried the same experiment with a hundred Americans of the same education and position, similarly gathered in a convention from every State in the Union.

I do not in the least mean that people are more commonplace in America than in England, or that the Americans are less ideal than the English. Neither of these statements would be true. On the contrary, the average American is more alive to new ideas, more easily touched through his imagination or his emotions, than the average Englishman or Frenchman. I mean only that the native-born Americans appear to vary less, in fundamentals, from what may be called the dominant American type than Englishmen, Germans, Frenchmen, Spaniards, or Italians do from any type which could be taken as the dominant type in any of those nations. Or, to put the same thing differently, it is rather more difficult to take any assemblage of attributes in any of these European countries and call it the national type than it is to do the like in the United States. . . .

Life in America is in most ways pleasanter, easier, simpler, than in Europe; it floats in a sense of happiness like that of a radiant summer morning. But life in any of the great European centres is capable of an intensity, a richness blended of many elements, which has not yet been reached in America. There are more problems in Europe calling for solution; there is more passion in the struggles that rage round them; the past more frequently kindles the present with a glow of imaginative light. In whichever country of Europe one dwells, one feels that the other countries are near, that the fortunes of their peoples are bound up with the fortunes of one's own, that ideas are shooting to and fro between them. The web of history woven day by day all over Europe is vast and of many colours: it is fateful to every European. But in America it is only the philosopher who can feel that it will ultimately be fateful to Americans also; to the ordinary man the Old World seems far off, severed by a dissociating ocean, its mighty burden with little meaning for him.

Those who have observed the uniformity I have been attempting to describe have commonly set it down, as Europeans do most American phenomena, to what they call Democracy. Democratic government has in reality not much to do with it, except in so far as such a government helps to induce that deference of individuals to the mass which strengthens a dominant type, whether of ideas, of institutions, or of manners. More must be ascribed to the equality of material conditions, still more general than in Europe, to the fact that nearly every one is engaged either in agriculture, or in commerce, or in some handicraft, to the extraordinary mobility of the population, which in migrating from one part of the country to another brings the characteristics of each part into the others, to the diffusion of education, to the cheapness of literature and universal habit of reading, which enable every one to know what every one else is thinking, but above all to the newness of the country, and the fact that four-fifths of it have been made all at a stroke, and therefore all of a piece, as compared with the slow growth by which European countries have developed. Newness is the cause of uniformity, not merely in the external aspect of cities, villages, farmhouses, but in other things also, for the institutions and social habits which belonged a century ago to a group of small communities on the Atlantic coast, have been suddenly extended over an immense area, each band of settlers naturally seeking to retain its customs, and to plant in the new soil shoots from which trees like those of the old home might spring up. The variety of European countries is due not only to the fact that their race-elements have not yet become thoroughly commingled, but also that many old institutions have survived among the new ones; as in a city that grows but slowly, old buildings are not cleared away to make room for others more suited to modern commerce, but are allowed to stand, sometimes empty and unused, sometimes half adapted to new purposes. This scarcely happens in America. Doubtless many American institutions are old, and were old before they were carried across the Atlantic. But they have generally received new dress, which, in adapting them to the needs of to-day, conceals their ancient character; and the form in which they have been diffused or reproduced in the different States of the Union is in all those States practically identical.

SUGGESTIONS FOR FURTHER READING

Ray Billington and Martin Ridge, *Westward Expansion: A History of the American Frontier*, 5th edition (New York: Macmillan Publishing Co., Inc., 1982).

Stanley M. Elkins and Eric McKitrick, *The Age of Federalism* (New York: Oxford University Press, 1993).

Max Farrand, ed., *The Records of the Federal Convention of 1787*, 3 vols., (New Haven: Yale University Press, 1966).

Felix Gilbert, *To the Farewell Address: Ideas of Early American Foreign Policy* (Princeton, NJ: Princeton University Press, 1961).

Jack P. Greene, ed., *Colonies to Nation 1763–1789: A Documentary History of the American Revolution* (New York: W. W. Norton & Co., 1967).

Louis Hartz, *The Liberal Tradition in America: An Interpretation of American Political Thought Since the Revolution* (New York: Harcourt Brace Jovanovich, 1955).

Michael G. Kammen, *People of Paradox: An Inquiry Concerning the Origins of American Civilization* (Ithaca, NY: Cornell University Press, 1990).

Marvin Meyers, ed., *The Mind of the Founder: Sources of the Political Thought of James Madison* (Hanover, MA: University Press of New England, 1973).

Stephen B. Oates, *With Malice Toward None: The Life of Abraham Lincoln* (New York: Harper & Row, 1977).

Herbert J. Storing, *What the Anti-Federalists Were For*, vol. 1 of *The Complete Anti-Federalist*, 7 vols. (Chicago: University of Chicago Press, 1981).

Alexis de Tocqueville, *Democracy in America*, edited by J. P. Mayer, translated by George Lawrence (New York: Harper Collins Publishers, 1969).

Garry Wills, *Lincoln at Gettysburg: The Words that Remade America* (New York: Simon & Schuster, 1992).

Gordon S. Wood, *The Creation of the American Republic: 1776–1787* (New York: W. W. Norton & Co., 1969).

John R. Wunder, *"Retained by the People: A History of American Indians and the Bill of Rights"* (New York: Oxford University Press, 1994).

PART II

Gender and Politics: Citizenship, Equality, and Difference

PART II

Gender and Politics:
Citizenship, Equality, and Difference

And, by the way, in the new code of laws which I suppose it will be necessary for you to make, I desire you would remember the ladies and be more generous and favorable to them than your ancestors. Do not put such unlimited power into the hands of the husbands. Remember, all men would be tyrants if they could. If particular care and attention is not paid to the ladies, we are determined to foment a rebellion, and will not hold ourselves bound by any laws in which we have no voice or representation.

—ABIGAIL ADAMS, in a letter to John Adams, 1776

It is no coincidence that Abigail Adams wrote the above remarks in the same year as the Declaration of Independence. Women in colonial America had few political rights. They could not vote nor serve on juries. A married woman, as was the case under British common law, had even fewer rights than a single one, based on the belief that her legal rights were covered by her husband's. We should not be surprised if a politically astute woman of the founding era like Abigail Adams took such staples of American revolutionary political ideas as that one should not be bound by laws one has no role in making, and even that one has a right to rebel against illegitimate government, and applied them to gender relations. What better time to reconsider relations of the sexes, and to do so in light of liberal and republican ideas, than during a revolution when so many other changes in politics and society were under way? John Adams, in the response to Abigail reproduced here, is clearly uncomfortable with the implications his wife draws from revolutionary political thought and responds in a mocking way. His very mockery suggests, however, that she struck a nerve.

Free American women played an important role in the Revolutionary War, as exemplified in the 1780 piece, "Sentiments of An American Woman," reproduced here. The author of this anonymously published Philadelphia Broadside notes the contribution of women to the revolutionary cause in supplying bandages for the troops and forgoing such luxuries as tea and fancy fabrics, thereby honoring the boycott of British goods. At the same time, she points to great queens of the past, like Elizabeth I and Catherine the Great, as well as to Old Testament and Roman republican heroines, and thus suggests that American women are capable of even greater political contributions in their own right.

The 1780 Philadelphia Broadside is deeply influenced by republican political thought and language. It expresses forcefully the view that women throughout history have made great contributions to the cause of *public liberty*. It does not ask for or assert the rights of women *as individuals* (as Adams begins to do in a letter that owes a greater debt to liberalism), but rather focuses on the contributions of women to the cause of the liberty of a whole people to govern themselves. "Born for liberty, disdaining to bear the irons of a tyrannic Government," the great women of the past discussed by the author "have extended the empire of liberty, and ... broken the chains of slavery, forged by tyrants in the times of ignorance and barbarity." The contrast here is between a people who are free to make laws by which they will be bound versus one who lives under the yoke of tyranny. This focus on the common good of a free people and the role of women in defending it—whether through roles as supportive wives and mothers to republican citizen-soldiers, or through more direct means like the Roman heroines the author of the Broadside so admires—is a hallmark of republican political thought and emphasizes the special role of women in it.

Judith Sargent Murray passionately proclaims the equality of the sexes: "Yes, ye lordly, ye haughty sex, our souls are by nature *equal* to yours." Murray is most interested in this piece in supporting improved education for women while affirming women's capacity for self-development and the contributions her sex could make to the betterment of the species if opportunities were not denied it. It was left, however, to a later generation of women activists, who gradually coalesced around the cause of women's suffrage, to pick up the liberal egalitarian thread of argument we find in Abigail Adams and in Murray. Many of the suffragists were introduced to politics through the abolitionist movement prior to the Civil War. Women, including Lucretia Mott, Susan B. Anthony, Elizabeth Cady Stanton, and countless others, played crucial roles in antislavery societies throughout the north. Sojourner Truth, a former slave who spoke widely to abolitionist and suffragist audiences, brings together the denial of rights to blacks and to women in a particularly personal and poignant way. Many white suffragists, it must be noted, were later to feel betrayed by male abolitionists when, after the war, such men as Wendell Phillips and Frederick Douglass were to tell them to "wait their turn." That is, they were advised to wait until the vote was secured for African-Americans before pushing their demands for the vote for women. The abolitionist experience and the war itself which, like the Revolutionary War before and World War II after, forced women into greater economic self-reliance as men were off fighting, profoundly shaped the women's movement for the latter half of the nineteenth century.

Susan B. Anthony was the great organizer of the suffragist cause, while Elizabeth Cady Stanton was a better—and more militant—theorist. Both Anthony and Stanton not only affirmed women's equality but argued that once this was recognized, there was no legitimate reason for denying women the full rights of citizenship, including the vote. The latter is represented here in two works, first, the "Declaration of Sentiments and Resolutions" of the convention at Seneca Falls in 1848, a document based upon the Declaration of Independence. Stanton's 1890 speech points toward concerns emphasized by later, more radical feminists, as she looks at a wide range of social policies and practices that harm women, and at how they should be changed. The issue for her is not simply to gain the vote for women, but what they may do with it to improve their lives.

The writings by Emma Goldman, bell hooks, and Catharine MacKinnon can all be described as "radical feminist" in orientation. Radical feminists seek not simply to include women in a political and economic system they see as basically sound but, rather, to transform a system they see as fundamentally oppressive and dehumanizing. Goldman's 1917 writing criticizes the goal of women's suffrage not because she denies the premise of gender equality but because she believes the society needs to be radically transformed to truly meet the economic, sexual, and spiritual needs of women. It was not that the demand for suffrage asked too much, but rather that it asked far too little. Bell hooks also sees oppression of women as a necessary consequence of a liberal capitalist political order and challenges the women's movement to move beyond such ameliorative demands as "equal pay for equal work" and to challenge the legitimacy of class inequality which, she believes, gives rise to sexual oppression. MacKinnon's piece is also radical in its critique of the First Amendment, which she interprets as protecting access to pornography. She suggests that our entire political order—even our most cherished basic liberties—is built upon the exclusion of women and does violence to women.

When one discusses half the species, it should be clear that no single political creed is going to represent all women any more than it would all men. Radical feminism, which itself comes in diverse forms, is one influential strain of contemporary political thought. It is not the only or even a majority one, however, and many women do not consider themselves feminists at all. Contemporary "liberal feminism" is represented by the 1966 founding "Statement of Purpose" of the National Organization for Women. This statement and the organization itself represent a continuation and broadening of the goals of suffragists like Susan B. Anthony.

NOW states as its objective to "take action to bring women into full participation in the mainstream of American society now, exercising all the privileges and responsibilities thereof in truly equal partnership with men."

Betty Friedan was a co-author of NOW's founding statement and has contributed subsequently to feminist thought and action. In her 1981 work, *The Second Stage*, Friedan contends that the contemporary women's movement faces issues it did not entirely foresee when NOW was founded. If at that time the goal was equality in public spheres of education, the workplace, and politics, feminism today must not abandon equality but must recognize as well the deep commitments many women have to raising families. It should pay attention to how these commitments can be reconciled. Friedan would move to the center of the agenda, policies that make it easier to meet the demands of both family and work outside of the home. This includes such "family policies" as child care allowances, maternity and paternity leave policies, and flextime. Such a focus, Friedan suggests, could also bridge the gap between the middle-class liberal women who have always been NOW's core constituency and working-class women of all races, who have sensed a certain ignorance or indifference to their plight. It would address also many of the concerns of conservative women who have complained of a belittling of family and motherhood on the part of liberal feminists.

Letters of Abigail and John Adams (1776)

Editor's Introduction: The following letter written by Abigail Adams (1744–1818), just months before the signing of the Declaration of Independence, is frequently cited as one of the earliest feminist writings in America. During the Revolutionary War, Abigail Adams was left alone to manage the family farm in Braintree, Massachusetts while her husband, John Adams (1735–1826), was serving the new nation in a variety of political capacities. He was later to become the first Vice President and the second President of the United States. While initially reluctant to take on this responsibility, Abigail became a sound manager and maintained the farm in stable financial condition during the war. This experience no doubt fostered a spirit of independence as well as patriotism. Indeed, Abigail made numerous personal sacrifices for the war effort, sacrifices she saw as no more than her duty. At the time of the letters reprinted here, John Adams was serving in the Second Continental Congress in Philadelphia. Abigail calls for the political rights of women in the language of rebellion and representation common among American revolutionaries. While her husband had commented often that Abigail had the cast of mind to be an excellent statesman, he could not bring himself to take her request to "remember the ladies" seriously. His jesting reply to his wife illustrates the general dismissal of women's claims to political and civil rights at this time.

*   *   *

Abigail Adams, 31 March, 1776

I wish you would ever write me a letter half as long as I write you, and tell me, if you may, where your fleet are gone; what sort of defense Virginia can make against our common enemy; whether it is so situated as to make an able defense. Are not the gentry lords, and the common people vassals? Are they not like the uncivilized vassals Britain represents us to be? I hope their riflemen, who have shown themselves very savage and even blood-thirsty, are not a specimen of the generality of the people. I am willing to allow the colony great merit for having produced a Washington; but they have been shamefully duped by a Dunmore.

I have sometimes been ready to think that the passion for liberty cannot be equally strong in the breasts of those who have been accustomed

Source: Charles Francis Adams, *Familiar Letters of John Adams and his Wife Abigail Adams, During the Revolution* (Hurd and Houghton, The Riverside Press, Cambridge, MA, 1876).

to deprive their fellow creatures of theirs. Of this I am certain, that it is not founded upon the generous and Christian principle of doing to others as we would that others should do unto us.

Do not you want to see Boston? I am fearful of the small-pox, or I should have been in before this time. I got Mr. Crane to go to our house and see what state it was in. I find it has been occupied by one of the doctors of a regiment; very dirty, but no other damage has been done to it. The few things which were left in it are all gone. I look upon it as a new acquisition of property—a property which one month ago I did not value at a single shilling, and would with pleasure have seen it in flames.

The town in general is left in a better state than we expected; more owing to a precipitate flight than any regard to the inhabitants; though some individuals discovered a sense of honor and justice, and have left the rent of the houses in which they were, for the owners, and the furniture unhurt, or, if damaged, sufficient to make it good. Others have committed abominable ravages. The mansionhouse of your President is safe, and the furniture unhurt; while the house and furniture of the Solicitor General have fallen prey to their own merciless party. Surely the very fiends feel a reverential awe for virtue and patriotism, whilst they detest the parricide and traitor.

I feel very differently at the approach of spring from what I did a month ago. We knew not then whether we could plant or sow with safety, whether where we had tilled we could reap the fruits of our own industry, whether we could rest in our own cottages or whether we should be driven from the seacoast to seek shelter in the wilderness; but now we feel a temporary peace, and the poor fugitives are returning to their deserted habitations.

Though we felicitate ourselves, we sympathize with those who are trembling lest the lot of Boston should be theirs. But they cannot be in similar circumstances unless pusillanimity and cowardice should take possession of them. They have time and warning given them to see the evil and shun it.

I long to hear that you have declared an independency. And, by the way, in the new code of laws which I suppose it will be necessary for you to make, I desire you would remember the ladies and be more generous and favorable to them than your ancestors. Do not put such unlimited power into the hands of the husbands. Remember, all men would be tyrants if they could. If particular care and attention is not paid to the ladies, we are determined to foment a rebellion, and will not hold ourselves bound by any laws in which we have no voice or representation.

That your sex are naturally tyrannical is a truth so thoroughly established as to admit of no dispute; but such of you as wish to be happy willingly give up the harsh title of master for the more tender and endearing one of friend. Why, then, not put it out of the power of the vicious and the lawless to use us with cruelty and indignity with impunity? Men of sense in all ages abhor those customs which treat us only as the vassals of your sex; regard us then as beings placed by Providence under your protection, and in imitation of the Supreme Being make use of that power only for our happiness.

[Text omitted]

John Adams. 14 April.

You justly complain of my short letters, but the critical state of things and the multiplicity of avocations must plead my excuse. You ask where the fleet is? The inclosed papers will inform you. You ask what sort of defense Virginia can make? I believe they will make an able defense. Their militia and minute-men have been some time employed in training themselves, and they have nine battalions of regulars, as they call them, maintained among them, under good officers, at the Continental expense. They have set up a number of manufactories of firearms, which are busily employed. They are tolerably supplied with powder, and are successful and assiduous in making saltpetre. Their neighboring sister, or rather daughter colony of North Carolina, which is a warlike colony, and has several battalions at the Continental expense, as well as a pretty good militia, are ready to assist them, and they are in very good spirits and seem determined to make a brave resistance. The gentry are very rich, and the common people very poor. This inequality of property gives an aristocratical turn to all their proceedings, and occasions a strong aversion in their patricians to "Common Sense." (Paine's pamphlet) But the spirit of these Barons is coming down, and it must submit. It is very true, as you observe, they have been duped by Dunmore. But this is a common case. All the colonies are duped, more or less, at one time and another. A more egregious bubble was never blown up than the story of Commissioners coming to treat with the Congress, yet it has gained credit like a charm, not only with, but against the clearest evidence. I never shall forget the delusion which seized our best and most sagacious friends, the dear inhabitants of Boston, the winter before last. Credulity and the want of foresight are imperfections in the human character, that no politician can sufficiently guard against.

[Text omitted]

Your description of your own *gaiete de cour* charms me. Thanks be to God, you have just cause to rejoice, and may the bright prospect be obscured by no cloud. As to declarations of independency, be patient.

Read our privateering laws and our commercial laws. What signifies a word?

As to your extraordinary code of laws, I cannot but laugh. We have been told that our struggle has loosened the bonds of government everywhere; that children and apprentices were disobedient; that schools and colleges were grown turbulent; that Indians slighted their guardians, and negroes grew insolent to their masters. But your letter was the first intimation that another tribe, more numerous and powerful than all the rest, were grown discontented. This is rather too coarse a compliment, but you are so saucy, I won't blot it out. Depend upon it, we know better than to repeal our masculine systems. Although they are in full force, you know they are little more than theory. We dare not exert our power in its full latitude. We are obliged to go fair and softly, and, in practice, you know we are the subjects. We have only the name of masters, and rather than give up this, which would completely subject us to the despotism of the petticoat, I hope General Washington and all our brave heroes would fight; I am sure every good politician would plot, as long as he would against despotism, empire, monarchy, aristocracy, oligarchy, or ochlocracy. A fine story, indeed! I begin to think the ministry as deep as they are wicked. After stirring up Tories, land-jobbers, trimmers, bigots, Canadians, Indians, negroes, Hanoverians, Hessians, Russians, Irish Roman Catholics, Scotch renegadoes, at last they have stimulated the __ to demand new privileges and threaten to rebel.

Philadelphia Broadside,
"The Sentiments of an American Woman" (1780)

Editor's Introduction: This broadside of 1780 announced the role Philadelphia women would play in advancing the cause of the American Revolution by raising contributions for soldiers. The campaign was organized by Esther DeBerdt Reed, wife of the president of Pennsylvania, and Sarah Franklin Bache, Benjamin Franklin's daughter. The women raised a substantial amount of money by traveling from door to door soliciting donations. Though the women preferred to give this money directly to the soldiers in the form of cash bonuses, General George Washington refused their request. In fear that the cash would be spent unwisely if deposited in the general fund or that it would replace the taxes earmarked for the army, the women sewed shirts for the soldiers from linen purchased with the money raised. Each shirt was inscribed with the name of its seamstress, providing a personal touch and a gesture of solidarity from the women of Philadelphia. The selection which follows emphasizes the patriotism of women and the sacrifices they are willing to make in times of war.

* * *

On the commencement of actual war, the Women of America manifested a firm resolution to contribute as much as could depend on them, to the deliverance of their country. Animated by the purest patriotism, they are sensible of sorrow at this day, in not offering more than barren wishes for the success of so glorious a Revolution. They aspire to render themselves more really useful, and this sentiment is universal from the north to the south of the Thirteen United States. Our ambition is kindled by the fame of those heroines of antiquity, who have rendered their sex illustrious, and have proved to the universe, that, if the weakness of our Constitution, if opinion and manners did not forbid us to march to glory by the same paths as the Men, we should at least equal, and sometimes surpass them in our love for the public good. I glory in all that which my sex has done great and commendable. I call to mind with enthusiasm and with admiration, all those acts of courage, of constancy and patriotism, which history has transmitted to us: The people favoured by Heaven, preserved from destruction by the virtues, the zeal and the resolution of Deborah, of Judith, of Esther! The fortitude of the mother of the Macchabees, in giving up her sons to die before her eyes: Rome saved from the

Source: Collections of the American Antiquarian Society

fury of a victorious enemy by the efforts of Volumnia, and other Roman Ladies: So many famous sieges where the Women have been forgetting the weakness of their sex, building new walls, digging trenches with their feeble hands, furnishing arms to their defenders, they themselves darting the missile weapons on the enemy, resigning the ornaments of their apparel, and their fortune, to fill the public treasury, and to hasten the deliverance of their country, burying themselves under its ruins, throwing themselves into the flames rather than submit to the disgrace of humiliation before a proud enemy.

Born for liberty, disdaining to bear the irons of a tyrannic Government, we associate ourselves to the grandeur of those Sovereigns, cherished and revered, who have held with so much splendor the scepter of the greatest States, The Batildas, the Elizabeths, the Maries, the Catherines, who have extended the empire of liberty, and contented to reign by sweetness and justice, have broken the chains of slavery, forged by tyrants in the times of ignorance and barbarity. The Spanish Women, do they not make, at this moment, the most patriotic sacrifices, to encrease the means of victory in the hands of their Sovereign. He is a friend to the French Nation. They are our allies. We call to mind, doubly interested, that it was a French Maid who kindled up among her fellow-citizens, the flame of patriotism buried under long misfortunes: It was the Maid of Orleans who drove from the kingdom of France the ancestors of those same British, whose odious yoke we have shaken off, and whom it is necessary that we drive from this Continent.

But I must limit myself to the recollection of this small number of achievements. Who knows if persons disposed to censure, and sometimes too severely with regard to us, may not disapprove our appearing acquainted even with the actions of which our sex boasts? We are at least certain, that he cannot be a good citizen who will not applaud our efforts for the relief of the armies which defend our lives, our possessions, our liberty? The situation of our soldiery has been represented to me; the evils inseparable from war, and the firm and generous spirit which has enabled them to support these. But it has been said that they may apprehend, that, in the course of a long war, the view of their distresses may be lost, and their services be forgotten. Forgotten! Never; I can answer in the name of all my sex. Brave Americans, your disinterestedness, your courage, and your constancy will always be dear to America, as long as she shall preserve her virtue.

We know that at a distance from the theater of war, if we enjoy any tranquility, it is the fruit of your watchings, your labors, your dangers. If I live happy in the midst of my family, if my husband cultivates his field, and reaps his harvest in peace, if, surrounded with my children, I myself nourish the youngest, and press it to my bosom, without being afraid of feeling myself separated from it, by a ferocious enemy, if the house in which we dwell, if our barns, our orchards are safe in the present time from the hands of those incendiaries, it is to you that we owe it. And shall we hesitate to evidence to you our gratitude? Shall we hesitate to wear a clothing more simple, hair dressed less elegant, while at the price of this small privation, we shall deserve your benedictions. Who, amongst us, will not renounce with the highest pleasure, those vain ornaments, when she shall consider that the valiant defenders of America will be able to draw some advantage from the money which she may have laid out in these that they will be better defended from the rigours of the seasons, that after their painful toils, they will receive some extraordinary and unexpected relief; that these presents will perhaps be valued by them at a greater price, when they will have it in their power to say: **This is the offering of the Ladies**. The time is arrived to display the same sentiments which animated us at the beginning of the Revolution, when we renounced the use of teas, however agreeable to our taste, rather than receive them from our persecutors, when we made it appear to them that we placed former necessaries in the rank of superfluities, when our liberty was interested; when our republican and laborious hands spun the flax, prepared the linen intended for the use of our soldiers, when exiles and fugitives we supported with courage all the evils which are the concomitants of war. Let us not lose a moment, let us be engaged to offer the homage of our gratitude at the altar of military valour, and you, our brave deliverers, while mercenary slaves combat to cause you to share with them, the irons with which they are loaded, receive with a free hand our offering, the purest which can be presented to your virtue.

By an American Woman.

Judith Sargent Murray,
"On the Equality of the Sexes" (1790)

Editor's Introduction: Judith Sargent Murray (1751–1820) was born to a progressive merchant family in Gloucester, Massachusetts, in 1751. The Sargent family allowed Murray to study with her brother, to which she alludes in the following selection. This education provided her with the necessary knowledge and skills to become a proficient writer while also engendering an enduring commitment to the education of women.

Murray argues that men and women are by nature equally capable of intellectual attainment, though this quality is not nurtured in women. Women suffer a lack of mental cultivation but so, she suggests, do men as they are denied the intellectual contributions that half the species could offer and even denied more interesting and more virtuous partners. Murray draws upon liberal and republican ideals in making her case for the education of women by asserting the moral equality of persons, their natural desires for personal independence and self-development, and by describing the good such attainment can do for others.

Murray is best known for a collection of essays on the education of women entitled *The Gleaner*. She is also the first native-born female dramatist to have her plays performed professionally in the United States.

* * *

Is it upon mature consideration we adopt the idea, that nature is thus partial in her distributions? Is it indeed a fact, that she hath yielded to one half of the human species so unquestionable a mental superiority? I know that to both sexes elevated understandings, and the reverse, are common. But, suffer me to ask, in what the minds of females are so notoriously deficient, or unequal. May not the intellectual powers be ranged under their four heads—imagination, reason, memory and judgment. The province of imagination has long since been surrendered up to us, and we have been crowned undoubted sovereigns of the regions of fancy. Invention is perhaps the most arduous effort of the mind; this branch of imagination hath been particularly ceded to us, and we have been time out of mind invested with that creative faculty. Observe the variety of fashions (here I bar the contemptuous smile) which distinguish

Source: Judith Sargent Murray, "On the Equality of the Sexes," The *Massachusetts Magazine*, March 1790, pp. 132–135, and April 1790, pp. 223–226. Reprinted with permission of University Microfilms, Inc.

and adorn the female world; how continually are they changing, insomuch that they almost render the whole man's assertion problematical, and we are ready to say, *there is something new under the sun*. Now, what a playfulness, what an exuberance of fancy, what strength of inventive imagination, doth this continual variation discover? Again, it hath been observed, that if the turpitude of the conduct of our sex, hath been ever so enormous, so extremely ready are we that the very first thought presents us with an apology so plausible, as to produce our actions even in an amiable light. Another instance of our creative powers, is our talent for slander; how ingenious are we at inventive scandal? what a formidable story can we in a moment fabricate merely from the force of a prolifick imagination? how many reputations, in the fertile brain of a female, have been utterly despoiled? how industrious are we at improving a hint? suspicion how easily do we convert into conviction, and conviction, embellished by the power of eloquence, stalks abroad to the surprise and confusion of unsuspecting innocence. Perhaps it will be asked if I furnish these facts as instances of excellency in our sex. Certainly not; but as proofs of a creative faculty, of a lively imagination. Assuredly great activity of mind is thereby discovered, and was this activity properly directed, what beneficial effects would follow. Is the needle and kitchen sufficient to employ the operations of a soul thus organized? I should conceive not. Nay, it is a truth that those very departments leave the intelligent principle vacant, and at liberty for speculation. Are we deficient in reason? We can only reason from what we know, and if opportunity of acquiring knowledge hath been denied us, the inferiority of our sex cannot fairly be deduced from thence. Memory, I believe, will be allowed us in common, since every one's experience must testify, that a loquacious old woman is as frequently met with, as a communicative old man; their subjects are alike drawn from the fund of other times, and the transactions of their youth, or of maturer life, entertain, or perhaps fatigue you, in the evening of their lives. "But our judgment is not so strong—we do not distinguish so well." Yet it may be questioned, from what doth this superiority, in thus discriminating faculty of the soul, proceed. May we not trace its source in the difference of education, and continued advantages? Will it be said that the judgment of a male of two years old, is more sage than that of a female's of the same age? I believe the reverse is generally observed to be true. But from that period what partiality! how is the one exalted and the other depressed, by the contrary modes of education which are adopted! the one is taught to aspire, and the other is early confined and limited. As their years increase, the sister must be wholly domesticated, while the brother is led by the hand through all the flowery paths of science. Grant that their minds are by nature equal, yet who shall wonder at the *apparent* superiority, if indeed custom becomes *second nature*;

nay if it taketh place of nature, and that it doth the experience of each day will evince. At length arrived at womanhood, the uncultivated fair one feels a void, which the employments allotted her are by no means capable of filling. What can she do? to books, she may not apply; or if she doth, *to those only of the novel kind*, lest she merit the appellation of a *learned lady*; and what ideas have been affixed to this term, the observation of many can testify. Fashion, scandal and sometimes what is still more reprehensible, are then called in to her relief; and who can say to what lengths the liberties she takes may proceed. Meantime she herself is most unhappy; she feels the want of a cultivated mind. Is she single, she in vain seeks to fill up time from sexual employments or amusements. Is she united to a person whose soul nature made equal to her own, education hath set him so far above her, that in those entertainments which are productive of such rational felicity, she is not qualified to accompany him. She experiences a mortifying consciousness of inferiority, which embitters eveiy enjoyment. Doth the person to whom her adverse fate hath consigned her, possess a mind incapable of improvement, she is equally wretched, in being so closely connected with an individual whom she cannot but despise. Now, was she permitted the same instructors as her brother, (with an eye however to their particular departments) for the employment of a rational mind an ample field would be opened. In astronomy she might catch a glimpse of the immensity of the Deity, and thence she would form amazing conceptions of the august and supreme Intelligence. In geography she would admire Jehova in the midst of his benevolence; thus adapting this globe to the various wants and amusements of its inhabitants. In natural philosophy she would adore the infinite majesty of heaven, clothed in condescension; and as she traversed the reptile world, she would hail the goodness of a creating God. A mind, thus filled, would have little room for the trifles with which our sex are, with too much justice, accused of amusing themselves, and they would thus be rendered fit companions for those, who should one day wear them as their crown. Fashions, in their variety, would then give place to conjectures, which might perhaps conduce to the improvement of the literary world; and there would be no leisure for slander or detraction. Reputation would not then be blasted, but serious speculations would occupy the lively imaginations of the sex. Unnecessary visits would be precluded, and that custom would only be indulged by way of relaxation, or to answer the demands of consanguinity and friendship. Females would become discreet, their judgments would be invigorated, and their partners for life being circumspectly chosen, an unhappy Hymen would then be as rare, as is now the reverse.

Will it be urged that those acquirements would supersede our domestick duties, I answer that every requisite in female economy is easily attained; and, with truth I can add, that when once attained, they require no further *mental attention*. Nay, while we are pursuing the needle, or the superintendency of the family, I repeat, that our minds are at full liberty for reflection; that imagination may exert itself in full vigor; and that if a just foundation early laid, our ideas will then be worthy of rational beings. If we were industrious we might easily find time to arrange them upon paper, or should avocations press too hard for such an indulgence, the hours allotted for conversation would at least become more refined and rational. Should it still be vociferated, "Your domestick employments are sufficient"—I would calmly ask, is it reasonable, that a candidate for immortality, for the joys of heaven, an intelligent being, who is to spend an eternity in contemplating the works of Deity, should at present be so degraded, as to be allowed no other ideas, than those which are suggested by the mechanism of a pudding, or the sewing of the seams of a garment? Pity that all such censurers of female improvement do not go one step further, and deny their future existence; to be consistent they surely ought.

Yes, ye lordly, ye haughty sex, our souls are by nature *equal* to yours; the same breath of God animates, enlivens, and invigorates us; and that we are not fallen lower than yourselves, let those witness who have greatly towered above the various discouragements by which they have been so heavily oppressed; and though I am unacquainted with the list of celebrated characters on either side, yet from the observations I have made in the contracted circle in which I have moved, I dare confidently believe, that from the commencement of time to the present day, there hath been as many females, as males, who, by the *mere force of natural powers*, have merited the crown of applause; who *thus unassisted*, have seized the wreath of fame. I know there are who assert, that as the animal powers of the one sex are superiour, of course their mental faculties also must be stronger; thus attributing strength of mind to the transient organization of this earth born tenement. But if this reasoning is just, man must be content to yield the palm to many of the brute creation, since by not a few of his brethren of the field, he is far surpassed in bodily strength. Moreover, was this argument admitted, it would prove too much, for occular demonstration evinceth, that there are many robust masculine ladies, and effeminate gentlemen. Yet I fancy that Mr. Pope, though clogged with an enervated body, and distinguished by a diminutive stature, could nevertheless lay claim to greatness of soul; and perhaps there are many other instances which might be adduced to combat so unphilosophical an opinion. Do we not often see, that when the clay built tabernacle is well nigh dissolved, when it is just ready to mingle with the parent soil, the immortal inhabitant aspires to, and even attaineth heights the most sublime, and which were before wholly unexplored. Besides, were we to grant that animal strength proved anything, taking into consideration the accustomed impartiality of nature, we should be induced to imagine, that she had invested the female mind with superiour strength as an equivalent for the bodily powers of man. But waving this however palpable advantage, for *equality* only, we wish to contend.

CONSTANTIA

By way of supplement to the forgoing pages, I subjoin the following extract from a letter wrote to a friend in the December of 1780.

And now assist me, O thou genius of my sex, while I undertake the arduous task of endeavouring to combat that vulgar, that almost universal errour, which hath, it seems enlisted even Mr. P_____ under its banners. The superiority of your sex hath, I grant, been time out of mind esteemed a truth incontrovertible; in consequence of which persuasion, every plan of education hath been calculated to establish this favourite tenet. Not long since, weak and presuming as I was, I amused myself with selecting some arguments from nature, reason and experience, against this so generally received idea. I confess that to sacred testimonies I had not recourse. I held them to be merely metaphorical, and thus regarding them, I could not persuade myself that there was any propriety in bringing them to decide in this *very important debate*. However, as you, sir, confine yourself entirely to the sacred oracles, I mean to bend the whole of my artillery against those supposed proofs, which you have from thence provided, and from which you have formed an intrenchment *apparently* so invulnerable. And first, to begin with our great progenitors; but here, suffer me to promise, that it is for mental strength I mean to contend, for with respect to animal powers, I yield them undisputed to that sex, which enjoys them in common with the lion, the tyger, and many other beasts of prey; therefore your observations respecting *the rib, under the arm, at a distance from the head, &c.&c.* in no sort militate against my view. Well, but the woman was first in the transgression. Strange how blind *self love* renders you men; were you not wholly absorbed in a partial admiration of your own abilities, you would long since have acknowledged the force of what I am now going to urge. It is true some ignoramuses have, absurdly enough informed us, that the beauteous fair of paradise, was seduced from her obedience, by a malignant demon, *in the guise of a baleful serpent*; but we, who are better informed, know that the fallen spirit presented himself to her view, *a shining angel still*; for thus, saith the criticks in the Hebrew tongue, ought the word to be rendered. Let us examine her motive—Hark! the seraph declares that she shall attain a perfection of knowledge; for is there aught which is not comprehended under one or other of the terms *good* and *evil*. It doth not appear that she was governed by any one sensual appetite; but merely by a desire of adorning her mind; a laudable ambition fired her soul, and a thirst for knowledge impelled the predilection so fatal in its consequences. Adam could not plead the same deception; assuredly he was not deceived; nor ought we to admire his superiour strength, or wonder at his sagacity, when we so often confess that example is much more influential than precept. His gentle partner stood before him, a melancholy instance of direful effects of disobedience; he saw her not possessed of that wisdom which she had fondly hoped to obtain, but he beheld the once blooming female, disrobed of that innocence, which had heretofore rendered her so lovely. To him then deception became impossible, as he had proof positive of the fallacy of the argument, which the deceiver had suggested. What then could be his inducement to burst the barriers, and to fly directly in the face of that command, which *immediately* from the mouth of Deity *he* had received, since, I say, he could not plead the fascinating stimulus, the accumulation of knowledge, as indisputable conviction was so visibly portrayed before him. What mighty cause impelled him to sacrifice myriads of beings yet unborn, and by one impious act, which *he saw* would be productive of such fatal effect, entail undistinguished ruin upon a race of beings, which he was yet to produce. Blush, ye vaunters of fortitude; ye boasters of resolution; ye haughty lords of the creation; blush when ye remember, that he was influenced by no other motive than a bare pusillanimous attachment to a woman! by sentiments so exquisitely soft, that all his sons have, from that period, when they have designed to degrade them, described as highly feminine. Thus it should see, that all the arts of the grand deceiver (since means adequate to the purpose are, I conceive, invariably pursued) were requisite to mislead our general mother, while the father of mankind forfeited his own, and relinquished the happiness of posterity, merely in compliance with the blandishments of a female.

Elizabeth Cady Stanton, Lucretia Mott, et al., "Declaration of Sentiments and Resolutions," Seneca Falls (1848)

Editor's Introduction: On July 19, 1848, a convention of some three hundred people met in Seneca Falls, New York, to consider the "social, civil, and religious condition and rights of women." The two key figures in calling the convention were Lucretia Mott, a noted spokesperson for women's and abolitionist causes, and Elizabeth Cady Stanton (1815–1902). Mott was Stanton's senior and had, in fact, played a considerable role in introducing Stanton to important feminist writings, such as those by the British political thinker Mary Wollstonecraft, and to political allies. Stanton resided with her family in Seneca Falls, and it was her idea to hold the convention there. It was also her idea to base the convention's Declaration on the Declaration of Independence.

Like the 1776 Declaration, this one argues for the moral equality of persons which gives rise to equal inalienable rights but, unlike the earlier document, it makes clear that women count as "persons." Stanton's influence pushed nineteenth century feminist thought in a new direction. Whereas earlier writers, like Judith Sargent Murray, pushed for greater education for women, they rarely sought the degree of legal and political reform that Stanton urged. Eleven of the resolutions of the convention passed unanimously. The twelfth, demanding the right to vote, passed by a narrow margin and only after an impassioned plea by former slave and abolitionist, Frederick Douglass (see Part IV).

Prior to the Civil War, there was considerable cooperation between abolitionists and feminists. White women played important roles in abolitionist societies throughout the north. Relations between the nineteenth century women's movement and that for racial equality grew strained after the war, especially as the right to vote was extended to blacks in the Fifteenth Amendment to the Constitution but still denied to women.

*   *   *

When, in the course of human events, it becomes necessary for one portion of the family of man to assume among the people of the earth a position different from that which they have hitherto occupied, but one

Source: Elizabeth Cady Stanton, Susan B. Anthony, and Matilda Joslyn Gage, eds., *History of Woman Suffrage*, Vol. 1, (N. Stratford, NH: Ayer Co. Publishers, 1969). Reprinted by permission of Ayer Co. Publishers.

to which the laws of nature and of nature's God entitle them, a decent respect to the opinions of mankind requires that they should declare the causes that impel them to such a course.

We hold these truths to be self-evident: that all men and women are created equal; that they are endowed by their Creator with certain inalienable rights; that among these are life, liberty, and the pursuit of happiness; that to secure these rights governments are instituted, deriving their just powers from the consent of the governed. Whenever any form of government becomes destructive of these ends, it is the right of those who suffer from it to refuse allegiance to it, and to insist upon the institution of new government, laying its foundation on such principles, and organizing its powers in such form, as to them shall seem most likely to effect their safety and happiness. Prudence indeed, will dictate that governments long established should not be changed for light and transient causes; and accordingly all experience hath shown that mankind are more disposed to suffer, while evils are sufferable, than to right themselves by abolishing the forms to which they were accustomed. But when a long train of abuses and usurpations, pursuing invariably the same object evinces a design to reduce them under absolute despotism, it is their duty to throw off such government, and to provide new guards for their future security. Such has been the patient sufferance of the women under this government, and such is now the necessity which constrains them to demand the equal station to which they are entitled.

The history of mankind is a history of repeated injuries and usurpations on the part of man toward woman, having in direct object the establishment of an absolute tyranny over her. To prove this, let facts be submitted to a candid world.

He has never permitted her to exercise her inalienable right to the elective franchise.

He has compelled her to submit to laws, in the formation of which she had no voice.

He has withheld from her rights which are given to the most ignorant and degraded men—both natives and foreigners.

Having deprived her of this first right of a citizen, the elective franchise, thereby leaving her without representation in the halls of legislation, he has oppressed her on all sides.

He has made her, if married, in the eye of the law, civilly dead.

He has taken from her all right in property, even to the wages she earns.

He has made her, morally, an irresponsible being, as she can commit many crimes with impunity, provided they be done in the presence of her husband. In the covenant of marriage, she is compelled to promise obedience to her husband, he becoming, to all intents and purposes, her master—the law giving him power to deprive her of her liberty, and to administer chastisement.

He has so framed the laws of divorce, as to what shall be the proper causes, and in case of separation, to whom the guardianship of the children shall be given, as to be wholly regardless of the happiness of women— the law, in all cases, going upon a false supposition of the supremacy of man, and giving all power into his hands.

After depriving her of all rights as a married woman, if single, and the owner of property, he has taxed her to support a government which recognizes her only when her property can be made profitable to it.

He has monopolized nearly all the profitable employments, and from those she is permitted to follow, she receives but a scanty remuneration. He closes against her all the avenues to wealth and distinction which he considers most honorable to himself. As a teacher of theology, medicine, or law, she is not known.

He has denied her the facilities for obtaining a thorough education, all colleges being closed against her.

He allows her in Church, as well as State, but a subordinate position, claiming Apolstolic authority for her exclusion from the ministry, and, with some exceptions, from any public participation in the affairs of the Church.

He has created a false public sentiment by giving to the world a different code of morals for men and women, by which moral delinquencies which exclude women from society, are not only tolerated, but deemed of little account in man.

He has usurped the prerogative of Jehovah himself, claiming it as his right to assign for her a sphere of action, when that belongs to her conscience and to her God.

He has endeavored, in every way that he could, to destroy her confidence in her own powers, to lessen her self-respect, and to make her willing to lead a dependent and abject life.

Now, in view of this entire disfranchisement of one-half the people of this country, their social and religious degradation—in view of the unjust laws above mentioned, and because women do feel themselves aggrieved, oppressed, and fraudulently deprived of their most sacred rights, we insist that they have immediate admission to all the rights and privileges which belong to them as citizens of the United States.

In entering upon the great work before us, we anticipate no small amount of misconception, misrepresentation, and ridicule; but we shall use every instrumentality within our power to effect our object. We shall employ agents, circulate tracts, petition the State and National legislatures, and endeavor to enlist the pulpit and the press in our behalf. We hope this Convention will be followed by a series of Conventions embracing every part of the country.

The following resolutions were discussed by Lucretia Mott, Thomas and Mary Ann McClintock, Amy Post, Catharine A. F. Stebbins, and others, and were adopted:

WHEREAS, The great precept of nature is conceded to be, that "man shall pursue his own true and substantial happiness." Blackstone in his Commentaries remarks, that this law of Nature being coeval with mankind, and dictated by God himself, is of course superior in obligation to any other. It is binding over all the globe, in all countries and at all times; no human laws are of any validity if contrary to this, and such of them as are valid, derive all their force and all their validity, and all their authority, mediately and immediately, from this original; therefore,

Resolved, That such laws as conflict, in any way, with the true and substantial happiness of woman, are contrary to the great precept of nature and of no validity, for this is "superior in obligation to any other."

Resolved, That all laws which prevent woman from occupying such a station in society as her conscience shall dictate, or which place her in a position inferior to that of man, are contrary to the great precept of nature, and therefore of no force or authority.

Resolved, That woman is man's equal—was intended to be so by the Creator, and the highest good of the race demands that she should be recognized as such.

Resolved, That the women of this country ought to be enlightened in regard to the laws under which they live, that they may no longer publish their degradation by declaring themselves satisfied with their present position, nor their ignorance, by asserting that they have all the rights they want.

Resolved, That inasmuch as man, while claiming for himself intellectual superiority, does accord to woman moral superiority, it is preeminently his duty to encourage her to speak and teach, as she has an opportunity, in all religious assemblies.

Resolved, That the same amount of virtue, delicacy, and refinement of behavior that is required of woman in the social state, should also be required of man, and the same transgressions should be visited with equal severity on both man and woman.

Resolved, That the objection of indelicacy and impropriety, which is so often brought against woman when she addresses a public audience, comes with a very ill-grace from those who encourage, by their attendance, her appearance on the stage, in the concert, or in feats of the circus.

Resolved, That woman has too long rested satisfied in the circumscribed limits which corrupt customs and a perverted application of the Scriptures have marked out for her, and that it is time she should move in the enlarged sphere which her great Creator has assigned her.

Resolved, That it is the duty of the women of this country to secure to themselves their sacred right to the elective franchise.

Resolved, That the equality of human rights results necessarily from the fact of the identity of the race in capabilities and responsibilities.

Resolved, therefore, That, being invested by the Creator with the same capabilities, and the same consciousness of responsibility for their exercise, it is demonstrably the right and duty of woman, equally with man, to promote every righteous cause by every righteous means; and especially in regard to the great subjects of morals and religion, it is self-evidently her right to participate with her brother in teaching them, both in private and in public, by writing and by speaking, by any instrumentalities proper to be used, and in any assemblies proper to be held; and this being a self-evident truth growing out of the divinely implanted principles of human nature, any custom or authority adverse to it, whether modern or wearing the hoary sanction of antiquity, is to be regarded as a self-evident falsehood, and at war with mankind.

[At the last session Lucretia Mott offered and spoke to the following resolution:]

Resolved, That the speedy success of our cause depends upon the zealous and untiring efforts of both men and women, for the overthrow of the monopoly of the pulpit, and for the securing to woman an equal participation with men in the various trades, professions, and commerce.

Frances D. Gage, Sojourner Truth, "A'n't I A Woman?" (1851)

Editor's Introduction: Sojourner Truth (c. 1795–1883) was born a slave in Ulster County, New York, and given the name Isabella Baumfree. Isabella bore seven children under the dehumanizing conditions of slavery. When Isabella's owner refused to accept the New York emancipation act of 1827, she fled and was taken in by a Quaker family. Isabella's spirituality grew with her developing consciousness of the wrongs of slavery and her increasing awareness of the similarities between slavery and domestic service work for whites. Once emancipated and her children secured, Isabella traveled to New York City in hopes of finding a better job, a religious community, and an environment in which her family could reunite. Over time she became discouraged by the poverty and violence of New York City and followed her religious convictions to become a missionary of God's word. At this time, Isabella felt a new spirituality which converged in her beliefs about work and religion. From now on she would no longer work as a domestic servant but would follow her religious calling. This was the birth of Sojourner Truth.

Though unable to read or write, Sojourner Truth traveled the country preaching and singing the hymns of the Lord, and lecturing on the rights of blacks and women. Her striking height and presence combined with a rich, deep voice allowed Truth to make an impression on audiences where others dared not speak. The following selection is a speech, as recalled by reformer Frances Dana Gage, to a woman's suffrage convention held in Akron, Ohio, in 1851.

*   *   *

The leaders of the movement trembled on seeing a tall, gaunt black woman in gray dress and white turban, surmounted with an uncouth sun-bonnet, march deliberately into the church, walk with the air of a queen up the aisle, and take her seat upon the pulpit steps. A buzz of disapprobation was heard all over the house, and there fell on the listening ear, "An abolition affair!" "Woman's rights and niggers!" "I told you so!" "Go it, darkey!"

I chanced on that occasion to wear my first laurels in public life as president of the meeting. At my request order was restored, and the

Source: Elizabeth Cady Stanton, Susan B. Anthony, Matilda Joslyn Gage, eds., *History of Woman Suffrage* (N. Stratford, NH: Ayer Co. Publishers, 1969). Reprinted by permission of Ayer Co. Publishers.

business of the Convention went on. Morning, afternoon, and evening exercises came and went. Through all these sessions old Sojourner, quiet and reticent as the "Lybian Statue," sat crouched against the wall on the corner of the pulpit stairs, her sun-bonnet shading her eyes, her elbows on her knees, her chin resting upon her broad, hard palms. At intermission she was busy selling the "Life of Sojourner Truth," a narrative of her own strange and adventurous life. Again and again, timorous and trembling ones came to me and said, with earnestness, "Don't let her speak, Mrs. Gage, it will ruin us. Every newspaper in the land will have our cause mixed up with abolition and niggers, and we shall be utterly denounced." My only answer was, "We shall see when the time comes."

The second day the work waxed warm. Methodist, Baptist, Episcopal, Presbyterian, and Universalist ministers came in to hear and discuss the resolutions presented. One claimed superior rights and privileges for man, on the ground of "superior intellect"; another, because of the "manhood of Christ; if God had desired the equality of woman, He would have given some token of His will through the birth, life, and death of the Saviour." Another gave us a theological view of the "sin of our first mother."

There were very few women in those days who dared to "speak in meeting;" and the august teachers of the people were seemingly getting the better of us, while the boys in the galleries, and the sneers among the pews, were hugely enjoying the discomfiture, as they supposed, of the "strong-minded." Some of the tender-skinned friends were on the point of losing dignity, and the atmosphere betokened a storm. When, slowly from her seat in the corner rose Sojourner Truth, who till now, had scarcely lifted her head. "Don't let her speak!" gasped half a dozen in my ear. She moved slowly and solemnly to the front, laid her old bonnet at her feet, and turned her great speaking eyes to me. There was a hissing sound of disapprobation above and below. I rose and announced "Sojourner Truth," and begged the audience to keep silence for a few moments.

The tumult subsided at once, and every eye was fixed on this almost Amazon form, which stood nearly six feet high, head erect, and eyes piercing the upper air like one in a dream. At her first word there was a profound hush. She spoke in deep tones, which though not loud, reached every ear in the house, and away through the throng at the doors and windows.

"Wall, chilern, whar dar is so much racket dar must be somethin' out o' kilter. I tink dat 'twixt de niggers of de Souf and de womin at de Norf, all talkin' bout rights, de white men will be in a fix pretty soon. But what's all dis here talkin' 'bout?

"Dat man ober dar say dat womin needs to be helped into carriages, and lifted ober ditches, and to hab de best place everywhar. Nobody eber

helps me into carriages, or ober mud-puddles, or gibs me any best place!"
And raising herself to her full height, and her voice to a pitch like rolling
thunder, she asked, "And a'n't I a woman? Look at me! Look at my arm!
(and she bared her right arm to the shoulder, showing her tremendous
muscular power). I have ploughed, and planted, and gathered into barns,
and no man could head me! And a'n't I a woman? I could work as much
and eat as much as a man—when I could get it—and bear de lash as
well! And a'n't I a woman? I have borne thirteen chilern, and seen 'em
mos' all sold off to slavery, and when I cried out with my mother's grief,
none but Jesus heard me! And a'n't I a woman?

"Den dey talks 'bout dis ting in de head; what dis dey call it?"
("Intellect," whispered some one near.) "Dat's it honey. What's dat got
to do wid womin's rights or nigger's rights? If my cup won't hold but a
pint, and yourn holds a quart, wouldn't ye be mean not to let me have
all little half-measure full?" And she pointed her significant finger, and
sent a keen glance at the minister who had made the argument. The
cheering was long and loud.

"Den dat little man in black dar, he say women can't have as much
rights as men, 'cause Christ wasn't a woman! Whar did your Christ come
from?" Rolling thunder couldn't have stilled that crowd, as did those
deep, wonderful tones, as she stood there with outstretched arms and
eyes of fire. Raising her voice still louder, she repeated, "Whar did your
Christ come from? From God and a woman! Man had nothin' to do wid
Him." Oh, what a rebuke that was to that little man.

Turning again to another objector, she took up the defense of Mother
Eve. I can not follow her through it all. It was pointed and witty, and
solemn; eliciting at almost every sentence deafening applause; and she
ended by asserting; "If de fust woman God ever made was strong enough
to turn de world upside down all alone, dese women togedder (and she
glanced her eye over the platform) ought to be able to turn it back, and
get it right side up again! And now dey is asking to do it, de men better
let'em." Long-continued cheering greeted this. "Bleeged to ye for hearin'
on me, and now ole Sojourner han't got nothin' more to say."

Amid roars of applause, she returned to her corner, leaving more
than one of us with streaming eyes, and hearts beating with gratitude.
She had taken us up in her strong arms and carried us safely over the
slough of difficulty turning the whole tide in our favor. I have never in
my life seen anything like the magical influence that subdued the mobbish
spirit of the day, and turned the sneers and jeers of an excited crowd into
notes of respect and admiration. Hundreds rushed up to shake hands
with her, and congratulate the glorious old mother, and bid her God-
speed on her mission of "testifyin' agin concerning the wickedness of this
'ere people."

Susan B. Anthony,
"Constitutional Argument" (1872)

Editor's Introduction: Susan B. Anthony (1820–1906) was born into an abolitionist Quaker family. Her first exposure to politics came through the temperance movement in the 1850s. The transition from temperance issues to more purely feminist ones was a natural transition, as the anti-alcohol movement largely grew out of a concern over abuses men committed against women while under the influence. Anthony was perhaps the greatest organizer and strategist of the movement for women's suffrage in the nineteenth century. Her prodigious energies and sense of practical politics molded her into an effective political leader.

After speaking and lobbying for women's suffrage for some years, Anthony decided to take matters into her own hands in 1872 when she cast a ballot in the presidential election. She and fifty other women registered to vote, but only sixteen actually did so. Anthony suspected that the election officials would be charged for allowing her to vote and offered to pay all of their expenses. However, much to Anthony's surprise, she was arrested and charged with a criminal act two weeks after voting.

The following speech is one Anthony made on several occasions prior to her trial. In it, she relies on liberal and republican arguments to defend her actions and appeals specifically to the Declaration of Independence and the Constitution. She asserts a "natural right" of all members of a political community to vote and claims emphatically that women are entitled to the same rights as men in this and every other regard. They have, in short, the same moral status as men and deserve to be treated with the same concern and respect under law. Anthony's analogy between wives under the law of her day and slaves takes matters further and begins to challenge power relations in the private as well as public sphere though she never pressed this theme as persistently as did Elizabeth Cady Stanton.

To finish the story, Anthony did indeed go to trial for her offense. After Judge Hunt heard the arguments of the prosecution and defense, he directed the jury to bring in a verdict of guilty. The jurors did not have the opportunity to discuss the case nor to decide the verdict for themselves. Though Anthony was convicted, her courage and commitment strengthened popular belief in women's right to vote.

Source: Ida Husted Harper, *The Life and Work of Susan B. Anthony Vol.* 2 (Indianapolis: The Hollenbeck Press, 1898).

*   *   *

Friends and Fellow-Citizens: —I stand before you under indictment for the alleged crime of having voted at the last presidential election, without having a lawful right to vote. It shall be my work this evening to prove to you that in thus doing, I not only committed no crime, but instead simply exercised my citizen's right, guaranteed to me and all United States citizens by the National Constitution beyond the power of any State to deny.

Our democratic-republican government is based on the idea of the natural right of every individual member thereof to a voice and a vote in making and executing the laws. We assert the province of government to be to secure the people in the enjoyment of their inalienable rights. We throw to the winds the old dogma that government can give rights. No one denies that before governments were organized each individual possessed the right to protect his own life, liberty and property. When 100 to 1,000,000 people enter into a free government, they do not barter away their natural rights; they simply pledge themselves to protect each other in the enjoyment of them through prescribed judicial and legislative tribunals. They agree to abandon the methods of brute force in the adjustment of their differences and adopt those of civilization. . . . The Declaration of Independence, the United States Constitution, the constitutions of the several States and the organic laws of the Territories, all alike propose to *protect* the people in the exercise of their God-given rights. Not one of them pretends to bestow rights.

> All men are created equal, and endowed by their Creator with certain inalienable rights. Among these are life, liberty and the pursuit of happiness. To secure these, governments are instituted among men, deriving their just powers from the consent of the governed.

Here is no shadow of government authority over rights, or exclusion of any class from their full and equal enjoyment. Here is pronounced the right of all men, and "consequently," as the Quaker preacher said, "of all women," to a voice in the government. And here, in this first paragraph of the Declaration, is the assertion of the natural right of all to the ballot; for how can "the consent of the governed" be given, if the right to vote be denied? The women, dissatisfied as they are with this form of government, that enforces taxation without representation—that compels them to obey laws to which they never have given their consent—that imprisons and hangs them without a trial by a jury of their peers—that robs them, in marriage, of the custody of their own persons, wages and children— are this half of the people who are left wholly at the mercy of the other half, in direct violation of the spirit and letter of the declarations of the framers of this government, every one of which was based on the immutable principle of equal rights to all. By these declarations, kings, popes, priests, aristocrats, all were alike dethroned and placed on a common level, politically, with the lowliest born subject or serf. By them, too, men, as such, were deprived of their divine right to rule and placed on a political level with women. By the practice of these declarations all class and caste distinctions would be abolished, and slave, serf, plebeian, wife, woman, all alike rise from their subject position to the broader platform of equality.

The preamble of the Federal Constitution says:

We, the people of the United States, in order to form a more perfect union, establish justice, insure domestic tranquillity, provide for the common defense, promote the general welfare and secure the blessings of liberty to ourselves and our posterity, do ordain and establish this Constitution for the United States of America.

It was we, the people, not we, the white male citizens, nor we, the male citizens; but we, the whole people, who formed this Union. We formed it not to give the blessings of liberty but to secure them; not to the half of ourselves and the half of our posterity, but to the whole people—women as well as men. It is downright mockery to talk to women of their enjoyment of the blessings of liberty while they are denied the only means of securing them provided by this democratic-republican government—the ballot.

The early journals of Congress show that, when the committee reported to that body the original articles of confederation, the very first one which became the subject of discussion was that respecting equality of suffrage. . . .

James Madison said:

Under every view of the subject, it seems indispensable that the mass of the citizens should not be without a voice in making the laws which they are to obey, and in choosing the magistrates who are to administer them. . . . Let it be remembered, finally, that is has ever been the pride and the boast of America that the rights for which she contended were the rights of human nature.

These assertions by the framers of the United States Constitution of the equal and natural right of all the people to a voice in the government, have been affirmed and reaffirmed by the leading statesmen of the nation throughout the entire history of our government. Thaddeus Stevens, of

Pennsylvania, said in 1866: "I have made up my mind that elective franchise is one of the inalienable rights meant to be secured by the Declaration of Independence." . . .

Charles Sumner, in his brave protests against the Fourteenth and Fifteenth Amendments, insisted that so soon as by the Thirteenth Amendment the slaves became free men, the original powers of the United States Constitution guaranteed to them equal rights—the right to vote and to be voted for. . . .

The preamble of the constitution of the State of New York declares the same purpose. It says: "We, the people of the State of New York, grateful to Almighty God for our freedom, in order to secure its blessings, do establish this constitution." Here is not the slightest intimation either of receiving freedom from the United States Constitution, or of the State's conferring the blessings of liberty upon the people; and the same is true of every other State constitution. Each and all declare rights God-given, and that to secure the people in the enjoyment of their inalienable rights is their one and only object in ordaining and establishing government. All of the State constitutions are equally emphatic in their recognition of the ballot as the means of securing the people in the enjoyment of these rights. . . .

I submit that in view of the explicit assertions of the equal right of the whole people, both in the preamble and previous article of the constitution, this omission of the adjective "female" should not be construed into a denial; but instead should be considered as of no effect. . . . No barriers whatever stand today between women and the exercise of their right to vote save those of precedent and prejudice, which refuse to expunge the word "male" from the constitution.

When, in 1871, I asked that senator to declare the power of the United States Constitution to protect women in their right to vote—as he had done for black men—he handed me a copy of all his speeches during that reconstruction period, and said:

> Put "sex" where I have "race" or "color," and you have here the best and strongest argument I can make for woman. There is not a doubt but women have the constitutional right to vote, and I will never vote for a Sixteenth Amendment to guarantee it to them. I voted for both the Fourteenth and Fifteenth under protest; would never have done it but for the pressing emergency of that hour; would have insisted that the power of the original Constitution to protect all citizens in the equal enjoyment of their rights should have been vindicated through the courts. But the newly-made freedmen had neither the intelligence, wealth nor time to await that slow process. Women do possess all these in an eminent degree, and I

insist that they shall appeal to the courts, and through them establish the powers of our American magna charta to protect every citizen of the republic.

But, friends, when in accordance with Senator Sumner's counsel I went to the ballot-box, last November, and exercised my citizen's right to vote, the courts did not wait for me to appeal to them—they appealed to me, and indicted me on the charge of having voted illegally. Putting sex where he did color, Senator Sumner would have said:

Qualifications can be in their nature permanent or insurmountable. Sex can not be a qualification any more than size, race, color or previous condition of servitude. A permanent or insurmountable qualification is equivalent to a deprivation of the suffrage. In other words, it is the tyranny of taxation without representation, against which our Revolutionary mothers, as well as fathers, rebelled.

For any State to make sex a qualification, which must ever result in the disfranchisement of one entire half of the people, is to pass a bill of attainder, an ex post facto law, and is therefore a violation of the supreme law of the land. By it the blessings of liberty are forever withheld from women and their female posterity. For them, this government has no just powers derived from the consent of the governed. For them this government is not a democracy; it is not a republic. It is the most odious aristocracy every established on the face of the globe. An oligarchy of wealth, where the rich govern the poor; an oligarchy of learning, where the educated govern the ignorant; or even an oligarchy of race, where the Saxon rules the African, might be endured; but the oligarchy of sex which makes father, brothers, husband, sons, the oligarchs over the mother and sisters, the wife and daughters of every household; which ordains all men sovereigns, all women subjects—carries discord and rebellion into every home of the nation. This most odious aristocracy exists, too, in the face of Section 4, Article IV, which says: "The United States shall guarantee to every State in the Union a republican form of government."

It is urged that the use of the masculine pronouns *he*, *his* and *him* in all the constitutions and laws, is proof that only men were meant to be included in their provisions. If you insist on this version of the letter of the law, we shall insist that you be consistent and accept the other horn of the dilemma, which would compel you to exempt women from taxation for the support of the government and from penalties for the violation of laws. There is no *she* or *her* or *hers* in the tax laws, and this is equally true of all criminal laws.

Take for example the civil rights law which I am charged with having violated; not only are all the pronouns in it masculine, but everybody knows that it was intended expressly to hinder the rebel men from voting. It reads, " If any person shall knowingly vote without *his* having a lawful right." . . . . I insist if government officials may thus manipulate the pronouns to tax, fine, imprison and hang women, it is their duty to thus change them in order to protect us in our right to vote. . . .

Though the words persons, people, inhabitants, electors, citizens, are all used indiscriminately in the national and State constitutions, there was always a conflict of opinion, prior to the war, as to whether they were synonymous terms, but whatever room there was for doubt, under the old regime, the adoption of the Fourteenth Amendment settled that question forever in its first sentence:

All persons born or naturalized in the United States, and subject to the jurisdiction thereof, are citizens of the United States, and of the State wherein they reside.

The second settles the equal status of all citizens:

No State shall make or enforce any law which shall abridge the privileges or immunities of citizens of the United States; nor shall any State deprive any person of life, liberty or property without due process of law, or deny to any person within its jurisdiction the equal protection of the laws.

The only question left to be settled now is: Are women persons? I scarcely believe any of our opponents will have the hardihood to say they are not. Being persons, then, women are citizens, and no State has a right to make any new law, or to enforce any old law, which shall abridge their privileges or immunities. Hence, every discrimination against women in the constitutions and laws of the several States is today null and void, precisely as is every one against negroes.

Is the right to vote one of the privileges or immunities of citizens? I think the disfranchised ex-rebels and ex-State prisoners all will agree that it is not only one of them, but the one without which all the others are nothing. Seek first the kingdom of the ballot and all things else shall be added, is the political injunction. . . .

[Text omitted]

If the Fourteenth Amendment does not secure to all citizens the right to vote, for what purpose was that grand old charter of the fathers lumbered with its unwieldy proportions? The Republican party . . .

pretended it was to do something for black men; and if that something were not to secure them in their right to vote and hold office, what could it have been? For by the Thirteenth Amendment black men had become people, and hence were entitled to all the privileges and immunities of the government, precisely as were the women of the country and foreign men not naturalized. According to Associate-Justice Washington, they already had:

> Protection of the government, the enjoyment of life and liberty, with the right to acquire and possess property of every kind, and to pursue and obtain happiness and safety, subject to such restraints as the government may justly prescribe for the general welfare of the whole; the right of a citizen of one State to pass through or to reside in any other State for the purpose of trade, agriculture, professional pursuit, or otherwise; to claim the benefit of the writ of habeas corpus, to institute and maintain actions of any kind in the courts of the State; to take, hold, and dispose of property, either real or personal, and an exemption from higher taxes or impositions than are paid by the other citizens of the State.

Thus, you see, those newly-freed men were in possession of every possible right, privilege and immunity of the government, except that of suffrage, and hence needed no constitutional amendment for any other purpose. What right in this country has the Irishman the day after he receives his naturalization papers that he did not possess the day before, save the right to vote and hold office? The Chinamen now crowding our Pacific coast are in precisely the same position. What privilege or immunity has California or Oregon the right to deny them, save that of the ballot? Clearly, then, if the Fourteenth Amendment was not to secure to black men their right to vote it did nothing for them, since they possessed everything else before. But if it was intended to prohibit the States from denying or abridging their right to vote, then it did the same for all persons, white women included, born or naturalized in the United States; for the amendment does not say that all male persons of African descent, but that all persons are citizens.

The second section is simply a threat to punish the States by reducing their representation on the floor of Congress, should they disfranchise any of their male citizens, and can not be construed into a sanction to disfranchise female citizens, nor does it in any wise weaken or invalidate the universal guarantee of the first section.

However much the doctors of the law may disagree as to whether people and citizens, in the original Constitution, were one and the same, or whether the privileges and immunities in the Fourteenth Amendment include the right of suffrage, the question of the citizen's right to vote is forever settled by the Fifteenth Amendment. "The right of citizens of the United States to vote shall not be denied or abridged by the United States, or by any State, on account of race, color, or previous condition of servitude." How can the State deny or abridge the right of the citizen, if the citizen does not possess it? There is no escape from the conclusion that to vote is the citizen's right, and the specifications of race, color or previous condition of servitude can in no way impair the force of that emphatic assertion that the citizen's right to vote shall not be denied or abridged. . . .

If once we establish the false principle that United States citizenship does not carry with it the right to vote in every State in this Union, there is no end to the petty tricks and cunning devices which will be attempted to exclude one and another class of citizens from the right of suffrage. It will not always be the men combining to disfranchise all women; native born men combining to abridge the rights of all naturalized citizens, as in Rhode Island. It will not always be the rich and educated who may combine to cut off the poor and ignorant; but we may live to see the hard-working, uncultivated day laborers, foreign and native born, learning the power of the ballot and their vast majority of numbers, combine and amend State constitutions so as to disfranchise the Vanderbilts, the Stewarts, the Conklings and the Fentons. It is a poor rule that won't work more ways than one. Establish this precedent, admit the State's right to deny suffrage, and there is no limit to the confusion, discord and disruption that may await us. There is and can be but one safe principle of government—equal rights to all. Discrimination against any class on account of color, race, nativity, sex, property, culture, can but embitter and disaffect that class, and thereby endanger the safety of the whole people. Clearly, then, the national government not only must define the rights of citizens, but must stretch out its powerful hand and protect them in every State in this Union.

If, however, you will insist that the Fifteenth Amendment's emphatic interdiction against robbing United States citizens of their suffrage "on account of race, color or previous condition of servitude," is a recognition of the right of either the United States or any State to deprive them of the ballot for any or all other reasons, I will prove to you that the class of citizens for whom I now plead are, by all the principles of our government and many of the laws of the States, included under the term "previous conditions of servitude."

Consider first married women and their legal status. What is servitude? "The condition of a slave." What is a slave? "A person who is robbed of the proceeds of his labor; a person who is subject to the will of another." By the laws of Georgia, South Carolina and all the States of the South, the negro had no right to the custody and control of his person. He belonged to his master. If he were disobedient, the master had the right to use correction. If the negro did not like the correction and ran away, the master had the right to use coercion to bring him back. By the laws of almost every State in this Union today, North, as well as South, the married woman has no right to the custody and control of her person. The wife belongs to the husband: and if she refuse obedience he may use moderate correction, and if she do not like his moderate correction and leave his "bed and board," the husband may use moderate coercion to bring her back. The little word "moderate," you see, is the saving clause for the wife, and would doubtless be overstepped should her offended husband administer his correction with the "cat-o'-nine-tails," or accomplish his coercion with blood-hounds.

Again the slave had no right to earnings of his hands, they belonged to his master; no right to the custody of his children, they belonged to his master; no right to sue or be sued, or to testify in the courts. If he committed a crime, it was the master who must sue or be sued. In many of the States there has been special legislation, giving married women the right to property inherited or received by bequest, or earned by the pursuit of any avocation outside the home; also giving them the right to sue and be sued in matters pertaining to such separate property; but not a single State of this Union has ever secured the wife in the enjoyment of her right to equal ownership of the joint earnings of the marriage copartnership. And since, in the nature of things, the vast majority of married women never earn a dollar by work outside their families, or inherit a dollar from their fathers, it follows that from the day of their marriage to the day of the death of their husbands not one of them ever has a dollar, except it shall please her husband to let her have it. . . .

A good farmer's wife in Illinois, who had all the rights she wanted, had made for herself a full set of false teeth. The dentist pronounced them an admirable fit, and the wife declared it gave her fits to wear them. The dentist sued the husband for his bill; his counsel brought the wife as witness; the judge ruled her off the stand, saying, "A married woman can not be a witness in matters of joint interest between herself and her husband." Think of it, ye good wives, the false teeth in your mouths are a joint interest with your husbands, about which you are legally incompetent to speak! If a married woman is injured by accident, in nearly all of the States it is her husband who must sue, and it is to him that the damages will be awarded. . . . Isn't such a position humiliating enough to be called "servitude?" That husband sued and obtained damages for the loss of the services of his wife, precisely as he would have done had it been his ox, cow or horse; and exactly as the master, under the old regime, would have recovered for the services of his slave.

I submit the question, if the deprivation by law of the ownership of one's own person, wages, property, children, the denial of the right as an individual to sue and be sued and testify in the courts, is not a condition of servitude most bitter and absolute, even though under the sacred name of marriage?. . . . The facts also prove that, by all the great fundamental principles of our free government, not only married women but the entire womanhood of the nation are in a "condition of servitude" as surely as were our Revolutionary fathers when they rebelled against King George. Women are taxed without representation, governed without their consent, tried, convicted and punished without a jury of their peers. Is all this tyranny any less humiliating and degrading to women under our democratic-republican government today than it was to men under their aristocratic, monarchical government one hundred years ago? . . .

Is anything further needed to prove woman's condition of servitude sufficient to entitle her to the guarantees of the Fifteenth Amendment? . . . I admit that, prior to the rebellion, by common consent, the right to enslave, as well as to disfranchise both native and foreign born persons, was conceded to the States. But the one grand principle settled by the war and the reconstruction legislation, is the supremacy of the national government to protect the citizens of the United States in their right to freedom and the elective franchise, against any and every interference on the part of the several States; and again and again have the American people asserted the triumph of this principle by their overwhelming majorities for Lincoln and Grant.

[Text omitted]

Benjamin F. Butler, in a recent letter to me, said: "I do not believe anybody in Congress doubts that the Constitution authorizes the right of women to vote, precisely as it authorizes trial by jury and many other like rights guaranteed to citizens."

It is upon this just interpretation of the United States Constitution that our National Woman Suffrage Association, which celebrates the twenty-fifth anniversary of the woman's rights movement next May in New York City, has based all its arguments and action since the passage of these amendments. We no longer petition legislature or Congress to give us the right to vote, but appeal to women everywhere to exercise their too long neglected "citizen's right." We appeal to the inspectors of election to receive the votes of all United States citizens, as it is their duty to do. We appeal to United States commissioners and marshals to arrest, as is their duty, the inspectors who reject the votes of United States citizens, and leave alone those who perform their duties and accept these votes. We ask the juries to return verdicts of "not guilty" in the cases of law-abiding United States citizens who cast their votes, and inspectors of election who receive and count them.

We ask the judges to enter unprejudiced opinions of the law, and wherever there is room for doubt to give the benefit to the side of liberty and equal rights for women, remembering that, as Sumner says, "The true rule of interpretation under our National Constitution, especially since its amendments, is that anything *for* human rights is constitutional, everything *against* human rights unconstitutional." It is on this line that we propose to fight our battle for the ballot—peaceably but nevertheless persistently—until we achieve complete triumph and all United States citizens, men and women alike, are recognized as equals in the government.

Elizabeth Cady Stanton,
"Address to the Founding Convention of the National American Woman Suffrage Association" (1890)

Editor's Introduction: Stanton (1815–1902) delivered the following speech at a convention called to merge two women's suffrage associations and thereby provide a stronger voice for the movement. Stanton also hoped to offer it a new direction.

Unlike other supporters of women's suffrage, including Susan B. Anthony, Stanton wished to see the women's movement take a more radical turn. It was not enough for her that women simply receive the vote. Rather, the vote should be used to shape policies that affected women. Among Stanton's goals were liberalized divorce laws, laws protecting women from spousal abuse, and "self-sovereignty" which spoke to the right of women to control their bodies in sexual relationships. Stanton was also critical of religious influence on the social status of women, believing that Christianity historically had degraded women. Indeed, one of the major projects of her later life was to publish "The Women's Bible," which was a satirical commentary on passages from the Old and New Testaments that pertained to women.

Stanton's social agenda reflected her concern with the oppression of women in all aspects of social life, including the family. It put her at odds with Anthony and others who tended to focus on suffrage itself and to a lesser degree on economic concerns of women workers. In these ways, Stanton grew increasingly out of step with more mainstream middle-class white feminists in her later years and is a precursor to radical feminism today.

*   *   *

. . . The chief barriers in the way to a more pronounced success in our movement have been: 1st, the apathy and indifference of society to all reforms. 2nd: Our lack of thorough and widespread organization. . . . [A]s to organization, for many years, we had no forces to organize. Each individual was a free lance to say or do whatsoever she listed. . . . [N]ow after twenty years of grand work in different lines, we have come to the conclusion that in Union there is strength, and added Power in thorough

---

Source: *Elizabeth Cady Stanton Papers,* Library of Congress.

organization. In uniting all our forces today under one banner, with the hearty cooperation of every friend of the movement, victory might soon be ours. . . . Isolated effort is of little value in carrying any great measure. . . . With all our forces molded together and concentrated on one point, our influence on the near future will, I know, prove irresistible. . . .

In view of the many vital questions now up for consideration in which women are especially interested, it seems to me that the time has come for more aggressive measures, more self assertion on our part than was ever manifested before. . . .

For fifty years we have been plaintiffs at the bar of justice and three generations of statesman, judges, and reformers have exhausted their able arguments and eloquent appeals in the courts and before the people. But as the Bench, the Bar and the Jury are all men, we are non-suited every time, and yet, some men tell us we must be patient and persuasive, that we must be womanly. My friends, what is man's idea of womanly? It is to have a manner that pleases him, quiet, deferential, submissive, that approaches him as a subject does a master. He wants no self-assertion on our part, no defiance, no vehement arraigning of him as a robber and a criminal. While the grand motto, "resistance to tyrants is obedience to God," has echoed and reechoed around the globe electrifying the lovers of liberty in every latitude and making crowned heads tremble, while every right achieved by the oppressed has been wrung from tyrants by force, while the darkest page of human history is the outrages on women, shall men tell us today to be patient, persuasive, womanly? What do we know as yet as to what is womanly? The women we have seen thus far have been with rare exceptions the mere echoes of men. . . . Patience and persuasiveness are beautiful virtues in dealing with children and the feeble minded adults, but with those who have the gift of reason and understand the principles of justice, it is our duty to compel them to act up to the highest light that is in them and as promptly as possible. . . .

As women are taking an active part in pressing on the consideration of Congress many narrow sectarian measures, such as more rigid Sunday laws, to stop travel and distribution of mail on that day, and intend to introduce the name of God into the constitution, this action on the part of some women is used as an argument for the disfranchisement of all. I hope this convention will declare that the Woman Suffrage Association is opposed to all Union of Church and State and pledges itself as far as possible, to maintain the secular nature of our government. As Sunday is the only day the laboring man can escape from the cities, to stop the street cars, omnibuses and rail roads would indeed be a lamentable exercise of arbitrary authority. No, no the duty of the state is to protect those who do the work of the world in the largest liberty and instead of shutting them up in their gloomy tenement houses on Sunday, we should open wide the parks, horticultural gardens, the museums, the libraries, the galleries of art, the music halls, where they can listen to the divine melodies of the great masters. All these are questions of legislation and what influence women will exert as voters is already being canvassed, hence the importance of this Association expressing its opinions on all questions in which woman's social, civil, religious, and political rights are involved.

Consider the thousands of women with babies in their arms year after year who have no change to the dull routine of their lives, except on Sunday when their husbands can go with them on some little excursion by land or sea, suddenly compelled to stay at home by passage of a rigid Sunday law, secured by the votes of those who can drive about at pleasure in their own carriages and go wherever they may desire. It is puerile to say "no matter how we use the ballot the right is ours," but if the presumption that we will use it wisely enters into the chance of our obtaining it, it is desirable for the public to know our opinions on practical questions of morals and politics.

We must demand a voice too in another field of labor, thus far bounded, fenced and titled by man alone, where according to his own statistics one may now gather more thorns and thistles than fruits and flowers. And this is the home. Many propositions are now floating about as to the laws regulating our family relations. . . . The message I should like to go out from this convention is that there should be no further legislation on the questions of marriage and divorce until woman has a voice in the state and national governments. Surely here is a relation in which above all others there should be equality; a relation in which woman really has a deeper interest than man and if the laws favor either party it should be the wife and mother. Marriage is a mere incident in a man's life. He has business interests and ambitions in other directions but as a general thing it is all of life to woman where all her interests and ambitions center. And if the conditions of her surroundings there are discordant and degrading she is indeed most unfortunate and needs the protection of the laws to set her free rather than hold her in bondage.

And yet it is proposed to have a national law restricting the right of divorce to a narrower basis. . . . Congress has already made an appropriation for a Report on the Question which shows that there are 10,000 divorces annually in the United States and other statisticians say, the majority asked for by women. If liberal divorce laws for wives are what Canada was for the slaves, a door of escape from bondage, we had better consult the women before we close the avenues to freedom. Where discontent is rocked in every cradle and complaints to heaven going up with every prayer, talk not of the sacredness of such relations, nor of the best interests of society requiring their permanent establishment. The best interests of society and the individual always lie in the same direction.

Hence the state as well as the family is interested in building the home on solid foundation.

Some may say that none of these questions legitimately belong on this platform, but as they have been discussed on the women's rights platform from the beginning they probably always will be. Wherever and whatever any class of women suffer whether in the home, the church, the courts, in the world of work, in the statute books, a voice in their behalf should be heard in our conventions. We must manifest a broad catholic spirit for all shades of opinions in which we may differ and recognize the equal right of all parties, sects and races, tribes and colors. Colored women, Indian women, Mormon women and women from every quarter of the globe have been heard in these Washington conventions and I trust they always will be.

The enfranchisement of woman is not a question to be carried by political clap-trap, by strategem or art, but by the slow process of education, by constant agitation and in new directions, attacking in turn every stronghold of the enemy. . . . Let us . . . stir up a whole group of new victims from time to time, by turning our guns on new strongholds. Agitation is the advance guard of education. When any principle or question is up for discussion, let us seize on it and show its connection, whether nearly or remotely, with woman's disfranchisement. There is such a thing as being too anxious lest someone "hurt the cause" by what he or she must say or do; or perhaps the very thing you fear is exactly what should be done. It is impossible for any one to tell what people are ready to hear. . . .

Another question demanding consideration on our platform, is the race problem that was supposed to be settled a quarter of a century ago by the proclamation of emancipation. . . . How comes it . . . that the race problem is again up for discussion in Congress and the civil rights bill in our hotels? Because every fundamental principle by which [the freedman] was emancipated and enfranchised was immediately denied in its application to women. . . . The denial of principle in the case of women at the North has reacted in the denial of the same principle in the case of the Freedman of the South, and now our statesmen are at their wits' ends to know what to do with the Freedman and are actually proposing to colonize him. If the Russian system is to be adopted and all discontented citizens are to be sent to some Siberia, our turn will come next. Hence we had better make a stand on the Freedman and demand justice for him as well as ourselves. It is justice, and that alone that can end the impossible conflict between freedom and slavery going on in every nation on the globe. That is all the Nihilists, the socialists, the Communists ask, and that is all Ireland asks, and the Freedmen and women of this Republic ask no more.

Emma Goldman,
"Woman Suffrage" (1917)

Editor's Introduction: Emma Goldman (1869–1940) was born in Russia and emigrated to America at the age of seventeen. In 1887, after a trial and conviction based upon scant evidence, four anarchists were hanged for the bombing of Chicago's Haymarket Square. This event became the critical moment in Goldman's life and prompted her to dedicate herself to the cause of anarchism. Goldman rejected all institutions of force and exploitation, among which she included private property, wage slavery, religion, the state, and marriage. As a radical feminist, Goldman despised the institutions which impoverished women not only economically, but also in terms of personal development. She was an ardent supporter of free love and believed strongly that women should feel free to express their individual personalities unconstrained by social conventions. Goldman has particularly harsh words for the prim and proper "Victorian" ladies of her day—including many feminists—who saw themselves as men's moral superiors and women's social function as civilizing men.

The following selection outlines Goldman's thoughts on woman suffrage. Her dissatisfaction with suffrage as a means to women's well-being led many to claim that she was an enemy of women as well as the state. However, Goldman's displeasure with the suffrage movement is not a position of antifeminism but rather a radical call for freedom and equality. She simply did not believe that suffrage would truly liberate women without enormous, revolutionary changes in American society.

Goldman was deported from the United States in 1919 after hindering conscription on the eve of the First World War. After several years of disillusionment with the Bolshevik Revolution in Russia, Goldman moved to England and then aided the Spanish anarchists during the Spanish Civil War. She died on May 14, 1940, after suffering a stroke three months before. Her body was buried next to the Haymarket anarchists, whose deaths had shaped her life for fifty years.

*　　　*　　　*

We boast of the age of advancement, of science, and progress. Is it not strange, then, that we still believe in fetich worship? True, our fetiches have different form and substance, yet in their power over the human mind they are still as disastrous as were those of old.

Source: Alix Kates Shulman, ed., *Red Emma Speaks* (New York: Schocken Books, 1983). Reprinted by permission of Alix Kates Shulman.

Our modern fetich is universal suffrage. Those who have not yet achieved that goal fight bloody revolutions to obtain it, and those who have enjoyed its reign bring heavy sacrifice to the altar of this omnipotent deity. Woe to the heretic who dare question that divinity!

Woman, even more than man, is a fetich worshiper, and though her idols may change, she is ever on her knees, ever holding up her hands, ever blind to the fact that her god has feet of clay. Thus woman has been the greatest supporter of all deities from time immemorial. Thus, too, she has had to pay the price that only gods can exact—her freedom, her heart's blood, her very life.

Nietzsche's memorable maxim, "When you go to woman, take the whip along," is considered very brutal, yet Nietzsche expressed in one sentence the attitude of woman towards her gods.

Religion, especially the Christian religion, has condemned woman to the life of an inferior, a slave. It has thwarted her nature and fettered her soul, yet the Christian religion has no greater supporter, none more devout, than woman. Indeed, it is safe to say that religion would have long ceased to be a factor in the lives of the people, if it were not for the support it receives from woman. The most ardent churchworkers, the most tireless missionaries the world over, are women, always sacrificing on the altar of the gods that have chained her spirit and enslaved her body.

The insatiable monster, war, robs woman of all that is dear and precious to her. It exacts her brothers, lovers, sons, and in return gives her a life of loneliness and despair. Yet the greatest supporter and worshiper of war is woman. She it is who instills the love of conquest and power into her children; she it is who whispers the glories of war into the ears of her little ones, and who rocks her baby to sleep with the tunes of trumpets and the noise of guns. It is woman, too, who crowns the victor on his return from the battlefield. Yes, it is woman who pays the highest price to that insatiable monster, war.

Then there is the home. What a terrible fetich it is! How it saps the very life-energy of woman—this modern prison with golden bars. Its shining aspect blinds woman to the price she would have to pay as wife, mother, and housekeeper. Yet woman clings tenaciously to the home, to the power that holds her in bondage.

It may be said that because woman recognizes the awful toll she is made to pay to the Church, State, and the home, she wants suffrage to set herself free. That may be true of the few; the majority of suffragists repudiate utterly such blasphemy. On the contrary, they insist always that it is woman suffrage which will make her a better Christian and homekeeper, a staunch citizen of the State. Thus suffrage is only a means of strengthening the omnipotence of the very gods that woman has served from time immemorial.

[Text omitted]

Woman's demand for equal suffrage is based largely on the contention that woman must have the equal right in all affairs of society. No one could, possibly, refute that, if suffrage were a right. Alas, for the ignorance of the human mind, which can see a right in an imposition. Or is it not the most brutal imposition for one set of people to make laws that another set is coerced by force to obey? Yet woman clamors for that "golden opportunity" that has wrought so much misery in the world, and robbed man of his integrity and self-reliance; an imposition which has thoroughly corrupted the people, and made them absolute prey in the hands of unscrupulous politicians.

The poor, stupid, free American citizen! Free to starve, free to tramp the highways of this great country, he enjoys universal suffrage, and, by that right, he has forged chains about his limbs. The reward that he receives is stringent labor laws prohibiting the right of boycott, of picketing, in fact, of everything, except the right to be robbed of the fruits of his labor. Yet all these disastrous results of the twentieth-century fetich have taught woman nothing. But, then, woman will purify politics, we are assured.

Needless to say, I am not opposed to woman suffrage on the conventional ground that she is not equal to it. I see neither physical, psychological, nor mental reasons why woman should not have the equal right to vote with man. But that can not possibly blind me to the absurd notion that woman will accomplish that wherein man has failed. If she would not make things worse, she certainly could not make them better. To assume, therefore, that she would succeed in purifying something which is not susceptible of purification, is to credit her with supernatural powers. Since woman's greatest misfortune has been that she was looked upon as either angel or devil, her true salvation lies in being placed on earth; namely, in being considered human, and therefore subject to all human follies and mistakes. Are we, then, to believe that two errors will make a right? Are we to assume that the poison already inherent in politics will be decreased, if women were to enter the political arena? The most ardent suffragists would hardly maintain such a folly.

As a matter of fact, the most advanced students of universal suffrage have come to realize that all existing systems of political power are absurd, and are completely inadequate to meet the pressing issues of life. This view is also borne out by a statement of one who is herself an ardent believer in woman suffrage, Dr. Helen L. Sumner. In her able work on *Equal Suffrage,* she says: "In Colorado, we find that equal suffrage serves to show in the most striking way the essential rottenness and degrading character of the existing system." Of course, Dr. Sumner has in mind a particular system of voting, but the same applies with equal force to the entire machinery of the representative system. With such a basis, it is difficult to understand how woman, as a political factor, would benefit either herself or the rest of mankind.

But, say our suffrage devotees, look at the countries and States where female suffrage exists. See what woman has accomplished—in Australia, New Zealand, Finland, the Scandinavian countries, and in our own four States, Idaho, Colorado, Wyoming, and Utah. Distance lends enchantment—or, to quote a Polish formula—"it is well where we are not." Thus one would assume that those countries and States are unlike other countries or States, that they have greater freedom, greater social and economic equality, a finer appreciation of human life, deeper understanding of the great social struggle, with all the vital questions it involves for the human race.

The women of Australia and New Zealand can vote, and help make the laws. Are the labor conditions better there than they are in England, where the suffragettes are making such a heroic struggle? Does there exist a greater motherhood, happier and freer children than in England? Is woman there no longer considered a mere sex commodity? Has she emancipated herself from the Puritanical double standard of morality for men and women? Certainly none but the ordinary female stump politician will dare answer these questions in the affirmative. If that be so, it seems ridiculous to point to Australia and New Zealand as the Mecca of equal suffrage accomplishments.

[Text omitted]

Not for a moment do I mean to imply that woman suffrage is responsible for this state of affairs. I do mean, however, that there is no reason to point to Australia as a wonder-worker of woman's accomplishment, since her influence has been unable to free labor from the thraldom of political bossism.

[Text omitted]

As to our own States where women vote, and which are constantly being pointed out as examples of marvels, what has been accomplished there through the ballot that women do not to a large extent enjoy in other States; or that they could not achieve through energetic efforts without the ballot?

True, in the suffrage States women are guaranteed equal rights to property; but of what avail is that right to the mass of women without property, the thousands of wage workers, who live from hand to mouth? That equal suffrage did not, and cannot, affect their condition is admitted even by Dr. Sumner, who certainly is in a position to know. As an ardent suffragist, and having been sent to Colorado by the Collegiate Equal Suffrage League of New York State to collect material in favor of suffrage, she would be the last to say anything derogatory; yet we are informed that "equal suffrage has but slightly affected the economic conditions of women. That women do not receive equal pay for equal work, and that though woman in Colorado has enjoyed school suffrage since 1876, women teachers are paid less than in California." . . . And where is the superior sense of justice that woman was to bring into the political field? Where was it in 1903, when the mine owners waged a guerrilla war against the Western Miners' Union; when General Bell established a reign of terror, pulling men out of bed at night, kidnapping them across the border line, throwing them into bull pens, declaring "to hell with the Constitution, the club is the Constitution"? Where were the women politicians then, and why did they not exercise the power of their vote? But they did. They helped to defeat the most fair-minded and liberal man, Governor Waite. The latter had to make way for the tool of the mine kings, Governor Peabody, the enemy of labor, the Tsar of Colorado. "Certainly male suffrage could have done nothing worse." Granted. Wherein, then, are the advantages to woman and society from woman suffrage? The oft-repeated assertion that woman will purify politics is also but a myth. It is not borne out by the people who know the political conditions of Idaho, Colorado, Wyoming, and Utah.

Woman, essentially a purist, is naturally bigoted and relentless in her effort to make others as good as she thinks they ought to be. Thus, in Idaho, she has disfranchised her sister of the street, and declared all women of "lewd character" unfit to vote. "Lewd" not being interpreted, of course, as prostitution *in* marriage. It goes without saying that illegal prostitution and gambling have been prohibited. In this regard the law must needs be of feminine gender: it always prohibits. Therein all laws are wonderful. They go no further, but their very tendencies open all the floodgates of hell. Prostitution and gambling have never done a more flourishing business than since the law has been set against them.

In Colorado, the Puritanism of woman has expressed itself in a more drastic form. "Men of notoriously unclean lives, and men connected with saloons, have been dropped from politics since women have the vote." Could Brother Comstock do more? Could all the Puritan fathers have done more? I wonder how many women realize the gravity of this would-be feat. I wonder if they understand that it is the very thing which, instead of elevating woman, has made her a political spy, a contemptible pry into the private affairs of people, not so much for the good of the cause, but because, as a Colorado woman said, "They like to get into houses they have never been in, and find out all they can, politically and otherwise." Yes, and into the human soul and its minutest nooks and corners. For nothing satisfies the craving of most women so much as scandal. And when did she ever enjoy such opportunities as are hers, the politician's?

"Notoriously unclean lives, and men connected with the saloons." Certainly, the lady vote gatherers can not be accused of much sense of proportion. Granting even that these busybodies can decide whose lives are clean enough for that eminently clean atmosphere, politics, must it follow that saloon-keepers belong to the same category? Unless it be American hypocrisy and bigotry, so manifest in the principle of Prohibition, which sanctions the spread of drunkenness among men and women of the rich class, yet keeps vigilant watch on the only place left to the poor man. *If* [for] no other reason, woman's narrow and purist attitude toward life makes her a greater danger to liberty wherever she has political power. Man has long overcome the superstitions that still engulf woman. In the economic competitive field, man has been compelled to exercise efficiency, judgment, ability, competency. He therefore had nether time nor inclination to measure everyone's morality with a Puritanic yardstick. In his political activities, too, he has not gone about blindfolded. He knows that quantity and not quality is the material for the political grinding mill, and, unless he is a sentimental reformer or an old fossil, he knows that politics can never be anything but a swamp.

Women who are at all conversant with the process of politics, know the nature of the beast, but in their self-sufficiency and egotism they make themselves believe that they have but to pet the beast, and he will become as gentle as a lamb, sweet and pure. As if women have not sold their votes, as if women politicians cannot be bought! If her body can be bought in return for material consideration, why not her vote? That it is being done in Colorado and in other States, is not denied even by those in favor of woman suffrage.

As I have said before, woman's narrow view of human affairs is not the only argument against her as a politician superior to man. There are others. Her life-long economic parasitism has utterly blurred her conception of the meaning of equality. She clamors for equal rights with man, yet we learn that "few women care to canvas in undesirable districts." How little equality means to them compared with the Russian women, who face hell itself for their ideal!

Woman demands the same rights as man, yet she is indignant that her presence does not strike him dead: he smokes, keeps his hat on, and does not jump from his seat like a flunkey. These may be trivial things, but they are nevertheless the key to the nature of American suffragists. To be sure, their English sisters have outgrown these silly notions. They have shown themselves equal to the greatest demands on their character and power of endurance. All honor to the heroism and sturdiness of the English suffragettes. Thanks to their energetic, aggressive methods, they have proved an inspiration to some of our own lifeless and spineless ladies. But after all, the suffragettes, too, are still lacking in appreciation of real equality. Else how is one to account for the tremendous, truly gigantic effort set in motion by those valiant fighters for a wretched little bill which will benefit a handful of propertied ladies, with absolutely no provision for the vast mass of working women? True, as politicians they must be opportunists, must take half-measures if they can not get all. But as intelligent and liberal women they ought to realize that if the ballot is a weapon, the disinherited need it more than the economically superior class, and that the latter already enjoy too much power by virtue of their economic superiority.

[Text omitted]

The American suffrage movement has been, until very recently, altogether a parlor affair, absolutely detached from the economic needs of the people. Thus Susan B. Anthony, no doubt an exceptional type of woman, was not only indifferent but antagonistic to labor; nor did she hesitate to manifest her antagonism when, in 1869, she advised women to take the places of striking printers in New York. I do not know whether her attitude had changed before her death.

There are, of course, some suffragists who are affiliated with working women—the Women's Trade Union League, for instance; but they are a small minority, and their activities are essentially economic. The rest look upon toil as a just provision of Providence. What would become of the rich, if not for the poor? What would become of these idle, parasitic ladies, who squander more in a week than their victims earn in a year, if not for the eighty million wage workers? Equality, who ever heard of such a thing?

Few countries have produced such arrogance and snobbishness as America. Particularly is this true of the American woman of the middle class. She not only considers herself the equal of man, but his superior, especially in her purity, goodness, and morality. Small wonder that the American suffragist claims for her vote the most miraculous powers. In her exalted conceit she does not see how truly enslaved she is, not so much by man, as by her own silly notions and traditions. Suffrage can not ameliorate that sad fact; it can only accentuate it, as indeed it does.

One of the great American women leaders claims that woman is entitled not only to equal pay, but that she ought to be legally entitled even to the pay of her husband. Failing to support her, he should be put in convict stripes, and his earnings in prison be collected by his equal wife. Does not another brilliant exponent of the cause claim for woman that her vote will abolish the social evil, which has been fought in vain by the collective efforts of the most illustrious minds the world over? It is indeed to be regretted that the alleged creator of the universe has already presented us with his wonderful scheme of things, else woman suffrage would surely enable woman to outdo him completely.

Nothing is so dangerous as the dissection of a fetich. If we have outlived the time when such heresy was punishable by the stake, we have not outlived the narrow spirit of condemnation of those who dare differ with accepted notions. Therefore I shall probably be put down as an opponent of woman. But that can not deter me from looking the question squarely in the face. I repeat what I have said in the beginning: I do not believe that woman will make politics worse; nor can I believe that she could make it better. If, then, she cannot improve on man's mistakes, why perpetrate the latter?

History may be a compilation of lies; nevertheless, it contains a few truths, and they are the only guide we have for the future. The history of the political activities of men proves that they have given him absolutely nothing that he could not have achieved in a more direct, less costly, and more lasting manner. As a matter of fact, every inch of ground he has gained has been through a constant fight, a ceaseless struggle for self-assertion, and not through suffrage. There is no reason whatever to assume that woman, in her climb to emancipation, has been, or will be, helped by the ballot.

In the darkest of all countries, Russia, with her absolute despotism, woman has become man's equal, not through the ballot, but by her will to be and to do. Not only has she conquered for herself every avenue of learning and vocation, but she has won man's esteem, his respect, his comradeship; aye, even more than that: she has gained the admiration, the respect of the whole world. That, too, not through suffrage, but by her wonderful heroism, her fortitude, her ability, willpower, and her endurance in her struggle for liberty. Where are the women in any suffrage country or State that can lay claim to such a victory? When we consider the accomplishments of woman in America, we find also that something deeper and more powerful than suffrage has helped her in the march to emancipation.

It is just sixty-two years ago since a handful of women at the Seneca Falls Convention set forth a few demands for their right to equal education with men, and access to the various professions, trades, etc. What wonderful accomplishments, what wonderful triumphs! Who but the most ignorant dare speak of woman as a mere domestic drudge? Who dare suggest that this or that profession should not be open to her? For over sixty years she has molded a new atmosphere and a new life for herself. She has become a world-power in every domain of human thought and activity. And all that without suffrage, without the right to make laws, without the "privilege" of becoming a judge, a jailer, or an executioner.

Yes, I may be considered an enemy of woman; but if I can help her see the light, I shall not complain.

The misfortune of woman is not that she is unable to do the work of a man, but that she is wasting her life-force to outdo him, with a tradition of centuries which has left her physically incapable of keeping pace with him. Oh, I know some have succeeded, but at what cost, at what terrific cost! The import is not the kind of work woman does, but rather the quality of the work she furnishes. She can give suffrage or the ballot no new quality, nor can she receive anything from it that will enhance her own quality. Her development, her freedom, her independence, must come from and through herself. First, by asserting herself as a personality, and not as a sex commodity. Second, by refusing the right to anyone over her body; by refusing to bear children, unless she wants them; by refusing to be a servant to God, the State, society, the husband, the family, etc., by making her life simpler, but deeper and richer. That is, by trying to learn the meaning and substance of life in all its complexities, by freeing herself from the fear of public opinion and public condemnation. Only that, and not the ballot, will set woman free, will make her a force hitherto unknown in the world, a force for real love, for peace, for harmony; a force of divine fire, of life-giving; a creator of free men and women.

The National Organization for Women, "Statement of Purpose" (1966)

Editor's Introduction: The National Organization for Women was founded in 1966 and is still the largest grassroots organization dedicated to women's issues in the country. As of 1995, it has over 250,000 members in six hundred local chapters, and a national office in Washington, D.C. NOW was formed in order to integrate women more fully into the economic, social, and political institutions of American society. The following is the founding statement for the organization and it sets out NOW's guiding principles. It was coauthored by Betty Friedan, who became NOW's first president, and Dr. Pauli Murray, an African-American Episcopal minister. It was written shortly after the passage of the Civil Rights Act of 1964, which outlawed race-based discrimination in public accommodations such as restaurants, hotels, and public transportation, and the Voting Rights Act of 1965, which sought to end discrimination in the exercise of the franchise. Not unlike the suffragists of a century earlier, NOW takes a cue from such race-related legislation and formulates demands for the end to discrimination against women in education and employment. Though NOW's sights are set largely on political and legal reforms, the statement also advocates social reforms such as a more equitable sharing between men and women of labor in the home and presentation of a more well-rounded portrait of women's lives in mass media.

*　　　*　　　*

NOTICE: This is a historic document, which was adopted at NOW's first National Conference in Washington, D.C., on October 29, 1966. The words are those of the 1960s, and do not reflect current language or NOW's current priorities.

We, men and women who hereby constitute ourselves as the National Organization for Women, believe that the time has come for a new movement toward true equality for all women in America, and toward a fully equal partnership of the sexes, as part of the world-wide revolution of human rights now taking place within and beyond our national borders.

The purpose of NOW is to take action to bring women into full participation in the mainstream of American society now, exercising all the privileges and responsibilities thereof in truly equal partnership with men.

Source: Reprinted by permission of the National Organization for Women.

We believe the time has come to move beyond the abstract argument, discussion and symposia over the status and special nature of women which has raged in America in recent years; the time has come to confront, with concrete action, the conditions that now prevent women from enjoying the equality of opportunity and freedom of choice which is their right, as individual Americans, and as human beings.

NOW is dedicated to the proposition that women, first and foremost, are human beings, who, like all other people in our society, must have the chance to develop their fullest human potential. We believe that women can achieve such equality only by accepting to the full the challenges and responsibilities they share with all other people in our society, as part of the decision-making mainstream of American political, economic and social life.

We organize to initiate or support action, nationally, or in any part of this nation, by individuals or organizations, to break through the silken curtain of prejudice and discrimination against women in government, industry, the professions, the churches, the political parties, the judiciary, the labor unions, in education, science, medicine, law, religion and every other field of importance in American society.

Enormous changes taking place in our society make it both possible and urgently necessary to advance the unfinished revolution of women toward true equality, now. With a life span lengthened to nearly 75 years it is no longer either necessary or possible for women to devote the greater part of their lives to child-rearing; yet childbearing and rearing—which continues to be a most important part of most women's lives—still is used to justify barring women from equal professional and economic participation and advance.

Today's technology has reduced most of the productive chores which women once performed in the home and in mass-production industries based upon routine unskilled labor. This same technology has virtually eliminated the quality of muscular strength as a criterion for filling most jobs, while intensifying American industry's need for creative intelligence. In view of this new industrial revolution created by automation in the mid-twentieth century, women can and must participate in old and new fields of society in full equality—or become permanent outsiders.

Despite all the talk about the status of American women in recent years, the actual position of women in the United States has declined, and is declining, to an alarming degree throughout the 1950's and 60's. Although 46.4% of all American women between the ages of 18 and 65 now work outside the home, the overwhelming majority—75%—are in routine clerical, sales, or factory jobs, or they are household workers, cleaning women, hospital attendants. About two-thirds of Negro women workers are in the lowest paid service occupations. Working women are becoming increasingly—not less—concentrated on the bottom of the job ladder. As a consequence full-time women workers today earn on the average only 60% of what men earn, and that wage gap has been increasing over the past twenty-five years in every major industry group. In 1964, of all women with a yearly income, 89% earned under $5,000 a year; half of all full-time year round women workers earned less than $3,690; only 1.4% of full-time year round women workers had an annual income of $10,000 or more.

Further, with higher education increasingly essential in today's society, too few women are entering and finishing college or going on to graduate or professional school. Today, women earn only one in three of the B.A.'s and M.A.'s granted, and one in ten of the Ph.D.'s.

In all the professions considered of importance to society, and in the executive ranks of industry and government, women are losing ground. Where they are present it is only a token handful. Women comprise less than 1% of federal judges; less than 4% of all lawyers; 7% of doctors. Yet women represent 51% of the U.S. population. And, increasingly, men are replacing women in the top positions in secondary and elementary schools, in social work, and in libraries—once thought to be women's fields.

Official pronouncements of the advance in the status of women hide not only the reality of this dangerous decline, but the fact that nothing is being done to stop it. The excellent reports of the President's Commission on the Status of Women and of the State Commissions have not been fully implemented. Such Commissions have power only to advise. They have no power to enforce their recommendation; nor have they the freedom to organize American women and men to press for action on them. The reports of these commissions have, however, created a basis upon which it is now possible to build. Discrimination in employment on the basis of sex is now prohibited by federal law, in Title VII of the Civil Rights Act of 1964. But although nearly one-third of the cases brought before the Equal Employment Opportunity Commission during the first year dealt with sex discrimination and the proportion is increasing dramatically, the Commission has not made clear its intention to enforce the law with the same seriousness on behalf of women as of other victims of discrimination. Many of these cases were Negro women, who are the victims of double discrimination of race and sex. Until now, too few women's organizations and official spokesmen have been willing to speak out against these dangers facing women. Too many women have been restrained by the fear of being called "feminist." There is no civil rights movement to speak for women, as there has been for Negroes and other victims of discrimination. The National Organization for Women must therefore begin to speak.

WE BELIEVE that the power of American law, and the protection guaranteed by the U.S. Constitution to the civil rights of all individuals, must be effectively applied and enforced to isolate and remove patterns of sex discrimination, to ensure equality of opportunity in employment and education, and equality of civil and political rights and responsibilities on behalf of women, as well as for Negroes and other deprived groups.

We realize that women's problems are linked to many broader questions of social justice; their solution will require concerted action by many groups. Therefore, convinced that human rights for all are indivisible, we expect to give active support to the common cause of equal rights for all those who suffer discrimination and deprivation, and we call upon other organizations committed to such goals to support our efforts toward equality for women.

WE DO NOT ACCEPT the token appointment of a few women to high-level positions in government and industry as a substitute for serious continuing effort to recruit and advance women according to their individual abilities. To this end, we urge American government and industry to mobilize the same resources of ingenuity and command with which they have solved problems of far greater difficulty than those now impeding the progress of women.

WE BELIEVE that this nation has a capacity at least as great as other nations, to innovate new social institutions which will enable women to enjoy the true equality of opportunity and responsibility in society, without conflict with their responsibilities as mothers and homemakers. In such innovations, America does not lead the Western world, but lags by decades behind many European countries. We do not accept the traditional assumption that a woman has to choose between marriage and motherhood, on the one hand, and serious participation in industry or the professions on the other. We question the present expectation that all normal women will retire from job or profession for 10 or 15 years, to devote their full time to raising children, only to reenter the job market at a relatively minor level. This, in itself, is a deterrent to the aspirations of women, to their acceptance into management or professional training courses, and to the very possibility of equality of opportunity or real choice, for all but a few women. Above all, we reject the assumption that these problems are the unique responsibility of each individual woman, rather than a basic social dilemma which society must solve. True equality of opportunity and freedom of choice for women requires such practical, and possible innovations as a nationwide network of child-care centers, which will make it unnecessary for women to retire completely from society until their children are grown, and national programs to provide retraining for women who have chosen to care for their children full-time.

WE BELIEVE that it is as essential for every girl to be educated to her full potential of human ability as it is for every boy—with the knowledge that such education is the key to effective participation in today's economy and that, for a girl as for a boy, education can only be serious where there is expectation that it will be used in society. We believe that American educators are capable of devising means of imparting such expectations to girl students. Moreover, we consider the decline in the proportion of women receiving higher and professional education to be evidence of discrimination. This discrimination may take the form of quotas against the admission of women to colleges, and professional schools; lack of encouragement by parents, counselors and educators; denial of loans or fellowships; or the traditional or arbitrary procedures in graduate and professional training geared in terms of men, which inadvertently discriminate against women. We believe that the same serious attention must be given to high school dropouts who are girls as to boys.

WE REJECT the current assumptions that a man must carry the sole burden of supporting himself, his wife, and family, and that a woman is automatically entitled to lifelong support by a man upon her marriage, or that marriage, home and family are primarily woman's world and responsibility—hers, to dominate—his to support. We believe that a true partnership between the sexes demands a different concept of marriage, an equitable sharing of the responsibilities of home and children and of the economic burdens of their support. We believe that proper recognition should be given to the economic and social value of homemaking and child-care. To these ends, we will seek to open a reexamination of laws and mores governing marriage and divorce, for we believe that the current state of "half-equity" between the sexes discriminates against both men and women, and is the cause of much unnecessary hostility between the sexes.

WE BELIEVE that women must now exercise their political rights and responsibilities as American citizens. They must refuse to be segregated on the basis of sex into separate-and-not-equal ladies' auxiliaries in the political parties, and they must demand representation according to their numbers in the regularly constituted party committees—at local, state, and national levels—and in the informal power structure, participating fully in the selection of candidates and political decision-making, and running for office themselves.

IN THE INTERESTS OF THE HUMAN DIGNITY OF WOMEN, we will protest, and endeavor to change, the false image of women now prevalent in the mass media, and in the texts, ceremonies, laws, and practices of our major social institutions. Such images perpetuate contempt for women by society and by women for themselves. We are similarly opposed to all policies and practices—in church, state, college, factory, or office—which, in the guise of protectiveness, not only deny opportunities but also foster in women self-denigration, dependence, and evasion of responsibility, undermine their confidence in their own abilities and foster contempt for women.

NOW WILL HOLD ITSELF INDEPENDENT OF ANY POLITICAL PARTY in order to mobilize the political power of all women and men intent on our goals. We will strive to ensure that no party, candidate, president, senator, governor, congressman, or any public official who betrays or ignores the principle of full equality between the sexes is elected or appointed to office. If it is necessary to mobilize the votes of men and women who believe in our cause, in order to win for women the final right to be fully free and equal human beings, we so commit ourselves.

WE BELIEVE THAT women will do most to create a new image of women by acting now, and by speaking out in behalf of their own equality, freedom, and human dignity—not in pleas for special privilege, nor in enmity toward men, who are also victims of the current, half-equality between the sexes—but in an active, self-respecting partnership with men. By so doing, women will develop confidence in their own ability to determine actively, in partnership with men, the conditions of their life, their choices, their future and their society.

bell hooks,
"Feminism: A Movement To End Sexist Oppression" (1984)

Editor's Introduction: bell hooks (1952–   ) is now a Distinguished Professor of English at City College in New York, prior to which she was Professor in Women Studies and American Literature at Oberlin College. She is a feminist theorist and critic of popular culture. She prefers not to use the term women's movement when discussing feminism because she believes this movement must include all people in its struggles for freedom and equality across barriers of race, class, and gender. In her writings, hooks criticizes and struggles with the mechanisms of oppression, yet she also provides hope and encouragement to her readers. She, like Emma Goldman before her, is critical of liberal feminists (as represented, for example, by the National Organization for Women) and believes that society must be radically transformed to meet the needs of women as well as men. Liberal feminism in her view has been indifferent to the needs of poor and minority women and misguided in accepting capitalism as a just economic and social system.

Hooks took her pseudonym from her great-grandmother as homage to those black, working- and middle-class women who worked hard and courageously over the years and gained little mainstream recognition. Her decision to use lowercase lettering reflects her rejection of the academic tradition of emphasizing the author over the idea, though, ironically, it has become her distinctive trademark.

*   *   *

A central problem within feminist discourse has been our inability to either arrive at a consensus of opinion about what feminism is or accept definition(s) that could serve as points of unification. Without agreed upon definition(s), we lack a sound foundation on which to construct theory or engage in overall meaningful praxis. Expressing her frustrations with the absence of clear definitions in a recent essay, "Towards A Revolutionary Ethics," Carmen Vasquez comments:

> We can't even agree on what a "Feminist" is, never mind what she would believe in and how she defines the principles that constitute

Source: bell hooks, *Feminist theory: from margin to center* (South End Press. Boston, 1984). Reprinted by permission of South End Press.

honor among us. In key with the American capitalist obsession for individualism and anything goes so long as it gets you what you want. Feminism in American has come to mean anything you like, honey. There are as many definitions of Feminism as there are feminists, some of my sisters say, with a chuckle. I don't think it's funny.

It is not funny. It indicates a growing disinterest in feminism as a radical political movement. It is a despairing gesture expressive of the belief that solidarity between women is not possible. It is a sign that the political naivete which has traditionally characterized woman's lot in male-dominated culture abounds.

Most people in the United States think of feminism or the more commonly used term "women's lib" as a movement that aims to make women the social equals of men. This broad definition, popularized by the media and mainstream segments of the movement, raises problematic questions. Since men are not equals in white supremacist, capitalist, patriarchal class structure, which men do women want to be equal to? Do women share a common vision of what equality means? Implicit in this simplistic definition of women's liberation is a dismissal of race and class as factors that, in conjunction with sexism, determine the extent to which an individual will be discriminated against, exploited, or oppressed. Bourgeois white women interested in women's rights issues have been satisfied with simple definitions for obvious reasons. Rhetorically placing themselves in the same social category as oppressed women, they were not anxious to call attention to race and class privilege.

Women in lower class and poor groups, particularly those who are non-white, would not have defined women's liberation as women gaining social equality with men since they are continually reminded in their everyday lives that all women do not share a common social status. Concurrently, they know that many males in their social groups are exploited and oppressed. Knowing that men in their groups do not have social, political, and economic power, they would not deem it liberatory to share their social status. While they are aware that sexism enables men in their respective groups to have privileges denied them, they are more likely to see exaggerated expressions of male chauvinism among their peers as stemming from the male's sense of himself as powerless and ineffectual in relation to ruling male groups, rather than an expression of an overall privileged social status. From the very onset of the women's liberation movement, these women were suspicious of feminism precisely because they recognized the limitation inherent in its definition. They recognized the possibility that feminism defined as social equality with men might easily become a movement that would primarily affect the social standing of white women in middle and upper class groups while affecting only in a very marginal way the social status of working class and poor women.

[Text omitted]

It is now evident that many women active in feminist movement were interested in reform as an end in itself, not as a stage in the progression towards revolutionary transformation. Even though Zillah Eisenstein can optimistically point to the potential radicalism of liberal women who work for social reform in *The Radical Future of Liberal Feminism,* the process by which this radicalism will surface is unclear.

[Text omitted]

The positive impact of liberal reforms on women's lives should not lead to the assumption that they eradicate systems of domination. Nowhere in these demands is there an emphasis on eradicating the politic of domination, yet it would need to be abolished if any of these demands were to be met. The lack of any emphasis on domination is consistent with the liberal feminist belief that women can achieve equality with men of their class without challenging and changing the cultural basis of group oppression. It is this belief that negates the likelihood that the potential radicalism of liberal feminism will ever be realized.

[Text omitted]

Although liberal perspectives on feminism include reforms that would have radical implications for society, these are reforms which will be resisted precisely because they would set the stage for revolutionary transformation were they implemented. It is evident that society is more responsive to the "feminist" demands that are not threatening, that may even help maintain the status quo.

[Text omitted]

Liberal women have not been alone in drawing upon the dynamism of feminism to further their interests. The great majority of women who have benefited in any way from feminist-generated social reforms do not want to be seen as advocates of feminism. . . . They are either reluctant to make a public commitment to feminist movement or sneer at the term. Individual African-American, Native American Indian, Asian American, and Hispanic American women find themselves isolated if they support feminist movement. Even women who may achieve fame and notoriety (as well as increased economic income) in response to attention given their work by large numbers of women who support feminism may deflect attention away from their engagement with feminist movement. They may even go so far as to create other terms that express their concern with women's issues so as to avoid using the term feminist. The creation of new terms that have no relationship to organized political activity tend to provide women who may already be reluctant to explore feminism with ready excuses to explain their reluctance to participate. This illustrates an uncritical acceptance of distorted definitions of feminism rather than a demand for redefinition. They may support specific issues while divorcing themselves from what they assume is feminist movement.

[Text omitted]

Many women are reluctant to advocate feminism because they are uncertain about the meaning of the term. Other women from exploited and oppressed ethnic groups dismiss the term because they do not wish to be perceived as supporting a racist movement; feminism is often equated with white women's rights efforts. Large numbers of women see feminism as synonymous with lesbianism; their homophobia leads them to reject association with any group identified as pro-lesbian. Some women fear the word "feminism" because they shun identification with any political movement, especially one perceived as radical. Of course there are women who do not wish to be associated with women's rights movement in any form so they reject and oppose feminist movement. Most women are more familiar with negative perspectives on "women's lib" than the positive significations of feminism. It is this term's positive political significance and power that we must now struggle to recover and maintain.

Currently feminism seems to be a term without any clear significance. The "anything goes" approach to the definition of the word has rendered it practically meaningless. What is meant by "anything goes" is usually that any woman who wants social equality with men regardless of her political perspective (she can be a conservative right-winger or a nationalist communist) can label herself feminist. Most attempts at defining feminism reflect the class nature of the movement. Definitions are usually liberal in origin and focus on the individual woman's right to freedom and self-determination.

[Text omitted]

Many feminist radicals now know that neither a feminism that focuses on woman as an autonomous human being worthy of personal freedom nor one that focuses on the attainment of equality of opportunity with men can rid society of sexism and male domination. Feminism is a struggle to end sexist oppression. Therefore, it is necessarily a struggle to eradicate the ideology of domination that permeates Western culture on various levels as well as a commitment to reorganizing society so that the self-development of people can take precedence over imperialism, economic expansion, and material desires. Defined in this way, it is unlikely that women would join feminist movement simply because we are biologically the same. A commitment to feminism so defined would demand that each individual participant acquire a critical political consciousness based on ideas and beliefs.

All too often the slogan "the personal is political" (which was first used to stress that woman's everyday reality is informed and shaped by politics and is necessarily political) became a means of encouraging women to think that the experience of discrimination, exploitation, or oppression automatically corresponded with an understanding of the ideological and institutional apparatus shaping one's social status. As a consequence, many women who had not fully examined their situation never developed a sophisticated understanding of their political reality and its relationship to that of women as a collective group. They were encouraged to focus on giving voice to personal experience. Like revolutionaries working to change the lot of colonized people globally, it is necessary for feminist activists to stress that the ability to see and describe one's own reality is a significant step in the long process of self-recovery; but it is only a beginning. When women internalized the idea that describing their own woe was synonymous with developing a critical political consciousness, the progress of feminist movement was stalled. Starting from such incomplete perspectives, it is not surprising that theories and strategies were developed that were collectively inadequate and misguided. To correct this inadequacy in past analysis, we must now encourage women to develop a keen, comprehensive understanding of women's political reality. Broader perspectives can only emerge as we examine both the personal that is political, the politics of society as a whole, and global revolutionary politics.

Feminism defined in political terms that stress collective as well as individual experience challenges women to enter a new domain—to leave behind the apolitical stance sexism decrees is our lot and develop political consciousness. Women know from our everyday lives that many of us rarely discuss politics. Even when women talked about sexist politics in the heyday of contemporary feminism, rather than allow this engagement with serious political matters to lead to complex, in-depth analysis of women's social status, we insisted that men were "the enemy," the cause of all our problems. As a consequence, we examined almost exclusively women's relationship to male supremacy and the ideology of sexism. . . . By repudiating the popular notion that the focus of feminist movement should be social equality of the sexes and emphasizing eradicating the cultural basis of group oppression, our own analysis would require an exploration of all aspects of women's political reality. This would mean that race and class oppression would be recognized as feminist issues with as much relevance as sexism.

When feminism is defined in such a way that it calls attention to the diversity of women's social and political reality, it centralizes the experiences of all women, especially the women whose social conditions have been least written about, studied, or changed by political movements. When we cease to focus on the simplistic stance "men are the enemy," we are compelled to examine systems of domination and our role in their maintenance and perpetuation. Lack of adequate definition made it easy for bourgeois women, whether liberal or radical in perspective, to maintain their dominance over the leadership of the movement and its direction. This hegemony continues to exist in most feminist organizations. Exploited and oppressed groups of women are usually encouraged by those in power to feel that their situation is hopeless, that they can do nothing to break the pattern of domination. Given such socialization, these women have often felt that our only response to white, bourgeois, hegemonic dominance of feminist movement is to trash, reject, or dismiss feminism. This reaction is in no way threatening to the women who wish to maintain control over the direction of feminist theory and praxis. They prefer us to be silent, passively accepting their ideas. They prefer us speaking against "them" rather than developing our own ideas about feminist movement.

Feminism is the struggle to end sexist oppression. Its aim is not to benefit solely any specific group of women, any particular race or class of women. It does not privilege women over men. It has the power to transform in a meaningful way all our lives. Most importantly, feminism is neither a lifestyle nor a ready-made identity or role one can step into. Diverting energy from feminist movement that aims to change society, many women concentrate on the development of a counter-culture, a woman-centered world wherein participants have little contact with men. Such attempts do not indicate a respect or concern for the vast majority of women who are unable to integrate their cultural expressions with the visions offered by alternative woman-centered communities.

[Text omitted]

Equating feminist struggle with living in a counter-cultural, woman-centered world erected barriers that closed the movement off from most women. Despite sexist discrimination, exploitation, or oppression, many women feel their lives as they live them are important and valuable. Naturally the suggestion that these lives could be simply left or abandoned for an alternative "feminist" lifestyle met with resistance. Feeling their life experiences devalued, deemed solely negative and worthless, many women responded by vehemently attacking feminism. By rejecting the notion of an alternative feminist "lifestyle" that can emerge only when women create a subculture (whether it is living space or even space like women's studies that at many campuses has become exclusive) and insisting that feminist struggle can begin wherever an individual woman is, we create a movement that focuses on our collective experience, a movement that is continually mass-based.

[Text omitted]

Focusing on feminism as political commitment, we resist the emphasis on individual identity and lifestyle. (This should not be confused with the very real need to unite theory and practice.) Such resistance engages us in revolutionary praxis. The ethics of Western society informed by imperialism and capitalism are personal rather than social. They teach us that the individual good is more important than the collective good and consequently that individual change is of greater significance than collective change. This particular form of cultural imperialism has been reproduced in feminist movement in the form of individual women equating the fact that their lives have been changed in a meaningful way by feminism "as is" with a policy of no change need occur in the theory and praxis even if it has little or no impact on society as a whole, or on masses of women.

To emphasize that engagement with feminist struggle as political commitment we could avoid using the phrase "I am a feminist" (a linguistic structure designed to refer to some personal aspect of identity and self-definition) and could state "I advocate feminism." Because there has been undue emphasis placed on feminism as an identity or lifestyle, people usually resort to stereotyped perspectives on feminism. Deflecting attention away from stereotypes is necessary if we are to revise our strategy and direction. I have found that saying "I am a feminist" usually means I am plugged into preconceived notions of identity, role, or behavior. When I say "I advocate feminism" the response is usually, "what is feminism?" A phrase like "I advocate" does not imply the kind of absolutism that is suggested by "I am." It does not engage us in the either/or dualistic thinking that is the central ideological component of all systems of domination in Western society. It implies that a choice has been made, the commitment to feminism is an act of will. It does not suggest that by committing oneself to feminism, the possibility of supporting other political movements is negated.

As a black woman interested in feminist movement, I am often asked whether being black is more important than being a woman; whether feminist struggle to end sexist oppression is more important than the struggle to end racism and vice-versa. All such questions are rooted in competitive either/or thinking, the belief that the self is formed in opposition to an other. Therefore one is a feminist because you are not something else. Most people are socialized to think in terms of opposition rather than compatibility. Rather than see anti-racist work as totally compatible with working to end sexist oppression, they are often seen as two movements competing for first place. When asked "Are you a feminist?" it appears that an affirmative answer is translated to mean that one is concerned with no political issues other than feminism. When one is black, an affirmative response is likely to be heard as a devaluation of struggle to end racism. Given the fear of being misunderstood, it has been difficult for black women and women in exploited and oppressed ethnic groups to give expression to their interest in feminist concerns. They have been wary of saying "I am a feminist." The shift in expression from "I am a feminist" to "I advocate feminism" could serve as a useful strategy for eliminating the focus on identity and lifestyle. It could serve as a way women who are concerned about feminism as well as other political movements could express their support while avoiding linguistic structures that give primacy to one particular group. It would also encourage greater exploration in feminist theory.

[Text omitted]

Since bourgeois white women had defined feminism in such a way as to make it appear that it had no real significance for black women, they could then conclude that black women need not contribute to developing theory. We were to provide the colorful life stories to document and validate the prevailing set of theoretical assumptions. Focus on social equality with men as a definition of feminism led to an emphasis on discrimination, male attitudes, and legalistic reforms. Feminism as a movement to end sexist oppression directs our attention to systems of domination and the inter-relatedness of sex, race, and class oppression. Therefore, it compels us to centralize the experiences and the social predicaments of women who bear the brunt of sexist oppression as a way to understand the collective social status of women in the United States. Defining feminism as a movement to end sexist oppression is crucial for the development of theory because it is a starting point indicating the direction of exploration and analysis.

The foundation of future feminist struggle must be solidly based on a recognition of the need to eradicate the underlying cultural basis and causes of sexism and other forms of group oppression. Without challenging and changing these philosophical structures, no feminist reforms will have a long range impact. Consequently, it is now necessary for advocates of feminism to collectively acknowledge that our struggle cannot be defined as a movement to gain social equality with men; that terms like "liberal feminist" and "bourgeois feminist" represent contradictions that must be resolved so that feminism will not be continually co-opted to serve the opportunistic ends of special interest groups.

Catharine A. MacKinnon,
"The Sexual Politics of the First Amendment"
(1986)

Editor's Introduction: Catharine MacKinnon (1946–   ) is currently Professor of Law at the University of Michigan Law School. MacKinnon is known as a feminist, political activist, legal scholar, and educator. Her work has been influential in the framing of sexual harassment law. With Andrea Dworkin, MacKinnon introduced antipornography ordinances in Indianapolis and Minneapolis, which were later struck down as violations of free speech.

In the following selection, a speech made by MacKinnon at the Seventeenth Annual Conference on Women and the Law, held March 23, 1986, MacKinnon outlines her understanding of the gendered nature of the First Amendment, especially in regard to pornography. MacKinnon essentially draws no distinction between violence toward women and the depiction of such violence in film or literary representations. She argues that the latter is entitled to no more protection than the former. In contrast, the Supreme Court has held that "obscene" speech is not protected by the First Amendment, but it has left wide latitude for local communities to define obscenity and impose local restrictions. MacKinnon's attack on "First Amendment absolutism" troubles civil libertarians, who fear that it opens the door to banning not just pornography but political and artistic expression as well. MacKinnon considers the Court's position and such criticisms in what follows.

*   *   *

The Constitution of the United States, contrary to any impression you may have received, is a piece of paper with words written on it. Because it is old, it is considered a document. When it is interpreted by particular people under particular conditions, it becomes a text. Because it is backed up by the power of the state, it is a law.

Feminism, by contrast, springs from the impulse to self-respect in every woman. From this have come some fairly elegant things: a metaphysics of mind, a theory of knowledge, an approach to ethics, and a concept of social action. Aspiring to the point of view of all women on

---

* Catharine A. MacKinnon, *Feminism Unmodified: Discourses on Life and Law* (Cambridge, Mass: Harvard University Press, 1987). Reprinted by permission of the publishers.

social life as a whole, feminism has expressed itself as a political movement for civil equality.

Looking at the Constitution through the lens of feminism, initially one sees exclusion of women from the Constitution. This is simply to say that we had no voice in the constituting document of this state. From that one can suppose that those who did constitute it may not have had the realities of our situation in mind.

Next one notices that the Constitution as interpreted is structured around what can generically be called the public, or state action. This constituting document pervasively assumes that those guarantees of freedoms that must be secured to citizens begin where law begins, with the public order. This posture is exalted as "negative liberty" and is a cornerstone of the liberal state. You notice this from the feminist standpoint because women are oppressed socially, prior to law, without express state acts, often in intimate contexts. For women this structure means that those domains in which women are distinctively subordinated are assumed by the Constitution to be the domain of freedom.

Finally, combining these first two observations, one sees that women are not given affirmative access to those rights we need most. Equality, for example. Equality, in the words of Andrea Dworkin, was tacked on to the Constitution with spit and a prayer. And, let me also say, late.

If we apply these observations to the First Amendment, our exclusion means that the First Amendment was conceived by white men from the point of view of their social position. Some of them owned slaves; most of them owned women. They wrote it to guarantee their freedom to keep something they felt at risk of losing. Namely—and this gets to my next point—speech which they did not want lost through state action. They wrote the First Amendment so their speech would not be threatened by this powerful instrument they were creating, the federal government. You recall that it reads, "Congress shall make no law abridging . . . the freedom of speech." They were *creating* that body. They were worried that it would abridge something they *did have.* You can tell that they had speech, because what they said was written down: it became a document, it has been interpreted, it is the law of the state.

By contrast with those who wrote the First Amendment so they could keep what they had, those who didn't have it didn't get it. Those whose speech was silenced prior to law, prior to any operation of the state's prohibition of it, were not secured freedom of speech. Their speech was not regarded as something that had to be—and this gets to my next point—affirmatively guaranteed. Looking at the history of the First Amendment from this perspective, reprehensible examples of state attempts to suppress speech exist. But they constitute a history of comparative privilege in contrast with the history of silence of those whose speech has never been able to exist for the state even to contemplate abridging it.

A few affirmative guarantees of access to speech do exist. The *Red Lion* decision is one, although it may be slated for extinction. Because certain avenues of speech are inherently restricted—for instance, there are only so many broadcast frequencies—according to the *Red Lion* doctrine of fairness in access to broadcast media, some people's access has to be restricted in the interest of providing access to all. In other words, the speech of those who could buy up all the speech there is, is restricted. Conceptually, this doctrine works exactly like affirmative action. The speech of those who might be the only ones there, is not there, so that others' can be.

With a few exceptions like that we find no guarantees of access to speech. Take, for example, literacy. Even after it became clear that the Constitution applied to the states, nobody argued that the segregation of schools that created inferior conditions of access to literacy for Blacks violated their First Amendment rights. Or the slave codes that made it a crime to teach a slave to read and write or to advocate their freedom. Some of those folks who struggled for civil rights for Black people must have thought of this, but I never heard their lawyers argue it. If access to the means of speech is effectively socially precluded on the basis of race or class or gender, freedom from state burdens on speech does not meaningfully guarantee the freedom to speak.

First Amendment absolutism, the view that speech must be absolutely protected, is not the law of the First Amendment. It is the conscience, the superego of the First Amendment, the implicit standard from which all deviations must be justified. It is also an advocacy position typically presented in debate as if it were legal fact. Consider for example that First Amendment bog, the distinction between speech and conduct. Most conduct is expressive as well as active; words are as often tantamount to acts as they are vehicles for removed cerebration. Case law knows this. But the first question, the great divide, the beginning and the end, is still the absolutist question, "Is it speech or isn't it?"

First Amendment absolutism was forged in the crucible of obscenity litigation. Probably its most inspired expositions, its most passionate defenses, are to be found in Justice Douglas's dissents in obscenity cases. This is no coincidence. Believe him when he says that pornography is at the core of the First Amendment. Absolutism has developed through obscenity litigation, I think, because pornography's protection fits perfectly with the power relations embedded in First Amendment structure and jurisprudence from the start. Pornography is exactly that speech of men that silences the speech of women. I take it seriously when Justice Douglas speaking on pornography and others preaching absolutism say that pornography has to be protected speech or else free expression will not mean what it has always meant in this country.

I must also say that the First Amendment has become a sexual fetish through years of absolutist writing in the melodrama mode in *Playboy* in particular. You know those superheated articles where freedom of speech is extolled and its imminent repression is invoked. Behaviorally, *Playboy's* consumers are reading about the First Amendment, masturbating to the women, reading about the First Amendment, masturbating to the women, reading about the First Amendment, masturbating to the women. It makes subliminal seduction look subtle. What is conveyed is not only that using women is as legitimate as thinking about the Constitution, but also that if you don't support these views about the Constitution, you won't be able to use these women.

This general approach affects even religious groups. I love to go speaking against pornography when the sponsors dig up some religious types, thinking they will make me look bad because they will agree with me. Then the ministers come on and say, "This is the first time we've ever agreed with the ACLU about anything . . . why, what she's advocating would *violate the First Amendment.*" This isn't their view universally, I guess, but it has been my experience repeatedly, and I have personally never had a minister support me on the air. One of them finally explained it. The First Amendment, he said, also guarantees the freedom of religion. So this is not only what we already know: regardless of one's politics and one's moral views, one is into using women largely. It is also that, consistent with this, First Amendment absolutism resonates historically in the context of the long-term collaboration in misogyny between church and state. Don't let them tell you they're "separate" in that.

In pursuit of absolute freedom of speech, the ACLU has been a major institution in defending, and now I describe their behavior, the Nazis, the Klan, and the pornographers. I am waiting for them to add the antiabortionists, including the expressive conduct of their violence. Think about one of their favorite metaphors, a capitalist metaphor, the marketplace of ideas. Think about whether the speech of the Nazis has historically enhanced the speech of the Jews. Has the speech of the Klan expanded the speech of Blacks? Has the so-called speech of the pornographers enlarged the speech of women? In this context, apply to what they call the marketplace of ideas the question we were asked to consider in the keynote speech by Winona LaDuke: Is there a relationship between our poverty in speech and their wealth?

As many of you may know, Andrea Dworkin and I, with a lot of others, have been working to establish a law that recognizes pornography as a violation of the civil rights of women in particular. It recognizes that pornography is a form of sex discrimination. Recently, in a fairly unprecedented display of contempt, the U.S. Supreme Court found that the Indianapolis version of our law violates the First Amendment. On a direct appeal, the Supreme Court invalidated a local ordinance by summary affirmance—no arguments, no briefs on the merits, no victims, no opinion, not so much as a single line of citation to controlling precedent. One is entitled to think that they would have put one there if they had had one.

The Court of Appeals opinion they affirmed expressly concedes that pornography violates women in all the ways Indianapolis found it did. The opinion never questioned that pornography is sex discrimination. Interesting enough, the Seventh Circuit, in an opinion by Judge Frank Easterbrook, conceded the issue of objective causation. The only problem was, the harm didn't matter as much as the materials mattered. They are valuable. So the law that prohibited the harm the materials caused was held to be content-based and impermissible discrimination on the basis of viewpoint.

This is a law that gives victims a civil action when they are coerced into pornography, when pornography is forced on them, when they are assaulted because of specific pornography, and when they are subordinated through the trafficking in pornography. Some of us thought that sex discrimination and sexual abuse were against public policy. We defined pornography as the sexually explicit subordination of women through pictures or words that also includes presentations of women being sexually abused. There is a list of the specific acts of sexual abuse. The law covers men, too. We were so careful that practices whose abusiveness some people publicly question—for example, submission, servility, and display—are not covered by the trafficking provision. So we're talking rape, torture, pain, humiliation: we're talking violence against women turned into sex.

Now we are told that pornography, which, granted, does the harm we say it does, this pornography as we define it is protected speech. It has speech value. You can tell it has value as speech because it is so effective in doing the harm that it does. (The passion of this rendition is mine, but the opinion really does say this.) The more harm, the more protection. This is now apparently the law of the First Amendment, at least where harm to women is the rationale. Judge LaDoris Cordell spoke earlier about the different legal standards for high-value and low-value speech, a doctrine that feminists who oppose pornography have always been averse to. But at least it is now clear that whatever the value of pornography is—and it is universally conceded to be low—the value of women is lower.

It is a matter of real interest to me exactly what the viewpoint element in our law is, according to Easterbrook's opinion. My best guess is that our law takes the point of view that women do not enjoy and deserve rape, and he saw that as just one point of view among many. Where do you suppose he got that idea? Another possible rendering is that our law takes the position that women should not be subordinated to men on the basis of sex, that women are or should be equal, and he regards relief to that end as the enforcement of a prohibited viewpoint.

Just what is and is not valuable, is and is not a viewpoint, is and is not against public policy was made even clearer the day after the summary affirmance. In the *Renton* case the Supreme Court revealed the conditions under which pornography can be restricted: it can be zoned beyond the city limits. It can be regulated this way on the basis of its "secondary effects"—which are, guess what, property values. But it cannot be regulated on the basis of its primary effects on the bodies of the women who had to be ground up to make it.

Do you think it makes any difference to the woman who is coerced into pornography or who has just hit the end of this society's chances for women that the product of her exploitation is sold on the other side of the tracks? Does it matter to the molested child or the rape victim that the offender who used the pornography to get himself up or to plan what he would do or to decide what "type" to do it to had to drive across town to get it? It *does* matter to the women who live or work in the neighborhoods into which the pornography is zoned. They pay in increased street harassment, in an atmosphere of terror and contempt for what other neighborhoods gain in keeping their property values up.

Reading the two decisions together, you see the Court doing what it has always done with pornography: making it available in private while decrying it in public. Pretending to be tough on pornography's effects, the *Renton* case *still gives it a place to exist*. Although obscenity is supposed to have such little value that it is not considered speech at all, *Renton* exposes the real bottom line of the First Amendment: the pornography stays. Anyone who doesn't think absolutism has made any progress, check that.

Why is it that obscenity law can exist and our trafficking provision cannot? Why can the law against child pornography exist and not our law against coercion? Why aren't obscenity and child pornography laws viewpoint laws? Obscenity, as Justice Brennan pointed out in his dissent in *Renton*, expresses a viewpoint: sexual mores should be more relaxed, and if they were, sex would look like pornography. Child pornography also presents a viewpoint: sex between adults and children is liberating, fulfilling, fun, and natural for the child. If one is concerned about the government taking a point of view through law, the laws against these things express the state's opposition to these viewpoints, to the extent of making them crimes to express. Why is a time-place-manner distinction all right in Renton, and not our forcing provision, which is kind of time-and-place-like and does not provide for actions against the pornographers at all? Why is it all right to make across-the-board, content-based distinctions like obscenity and child pornography, but not our trafficking provision, not our coercion provision?

When do you see a viewpoint as a viewpoint? When you don't agree with it. When is a viewpoint not a viewpoint? When it's yours. What is and is not a viewpoint, much less a prohibited one, is a matter of individual values and social consensus. The reason Judge Easterbrook saw a viewpoint in our law was because he disagrees with it. (I don't mean to personify it, because it isn't at all personal; I mean, it *is* him, personally, but it isn't him only or only him, as a person.) There is real social disagreement as to whether women are or should be subordinated to men. Especially in sex.

His approach obscured the fact that our law is not content-based at all; it is harm-based. A harm is an act, an activity. It is not just a mental event. Coercion is not an image. Force is not a representation. Assault is not a symbol. Trafficking is not simply advocacy. Subordination is an activity, not just a point of view. The problem is, pornography is both theory and practice, both a metaphor for and a means of the subordination of women. The Seventh Circuit allowed the fact that pornography has a theory to obscure the fact that it is a practice, the fact that it is a metaphor to obscure the fact that it is also a means.

I don't want you to misunderstand what I am about to say. Our law comes nowhere near anybody's speech rights, and the literatures of other inequalities do not relate to those inequalities in the same way pornography relates to sexism. But I risk your misunderstanding on both of these points in order to say that there have been serious movements for liberation in this world. This is by contrast with liberal movements. In serious movements for human freedom, speech is serious, both the attempt to get some for those who do not have any and the recognition that the so-called speech of the other side is a form of the practice of the other side. In union struggles, yellow-dog presses are attacked. Abolitionists attacked slave presses. The monarchist press was not tolerated by the revolutionaries who founded this country. When the White Circle League published a racist pamphlet, it was found to violate a criminal law against libeling groups. After World War II the Nazi press was restricted in Germany by law under the aegis of the Allies. Nicaragua considers it "immoral" and contrary to the progress of education and the cultural development of the people to publish, distribute, circulate, exhibit, transmit, or sell materials that, among other things, "stimulate viciousness," "lower human dignity," or to "use women as sexual or commercial objects."

The analogy Norma Ramos mentioned between the fight against pornography to sex equality and the fight against segregation to race equality makes the analogy between the Indianapolis case and *Brown v. Board of Education* evocative to me also. But I think we may be at an even prior point. The Supreme Court just told us that it is a constitutional right to traffic in our flesh, so long as it is done through pictures and words, and a legislature may not give us access to court to contest it. The Indianapolis case is the *Dred Scott* of the women's movement. The Supreme Court told Dred Scott, to the Constitution, you are property. It told women, to the Constitution, you are speech. The struggle against pornography is an abolitionist struggle to establish that just as buying and selling human beings never was anyone's property right, buying and selling women and children is no one's civil liberty.

SUGGESTIONS FOR FURTHER READING

Gloria Anzaldua, ed., *Making Face, Making Soul = Haciendo Caras: Creative and Critical Perspectives of Feminists of Color* (San Francisco: Aunt Lute Books, 1990).

Jacqueline Bernard, *Journey Toward Freedom: The Story of Sojourner Truth* (New York: W. W. Norton & Company, 1967).

Susan Brownmiller, *Against Our Will: Men, Women and Rape* (New York: Ballantine Books, 1993).

Ellen Carol DuBois, *Elizabeth Cady Stanton and Susan B. Anthony: Correspondence, Writings, Speeches* (New York: Schocken Books, 1981).

Jean Bethke Elshtain, *Public Man, Private Woman: Women in Social and Political Thought* (Princeton, NJ: Princeton University Press, 1981).

Susan Faludi, *Backlash: The Undeclared War Against American Women* (New York: Crown, 1991).

Betty Friedan, *The Feminine Mystique* (New York: Dell Publishing Co., 1983).

Betty Friedan, *The Second Stage*, revised edition (New York: Summit Books, 1986).

Paula Giddings, *When and Where I Enter: The Impact of Black Women on Race and Sex in America* (New York: Bantam Books, 1985).

Emma Goldman, *Living My Life* (New York: Alfred A. Knopf, 1931).

Linda K. Kerber, *Women of the Republic* (Chapel Hill: University of North Carolina–Chapel Hill, 1980).

Jane J. Mansbridge, *Why We Lost the ERA* (Chicago: University of Chicago Press, 1986).

Mary Beth Norton, *Liberty's Daughters* (Boston: Little, Brown and Company, 1980).

Christina Hoff Sommers, *Who Stole Feminism?: Women Have Betrayed Women* (New York: Simon & Schuster, 1995).

172

PART III

Immigration and National Identity: From the Melting Pot to Multiculturalism

PART III

Immigration and National Identity:
From the Melting Pot to Multiculturalism

I am not sure that we can, or that we ought, to accelerate Americanization. Thus far it has been a contagion with no artificial stimulus. When
we shall say: "Go to, we will Americanize you," there will be organized
effort to resist us, and the resistance will grow with our insistence."

—EDWARD STEINER[1]

Down with racism, down with Western Culture, up with diversity![2]

—Student chant, Stanford University, late 1980s

As a New Yorker who relocated to California, I found that a number
of adjustments and surprises awaited me. Among these was the discovery
that I am labeled by some Californians (including most the age of my
students) as an "Anglo." It seems that many Californians recognize ethnic
diversity among whites, Asians, African-Americans, and Latinos, but ethnic differences within these broad categories are not so well understood.
I can't help thinking what an historical irony this is and how it would
have struck my Italian-born father who, after World War II, could not
find a job in a New York law firm because the real Anglo-Americans who
ran these firms openly discriminated against Americans of Italian descent.
To the average Californian, he would be one of them.

On the one hand, my personal story speaks to the success of uncoerced "Americanization" that Steiner addresses in the passage quoted.
Aside from a few cultural affinities, like a taste for provolone or a cannoli
for dessert (and the former may be served on Jewish rye bread with
French mustard and the latter with Swiss mocha), it is not that wrong to
describe me, a second-generation American, as an "Anglo," taking that

---

[1] Edward A. Steiner, *The Confessions of a Hyphenated American* (New York: Fleming
H. Revell Company, 1916), p. 52.

[2] Quote in James Davison Hunter, *Culture Wars: The Struggle to Define America* (New
York: Basic Books, 1991), pp. 215–216.

term to mean a generic American white person. On the other hand, to define whites as Anglos, whether they be of Irish, Italian, Polish, or Russian descent, is to draw a dividing line between whites and peoples of color. It could be taken to suggest, somewhat ominously, that American political institutions and history are the province of one race and not the possession of all of us regardless of ethnicity, race, or creed. This seems to be what the Stanford students, who were protesting a western civilization course requirement, were saying when they linked racism with western—and "American"—culture and set it in opposition to "diversity." Their view, though largely unarticulated, raises troubling questions.

The United States is frequently described as a "nation of immigrants" and this is true as far as it goes. Almost all of us who are from families that came here voluntarily (we must not forget Africans brought here against their wills as slaves or Native Americans who migrated here in prehistory) have some memory, whether passed down orally or in writing, of their familial place of origin. That we are a land of immigrants is beyond question, but are we a *nation* of immigrants? The term "nation" usually refers to a people who share common customs, language, fables, heroes, etc. The French are a nation, as are the Japanese. French parents and schools teach their children of great semimythic heroes like Charlemagne, of the great achievements of French artists and writers from Chretien de Troyes in the Middle Ages to Henri Matisse, of the virtues of French wines and culinary habits, etc. But is America a nation in this sense? If so, what is it that we share? What are our common myths, customs, tastes, etc., that make us a nation? Or, if not a nation, are we something else? We are certainly a state, the latter being an area ruled by a single government or sovereign. And many states in the world are multinational—i.e., like India, they contain peoples who speak many languages and share little of a common culture.

Ultimately, the sorts of questions we've just raised in general theoretical terms become intensely personal for every immigrant to these shores. The immigrant must confront the question, "What does it mean to be an American?" She must ask further, "How does my becoming an American fit with my prior, or other, national identity?" Can I become an American, in other words, and remain true to what I already am? In this section we look at a variety of answers to these questions, offered by recent immigrants as well as by the children and grandchildren of immigrants who got here first.

We begin with Henri de Crevecoeur, a French immigrant in the late 1700s who is among the first to offer a "melting pot" thesis of Americanization. The voyage to the New World causes the immigrant to leave "behind him all his ancient prejudices and manners, receives new ones from the new mode of life he has embraced." We have encountered this largely environmental explanation of the uniformity of an American way of life in the writings of Frederick Jackson Turner and James Bryce.

It was not far into our history as an independent country, however, that immigration became a contentious issue. An early flare-up occurred over the Alien and Sedition Acts in the 1790s. We provide some background for this in the introduction to our excerpt from Madison's report to the Virginia legislature. Suffice it to say here that the controversy regarding the status of aliens was rooted in immediate political concerns. In the course of addressing these concerns, however, Madison discusses the civil rights of legal aliens in ways that are relevant through to the present. He asserts, for example, that aliens are entitled to constitutional protections and are not to be treated as a suspect class deserving of such punishment as deportation or detention without due process of law. The issue of the legal and moral status of immigrants—both naturalized citizens and alien residents—is reexplored in two Supreme Court decisions reproduced in abridged version. The first, *Korematsu v. United States*, concerns a legal challenge to the internment of Japanese-Americans during World War II. The second, *Plyler v. Doe*, considers whether the children of undocumented aliens are entitled to public education under the Constitution.

In addition to legal and political issues, mass immigration to the United States has been a source of cultural controversy throughout our history. In 1790, the national origins of those in the United States, excluding slaves for the moment, was roughly 61% English, 14% Scottish or Irish, 9% German, 3% Dutch, and a smattering of other nationalities, including French and Spanish. When one keeps in mind that there were substantial cultural and even linguistic differences between those from England and the Scottish and Irish, this indicates a considerable ethnic diversity going back to our very origins. From the 1830s up to the Civil War, the pace of immigration increased dramatically, with some five million immigrants, mostly Irish and German, entering the United States, some two million of whom were Roman Catholics. This gave rise to a strong nativist (i.e., anti-immigrant) response represented here with an 1855 writing from the Know-Nothing Party, "America for Americans." The Know-Nothings were strongly anti-Catholic, fearing that Catholics could not be good Americans and good democrats, as their first allegiance was to the pope and the authoritarian institution he represents. While this nativism took a particularly ugly turn, it has some intellectual roots in the sorts of arguments we explored in the debates between Federalists and Anti-Federalists, where the latter argued that cultural and religious homogeneity is a precondition of democratic government.

Another great "wave" of immigration occurred between 1890 and the beginning of World War I in 1914. In 1910, roughly 15% of the

American population were foreign-born, vastly more as a proportion of the population than is the case today. Immigrants in this period tended to be from southern and eastern Europe, including Italians, Russians, Poles, etc., and met with considerable hostility in their new land. This period gave rise to one of the most intense debates about immigration that our country has known. It culminated with the passage of the Immigration Act of 1924, which was very restrictive regarding the admission of new immigrants from these lands and favoring admission of the so-called "old" or western European immigrants. We reproduce three important writings from this period, those by Theodore Roosevelt, John Dewey, and Horace Kallen. Roosevelt's writing, taken from his book, *True Americanism*, represents about as strong a case for assimilation as one can imagine. To be an American, Roosevelt suggests, is essentially an act of forgetting and reconstitution. Forget one's land of origin, one's native language and culture, and adopt fully the American way of life. Roosevelt is urging that immigrants become what Crevecouer says they will become naturally, i.e., a homogeneous people without affinities for the Old World.

In response, Dewey and Kallen present somewhat different versions of what might be called today a multicultural argument. They defend the notion of the "hyphenated American," a term that was popularized in the early years of the twentieth century, along with the familiar metaphor of the "melting pot" (though with the opposite meaning). The hyphenated American, whether he be Irish-, German-, Spanish-American, etc., is one who maintains some cultural allegiance to his native land and customs but who develops a political allegiance to the United States. Kallen and Dewey would both reject the notion that we are a "nation" of immigrants, as much as we are a land of them. For them, unlike for Roosevelt, "true Americanism" is one that recognizes and finds itself strengthened by ethnic diversity.

The debate between the assimilationist and multicultural positions of the early 1900s will sound surprisingly familiar to students today. Questions regarding the economic and social costs of immigration are being raised with a new vigor in the 1990s. We see this, for example, in controversies such as that over Proposition 187 in California (see introduction to *Plyler v. Doe*), a ballot initiative that passed handily in 1994 and would deny, if fully implemented, education and health care expenditures on undocumented aliens. We see it too in debates about bilingualism versus English as an official language, and in arguments about multicultural curricula in colleges, such as that which sparked the protest at Stanford University. These debates, like the nativist movement in the 1850s and the controversies over "new immigrants" in the early years of this century, are driven by a third great "wave" of immigration that has been occurring since the 1970s. In 1970, the share of the American population who were foreign born had declined, according to the U.S. census, to a century low of 4.8%. That total has risen steadily since and, in 1994, the percent of the foreign born reached 8.7. This amounts to some twenty-two million people, mostly of Latin-American and Asian descent, a third of whom live in one state, California. Michael Walzer's article on multiculturalism addresses some of the issues at play today at a time when both ethnic self-assertiveness and nativism seem to be on the rise. We will address others in our conclusion.

One last word about these readings is in order. It is their purpose to highlight important themes regarding the legal, moral, and cultural responses of American citizens to immigrants and vice versa. They focus largely on debates in our past to shed light on the present. It is not our purpose, nor would it be possible, to represent the voices of many or all immigrant groups. Doing so is far less important than understanding the terms of the debate. It is hoped, however, that you will think about what these readings teach in light of your own life experiences and further reading on your own.

Hector St. Jean de Crevecoeur,
"Letters from an American Farmer" (1782)

Editor's Introduction: Hector St. Jean de Crevecoeur (1735–1813) was born in Normandy, France. In 1755, he joined the French forces fighting the French and Indian War in Canada as a mapmaker. Upon completing his military service in 1759, he settled in America, which would be his home for the next twenty years. Crevecoeur spent several years traveling before he married and bought a farm in New York in 1769. He wrote *Letters from an American Farmer* before his departure from America in 1780, and it was first published in London in 1782. Crevecoeur is best known for introducing the symbol of the "melting-pot" into American culture and for his depiction of Americans as a new race. His work also celebrates the beauty of nature and the simple virtues of the agrarian lifestyle. Both Benjamin Franklin and George Washington recommended his *Letters* to potential American immigrants.

*   *   *

What attachment can a poor European emigrant have for a country where he had nothing? The knowledge of the language, the love of a few kindred as poor as himself, were the only cords that tied him: his country is now that which gives him land, bread, protection, and consequence: *Ubi panis ibi patria*, is the motto of all emigrants. What then is the American, this new man? He is either an European, or the descendant of an European, hence that strange mixture of blood, which you will find in no other country. I could point out to you a family whose grandfather was an Englishman, whose wife was Dutch, whose son married a French woman, and whose present four sons have now four wives of different nations. He is an American, who, leaving behind him all his ancient prejudices and manners, receives new ones from the new mode of life he has embraced, the new government he obeys, and the new rank he holds. He becomes an American by being received in the broad lap of our great *Alma Mater*. Here individuals of all nations are melted into a new race of men, whose labours and posterity will one day cause great changes in the world. Americans are the western pilgrims, who are carrying along with them that great mass of arts, sciences, vigour, and industry which began long since in the east; they will finish the great circle. The Americans

Source: Hector St. John de Crevecoeur *Letters from an American Farmer* Introduction and Notes by Warren Barton Blake. (New York: E.P. Dutton & Co., 1908)

were once scattered all over Europe; here they are incorporated into one of the finest systems of population which has ever appeared, and which will hereafter become distinct by the power of the different climates they inhabit. The American ought therefore to love this country much better than that wherein either he or his forefathers were born. Here the rewards of his industry follow with equal steps the progress of his labour; his labour is founded on the basis of nature, *self-interest*; can it want a stronger allurement? Wives and children, who before in vain demanded of him a morsel of bread, now, fat and frolicsome, gladly help their father to clear those fields whence exuberant crops are to arise to feed and to clothe them all; without any part being claimed, either by a despotic prince, a rich abbot, or a mighty lord. Here religion demands but little of him; a small voluntary salary to the minister, and gratitude to God; can he refuse these? The American is a new man, who acts upon new principles; he must therefore entertain new ideas, and form new opinions. From involuntary idleness, servile dependence, penury, and useless labour, he has passed to toils of a very different nature, rewarded by ample subsistence—This is an American.

[Text omitted]

An European, when he first arrives, seems limited in his intentions, as well as in his views; but he very suddenly alters his scale; two hundred miles formerly appeared a very great distance, it is now but a trifle; he no sooner breathes out air than he forms schemes, and embarks in designs he never would have thought of in his own country. There the plenitude of society confines many useful ideas, and often extinguishes the most laudable schemes which here ripen into maturity. Thus Europeans become Americans.

But how is this accomplished in that crowd of low, indigent people, who flock here every year from all parts of Europe? I will tell you; they no sooner arrive than they immediately feel the good effects of that plenty of provisions we possess: they fare on our best food, and they are kindly entertained; their talents, character, and peculiar industry are immediately inquired into; they find countrymen everywhere disseminated, let them come from whatever part of Europe. Let me select one as an epitome of the rest; he is hired, he goes to work, and works moderately; instead of being employed by a haughty person, he finds himself with his equal, placed at the substantial table of the farmer, or else at an inferior one as good; his wages are high, his bed is not like that bed of sorrow on which he used to lie: if he behaves with propriety, and is faithful, he is caressed, and becomes as it were a member of the family. He begins to feel the effects of a sort of resurrection; hitherto he had not lived, but simply vegetated; he now feels himself a man, because he is treated as such; the laws of his own country had overlooked him in his insignificancy; the laws of this cover him with their mantle. Judge what an alteration there must arise in the mind and thoughts of this man; he begins to forget his former servitude and dependence, his heart involuntarily swells and glows; this first swell inspires him with those new thoughts which constitute an American. What love can he entertain for a country where his existence was a burthen to him; if he is a generous good man, the love of this new adoptive parent will sink deep into his heart. He looks around, and sees many a prosperous person, who but a few years before was as poor as himself. This encourages him much, he begins to form some little scheme, the first, alas, he ever formed in his life. If he is wise he thus spends two or three years, in which time he acquires knowledge, the use of tools, the modes of working the lands, felling trees, etc. This prepares the foundation of a good name, the most useful acquisition he can make. He is encouraged, he has gained friends; he is advised and directed, he feels bold, he purchases some land; he gives all the money he has brought over, as well as what he has earned, and trusts to the God of harvests for the discharge of the rest. His good name procures him credit. He is now possessed of the deed, conveying to him and his posterity the fee simple and absolute property of two hundred acres of land, situated on such a river. What an epocha in this man's life! He is become a freeholder, from perhaps a German boor—he is now an American, a Pennsylvanian, an English subject. He is naturalised, his name is enrolled with those of the other citizens of the province. Instead of being a vagrant, he has a place of residence; he is called the inhabitant of such a country, or of such a district, and for the first time in his life counts for something; for hitherto he has been a cypher. I only repeat what I have heard many say, and no wonder their hearts should glow, and be agitated with a multitude of feelings, not easy to describe. From nothing to start into being; from a servant to the rank of a master; from being the slave of some despotic prince, to become a free man, invested with lands, to which every municipal blessing is annexed! What a change indeed! It is in consequence of that change that he becomes an American. This great metamorphosis has a double effect, it extinguishes all his European prejudices, he forgets that mechanism of subordination, that servility of disposition which poverty had taught him; and sometimes he is apt to forget too much, often passing from one extreme to the other. If he is a good man, he forms schemes of future prosperity, he proposes to educate his children better than he has been educated himself; he thinks of future modes of conduct, feels an ardour to labour he never felt before. Pride steps in and leads him to everything that the laws do not forbid: he respects them; with a heartfelt gratitude he looks toward the east, toward the insular government from whose wisdom all his new felicity is derived, and under whose wings and protection he now lives. These reflections constitute him the good man and the good subject. Ye poor Europeans, ye, who sweat, and work for the great—ye, who are obliged to give so many sheaves to the church, so many to your lords, so many to your government, and have hardly any left for yourselves—ye, who are held in less estimation than favourite hunters or useless lap-dogs—ye, who only breathe the air of nature, because it cannot be withheld from you; it is here that ye can conceive the possibility of those feelings I have been describing; it is here the laws of naturalisation invite every one to partake of our great labours and felicity, to till unrented, untaxed lands! Many, corrupted beyond the power of amendment, have brought with them all their vices, and disregarding the advantages held to them, have gone on in their former career of iniquity, until they have been overtaken and punished by our laws. It is not every emigrant who succeeds; no, it is only the sober, the honest, and industrious: happy those to whom this transition has served as a powerful spur to labour, to prosperity, and to the good establishment of children, born in the days of their poverty; and who had no other portion to expect but the rags of their parents, had it not been for their happy emigration. Others again, have been led astray by this enchanting scene; their new pride, instead of leading them to the fields, has kept them in idleness; the idea of possessing lands is all that satisfies them— though surrounded with fertility, they have mouldered away their time in inactivity, misinformed husbandry, and ineffectual endeavours. How much wiser, in general, the honest Germans than almost all other Europeans; they hire themselves to some of their wealthy landsmen, and in that apprenticeship learn everything that is necessary. They attentively consider the prosperous industry of others, which imprints in their minds a strong desire of possessing the same advantages. This forcible idea never quits them, they launch forth, and by dint of sobriety, rigid parsimony, and the most persevering industry, they commonly succeed. Their astonishment at their first arrival from Germany is very great—it is to them a dream; the contrast must be powerful indeed; they observe their countrymen flourishing in every place; they travel through whole counties where not a word of English is spoken; and in the names and the language of the people, they retrace Germany. They have been an useful acquisition to this continent, and to Pennsylvania in particular; to them it owes some share of its prosperity: to their mechanical knowledge and patience it owes the finest mills in all America, the best teams of horses, and many other advantages. The recollection of their former poverty and slavery never quits them as long as they live.

James Madison, et al., "Report on the Resolutions ... Concerning the Alien and Sedition Acts" (1799)

Editor's Introduction: The Alien and Sedition Acts were four separate laws passed in 1798 during the Administration of John Adams in response to a foreign policy crisis regarding relations of the United States to France. Their passage precipitated the first great constitutional crisis for the new nation. In 1798 John Adams sent three commissioners to France to preserve peace between the countries, whose relations were strained due to the United States' declaration of neutrality in the war raging between France and Britain. The commissioners were asked to pay a large bribe to French officials before talks could occur. Documents pertaining to this event, referred to as the XYZ Affair, were then published in the American press and this heightened animosity toward France among supporters of Adams's Federalist Party.

Opposed to the Federalist Party were the Democratic-Republicans, most notably represented by James Madison and Thomas Jefferson, who tended to hold pro-French views. The Federalists passed the Alien and Sedition Acts in a highly partisan atmosphere in which each side was savaging the other in the press. These acts included the Naturalization Act, the Alien Act, the Alien Enemies Act, and the Sedition Act. The Naturalization Act increased the residency requirement for aliens requesting citizenship from five to fourteen years. The Alien Act allowed the President to deport any foreigner he regarded as dangerous to the United States, and the Alien Enemies Act, to detain enemy aliens during times of war. The Sedition Act criminalized false or scandalous works published against Congress or the President. Thomas Jefferson and James Madison opposed these acts in what have come to be known as the Virginia and Kentucky Resolutions. These resolutions accused the Federalists of violating constitutional protections of free speech and suggested that states had a right and duty to not enforce federal laws that violated the Constitution. This precipitated a constitutional crisis that was resolved only by the election of Jefferson in 1800 and the subsequent repeal of the acts.

The following selection is from a report to the committee of the Virginia legislature which considers Madison's Virginia Resolutions. In

Source: Gaillard Hunt, ed., *The Writings of James Madison* (New York: G. P. Putnam's Sons, 1906).

it, Madison expresses his views on the rights of aliens living in the United States and argues that they are entitled to constitutional protections. Specifically, he argues that aliens should not be deported or detained without proof of specific legal wrongdoing determined through due process of law. This issue of the moral, legal, and constitutional status of resident aliens recurs at numerous points in our history. It is worth reading this piece in conjunction with the 1982 Supreme Court decision, *Plyler v. Doe*, also in this volume.

*   *   *

Report of the Committee to whom were referred the Communications of various States, relative to the Resolutions of the last General Assembly of this State, concerning the Alien and Sedition Laws.

House of Delegates, Session of 1799–1800

[Text omitted]

The resolution next in order is contained in the following terms:
"That the General Assembly doth particularly protest against the palpable and alarming infractions of the Constitution in the two late cases of the 'Alien and Sedition Acts,' passed at the last session of Congress; the first of which exercises a power nowhere delegated to the Federal Government, and which, by uniting legislative and judicial powers to those of executive, subverts the general principles of a free Government, as well as the particular organization and positive provisions of the Federal Constitution; and the other of which acts exercises, in like manner, a power not delegated by the Constitution but, on the contrary, expressly and positively forbidden by one of the amendments thereto; a power which, more than any other, ought to produce universal alarm; because it is levelled against that right of freely examining the public characters and measures, and of free communication among the people thereon, which has ever been justly deemed the only effectual guardian of every other right."

The subject of this resolution having, it is presumed, more particularly led the General Assembly into the proceedings which they communicated to the other States, and being in itself of peculiar importance, it deserves the most critical and faithful investigation, for the length of which no other apology will be necessary.

The subject divides itself into—*first*, "The Alien Act"; *secondly*, "The Sedition Act."

Of the "Alien Act," it is affirmed by the resolution—1st. That it exercise a power nowhere delegated to the Federal Government. 2d. That it unites legislative and judicial powers to those of the Executive. 3d. That this union of power subverts the general principles of free government. 4th. That it subverts the particular organization and positive provisions of the Federal Constitution.

In order to clear the way for a correct view of the first position several observations will be premised.

I. In the first place, it is to be borne in mind that it being a characteristic feature of the Federal Constitution, as it was originally ratified, and an amendment thereto having precisely declared, "That the powers not delegated to the United States by the Constitution, nor prohibited by it to the States, are reserved to the States, respectively, or to the people"; it is incumbent in this as in every other exercise of power by the Federal Government, to prove from the Constitution that it grants the particular power exercised.

The next observation to be made is, that much confusion and fallacy have been thrown into the question by blending the two cases of *aliens, members of a hostile nation,* and *aliens, members of friendly nations.* These two cases are so obviously and so essentially distinct, that it occasions no little surprise that the distinction should have been disregarded; and the surprise is so much the greater, as it appears that the two cases are actually distinguished by two separate acts of Congress, passed at the same session, and comprised in the same publication; the one providing for the case of "alien enemies"; the other, "concerning aliens" indiscriminately, and, consequently, extending to aliens of every nation in peace and amity with the United States. With respect to alien enemies, no doubt has been intimated as to the Federal authority over them; the Constitution having expressly delegated to Congress the power to declare war against any nation, and, of course, to treat it and all its members as enemies. With respect to aliens who are not enemies, but members of nations in peace and amity with the United States, the power assumed by the act of Congress is denied to be constitutional; and it is, accordingly, against this act that the protest of the General Assembly is expressly and exclusively directed.

A third observation is, that were it admitted, as is contended, that the "act concerning aliens" has for its object, not a *penal,* but a *preventive* justice, it would still remain to be proved that it comes within the constitutional power of the Federal Legislature; and, if within its power, that the Legislature has exercised it in a constitutional manner.

In the administration of preventive justice the following principles have been held sacred: that some probable ground of suspicion be exhibited before some judicial authority; that it be supported by oath or affirmation; that the party may avoid being thrown into confinement by finding pledges or sureties for his legal conduct, sufficient in the judgment of some judicial authority; that he may have the benefit of a writ of *habeas corpus*, and thus obtain his release if wrongfully confined; and that he may at any time be discharged from his recognisance, or his confinement, and restored to his former liberty and rights on the order of the proper judicial authority, if it shall see sufficient cause.

All these principles of the only preventive justice known to American jurisprudence are violated by the Alien Act. The ground of suspicion is to be judged of, not by any judicial authority, but by the Executive Magistrate alone. No oath or affirmation is required. If the suspicion be held reasonable by the President, he may order the suspected alien to depart the territory of the United States, without the opportunity of avoiding the sentence by finding pledges for his future good conduct. As the President may limit the time of departure as he pleases, the benefit of the writ of *habeas corpus* may be suspended with respect to the party, although the Constitution ordains that it shall not be suspended unless when the public safety may require it, in case of rebellion or invasion—neither of which existed at the passage of the act; and the party being, under the sentence of the President, either removed form the United States, or being punished by imprisonment, or disqualification ever to become a citizen, on conviction of not obeying the order of removal, he cannot be discharged from the proceedings against him, and restored to the benefits of his former situation, although the *highest judicial authority* should see the most sufficient cause for it.

But, in the last place, it can never be admitted that the removal of aliens, authorized by the act, is to be considered, not as punishment for an offence, but as a measure of precaution and prevention. If the banishment of an alien from a country into which he has been invited as the asylum most auspicious to his happiness—a country where he may have formed the most tender connexions; where he may have invested his entire property, and acquired property of the real and permanent, as well as the movable and temporary kind; where he enjoys, under the laws, a greater share of the blessings of personal security, and personal liberty, than he can elsewhere hope for, and where he may have nearly completed his probationary title to citizenship; if, moreover, in the execution of the sentence against him, he is to be exposed, not only to the ordinary dangers of the sea, but to the peculiar casualties incident to a crisis of war and of unusual licentiousness on that element, and possibly to vindictive purposes which his emigration itself may have provoked; if a banishment of this sort be not punishment, and among the severest of punishments, it will be difficult to imagine a doom to which the name can be applied. And if it be a punishment, it will remain to be inquired whether it can be constitutionally inflicted, on mere suspicion, by the single will of the Executive Magistrate, on persons convicted of no personal offence against the laws of the land, nor involved in any offence against the law of nations, charged on the foreign State of which they are members.

One argument offered in justification of this power exercised over aliens is, that the admission of them into the country being of favor, not of right, the favor is at all times revocable.

To this argument it might be answered, that, allowing the truth of the inference, it would be no proof of what is required. A question would still occur, whether the Constitution had vested the discretionary power of admitting aliens in the Federal Government or in the State governments.

But it cannot be a true inference, that, because the admission of an alien is a favor, the favor may be revoked at pleasure. A grant of land to an individual may be of favor, not of right; but the moment the grant is made, the favor becomes a right, and must be forfeited before it can be taken away. To pardon a malefactor may be a favor, but the pardon is not, on that account, the less irrevocable. To admit an alien to naturalization, is as much a favor as to admit him to reside in the country; yet it cannot be pretended that a person naturalized can be deprived of the benefits any more than a native citizen can be disfranchised.

Again, it is said, that aliens not being parties to the Constitution, the rights and privileges which it secures cannot be at all claimed by them.

To this reasoning, also, it might be answered that, although aliens are not parties to the Constitution, it does not follow that the Constitution has vested in Congress an absolute power over them. The parties to the Constitution may have granted, or retained, or modified, the power over aliens, without regard to that particular consideration.

But a more direct reply is, that it does not follow, because aliens are not parties to the Constitution, as citizens are parties to it, that, whilst they actually conform to it, they have no right to its protection. Aliens are not more parties to the laws than they are parties to the Constitution; yet it will not be disputed that, as they owe, on one hand, a temporary obedience, they are entitled, in return, to their protection and advantage.

If aliens had no rights under the Constitution, they might not only be banished, but even capitally punished, without a jury or the other incidents to a fair trial. But so far has a contrary principle been carried, in every part of the United States, that, except on charges of treason, an alien has, besides all the common privileges, the special one of being tried by a jury, of which one-half may be also aliens.

It is said further, that, by the law and practice of nations, aliens may be removed, at discretion, for offences against the law of nations; that Congress are authorized to define and punish such offences; and that to be dangerous to the peace of society is, in aliens, one of those offences.

The distinction between alien enemies and alien friends is a clear and conclusive answer to this argument. Alien enemies are under the law of nations, and liable to be punished for offences against it. Alien friends, except in the single case of public ministers, are under the municipal law, and must be tried and punished according to that law only.

This argument also, by referring the alien act to the power of Congress to define and *punish* offences against the law of nations, yields the point that the act is of a *penal*, not merely of a preventive operation. It must, in truth, be so considered. And if it be a penal act, the punishment it inflicts must be justified by some offence that deserves it.

Know-Nothing Party,
"America For Americans" and
"The Silent Scourge" (1855)

Editor's Introduction: Immigration to the United States rose exponentially from 1830 or so up to the Civil War. In this thirty-year period more than five million immigrants, mostly Irish and Germans, arrived in this country. Of this number, more than two million were Roman Catholics. To put this in context, the entire United States population in 1860 was roughly 31 million. In the 1850s a number of nativist (i.e., antiforeign) organizations emerged, the most influential being the "Know-Nothings." Members of this society were pledged to secrecy. This gave rise to its name, as when asked about it, a member's pat reply was, "I know nothing." The Know-Nothings opposed immigration and were profoundly anti-Catholic. They saw themselves as upholders of Protestantism and also as protecting jobs for native-born workers. They eventually became a political party and ran a candidate, ex-President Millard Fillmore, for President in 1856. He carried only one state. The Know-Nothing Party disintegrated with the onset of the Civil War, though the nativist strain they represent has never entirely disappeared from American life.

*   *   *

AMERICA FOR AMERICANS
FROM THE NEW YORK MIRROR

Well, why not? Is there another country under the sun, that does not belong to its own, native-born people? Is there another country where the alien by birth, and often by openly boasted sympathy, is permitted to fill the most responsible offices, and preside over the most sacred trusts of the land? Is there another country that would place its secret archives and its diplomacy with foreign states, in other than native hands—with tried and trusty native hearts to back them? Is there another country that would even permit the foreigner to become a citizen, shielded by its laws and its flag, on terms such as we exact, leaving the political franchise out of sight? More than all else, is there a country, other than ours, that would acknowledge as a citizen, a patriot, a republican, or a safe man, one who stood bound by a religious oath or obligation, in political conflict with,

---

Source: *The Wide-Awake Gift: Know-Nothing Token for 1855.* Edited by "One of 'Em" (New York: J. C. Derby, 1855).

and which he deemed temporarily higher than, the Constitution and Civil Government of that country—to which he also professes to swear fealty?

America for the Americans, we say. And why not? Didn't they plant it, and battle for it through bloody revolution—and haven't they developed it, as only Americans could, into a nation of a century, and yet mightier than the oldest empire on earth? Why shouldn't they shape and rule the destinies of their own land—the land of their birth, their love, their altars, and their graves; the land red and rich with the blood and ashes, and hallowed by the memories of their fathers? Why not rule their own, particularly when the alien betrays the trust that should never have been given him, and the liberties of the land are thereby imperilled?

Lacks the American numbers, that he may not rule by the right of majority, to which is constitutionally given the political sovereignty of this land? Did he not, at the last numbering of the people, count seventeen and a half millions, native to the soil, against less than two and half millions of actually foreign born, and those born of foreigners coming among us for the last three quarters of a century? Has he not tried the mixed rule, with a tolerance unexampled, until it had plagued him worse than the lice and locust plagued the Egyptian? Has he not shared the trust of office and council, until foreign-born pauperism, vice and crime, stain the whole land—until a sheltered alien fraction have become rampant in their ingratitude and insolence? Has he not suffered burdens of tax, and reproach, and shame, by his ill-bestowed division of political power?

America for the Americans! That is the watchword that should ring through the length and breadth of the land, from the lips of the whole people. America for the Americans—to shape and to govern; to make great, and to keep great, strong and free, from home foes and foreign demagogues and hierarchs. In the hour of Revolutionary peril, Washington said, "Put none but Americans on guard to-night." At a later time, Jefferson wished "an ocean of fire rolled between the Old World and the New." To their children, the American people, the fathers and builders of the Republic, bequeathed it. "Eternal vigilance is the price of liberty!"— let the American be vigilant that the alien seize not his birth right.

America for the Americans! Shelter and welcome let them give to the emigrant and the exile, and make them citizens in so far as civil privileges are concerned. But let it be looked to that paupers and criminals are no longer shipped on us by foreign states. Let it be looked to that foreign nationalities in our midst are rooted out; that foreign regiments and battalions are disarmed; that the public laws and schools of the country are printed and taught in the language of the land; that no more charters for foreign titled or foreign charactered associations—benevolent, social or other—are granted by our Legislatures; that all National and State support given to Education, have not the shadow of sectarianism about it. There is work for Americans to do. They have slept on guard—if, indeed, they have been on guard—and the enemy have grown strong and riotous in their midst.

America for the Americans! We have had enough of "Young Irelands," "Young Germanys," and "Young Italys." We have had enough of insolent alien threat to suppress our "Puritan Sabbath," and amend our Constitution. We have been a patient camel, and borne foreign burden even to the back-breaking pound. But the time is come to right the wrong; the occasion is ripe for reform in whatever we have failed. The politico-religious foe is fully discovered—he must be squarely met, and put down. We want in this free land none of his political dictation. We want none of his religious mummeries—let him keep his "holy shirt of Treves," his "winking (pictorial) damsel of Rimini," his "toe-nails of the Apostle Peter," and his travail about the "Immaculacy of the Virgin Mary," in those lands that have been desolated with persecution, and repeopled with serfs and lazzaroni by the hierarchy to which he owes supreme religious and temporal obedience. Our feeling is earnest, not bitter. The matters of which we have written are great and grave ones, and we shall not be silent until we have aided in wholly securing *America for the Americans*!

THE SILENT SCOURGE

Never was the near future of political parties in this country so seething with anxious hopes, and doubts, and fears; never so pregnant with inexplicable terrors to time-servers and place-men; never so ominous to demagogues and hucksters in the field of politics as now. From the tap-room to the Senate Chamber, wherever party organization has heretofore stalked, confident and defiant—wherever the edict of the bully-governed caucus has decided nominations and appointments, and ruled with a rude, yet iron hand, the rank and file of the people—led like sheep to the slaughter—at the ballot-box, all is dismay and trembling. The mouthing impudence, so brazen and brow-beating until now, is as suddenly hushed as though the finger of death was on its lips; no grim skeleton ever brought such stillness to an Egyptian feast. All ears are open to hear, all eyes are staring to see, and all tongues are questioning the course of the silent scourge that has risen up in the land, invisible and secret as sleeping lightning, to rebuke and punish the traders and traitors who have so long corrupted the national franchise, and brought the country to shame—and nigh to ruin.

Who is it—what is it—where is it—this scourge, so potent and purifying? Who conceived it—who evoked it—and how and where is it to end, if, indeed, it end at all? Mighty and mysterious scourge! preceded by no rumbling, yet it stirs all the land, bursting like a sudden earthquake wherever its fires are called to purge Freedom's palladium, and make the ballot what the framers of the Republic intended,

-*"A weapon surer, yet,*
And mightier than the bayonet;
A weapon, that comes down as still
As snow flakes fall upon the sod,
And executes a freeman's will,
As lightnings do the will of God!"

East and West, and North and South—in the chief marts and capitals of the Union, its stroke has fallen swift and sure, and politicians and parties, stripped of every gauge of accustomed calculation, have only been aware of its presence when they saw their petted candidates and schemes rolling headlong in the ditch of overwhelming defeat. New Orleans, long at the mercy of insolent, foreign-born brawlers, bears witness! So does Washington, as it will, despite the executive guillotine that flashed its knife madly and in vain. So do St. Louis—where the Germans boasted that the American should be put down—and Philadelphia—desecrated too long by foreign-born mobs—and Mobile, and Norfolk, and many a lesser place we might name. And so, by-and-by, in our own city and State, this silent scourge will fall, and many a demagogue's back will writhe under the biting blow, and all true men will gladly confess that this is yet an American land, and that Americans can and will rule it, as they ought ever to have done.

And far wider than municipalities and States, the blow will be struck all over the Union, and the next occupant of the White House chair will owe his elevation—of which he must be worthy—to invisible hands. Even now, while no man can say of it more than is said of the wind, "It goeth and cometh as it listeth," there is fright and confusion in every political camp. The master demagogues, the whippers-in, the men who have been the leaders, the Sampsons of their hosts, grope stone-blind in the midst of their temples, waiting to be buried when the pillars shall be shaken by the coming scourge. The tricky place-men feel their doom at hand. They would trade to avert it, but they idly beat the air in their search for the angel of the scourge. Here he is, and there he is, they cry—but they find him not. One says the scourge is against that party, and another that it is against this; yet the only thing men know is this:—that it is against all men, and all parties, who have been false, or are likely—having the power—to be false to this Union, this American Republic.

If any party may seem—as one perhaps does—to have most severely felt the scourge, it is because that party has most betrayed and trampled on the principles that should accompany its sacred name; because its possession of that name—a pretentious cheat—has most enabled it to barter the officers and interests of the land to a foreign horde. No other party could have so sold a country, and raised up in its midst a sedition against its most cherished institutions and ideas—nor can this one do it longer, nor could it have done it, but for delusive name, and the easy temper until thoroughly aroused, of the American people. The game is now up! Neither coaxing nor threatening can stay the impending blow that is to punish the shameless traders and traitors, native or foreign, until every citizen shall be glad and proud to say, "I too am an American."

The secret forces that wield the silent scourge, clearly understand their work. They aim at the right mark. They strike no indiscriminate blows, but smite the jockeys who have curried the foreign horses (worse than the fabled Greek), who have seduced and misled the people, and for a time have played their game of place and plunder without check. These are the heads to lop off, be they little or big, be they representatives or executives. Its silence preserved, a party organization avoided, and eternal vigilance—the price of liberty—written on its front, and all men will yet bless this scourge. It will purify the land. It will bury all young or old foreignalities, and, placing the destinies of the country in American hands, at home and abroad, will make the name of American Republic honored and respected throughout the world—which is not the case now. We warn nobody, for we know nothing more than is open and visible, to all who choose to see. But we reckon a warning is felt, and that it has struck deep in the right quarter, and will strike deeper, until the joints of political schemers are made to rattle louder than did ever the "dry bones" in the valley. All we have to say is God speed the silent scourge, until its bravely begun work is triumphantly done!

Theodore Roosevelt,
"True Americanism" (1897)

Editor's Introduction: Theodore Roosevelt (1858–1919) became the 26th President of the United States after the assassination of William McKinley in 1901 and held that office until 1909. TR was a man of enormous energies and is known for using the presidency as a "bully pulpit," i.e., a vehicle to mold public opinion. Among his accomplishments as President were the building of the Panama Canal, curbing trusts (i.e., monopolistic corporations), and conservation efforts such as establishing many national parks.

In 1908, Israel Zangwill wrote "The Melting Pot," a drama that was performed throughout the country and became famous for promoting the idea that immigrants should assimilate by abandoning their prior ethnic and cultural identities. Zangwill dedicated this play to Theodore Roosevelt because of the latter's firm belief in the ideas the metaphor of the melting pot represented. Roosevelt does not support "hyphenated Americanism," or the legacy of continuing one's ethnic customs and traditions in the new land of America. For Roosevelt, all must achieve a singular loyalty to the language, customs, and political institutions of the United States. "Either a man is an American and nothing else," Roosevelt wrote, "or he is not an American at all." Roosevelt took a stand against extreme nativist organizations and attempted to assure the population that Jews, Catholics, and the Irish could be "true Americans" by including them in government. However, his ideas about assimilation were limited to white immigrants. He believed that the racial difference between whites and nonwhites made the assimilation of blacks and Asians virtually impossible and thereby threatened the unity of the United States.

Roosevelt's book, *True Americanism*, appeared in 1897 while the country was mired in one of the deepest economic depressions in its history. At the same time, millions of "new immigrants" were coming to America, mostly from southern and eastern Europe (some fourteen million immigrants arrived between 1890 and 1910). These immigrants were seen by many Americans (including many who had just immigrated to the United States a generation before), as threats to jobs and also as insular minorities who settled in city ghettoes and failed to adopt the language and culture of the United States. The following selection is best read in

---

Source: Theodore Roosevelt, *True Americanism* (New York : G. P. Putnam's Sons, The Knickerbocker Press, 1897)

conjunction with the pieces by Horace Kallen and John Dewey in this volume, both of whom offer a "multicultural" critique of Roosevelt's position.

*   *   *

We Americans have many grave problems to solve, many threatening evils to fight, and many deeds to do, if, as we hope and believe, we have the wisdom, the strength, the courage, and the virtue to do them. But we must face facts as they are. We must neither surrender ourselves to a foolish optimism, nor succumb to a timid and ignoble pessimism. Our nation is that one among all the nations of the earth which holds in its hands the fate of the coming years. We enjoy exceptional advantages, and are menaced by exceptional dangers; and all signs indicate that we shall either fail greatly or succeed greatly. I firmly believe that we shall succeed; but we must not foolishly blink the dangers by which we are threatened, for that is the way to fail. On the contrary, we must soberly set to work to find out all we can about the existence and extent of every evil, must acknowledge it to be such, and must then attack it with unyielding resolution. There are many such evils, and each must be fought after a separate fashion; yet there is one quality which we must bring to the solution of every problem,—that is, an intense and fervid Americanism. We shall never be successful over the dangers that confront us; we shall never achieve true greatness, nor reach the lofty ideal which the founders and preservers of our mighty Federal Republic have set before us, unless we are Americans in heart and soul, in spirit and purpose, keenly alive to the responsibility implied in the very name of American, and proud beyond measure of the glorious privilege of bearing it.

[Text omitted]

The mighty tide of immigration to our shore has brought in its train much of good and much of evil; and whether the good or the evil shall predominate depends mainly on whether these newcomers do or do not throw themselves heartily into our national life, cease to be European, and become Americans like the rest of us. More than a third of the people of the Northern States are of foreign birth or parentage. An immense number of them have become completely Americanized, and these stand on exactly the same plane as the descendants of any Puritan, Cavalier, or Knickerbocker among us, and do their full and honorable share of the nation's work. But where immigrants or the sons of immigrants, do not heartily and in good faith throw in their lot with us, but cling to the speech, the customs, the ways of life, and the habits of thought of the Old World which they have left, they thereby harm both themselves and us. If they remain alien elements, unassimilated, and with interests separate from ours, they are mere obstructions to the current of our national life, and, moreover, can get no good from it themselves. In fact, though we ourselves also suffer from their perversity, it is they who really suffer most. It is an immense benefit to the European immigrant to change him into an American citizen. To bear the name of American is to bear the most honorable of titles; and whoever does not so believe has no business to bear the name at all, and, if he comes from Europe, the sooner he goes back there the better. Besides, the man who does not become Americanized nevertheless fails to remain a European, and becomes nothing at all. The immigrant cannot possibly remain what he was, or continue to be a member of the Old-World society. If he tries to retain his old language, in a few generations it becomes a barbarous jargon; if he tries to retain his old customs and ways of life, in a few generations he becomes an uncouth boor. He has cut himself off from the Old World, and cannot retain his connections with it; and if he wishes ever to amount to anything he must throw himself heart and soul, and without reservation, into the new life to which he has come. It is urgently necessary to check and regulate our immigration by much more drastic laws than now exist; and this should be done both to keep out laborers who tend to depress the labor market, and to keep out races which do not assimilate readily with our own, and unworthy individuals of all races—not only criminals, idiots, and paupers, but anarchists of the Most and O'Donovan Rossa type.

From his own standpoint, it is beyond all question the wise thing for the immigrant to become thoroughly Americanized. Moreover, from our standpoint, we have a right to demand it. We freely extend the hand of welcome and of good-fellowship to every man, no matter what his creed or birthplace, who comes here honestly intent on becoming a good United States citizen like the rest of us; but we have a right and it is our duty to demand that he shall indeed become so, and shall not confuse the issues with which we are struggling by introducing among us Old-World quarrels and prejudices. There are certain ideas which he must give up. For instance, he must learn that American life is incompatible with the existence of any form of anarchy, or of any secret society having murder for its aim, whether at home or abroad; and he must learn that we exact full religious toleration and the complete separation of Church and State. Moreover, he must not bring in his Old-World religious race and national antipathies, but must merge them into love for our common country, and must take pride in the things which we can all take pride in. He must revere . . . but no other flag should even come second. He must learn to celebrate Washington's birthday rather than that of the Queen or Kaiser, and the Fourth of July instead of St. Patrick's Day. Our political and social questions must be settled on their own merits, and not complicated by quarrels between England and Ireland, or France and Germany, with which we have nothing to do; it is an outrage to fight an American political campaign with reference to questions of European politics. Above all, the immigrant must learn to talk and think and *be* United States.

Horace M. Kallen,
"Democracy Versus the Melting-Pot:
A Study of American Nationality" (1915)

Editor's Introduction: Horace Kallen (1882–1974) emigrated to the United States from Berenstadt, Germany (now Poland) at an early age. Kallen's father became the rabbi for a Boston congregation and was stern in raising his children. As a young man at Harvard University intrigued with American philosophy and psychology, Kallen became disillusioned with his Jewish heritage. Years later, Kallen would reclaim his Jewishness, but in a cultural and secular form.

The following selection was written during a tumultuous period when Kallen was a Professor of Psychology and Philosophy at the University of Wisconsin, a position he resigned in 1918 over issues of academic freedom. In 1919, Kallen became one of the founding scholars at the New School for Social Research in New York, which offered an environment encouraging to his ideas as well as to friendships with leading liberal intellectuals such as John Dewey.

Horace Kallen is known today as one of the first great defenders of the idea of cultural pluralism in the American context. Kallen's first articulation of this notion is found in the following piece. However, he continued to refine his ideas on this issue for many years. For Kallen, individuals become richer and fuller people by interacting with others who maintain differing cultural identities. Kallen's ideas are essentially liberal in that he thinks governments role should be to foster a climate of tolerance and mutual respect within which cultural identities emerge and are expressed. For these reasons, Kallen takes issue with the notion of the melting-pot and thereby with assimilation practices that attempt to devalue the ethnic differences of a pluralistic citizenry and mold them into one preferred identity.

*   *   *

It was, I think, an eminent lawyer who, backed by a ripe experience of inequalities before the law, pronounced the American Declaration of Independence to be a collection of "glittering generalities." Yet it cannot be that the implied slur was deserved. There is hardly room to doubt that the equally eminent gentlemen over whose signatures this orotund synthesis of the social and political philosophy of the eighteenth century

Source: *The Nation,* Vol. 100, Nos. 2590 and 2591 (1915).

appears conceived that they were subscribing to anything but the dull and sober truth when they underwrote the doctrine that God had created all men equal and had endowed them with certain inalienable rights, among these being life, liberty, and the pursuit of happiness. That this doctrine did not describe a condition, that it even contradicted conditions, that many of the signatories owned other men and bought and sold them, that many were eminent by birth, many by wealth, and only a few by merit—all this is acknowledged. Indeed, they were aware of these inequalities; they would probably have fought against their abolition. But they did not regard them as incompatible with the Declaration of Independence. For to them the Declaration was neither a pronouncement of abstract principles nor an exercise in formal logic. It was an instrument in a political and economic conflict, a weapon of offence and defence. The doctrine of "natural rights" which is its essence was formulated to shield social orders against the aggrandizement of persons acting under the doctrine of "divine right": its function was to afford sanction for refusing customary obedience to traditional superiority. Such also was the function of the Declaration. Across the water, in England, certain powers had laid claim to the acknowledgment of their traditional superiority to the colonists in America. Whereupon the colonists, through their representatives, the signatories to the Declaration, replied that they were quite as good as their traditional betters, and that no one should take from them certain possessions which were theirs.

To-day the descendants of the colonists are reformulating a declaration of independence. Again, as in 1776, Americans of British ancestry find that certain possessions of theirs which may be lumped under the word "Americanism," are in jeopardy. The danger comes once more, from a force across the water, but the force is this time regarded not as superior, but as inferior. The relationships of 1776 are, consequently, reversed. To conserve the inalienable rights of the colonists of 1776, it was necessary to declare all men equal; to conserve the inalienable rights of their descendants in 1914, it becomes necessary to declare all men unequal. In 1776 all men were as good as their betters; in 1914 men are permanently worse than their betters. "A nation may reason," writes Mr. Ross, "why burden ourselves with the rearing of children? Let them perish unborn in the womb of time. The immigrants will keep up the population. A people that has no more respect for its ancestors and no more pride of race than this deserves the extinction that surely awaits it."

Respect for ancestors, pride of race! Time was when these would have been repudiated as the enemies of democracy, as the antithesis of the fundamentals of our republic, with its belief that "a man's a man for a'that." And now they are being invoked in defence of democracy, against the "melting-pot." . . . How conscious their invocation is cannot be said.

But that they have unconsciously colored much of the social and political thinking of this country from the days of the Cincinnati on, seems to me unquestionable, and even more unquestionable that this apparently sudden and explicit conscious expression of them is the effect of an actual, felt menace. . . .

In 1776 the mass of white men in the colonies *were* actually, with respect to one another, rather free and rather equal. I refer, not so much to the absence of great differences in wealth, as to the fact that the whites were *like-minded*. They were possessed of ethnic and cultural unity; they were homogeneous with respect to ancestry and ideals. Their century-and-a-half-old tradition as Americans was continuous with their immemorially older tradition as Britons. They did not, until the economic-political quarrel with the mother country arose, regard themselves as other than Englishmen, sharing England's dangers and England's glories. When the quarrel came they remembered how they had left the mother country in search of religious liberty for themselves; how they had left Holland, where they had found this liberty, for fear of losing their ethnic and cultural identity, and what hardships they had borne for the sake of conserving both the liberty and the identity. Upon these they grafted that political liberty the love of which was innate, perhaps, but the expression of which was occasioned by the economic warfare with the merchants of England. This grafting was not, of course, conscious. The continuity established itself rather as a mood than as an articulate idea. The economic situation *was* only an occasion, and not a cause. The cause lay in the homogeneity of the people, their *like-mindedness*, and in their *self-consciousness*.

[Text omitted]

In the course of time the state, which began to be with the Declaration of Independence, became possessed of all the United States. French and Germans in Louisiana and Pennsylvania remained at home; but the descendants of the British colonists trekked across the continent, leaving tiny self-conscious nuclei of population in their wake, and so established ethnic and cultural standards for the whole country. Had the increase of these settlements borne the same proportion to the unit of population that it bore between 1810 and 1820, the Americans of British stock would have numbered today over 100,000,000. The inhabitants of the country do number over 100,000,000; but they are not the children of the colonists and pioneers: they are immigrants and the children of immigrants, and they are not British, but of all the other European stocks.

[Text omitted]

In sum, [W]hen we consider that portion of our population, which has taken root, we see that it has not stippled the country in small units of diverse ethnic groups. It forms rather a series of stripes or layers of varying sizes, moving east to west along the central axis of settlement, where towns are thickest; *i.e.*, from New York and Philadelphia, through Chicago and St. Louis, to San Francisco and Seattle. Stippling is absent even in the towns, where the variety of population is generally greater. Probably 90 per cent of that population is either foreign-born or of foreign stock; yet even so, the towns are aggregations, not units. Broadly divided into the sections inhabited by the rich and those inhabited by the poor, this economic division does not abolish, it only crosses, the ethnic one. There are rich and poor little Italys, Irelands, Hungarys, Germanys, and rich and poor Ghettoes. The *common* city life, which depends upon like-mindedness, is not inward, corporate, and inevitable, but external, inarticulate, and incidental, a reaction to the need of amusement and the need of protection, not the expression of a unity of heritage, mentality, and interest. Politics and education in our cities thus present the phenomenon of ethnic compromises not unknown in Austria-Hungary; concessions and appeals to "the Irish vote," "the Jewish vote," "the German vote"; compromise school committees where members represent each ethnic faction, until, as in Boston, one group grows strong enough to dominate the entire situation.

[Text omitted]

All the immigrants and their offspring are in the way of becoming "Americanized," if they remain in one place in the country long enough— say, six or seven years. The general notion, "Americanization," appears to denote the adoption of English speech, of American clothes and manners, of the American attitude in politics. It connotes the fusion of the various bloods, and a transmutation by "the miracle of assimilation": of Jews, Slavs, Poles, Frenchmen, Germans, Hindus, Scandinavians, into beings similar in background, tradition, outlook, and spirit to the descendants of the British colonists, the Anglo-Saxon stock. Broadly speaking, the elements of Americanism are somewhat external, the effect of environment; largely internal, the effect of heredity.

[Text omitted]

The array of forces for and against that like-mindedness which is the stuff and essence of nationality aligns itself as follows: For it make social imitation of the upper by the lower classes, the facility of communications, the national pastimes of baseball and motion-picture, the mobility of population, the cheapness of printing, and the public schools. Against it make the primary ethnic differences with which the population starts its stratification over an enormous extent of country, its industrial and economic stratification. We are an English-speaking country, but in no intimate and inevitable way, as in New Zealand or Australia, or even Canada. English is to us what Latin was to the Roman provinces and to the middle ages—the language of the upper and dominant class, the vehicle and symbol of culture: for the mass of our population it is a sort of Esperanto or Ido, a *lingua franca* necessary less in the spiritual than the economic contacts of the daily life. This mass is composed of elementals, peasant . . . —the proletarian foundation material of all forms of civilization. Their self-consciousness as groups is comparatively weak. This is a factor which favors their "assimilation," for the more cultivated a group is, the more it is aware of its individuality, and the less willing it is to surrender that individuality.

[Text omitted]

. . . This *natio*, reaching consciousness first in a reaction against America, then as an effect of the competition with Americanization, assumes spiritual forms other than religious: the parochial school, to hold its own with the public school, gets secularized while remaining national. *Natio* is what underlies the vehemence of the "Americanized" and the spiritual and political unrest of the Americans. It is the fundamental fact of American life to-day, and in light of it Mr. Wilson's resentment of the "hyphenated" American is both righteous and pathetic. But a hyphen attaches, in things of the spirit, also to the "pure" English American. His cultural mastery tends to be retrospective rather than prospective. At the present time there is no dominant American mind. Our spirit is inarticulate, not a voice, but a chorus of many voices each singing a rather different tune. How to get order out of this cacophony is the question for all those who are concerned about those things which alone justify wealth and power, concerned about justice, the arts, literature, philosophy, science. What must, what *shall* this cacophony become—a unison or a harmony?

[Text omitted]

Immigrants appear to pass through four phases in the course of being Americanized. In the first phase they exhibit economic eagerness, the greed of the unfed. Since external differences are a handicap in the economic struggle, they "assimilate," seeking thus to facilitate the attainment of economic independence. Once the proletarian level of such independence is reached, the process of assimilation slows down and tends to come to a stop. The immigrant group is still a national group, modified, sometimes improved, by environmental influences, but otherwise a solitary spiritual unit, which is seeking to find its way out on its own social level. This search brings to light permanent group distinctions, and the immigrant, like the Anglo-Saxon American, is thrown back upon himself and his ancestry. Then a process of dissimilation begins. The arts, life, and ideals of the nationality become central and paramount; ethnic and national differences change in status from disadvantages to distinctions. All the while the immigrant has been using the English language and behaving like an American in matters economic and political, and continues to do so. The institutions of the Republic have become the liberating cause and the background for the rise of the cultural consciousness and social autonomy of the immigrant Irishman, German, Scandinavian, Jew, Pole, or Bohemian. On the whole, Americanization has not represented nationality. Americanization has liberated nationality.

Hence, what troubles ... many ... Anglo-Saxon Americans is not really inequality; what troubles them is *difference.* Only things that are alike in fact and not abstractly, and only men that are alike in origin and in spirit and not abstractly, can be truly "equal" and maintain that inward unanimity of action and outlook which make a national life. The writers of the Declaration of Independence and of the Constitution were not confronted by the practical fact of ethnic dissimilarity among the whites of the country. Their descendants are confronted by it. Its existence, acceptance, and development provide one of the inevitable consequences of the democratic principle on which our theory of government is based, and the result at the present writing is to many worthies very unpleasant. Democratism and the Federal principle have worked together with economic greed and ethnic snobbishness to people the land with all the nationalities of Europe, and to convert the early American nation into the present American state. For in effect we are in the process of becoming a true federal state, such a state as men hope for as the outcome of the European war, a great republic consisting of a federation or commonwealth of nationalities.

[Text omitted]

The problems which these conditions give rise to are important, but not primarily important. Although they have occupied the minds of all our political theorists, they are problems of means, of instruments, not of ends. They concern the conditions of life, not the *kind of life,* and there appears to have been a general assumption that only one kind of human life is possible in America. But the same democracy which underlies the evils of the economic order underlies also the evils—and the promise— of the ethnic order. Because no individual is merely an individual, the political autonomy of the individual has meant and is beginning to realize in these United States the spiritual autonomy of his group. The process is as yet far from fruition. We are, in fact, at the parting of the ways. A genuine social alternative is before us, either of which parts we may realize if we will. In social construction the will is farther to the fact, for the fact is nothing more than the concord or conflict of wills. What do we *will* to make of the United States—a unison, singing the old Anglo-Saxon theme "America," the America of the New England school, or a harmony, in which that theme shall be dominant, perhaps, among others, but one among many, not the only one?

The mind reverts helplessly to the historic attempts at unison in Europe—the heroic failure of the pan-Hellenists, of the Romans, the disintegration and the diversification of the Christian Church, for a time the most successful unison in history; the present-day failures of Germany and of Russia. Here, however, the whole social situation is favorable, as it has never been at any time elsewhere—everything is favorable but the basic law of America itself, and the spirit of American institutions. To achieve unison—it can be achieved—would be to violate these. For the end determines the means, and this end would involve no other means than those used by Germany in Poland, in Schleswig-Holstein, and Alsace-Lorraine; by Russia in the Pale, in Poland, in Finland. Fundamentally it would require the complete nationalization of education, the abolition of every form of parochial and private school, the abolition of instruction in other tongues than English, and the concentration of the teaching of history and literature upon the English tradition. The other institutions of society would require treatment analogous to that administered by Germany to her European acquisitions. And all of this, even if meeting with no resistance, would not completely guarantee the survival as a unison of the older Americanism. For the programme would be applied to diverse ethnic types, and the reconstruction that, with the best will, they might spontaneously make of the tradition would more likely than not be a far cry from the original. It is, already.

[Text omitted]

The attainment of the other alternative, a harmony, also requires concerted public action. But the action would do no violence to our fundamental law and the spirit of our institutions, nor to the qualities of men. It would seek simply to eliminate the waste and the stupidity of our social organization, by way of freeing and strengthening the strong forces actually in operation. Starting with our existing ethnic and cultural groups, it would seek to provide conditions under which each may attain the perfection that is proper to its kind. The provision of such conditions is the primary intent of our fundamental law and the function of our institutions. And the various nationalities which compose our commonwealth must learn first of all this fact, which is perhaps, to most minds, the outstanding ideal content of "Americanism"—that democracy means self-realization through self-control, self-government, and that one is impossible without the other. . . .

[Text omitted]

Government, the state, under democratic conception, is merely an instrument, not an end. That it is often an abused instrument, that it is often seized by the powers that prey, that it makes frequent mistakes and considers only secondary ends, surface needs, which vary from moment to moment, is, of course, obvious; hence our social and political chaos. But that it is an instrument, flexibly adjustable to changing life, changing opinion, and needs, our whole electoral organization and party system declare. And as intelligence and wisdom prevail over "politics" and special interests, as the steady and continuous pressure of the inalienable qualities and purposes of human groups more and more dominate the confusion of our common life, the outlines of a possible great and truly democratic commonwealth become discernible.

Its form is that of the Federal republic; its substance a democracy of nationalities, cooperating voluntarily and autonomously in the enterprise of self-realization through the perfection of men according to their kind. The common language of the commonwealth, the language of its great political tradition, is English, but each nationality expresses its emotional and voluntary life in its own language, it is own inevitable aesthetic and intellectual forms. The common life of the commonwealth is politico-economic, and serves as the foundation and background for the realization of the distinctive individuality of each *natio* that composes it. Thus "American civilization" may come to mean the perfection of the cooperative harmonies of "European civilization," the waste, the squalor, and the distress of Europe being eliminated—a multiplicity in a unity, an orchestration of mankind. As in an orchestra, every type of instrument has its specific timbre and tonality, founded in its substance and form; as every type has its appropriate theme and melody in the whole symphony, so in society each ethnic group is the natural instrument, its spirit and culture are its theme and melody, and the harmony and dissonances and discords of them all make the symphony of civilization, with this difference: a musical symphony is written before it is played; in the symphony of civilization the playing is the writing, so that there is nothing so fixed and inevitable about its progressions as in music, so that within the limits set by nature they may vary at will, and the range and variety of the harmonies may become wider and richer and more beautiful.

But the question is, do the dominant classes in America want such a society?

John Dewey,
"Nationalizing Education," Address to the
National Education Association (1916)

Editor's Introduction: John Dewey (1859–1952), philosopher, psychologist, and educator, is one of the most influential American intellectuals of the twentieth century. Dewey was a follower of the most distinctly American school of philosophy, formulated by William James and C. S. Peirce and known as *pragmatism*. Dewey's greatest influence was in the field of education. He provided the philosophical groundwork for what became known as "progressive education," the goal of which was to involve the students more actively in the learning process. In one of his most important works, *Democracy and Education,* Dewey makes his case for infusing all aspects of the learning process with democratic values so that schools become a training ground for democratic citizenship. In the following speech to the National Education Association, Dewey addresses education in a multicultural society. He is concerned about the emergence of a jingoistic nationalism on the eve of the United States' entry into World War I and asks us to recognize the value of cultural pluralism. In doing so, he suggests that we can cultivate a positive, inclusive nationalism that recognizes the contributions of diverse ethnic groups to a distinctive American identity.

*   *   *

The words "nation" and "national" have two quite different meanings. We cannot profitably discuss the nationalizing of education unless we are clear as to the difference between the two. For one meaning indicates something desirable, something to be cultivated by education, while the other stands for something to be avoided as an evil plague. The idea which has given the movement toward nationality which has been such a feature of the last century its social vitality, is the consciousness of a community of history and purpose larger than that of the family, the parish, the sect, and the province. The upbuilding of national states has substituted a unity of feeling and aim, a freedom of intercourse, over wide areas, for earlier local isolations, suspicions, jealousies, and hatreds. It has forst men out of narrow sectionalisms into membership in a larger social unit, and created loyalty to a state which subordinates petty and selfish interests.

Source: National Education Association, Secretary's Office, Ann Arbor, MI, (1916).

One cannot say this, however, without being at once reminded that nationalism has had another side. With the possible exception of our own country, the national states of the modern world have been built up thru conflict. The development of a sense of unity within a charmed area has been accompanied by dislike, by hostility, to all without. Skilful politicians and other self-seekers have always known how to play cleverly upon patriotism and upon ignorance of other peoples, to identify nationalism with latent hatred of other nations. Without exaggeration, the present world-war may be the outcome of this aspect of nationalism, and to present it in its naked unloveliness.

In the past our geographical isolation has largely protected us from the harsh, selfish, and exclusive aspect of nationalism. The absence of pressure from without, the absence of active and urgent rivalry and hostility of powerful neighbors, has perhaps played a part in the failure to develop an adequate unity of sentiment and idea for the country as whole. Individualism of a go-as-you-please type has had too full swing. We have an inherited jealousy of any strong national governing agencies, and we have been inclined to let things drift rather than to think out a central, controlling policy. But the effect of the war has been to make us aware that the days of geographical isolation are at an end, and also to make us conscious that we are lacking in an integrated social sense and policy for our country as a whole, irrespective of classes and sections.

We are now faced by the difficulty of developing the good aspect of nationalism without its evil side—of developing a nationalism which is the friend and not the foe of internationalism. Since this is a matter of ideas, of emotions, of intellectual and moral disposition and outlook, it depends for its accomplishment upon educational agencies, not upon outward machinery. Among these educational agencies, the public school takes first rank. When sometime in the remote future the tale is summed up and the public, as distinct from the private and merely personal, achievement of the common school is recorded, the question which will have to be answered is, What has the American public school done toward subordinating a local, provincial, sectarian, and partisan spirit of mind to aims and interests which are common to all the men and women of the country—to what extent has it taught men to think and feel in ideas broad enough to be inclusive of the purposes and happiness of all sections and classes? For unless the agencies which form the mind and morals of the community can prevent the operation of those forces which are always making for a division of interests, class and sectional ideas and feelings will become dominant, and our democracy will fall to pieces.

Unfortunately, at the present time one result of the excitement which the war has produced is that many influential and well-meaning persons attempt to foster the growth of an inclusive nationalism by appeal to our fears, our suspicions, our jealousies, and our latent hatreds. . . . The situation makes it all the more necessary that those concerned with education should withstand popular clamor for a nationalism based upon hysterical excitedness or mechanical drill, or a combination of the two. We must ask what a real nationalism, a real Americanism, is like. For unless we know our own character and purpose, we are not likely to be intelligent in our selection of the means to further them.

I want to mention only two elements in the nationalism which our education should cultivate. The first is that the American nation is itself complex and compound. Strictly speaking, it is inter-racial and international in its make-up. It is composed of a multitude of peoples speaking different tongues, inheriting diverse traditions, cherishing varying ideals of life. This fact is basic to our nationalism as distinct from that of other peoples. Our national motto, "One from Many," cuts deep and extends far. It denotes a fact which doubtless adds to the difficulty of getting a genuine unity. But it also immensely enriches the possibilities of the result to be attained. No matter how loudly any one proclaims his Americanism, if he assumes that any one racial strain, any one component culture, no matter how early settled it was in our territory, or how effective it has proved in its own land, is to furnish a pattern to which all other strains and cultures are to conform, he is a traitor to an American nationalism. Our unity cannot be a homogeneous thing like that of the separate states of Europe from which our population is drawn; it must be a unity created by drawing out and composing into a harmonious whole the best, the most characteristic, which each contributing race and people has to offer.

I find that many who talk the loudest about the need of a supreme and unified Americanism of spirit really mean some special code or tradition to which they happen to be attacht. They have some pet tradition which they would impose upon all. In thus measuring the scope of Americanism by some single element which enters into it they are themselves false to the spirit of America. Neither Englandism nor New-Englandism, neither Puritan nor Cavalier, any more than Teuton or Slav, can do anything but furnish one note in a vast symphony.

The way to deal with hyphenism, in other words, is to welcome it, but to welcome it in the sense of extracting from each people its special good, so that it shall surrender into a common fund of wisdom and experience what it especially has to contribute. All of these surrenders and contributions taken together create the national spirit of America. The dangerous thing is for each factor to isolate itself, to try to live off its past, and then to attempt to impose itself upon other elements, or, at least, to keep itself intact and thus refuse to accept what other cultures have to offer, so as thereby to be transmuted into authentic Americanism.

In what is rightly objected to as hyphenism, the hyphen has become something which separates one people from other peoples, and thereby prevents American nationalism. Such terms as Irish-American or Hebrew-American or German-American are false terms because they seem to assume something which is already in existence called America, to which the other factor may be externally hitcht on. The fact is, the genuine American, the typical American, is himself a hyphenated character. This does not mean that he is part American and that some foreign ingredient is then added. It means that, as I have said, he is international and interracial in his make-up. He is not American plus Pole or German. But the American is himself Pole-German-English-French-Spanish-Italian-Greek-Irish-Scandinavian-Bohemian-Jew- and so on. The point is to see to it that the hyphen connects instead of separates. And this means at least that our public schools shall teach each factor to respect every other, and shall take pains to enlighten all as to the great past contributions of every strain in our composite make-up. I wish our teaching of American history in the schools would take more account of the great waves of migration by which our land for over three centuries has been continuously built up, and made every pupil conscious of the rich breadth of our national make-up. When every pupil recognizes all the factors which have gone into our being, he will continue to prize and reverence that coming from his own past; he will think of it as honored in being simply one factor in forming a whole, nobler and finer than itself.

In short, unless our education is nationalized in a way which recognizes that the peculiarity of our nationalism is its internationalism, we shall breed enmity and division in our frantic efforts to secure unity. The teachers of the country know this fact much better than do many of its politicians. While too often politicians have been fostering a vicious hyphenatedism and nationalism as a bid for votes, teachers have been engaged in transmuting beliefs and feelings once divided and opposed, into a new thing under the sun—a national spirit inclusive not exclusive, friendly not jealous. This they have done by the influence of personal contact, cooperative intercourse, and sharing in common tasks and hopes. The teacher who has been an active agent in furthering the common struggle of native-born, African, Jew, Italian, and perhaps a score of other peoples, to attain emancipation and enlightenment will never become a party to a conception of America as a nation which conceives of its history and its hopes as less broad than those of humanity—let politicians clamor for their own ends as they will.

The other point in the constitution of a genuine American nationalism to which I invite attention is that we have been occupied during the greater part of our history in subduing nature, not one another or other peoples. I once heard two foreign visitors coming from different countries discuss what had been imprest upon them as the chief trait of the American people. One said vigor, youthful and buoyant energy. The other said it was kindness, the disposition to live and let live, the absence of envy at the success of others. I like to think that while both of these ascribed traits have the same cause back of them, the latter statement goes deeper. Not that we have more virtue, native or acquired, than others, but that we have had more room, more opportunity. Consequently, the same conditions which have put a premium upon active and hopeful energy have permitted the kindlier instincts of man to express themselves. The spaciousness of a continent not previously monopolized by man has stimulated vigor and has also diverted activity from the struggle against fellow-man into the struggle against nature. When men make their gains by fighting in common a wilderness, they have not the motive for mutual distrust which comes when they get ahead only by fighting one another. . . .

But with respect to this point as well as with respect to our composite make-up, the situation is changing. We no longer have a large unoccupied continent. Pioneer days are past, and natural resources are possest. There is danger that the same causes which have set the hand of man against the neighbor in other countries will have the same effect here. Instead of sharing in a common fight against nature, we are already starting to fight against one another, class against class, haves against have-nots. The change puts a definite responsibility upon the schools to sustain our true national spirit. The virtues of mutual esteem, of human forbearance, and well-wishing, which in our earlier days were the unconscious products of circumstances, must now be the conscious fruit of an education which forms the deepest springs of character.

Teachers above all others have occasion to be distrest when the earlier idealism of welcome to the opprest is treated as sentimentalism, when sympathy for the unfortunate and those who have not had a fair chance is regarded as a weak indulgence fatal to efficiency. Our traditional disposition in these respects must now become a central motive in public education, not as a matter of condescension or patronizing, but as essential to the maintenance of a truly American spirit. All this puts a responsibility upon the schools which can be met only by widening the scope of educational facilities. The schools have now to make up to the disinherited masses by conscious instruction, by the development of personal power, skill, ability, and initiative, for the loss of external opportunities consequent upon the passing of our pioneer days. Otherwise power is likely to pass more and more into the hands of the wealthy, and we shall end with this same alliance between intellectual and artistic culture and economic power due to riches, which has been the curse of every civilization in the past, and which our fathers in their democratic idealism thought this nation was to put an end to.

Since the idea of the nation is equal opportunity for all, to nationalize education means to use the schools as a means for making this idea effective. There was a time when this could be done more or less well simply by providing schoolhouses, desks, blackboards, and perhaps books. But that day has past. Opportunities can be equalized only as the schools make it their active serious business to enable all alike to become masters of their own industrial fate. That growing movement which is called industrial or vocational education now hangs in the scales. If it is so constructed in practice as to produce merely more competent hands for subordinate clerical and shop positions, if its purpose is shaped to drill boys and girls into certain forms of automatic skill which will make them useful in carrying out the plans of others, it means that, instead of nationalizing education in the spirit of our nation, we have given up the battle and decided to refeudalize education.

[Text omitted]

Just because the circumstances of the war have brought the idea of the nation and the national to the foreground of everyone's thoughts, the most important thing is to bear in mind that there are nations and nations, this kind of nationalism and that. Unless I am mistaken, there are some now using the cry of an American nationalism, of an intensified national patriotism, to further ideas which characterize the European nations, especially those most active in the war, but which are treasonable to the ideal of our nation. Therefore, I have taken this part of your time to remind you of the fact that our nation and democracy are equivalent terms; that our democracy means amity and good will to all humanity (including those beyond our border), and equal opportunity for all within. Since as a nation we are composed of representatives of all nations who have come here to live in peace with one another and to escape the enmities and jealousies which characterize old-world nations, to nationalize our education means to make it an instrument in the active and constant suppression of the war spirit and in the positive cultivation of sentiments of respect and friendship for all men and women, wherever they live. Since our democracy means the substitution of equal opportunity for all for the old-world ideal of unequal opportunity for different classes, and the limitation of the individual by the class to which he belongs, to nationalize our education is to make the public school an energetic and willing instrument in developing initiative, courage, power, and personal ability in each individual. If we can get our education nationalized in spirit in these directions, the nationalizing of the administrative machinery will in the end take care of itself. So I appeal to teachers in the face of every hysterical wave of emotion, and of every subtle appeal of sinister class interest, to remember that they, above all others, are the consecrated servants of the democratic ideas in which alone this country is truly a distinctive nation—ideas of friendly and helpful intercourse between all and the equipment of every individual to serve the community by his own best powers in his own best way.

Korematsu v. United States, 323 U.S. 214 (1944)

Editor's Introduction: Shortly after the attack on Pearl Harbor, President Franklin Delano Roosevelt signed an executive order establishing the authority of the U.S. Army to evacuate Japanese-Americans from a military area which included much of the west coast. Some 110,000 Japanese-Americans were placed in internment camps during the war. Many of them lost their property, as well as having to spend years of their lives behind barbed wire. The order was based on unsubstantiated claims that many Japanese-Americans were aiding the Japanese Empire in preparing for a direct attack on the mainland. Mr. Korematsu, a citizen of Japanese descent whose home was in the excluded area, challenged the constitutionality of the executive order and lost.

Reprinted here are key sections of the majority opinion of the Supreme Court, and of the dissent. In the opinion for the majority, Justice Black is unwilling to intercede in what he sees as a defensible military decision. Justice Murphy's dissent describes the executive order as little more than "legalized racism" and argues that civil liberties cannot be denied constitutionally based on racial identity as opposed to specific findings of individual wrongdoing. His arguments are similar to points Madison makes regarding the treatment of aliens in the Virginia Resolutions, with the important difference that those detained were not aliens but American citizens. In 1988 Congress passed a law promising to pay restitution to former detainees, and roughly one billion dollars has been paid as of 1996.

*   *   *

MR JUSTICE BLACK delivered the opinion of the Court.

The petitioner, an American citizen of Japanese descent, was convicted in a federal district court for remaining in San Leandro, California, a "Military Area," contrary to Civilian Exclusion Order No. 34 of the Commanding General of the Western Command, U.S. Army, which directed that after May 9, 1942, all persons of Japanese ancestry should be excluded from that area. No question was raised as to petitioner's loyalty to the United States. The Circuit Court of Appeals affirmed, and the importance of the constitutional question involved caused us to grant certiorari.

It should be noted, to begin with, that all legal restrictions which curtail the civil rights of a single racial group are immediately suspect. That is not to say that all such restrictions are unconstitutional. It is to say that courts must subject them to the most rigid scrutiny. Pressing public necessity may sometimes justify the existence of such restrictions; racial antagonism never can.

In the instant case prosecution of the petitioner was begun by information charging violation of an Act of Congress, of March 21, 1942, 56 Stat. 173, which provides that "... whoever shall enter, remain in, leave, or commit any act in any military area or military zone prescribed, under the authority of an Executive order of the President, by the Secretary of War, or by any military commander designated by the Secretary of War, contrary to the restrictions applicable to any such area or zone or contrary to the order of the Secretary of War or any such military commander, shall, if it appears that he knew or should have known of the existence and extent of the restrictions or order and that his act was in violation thereof, be guilty of a misdemeanor and upon conviction shall be liable to a fine not to exceed $5,000 or to imprisonment for not more than one year, or both, for each offense."

Exclusion Order No. 34, which the petitioner knowingly and admittedly violated, was one of a number of military orders and proclamations, all of which were substantially based upon Executive Order No. 9066, 7 Fed. Reg. That order, issued after we were at war with Japan, declared that "the successful prosecution of the war requires every possible protection against espionage and against sabotage to national-defense material, national-defense premises, and national-defense utilities. . . ."

One of the series of orders and proclamations, a curfew order, which like the exclusion order here was promulgated pursuant to Executive Order 9066, subjected all persons of Japanese ancestry in prescribed West Coast military areas to remain in their residences from 8 p.m. to 6 a.m. As is the case with the exclusion order here, that prior curfew order was designed as a "protection against espionage and against sabotage." In *Hirabayashi v. United States*, 320 U.S. 81, we sustained a conviction obtained for violation of the curfew order. The *Hirabayashi* conviction and this one thus rest on the same 1942 Congressional Act and the same basic executive and military orders, all of which orders were aimed at the twin dangers of espionage and sabotage.

The 1942 Act was attacked in the *Hirabayashi* case as an unconstitutional delegation of power; it was contended that the curfew order and other orders on which it rested were beyond the war powers of the Congress, the military authorities and of the President, as Commander in Chief of the Army; and finally that to apply the curfew order against none but citizens of Japanese ancestry amounted to a constitutionally prohibited discrimination solely on account of race. To these questions, we gave the serious consideration which their importance justified. We upheld the curfew order as an exercise of the power of the government to take steps necessary to prevent espionage and sabotage in an area threatened by Japanese attack.

In the light of the principles we announced in the *Hirabayashi* case, we are unable to conclude that it was beyond the war power of Congress and the Executive to exclude those of Japanese ancestry from the West Coast war area at the time they did. True, exclusion from the area in which one's home is located is a far greater deprivation than constant confinement to the home from 8 p.m. to 6 a.m. Nothing short of apprehension by the proper military authorities of the gravest imminent danger to the public safety can constitutionally justify either. But exclusion from a threatened area, no less than curfew, has a definite and close relationship to the prevention of espionage and sabotage. The military authorities, charged with the primary responsibility of defending our shores, concluded that curfew provided inadequate protection and ordered exclusion. They did so, as pointed out in our *Hirabayashi* opinion, in accordance with Congressional authority to the military to say who should, and who should not, remain in the threatened areas.

In this case the petitioner challenges the assumptions upon which we rested our conclusions in the *Hirabayashi* case. He also urges that by May 1942, when Order No. 34 was promulgated, all danger of Japanese invasion of the West Coast had disappeared. After careful consideration of these contentions we are compelled to reject them.

Here, as in the *Hirabayashi* case, ". . . we cannot reject as unfounded the judgment of the military authorities and of Congress that there were disloyal members of that population, whose number and strength could not be precisely and quickly ascertained. We cannot say that the war-making branches of the Government did not have ground for believing that in a critical hour such persons could not readily be isolated and separately dealt with, and constituted a menace to the national defense and safety, which demanded that prompt and adequate measures be taken to guard against it."

Like curfew, exclusion of those of Japanese origin was deemed necessary because of the presence of an unascertained number of disloyal members of the group, most of whom we have no doubt were loyal to this country. It was because we could not reject the finding of the military authorities that it was impossible to bring about an immediate segregation of the disloyal from the loyal that we sustained the validity of the curfew order as applying to the whole group. In the instant case, temporary exclusion of the entire group was rested by the military on the same ground. The judgment that exclusion of the whole group was for the same reason a military imperative answers the contention that the exclusion was in the nature of group punishment based on antagonism to those of

Japanese origin. That there were members of the group who retained loyalties to Japan has been confirmed by investigations made subsequent to the exclusion. Approximately five thousand American citizens of Japanese ancestry refused to swear unqualified allegiance to the United States and to renounce allegiance to the Japanese Emperor, and several thousand evacuees requested repatriation to Japan.

We uphold the exclusion order as of the time it was made and when the petitioner violated it. In doing so, we are not unmindful of the hardships imposed by it upon a large group of American citizens. But hardships are part of war, and war is an aggregation of hardships. . . . All citizens alike, both in and out of uniform, feel the impact of war in greater or lesser measure. Citizenship has its responsibilities as well as its privileges, and in time of war the burden is always heavier. Compulsory exclusion of large groups of citizens from their homes, except under circumstances of direst emergency and peril, is inconsistent with our basic governmental institutions. But when under conditions of modern warfare our shores are threatened by hostile forces, the power to protect must be commensurate with the threatened danger.

[Text omitted]

It is said that we are dealing here with the case of imprisonment of a citizen in a concentration camp solely because of his ancestry, without evidence or inquiry concerning his loyalty and good disposition towards the United States. Our task would be simple, our duty clear, were this a case involving the imprisonment of a loyal citizen in a concentration camp because of racial prejudice. Regardless of the true nature of the assembly and relocation centers—and we deem it unjustifiable to call them concentration camps with all the ugly connotations that term implies—we are dealing specifically with nothing but an exclusion order. To cast this case into outlines of racial prejudice, without reference to the real military dangers which were presented, merely confuses the issue. Korematsu was not excluded from the Military Area because of hostility to him or his race. He was excluded because we are at war with the Japanese Empire, because the properly constituted military authorities feared an invasion of our West Coast and felt constrained to take proper security measures, because they decided that the military urgency of the situation demanded that all citizens of Japanese ancestry be segregated from the West Coast temporarily, and finally, because Congress, reposing its confidence in this time of war in our military leaders—as inevitably it must—determined that they should have the power to do just this. There was evidence of disloyalty on the part of some, the military authorities considered that the need for action was great, and time was short. We cannot—by availing ourselves of the calm perspective of hindsight—now say that at that time these actions were unjustified.

Affirmed.

[Text omitted]

MR. JUSTICE MURPHY, dissenting.

This exclusion of "all persons of Japanese ancestry, both alien and non-alien," from the Pacific Coast area on a plea of military necessity in the absence of martial law ought not to be approved. Such exclusion goes over "the very brink of constitutional power" and falls into the ugly abyss of racism.

In dealing with matters relating to the prosecution and progress of a war, we must accord great respect and consideration to the judgments of the military authorities who are on the scene and who have full knowledge of the military facts. The scope of their discretion must, as a matter of necessity and common sense, be wide. And their judgments ought not to be overruled lightly by those whose training and duties ill-equip them to deal intelligently with matters so vital to the physical security of the nation.

At the same time, however, it is essential that there be definite limits to military discretion, especially where martial law has not been declared. Individuals must not be left impoverished of their constitutional rights on a plea of military necessity that has neither substance nor support. Thus, like other claims conflicting with the asserted constitutional rights of the individual, the military claim must subject itself to the judicial process of having its reasonableness determined and its conflicts with other interests reconciled. "What are the allowable limits of military discretion, and whether or not they have been overstepped in a particular case, are judicial questions." *Sterling v. Constantin*, 287 U.S. 378, 401. The judicial test of whether the Government, on a plea of military necessity, can validly deprive an individual of any of his constitutional rights is whether the deprivation is reasonably related to a public danger that is so "immediate, imminent, and impending" as not to admit of delay and not to permit the intervention of ordinary constitutional processes to alleviate the danger. . . . Civilian Exclusion Order No. 34, banishing from a prescribed area of the Pacific Coast "all persons of Japanese ancestry, both alien and non-alien," clearly does not meet that test. Being an obvious racial discrimination, the order deprives all those within its scope of the equal protection of the laws as guaranteed by the Fifth Amendment. It further deprives these individuals of their constitutional rights to live and work where they will, to establish a home where they choose and to move about freely. In excommunicating them without benefit of hearings, this order also deprives them of all their constitutional rights to procedural due process. Yet no reasonable relation to an "immediate, imminent, and impending" public danger is evident to support this racial restriction which is one of the most sweeping and complete deprivations of constitutional rights in the history of this nation in the absence of martial law.

[Text omitted]

That this forced exclusion was the result in good measure of this erroneous assumption of racial guilt rather than bona fide military necessity is evidenced by the Commanding General's Final Report on the evacuation from the Pacific Coast area. In it he refers to all individuals of Japanese descent as "subversive," as belonging to "an enemy race" whose "racial strains are undiluted," and as constituting "over 112,000 potential enemies . . . at large today" along the Pacific Coast. In support of this blanket condemnation of all persons of Japanese descent, however, no reliable evidence is cited to show that such individuals were generally disloyal, or had generally so conducted themselves in this area as to constitute a special menace to defense installations or war industries, or had otherwise by their behavior furnished reasonable ground for their exclusion as a group.

Justification for the exclusion is sought, instead, mainly upon questionable racial and sociological grounds not ordinarily within the realm of expert military judgment, supplemented by certain semi-military conclusions drawn from an unwarranted use of circumstantial evidence. Individuals of Japanese ancestry are condemned because they are said to be "a large, unassimilated, tightly knit racial group, bound to an enemy nation by strong ties of race, culture, custom and religion." They are claimed to be given to "emperor worshiping ceremonies" and to "dual citizenship." Japanese language schools and allegedly pro-Japanese organizations are cited as evidence of possible group disloyalty, together with facts as to certain persons being educated and residing at length in Japan. It is intimated that many of these individuals deliberately resided "adjacent to strategic points," thus enabling them "to carry into execution a tremendous program of sabotage on a mass scale should any considerable number of them have been inclined to do so." The need for protective custody is also asserted. The report refers without identity to "numerous incidents of violence" as well as to other admittedly unverified or cumulative incidents. From this, plus certain other events not shown to have been connected with the Japanese Americans, it is concluded that the "situation was fraught with danger to the Japanese population itself" and that the general public "was ready to take matters into its own hands." Finally, it is intimated, though not directly charged or proved, that persons of Japanese ancestry were responsible for three minor isolated shellings and bombings of the Pacific Coast area, as well as for unidentified radio transmissions and night signaling.

[Text omitted]

The main reasons relied upon by those responsible for the forced evacuation, therefore, do not prove a reasonable relation between the group characteristics of Japanese Americans and the dangers of invasion, sabotage and espionage. The reasons appear, instead, to be largely an accumulation of much of the misinformation, half-truths and insinuations that for years have been directed against Japanese Americans by people with racial and economic prejudices—the same people who have been among the foremost advocates of the evacuation. . . .

[Text omitted]

I dissent, therefore, from this legalization of racism. Racial discrimination in any form and in any degree has no justifiable part whatever in our democratic way of life. It is unattractive in any setting but it is utterly revolting among a free people who have embraced the principles set forth in the Constitution of the United States. All residents of this nation are kin in some way by blood or culture to a foreign land. Yet they are primarily and necessarily a part of the new and distinct civilization of the United States. They must accordingly be treated at all times as the heirs of the American experiment and as entitled to all the rights and freedoms guaranteed by the Constitution.

Plyler v. Doe, 457 U.S. 202 (1982)

Editor's Introduction: The *Plyler* decision is among the most significant Supreme Court actions affecting the status of undocumented immigrants in the United States. The decision overturned a section of a Texas law (section @21.031) which withheld state funds from local school districts that would be used for the education of children not "legally admitted" into the United States. The constitutional issue was whether the "equal protection clause" of the Fourteenth Amendment disallowed this kind of distinction in the law—whether, in other words, states are compelled to pay for the education of children whose parents have illegally entered the country. In the majority opinion, Justice Brennan upheld a United States District Court decision which prevented the state of Texas from withholding funds for this purpose. He argues that though education is not a "fundamental right" and though undocumented aliens are not a "suspect class," (two important bases for prior Court decisions that have overturned state laws on equal protection grounds), the danger the law posed of creating an uneducated underclass with drastically diminished life prospects was so great as to justify striking down the law. Chief Justice Burger disagreed, arguing that though such a law is unwise policy, it is not therefore unconstitutional. Indeed, he suggests that in this case the Court is clearly overstepping its own constitutional function.

In *Plyler v. Doe,* the Court struggles to define how the constitutional guarantee of equal protection under the law, a central notion in our liberal tradition of political thought, applies to a specific class of persons, i.e., undocumented children. The case is, for this reason, theoretically interesting as well as practically important. It is also an important legal precedent. The California Ballot Proposition 187, passed by voters in the 1994 election, also bars state spending for the education of the children of undocumented immigrants. Given the Plyler precedent, the constitutionality of the nationally controversial Proposition 187 remains in question unless and until the Supreme Court takes up the issue again.

*   *   *

JUSTICE BRENNAN delivered the opinion of the Court.

The question presented by these cases is whether, consistent with the Equal Protection Clause of the Fourteenth Amendment, Texas may deny to undocumented school-age children the free public education that it provides to children who are citizens of the United States or legally admitted aliens.

Since the late 19th century, the United States has restricted immigration into this country. Unsanctioned entry into the United States is a crime

. . . , and those who have entered unlawfully are subject to deportation. . . . But despite the existence of these legal restrictions, a substantial number of persons have succeeded in unlawfully entering the United States, and now live within various States, including the State of Texas.

[Text omitted]

The Equal Protection Clause directs that "all persons similarly circumstanced shall be treated alike." . . . But so too, "[the] Constitution does not require things which are different in fact or opinion to be treated in law as though they were the same." *Tigner v. Texas,* 310 U.S. 141, 147 (1940). The initial discretion to determine what is "different" and what is "the same" resides in the legislatures of the States. A legislature must have substantial latitude to establish classifications that roughly approximate the nature of the problem perceived, that accommodate competing concerns both public and private, and that account for limitations on the practical ability of the State to remedy every ill. In applying the Equal Protection Clause to most forms of state action, we thus seek only the assurance that the classification at issue bears some fair relationship to a legitimate public purpose.

But we would not be faithful to our obligations under the Fourteenth Amendment if we applied so deferential a standard to every classification. The Equal Protection Clause was intended as a restriction on state legislative action inconsistent with elemental constitutional premises. Thus we have treated as presumptively invidious those classifications that disadvantage a "suspect class," or that impinge upon the exercise of a "fundamental right." With respect to such classifications, it is appropriate to enforce the mandate of equal protection by requiring the State to demonstrate that its classification has been precisely tailored to serve a compelling governmental interest. In addition, we have recognized that certain forms of legislative classification, while not facially invidious, nonetheless give rise to recurring constitutional difficulties; in these limited circumstances we have sought the assurance that the classification reflects a reasoned judgment consistent with the ideal of equal protection by inquiring whether it may fairly be viewed as furthering a substantial interest of the State. We turn to a consideration of the standard appropriate for the evaluation of @ 21.031.

Sheer incapability or lax enforcement of the laws barring entry into this country, coupled with the failure to establish an effective bar to the employment of undocumented aliens, has resulted in the creation of a substantial "shadow population" of illegal migrants—numbering in the millions—within our borders. This situation raises the specter of a permanent caste of undocumented resident aliens, encouraged by some to remain here as a source of cheap labor, but nevertheless denied the benefits that our society makes available to citizens and lawful residents. The existence of such an underclass presents most difficult problems for a Nation that prides itself on adherence to principles of equality under law.

The children who are plaintiffs in these cases are special members of this underclass. Persuasive arguments support the view that a State may withhold its beneficence from those whose very presence within the United States is the product of their own unlawful conduct. These arguments do not apply with the same force to classifications imposing disabilities on the minor children of such illegal entrants. At the least, those who elect to enter our territory by stealth and in violation of our law should be prepared to bear the consequences, including, but not limited to, deportation. But the children of those illegal entrants are not comparably situated. Their "parents have the ability to conform their conduct to societal norms," and presumably the ability to remove themselves from the State's jurisdiction; but the children who are plaintiffs in these cases "can affect neither their parents' conduct nor their own status." *Trimble v. Gordon*, 430 U.S. 762, 770 (1977). Even if the State found it expedient to control the conduct of adults by acting against their children, legislation directing the onus of a parent's misconduct against his children does not comport with fundamental conceptions of justice.

[Text omitted]

Of course, undocumented status is not irrelevant to any proper legislative goal. Nor is undocumented status an absolutely immutable characteristic since it is the product of conscious, indeed unlawful, action. But @ 21.031 is directed against children, and imposes its discriminatory burden on the basis of a legal characteristic over which children can have little control. It is thus difficult to conceive of a rational justification for penalizing these children for their presence within the United States. Yet that appears to be precisely the effect of @ 21.031.

Public education is not a "right" granted to individuals by the Constitution. . . . But neither is it merely some governmental "benefit" indistinguishable from other forms of social welfare legislation. Both the importance of education in maintaining our basic institutions, and the lasting impact of its deprivation on the life of the child, mark the distinction. The "American people have always regarded education and [the] acquisition of knowledge as matters of supreme importance." *Meyer v. Nebraska*, 262 U.S. 390, 400 (1923). We have recognized "the public schools as a most vital civic institution for the preservation of a democratic system of government," *Abington School District v. Schempp*, 374 U.S. 203, 230 (1963) (BRENNAN, J., concurring), and as the primary vehicle for transmitting "the values on which our society rests.". . . In addition, education provides the basic tools by which individuals might lead economically productive lives to the benefit of us all. In sum, education has a fundamental role in maintaining the fabric of our society. We cannot ignore the significant social costs borne by our Nation when select groups are denied the means to absorb the values and skills upon which our social order rests.

In addition to the pivotal role of education in sustaining our political and cultural heritage, denial of education to some isolated group of children poses an affront to one of the goals of the Equal Protection Clause: the abolition of governmental barriers presenting unreasonable obstacles to advancement on the basis of individual merit. Paradoxically, by depriving the children of any disfavored group of an education, we foreclose the means by which that group might raise the level of esteem in which it is held by the majority. But more directly, "education prepares individuals to be self-reliant and self-sufficient participants in society." *Wisconsin v. Yoder,* . . . . Illiteracy is an enduring disability. The inability to read and write will handicap the individual deprived of a basic education each and every day of his life. The inestimable toll of that deprivation on the social, economic, intellectual, and psychological well-being of the individual, and the obstacle it poses to individual achievement, make it most difficult to reconcile the cost or the principle of a status-based denial of basic education with the framework of equality embodied in the Equal Protection Clause. . . .

[Text omitted]

These well-settled principles allow us to determine the proper level of deference to be afforded @ 21.031. Undocumented aliens cannot be treated as a suspect class because their presence in this country in violation of federal law is not a "constitutional irrelevancy." Nor is education a fundamental right; a State need not justify by compelling necessity every variation in the manner in which education is provided to its population. . . . But more is involved in these cases than the abstract question whether @ 21.031 discriminates against a suspect class, or whether education is a fundamental right. Section 21.031 imposes a lifetime hardship on a discrete class of children not accountable for their disabling status. The stigma of illiteracy will mark them for the rest of their lives. By denying these children a basic education, we deny them the ability to live within the structure of our civic institutions, and foreclose any realistic possibility that they will contribute in even the smallest way to the progress of our Nation. In determining the rationality of @ 21.031, we may appropriately take into account its costs to the Nation and to the innocent children who are its victims. In light of these countervailing costs, the discrimination contained in @ 21.031 can hardly be considered rational unless it furthers some substantial goal of the State.

It is the State's principal argument, and apparently the view of the dissenting Justices, that the undocumented status of these children vel non establishes a sufficient rational basis for denying them benefits that a State might choose to afford other residents. . . . Indeed, in the State's view, Congress' apparent disapproval of the presence of these children within the United States, and the evasion of the federal regulatory program that is the mark of undocumented status, provides authority for its decision to impose upon them special disabilities. . . .

[Text omitted]

We are reluctant to impute to Congress the intention to withhold from these children, for so long as they are present in this country through no fault of their own, access to a basic education. In other contexts, undocumented status, coupled with some articulable federal policy, might enhance state authority with respect to the treatment of undocumented aliens. But in the area of special constitutional sensitivity presented by these cases, and in the absence of any contrary indication fairly discernible in the present legislative record, we perceive no national policy that supports the State in denying these children an elementary education. . . .

Appellants argue that the classification at issue furthers an interest in the "preservation of the state's limited resources for the education of its lawful residents." . . . Of course, a concern for the preservation of resources standing alone can hardly justify the classification used in allocating those resources. . . . Apart from the asserted state prerogative to act against undocumented children solely on the basis of their undocumented status—an asserted prerogative that carries only minimal force in the circumstances of these cases—we discern three colorable state interests that might support @ 21.031.

[Text omitted]

First, appellants appear to suggest that the State may seek to protect itself from an influx of illegal immigrants. While a State might have an interest in mitigating the potentially harsh economic effects of sudden shifts in population, @ 21.031 hardly offers an effective method of dealing with an urgent demographic or economic problem. There is no evidence in the record suggesting that illegal entrants impose any significant burden on the State's economy. To the contrary, the available evidence suggests that illegal aliens underutilize public services, while contributing their labor to the local economy and tax money to the state fisc. . . . The dominant incentive for illegal entry into the State of Texas is the availability of employment; few if any illegal immigrants come to this country, or presumably to the State of Texas, in order to avail themselves of a free education. Thus, even making the doubtful assumption that the net impact of illegal aliens on the economy of the State is negative, we think it clear that "[charging] tuition to undocumented children constitutes a ludicrously ineffectual attempt to stem the tide of illegal immigration," at least when compared with the alternative of prohibiting the employment of illegal aliens. . . .

Second, while it is apparent that a State may "not . . . reduce expenditures for education by barring [some arbitrarily chosen class of] children from its schools," *Shapiro v. Thompson*, 394 U.S. 618, 633 (1969), appellants suggest that undocumented children are appropriately singled out for exclusion because of the special burdens they impose on the State's ability to provide high-quality public education. But the record in no way supports the claim that exclusion of undocumented children is likely to improve the overall quality of education in the State. . . . Of course, even if improvement in the quality of education were a likely result of barring some number of children from the schools of the State, the State must support its selection of this group as the appropriate target for exclusion. In terms of educational cost and need, however, undocumented children are "basically indistinguishable" from legally resident alien children. . . .

Finally, appellants suggest that undocumented children are appropriately singled out because their unlawful presence within the United States renders them less likely than other children to remain within the boundaries of the State, and to put their education to productive social or political use within the State. Even assuming that such an interest is legitimate, it is an interest that is most difficult to quantify. The State has no assurance that any child, citizen or not, will employ the education provided by the State within the confines of the State's borders. In any event, the record is clear that many of the undocumented children disabled by this classification will remain in this country indefinitely, and that some will become lawful residents or citizens of the United States. It is difficult to understand precisely what the State hopes to achieve by promoting the creation and perpetuation of a subclass of illiterates within our boundaries, surely adding to the problems and costs of unemployment, welfare, and crime. It is thus clear that whatever savings might be achieved by denying these children an education, they are wholly insubstantial in light of the costs involved to these children, the State, and the Nation.

If the State is to deny a discrete group of innocent children the free public education that it offers to other children residing within its borders, that denial must be justified by a showing that it furthers some substantial state interest. No such showing was made here. Accordingly, the judgment of the Court of Appeals in each of these cases is

Affirmed.

[Text omitted]

DISSENT BY: BURGER

Were it our business to set the Nation's social policy, I would agree without hesitation that it is senseless for an enlightened society to deprive any children—including illegal aliens—of an elementary education. I fully agree that it would be folly—and wrong—to tolerate creation of a segment of society made up of illiterate persons, many having a limited or no command of our language. However, the Constitution does not constitute us as "Platonic Guardians" nor does it vest in this Court the authority to strike down laws because they do not meet our standards of desirable social policy, "wisdom," or "common sense." See *TVA v. Hill*, 437 U.S. 153, 194–195 (1978). We trespass on the assigned function of the political branches under our structure of limited and separated powers when we assume a policy making role as the Court does today.

[Text omitted]

The dispositive issue in these cases, simply put, is whether, for purposes of allocating its finite resources, a state has a legitimate reason to differentiate between persons who are lawfully within the state and those who are unlawfully there. The distinction the State of Texas has drawn—based not only upon its own legitimate interests but on classifications established by the Federal Government in its immigration laws and policies—is not unconstitutional.

The Court acknowledges that, except in those cases when state classifications disadvantage a "suspect class" or impinge upon a "fundamental right," the Equal Protection Clause permits a state "substantial latitude" in distinguishing between different groups of persons. . . . Moreover, the Court expressly—and correctly—rejects any suggestion that illegal aliens are a suspect class, . . . , or that education is a fundamental right. . . . Yet by patching together bits and pieces of what might be termed quasi-suspect-class and quasi-fundamental-rights analysis, the Court spins out a theory custom-tailored to the facts of these cases.

In the end, we are told little more than that the level of scrutiny employed to strike down the Texas law applies only when illegal alien children are deprived of a public education, see ante, at 223–224. If ever a court was guilty of an unabashedly result-oriented approach, this case is a prime example.

The Court first suggests that these illegal alien children, although not a suspect class, are entitled to special solicitude under the Equal Protection Clause because they lack "control" over or "responsibility" for their unlawful entry into this country. . . . Similarly, the Court appears to take the position that @ 21.031 is presumptively "irrational" because it has the effect of imposing "penalties" on "innocent" children. . . . However, the Equal Protection Clause does not preclude legislators from classifying among persons on the basis of factors and characteristics over which individuals may be said to lack "control." Indeed, in some circumstances persons generally, and children in particular, may have little control over or responsibility for such things as their ill health, need for public assistance, or place of residence. Yet a state legislature is not barred from considering, for example, relevant differences between the mentally healthy and the mentally ill, or between the residents of different counties, simply because these may be factors unrelated to individual choice or to any "wrongdoing." The Equal Protection Clause protects against arbitrary and irrational classifications, and against invidious discrimination stemming from prejudice and hostility; it is not an all-encompassing "equalizer" designed to eradicate every distinction for which persons are not "responsible."

[Text omitted]

The second strand of the Court's analysis rests on the premise that, although public education is not a constitutionally guaranteed right, "neither is it merely some governmental 'benefit' indistinguishable from other forms of social welfare legislation." . . . Whatever meaning or relevance this opaque observation might have in some other context, it simply has no bearing on the issues at hand. Indeed, it is never made clear what the Court's opinion means on this score.

The importance of education is beyond dispute. Yet we have held repeatedly that the importance of a governmental service does not elevate it to the status of a "fundamental right" for purposes of equal protection analysis. . . . In *San Antonio Independent School Dist.*, JUSTICE POWELL, speaking for the Court, expressly rejected the proposition that state laws dealing with public education are subject to special scrutiny under the Equal Protection Clause. Moreover, the Court points to no meaningful way to distinguish between education and other governmental benefits in this context. Is the Court suggesting that education is more "fundamental" than food, shelter, or medical care?

The Equal Protection Clause guarantees similar treatment of similarly situated persons, but it does not mandate a constitutional hierarchy of governmental services. . . . The central question in these cases, as in every equal protection case not involving truly fundamental rights "explicitly or implicitly guaranteed by the Constitution," is whether there is some legitimate basis for a legislative distinction between different classes of persons. The fact that the distinction is drawn in legislation affecting access to public education—as opposed to legislation allocating other important governmental benefits, such as public assistance, health care, or housing—cannot make a difference in the level of scrutiny applied.

Once it is conceded—as the Court does—that illegal aliens are not a suspect class, and that education is not a fundamental right, our inquiry should focus on and be limited to whether the legislative classification at issue bears a rational relationship to a legitimate state purpose. . . .

The State contends primarily that @ 21.031 serves to prevent undue depletion of its limited revenues available for education, and to preserve the fiscal integrity of the State's school-financing system against an ever-increasing flood of illegal aliens—aliens over whose entry or continued presence it has no control. Of course such fiscal concerns alone could not justify discrimination against a suspect class or an arbitrary and irrational denial of benefits to a particular group of persons. Yet I assume no Member of this Court would argue that prudent conservation of finite state revenues is per se an illegitimate goal. Indeed, the numerous classifications this Court has sustained in social welfare legislation were invariably related to the limited amount of revenues available to spend on any given program or set of programs. . . . The significant question here is whether the requirement of tuition from illegal aliens who attend the public schools—as well as from residents of other states, for example—is a rational and reasonable means of furthering the State's legitimate fiscal ends.

Without laboring what will undoubtedly seem obvious to many, it simply is not "irrational" for a state to conclude that it does not have the same responsibility to provide benefits for persons whose very presence in the state and this country is illegal as it does to provide for persons lawfully present. By definition, illegal aliens have no right whatever to be here, and the state may reasonably, and constitutionally, elect not to provide them with governmental services at the expense of those who are lawfully in the state. In *De Canas v. Bica*, 424 U.S. 351, 357 (1976), we held that a State may protect its "fiscal interests and lawfully resident labor force from the deleterious effects on its economy resulting from the employment of illegal aliens." And only recently this Court made clear that a State has a legitimate interest in protecting and preserving the quality of its schools and "the right of its own bona fide residents to attend such institutions on a preferential tuition basis." . . . The Court has failed to offer even a plausible explanation why illegality of residence in this country is not a factor that may legitimately bear upon the bona fides of state residence and entitlement to the benefits of lawful residence.

[Text omitted]

The Constitution does not provide a cure for every social ill, nor does it vest judges with a mandate to try to remedy every social problem. . . . Moreover, when this Court rushes in to remedy what it perceives to be the failings of the political processes, it deprives those processes of an opportunity to function. When the political institutions are not forced to exercise constitutionally allocated powers and responsibilities, those powers, like muscles not used, tend to atrophy. Today's cases, I regret to say, present yet another example of unwarranted judicial action which in the long run tends to contribute to the weakening of our political processes.

Congress, "vested by the Constitution with the responsibility of protecting our borders and legislating with respect to aliens," . . . bears primary responsibility for addressing the problems occasioned by the millions of illegal aliens flooding across our southern border. Similarly, it is for Congress, and not this Court, to assess the "social costs borne by our Nation when select groups are denied the means to absorb the values and skills upon which our social order rests." . . . While the "specter of a permanent caste" of illegal Mexican residents of the United States is indeed a disturbing one, . . . it is but one segment of a larger problem, which is for the political branches to solve. I find it difficult to believe that Congress would long tolerate such a self-destructive result—that it would fail to deport these illegal alien families or to provide for the education of their children. Yet instead of allowing the political processes to run their course—albeit with some delay—the Court seeks to do Congress' job for it, compensating for congressional inaction. It is not unreasonable to think that this encourages the political branches to pass their problems to the Judiciary.

The solution to this seemingly intractable problem is to defer to the political processes, unpalatable as that may be to some.

Michael Walzer,
"Multiculturalism and Individualism" (1994)

Editor's Introduction: Michael Walzer (1935–) is currently a Professor of Social Science at Princeton University. He is a political philosopher who is best known for his theories of pluralism and political community. In this selection, Walzer joins earlier writers like Dewey and Kallen in taking a rather benign view of cultural pluralism in the United States. Walzer recognizes the danger of fragmentation if intraethnic group loyalties overwhelm feelings of allegiance toward the citizenry and government of the whole nation. Yet he sees excessive individualism—not fragmentation along ethnic lines—as a far greater danger in contemporary American life. Various types of associations that have traditionally brought people together, such as trade unions, churches, even local PTAs, are weaker today than in the past, and especially so among the poor. Walzer suggests that a consequence is that too many people are sinking into loneliness and isolation. Virtually any common activity that brings them out of this is good for the political community. Finally, Walzer notes that, historically, many immigrants have been "Americanized" first by joining with those of the same ethnic identity, as in the Irish-American political machines in many big cities, and then gradually by becoming aware of and active in the broader political culture.

*   *   *

Two powerful centrifugal forces are at work in the United States today. One breaks loose whole groups of people from a presumptively common center; the other sends individuals flying off. Both these de-centering, separatist movements have their critics, who argue that the first is driven by a narrow-minded chauvinism and the second by mere selfishness. The separated groups appear to these critics as exclusive and intolerant tribes, the separated individuals as rootless and lonely egotists. Neither of these views is entirely wrong; neither is quite right. The two movements have to be considered together, set against the background of a democratic politics that opens a lot of room for centrifugal force. Understood in context, the two seem to me, despite the laws of physics, each one the other's remedy.

The first of these forces is an increasingly strong articulation of group difference. It's the articulation that is new, obviously, since difference

---

Source: *Dissent* Vol. 41, No. 2, 189–191, (1994). Reprinted by permission of *Dissent*.

itself—pluralism, even multiculturalism—has been a feature of American life from very early on. John Jay, in one of the *Federalist Papers*, describes the Americans as a people "descended from the same ancestors, speaking the same language, professing the same religion, attached to the same principles of government, very similar in manners and customs."

These lines were already inaccurate when Jay wrote them in the 1780s; they were utterly falsified in the course of the nineteenth century. Mass immigration turned the United States into a land of many different ancestors, languages, religions, manners, and customs. Principles of government are our only stable and common commitment. Democracy fixes the limits and sets the ground rules for American pluralism.

[Text omitted]

And yet the full-scale and fervent articulation of difference is a fairly recent phenomenon. A long history of prejudice, subordination, and fear worked against any public affirmation of minority "manners and customs" and so served to conceal the radical character of American pluralism. I want to be very clear about this history. At its extremes it was brutal, as conquered Native Americans and transported black slaves can testify; at its center, with regard to religion and ethnicity rather than race, it was relatively benign. An immigrant society welcomed new immigrants or, at least, made room for them, with a degree of reluctance and resistance considerably below the standards set elsewhere. Nonetheless, all our minorities learned to be quiet: timidity has been the mark of minority politics until very recent times.

I remember, for example, how in the 1930s and 1940s any sign of Jewish assertiveness—even the appearance of "too many" Jewish names among New Deal Democrats or CIO organizers or socialist or communist intellectuals—was greeted among Jews with a collective shudder. The communal elders said, "Sha!" Don't make noise; don't attract attention; don't push yourself forward; don't say anything provocative. They thought of themselves as guests in this country long after they had become citizens.

Today all that is, as they say, history. The United States in the 1990s is socially, though not economically (and the contrast is especially striking after the Reagan years), a more egalitarian place than it was fifty or sixty years ago. No one is shushing us anymore; no one is intimidated or quiet. Old racial and religious identities have taken on greater prominence in our public life; gender and sexual preference have been added to the mix; and the current wave of immigration from Asia and Latin America makes for significant new differences among American citizens and potential citizens. And all this is expressed, so it seems, all the time. The voices are loud, the accents various, and the result is not harmony—as in the old image of pluralism as a symphony, each group playing its own instrument (but who wrote the music?)—but a jangling discord. It is very much like the dissidence of Protestant dissent in the early years of the Reformation: many sects, dividing and subdividing; many prophets and would-be prophets, all talking at once.

In response to this cacophony, another group of prophets, liberal and neoconservative intellectuals, academics, and journalists, wring their hands and assure us that the country is falling apart, that our fiercely articulated multiculturalism is dangerously divisive, and that we desperately need to reassert the hegemony of a single culture. Curiously, this supposedly necessary and necessarily singular culture is often described as a high culture, as if it is our shared commitment to Shakespeare, Dickens, and James Joyce that has been holding us together all these years. (But surely high culture divides us, as it always has—and probably always will in any country with a strong egalitarian and populist strain. . . .) Democratic politics seems to me a more likely resource than the literary or philosophical canon. We need to think about how this resource might usefully be deployed.

But isn't it already deployed—given that multiculturalism conflicts take place in the democratic arena and requires of their protagonists a wide range of characteristically democratic skills and performances? If one studies the history of ethnic, racial, and religious associations in the United states, one sees, I think, that these have served again and again as vehicles of individual and group integration—despite (or, perhaps, because of) the political conflicts they generated. Even if the aim of associational life is to sustain difference, that aim has to be achieved *here*, under American conditions, and the result is commonly a new and unintended kind of differentiation—of American Catholics and Jews, say, not so much from one another or from the Protestant majority as from Catholics and Jews in other countries. Minority groups adapt themselves to the local political culture. And if their primary aim is self-defense, toleration, civil rights, a place in the sun, the result of success is more clearly still an Americanization of whatever differences are being defended. That doesn't mean that differences are defended quietly—quietness is not one of our political conventions. Becoming an American means learning not to be quiet. Nor is the success that is sought by one group always compatible with the success of all (or any of) the others. The conflicts are real, and even small-scale victories are often widely threatening.

The greater difficulties, however, come from failure, especially reiterated failure. It is associational weakness, and the anxieties and resentments it breeds, that pull people apart in dangerous ways. Leonard Jeffrie's African-American Studies Department at the City College of New York is hardly an example of institutional strength. The noisiest groups in our contemporary cacophony and the groups that make the most extreme demands are also the weakest. In American cities today, poor people, mostly members of minority groups, find it difficult to work together in any coherent way. Mutual assistance, cultural preservation, and self-defense are loudly affirmed but ineffectively enacted. The contemporary poor have no strongly based or well-funded institutions to focus their energies or discipline wayward members. They are socially exposed and vulnerable. This is the most depressing feature of our current situation: the large number of disorganized, powerless, and demoralized men and women, who are spoken for, and also exploited by, a growing company of racial and religious demagogues and tinhorn charismatics.

But weakness is a general feature of associational life in America today. Unions, churches, interest groups, ethnic organizations, political parties and sects, societies for self-improvement and good works, local philanthropies, neighborhood clubs and cooperatives, religious sodalities, brotherhoods and sisterhoods: this American civil society is wonderfully multitudinous. Most of the associations, however, are precariously established, skimpily funded, and always at risk. They have less reach and holding power than they once did. I can't cite statistics; I'm not sure that anyone is collecting the right sorts of statistics; but I suspect that the number of Americans who are unorganized, inactive, and undefended is on the rise. Why is this so?

The answer has to do in part with the second of the centrifugal forces at work in contemporary American society. This country is not only a pluralism of groups but also a pluralism of individuals. It is perhaps the most individualist society in human history. Compared to the men and women of any earlier, old-world country, we are radically liberated, all of us. We are free to plot our own course, plan our own lives, choose a career, a partner (or a succession of partners), a religion (or no religion), a politics (or an antipolitics), a life-style (any style)—free to "do our own thing." Personal freedom is certainly one of the extraordinary achievements of the "new order of the ages" celebrated on the Great Seal of the United States. The defense of this freedom against puritans and bigots is one of the enduring themes of American politics, making for its most zestful moments; the celebration of this freedom, and of the individuality and creativity it makes possible, is one of the enduring themes of our literature.

Nonetheless, personal freedom is not an unalloyed delight. For many of us lack the means and the power to "do our own thing" or even to find our own things to do. Empowerment is, with rare exceptions, a familial, class, or communal, not an individual, achievement. Resources are accumulated over generations, cooperatively. And without resources, individual men and women find themselves hard-pressed by economic

236 PART III: Immigration and National Identity

dislocations, natural disasters, governmental failures, and personal crises. They can't count on steady or significant communal support. Often they are on the run from family, class, and community, seeking a new life in this new world. If they make good their escape, they never look back; if they need to look back, they are likely to find the people they left behind barely able to support themselves.

Consider for a moment the cultural (ethnic, racial, and religious) groups that constitute our supposedly fierce and divisive multiculturalism. All these are voluntary associations, with a core of militants, activists, and believers and a wide periphery of more passive men and women—who are, in effect, cultural free-riders, enjoying an identity that they don't pay for with money, time, or energy. When these people find themselves in trouble they look for help from similarly identified men and women. But the help is uncertain, for these identities are mostly unearned, without depth. Footloose individuals are not reliable members. There are no borders around our cultural groups and, of course, no border police. Men and women are free to participate or not as they please, to come and go, withdraw entirely, or simply fade away into the peripheral distances. This freedom, again, is one of the advantages of an individualist society; at the same time, however, it doesn't make for strong or cohesive associations. Ultimately, I'm not sure that it makes for strong or self-confident individuals.

Rates of disengagement from cultural association and identity for the sake of the private pursuit of happiness (or the desperate search for economic survival) are so high these days that all the groups worry all the time about how to hold the periphery and ensure their own future. They are constantly fund raising; recruiting; scrambling for workers, allies, and endorsements; preaching against the dangers of assimilation, intermarriage, passing, and passivity. Lacking any sort of coercive power and unsure of their own persuasiveness, they demand governmental programs (targeted entitlements, quota systems) that will help them press their own members into line. From their perspective, the real alternative to multiculturalism is not a strong and substantive Americanism, but an empty or randomly filled individualism, a great drift of human flotsam and jetsam away from every creative center.

This is, again, a one-sided perspective, but by no means entirely wrongheaded. The critical conflict in American life today is not between multiculturalism and some kind of cultural hegemony or singularity, not between pluralism and unity or the many and the one, but between the manyness of groups and of individuals, between communities and private men and women. And this is a conflict in which we have no choice except to affirm the value of both sides. The two pluralisms make America what it is or sometimes is and set the pattern for what it should be. Taken together, but only together, they are entirely consistent with a common democratic citizenship.

Consider now the increasingly dissociated individuals of contemporary American society. Surely we ought to worry about the processes, even though these are also, some of them, emancipatory processes, which produce dissociation and are its products:

- the rising divorce rate;
- the growing number of people living alone (in what the census calls "single person households");
- the decline in memberships (in unions and churches, for example);
- the long-term decline in voting rates and party loyalty (most dramatic in local elections);
- the high rates of geographic mobility (which continually undercut neighborhood cohesiveness);
- the sudden appearance of homeless men and women; and
- the rising tide of random violence.

Add to all this the apparent stabilization of high levels of unemployment and underemployment, especially among young people, which intensifies all these processes and aggravates their effects on already vulnerable minority groups. Unemployment makes family ties brittle, cuts people off from unions and interest groups, drains communal resources, leads to political alienation and withdrawal, increases the temptations of a criminal life. The old maxim about idle hands and the devil's work isn't necessarily true, but it comes true whenever idleness is a condition that no one would choose.

I am inclined to think that these processes, on balance, are more worrying than the multicultural cacophony—if only because, in a democratic society, action-in-common is better than withdrawal and solitude, tumult is better than passivity, shared purposes (even when we don't approve) are better than private listlessness. It is probably true, moreover, that many of these dissociated individuals are available for political mobilizations of a sort that democracies ought to avoid. There are writers today, of course, who claim that multiculturalism is itself the product of such mobilizations: American society in their eyes stands at the brink not only of dissolution but of "Bosnian" civil war. In fact, we have had (so far) only intimations of an openly chauvinist and racist politics. We are at a point where we can still safely bring the pluralism of groups to the rescue of the pluralism of dissociated individuals.

Individuals are stronger, more confident, more savvy, when they are participants in a common life, responsible to and for other people.

No doubt, this relation doesn't hold for every common life; I am not recommending religious cults or political sects—though men and women who manage to pass through groups of that sort are often strengthened by the experience, educated for a more modest commonality. It is only in the context of associational activity that individuals learn to deliberate, argue, make decisions, and take responsibility. . . .

Individuals were indeed saved by congregational membership—saved from isolation, loneliness, feelings of inferiority, habitual inaction, incompetence, a kind of moral vacancy—and turned into useful citizens. But it is equally true that Britain was saved from Protestant repression by the strong individualism of these same useful citizens: that was a large part of their usefulness.

So, we need to strengthen associational ties, even if these ties connect some of us to some others and not everyone to everyone else. . . .

[Text omitted]

Engaged men and women tend to be widely engaged—active in many different associations both locally and nationally. This is one of the most common findings of political scientists and sociologists (and one of the most surprising: where do these people find the time?). It helps to explain why engagement works, in a pluralist society, to undercut racist or chauvinist political commitments and ideologies. The same people show up for union meetings, neighborhood projects, political canvassing, church committees, and—most reliably—in the voting booth on election day. They are, most of them, articulate, opinionated, skillful, sure of themselves, and fairly steady in their commitments. Some mysterious combination of responsibility, ambition, and meddlesomeness carries them from one meeting to another. Everyone complains (I mean that all of them complain) that there are so few of them. Is this an inevitability of social life, so that an increase in the number of associations would only stretch out the competent people, more and more thinly? I suspect that demand-side economists have a better story to tell about this "human capital." Multiply the calls for competent people, and people will appear. Multiply the opportunities for action-in-common, and activists will emerge to seize the opportunities. Some of them, no doubt, will be narrow-minded and bigoted, but the greater their number and the more diverse their activities, the less likely it is that narrow-mindedness and bigotry will prevail.

A certain sort of stridency is a feature of what we may one day come to recognize as *early* multiculturalism; it is especially evident among the newest and weakest, the least organized, groups. It is the product of a historical period when social equality outdistances economic equality. Stronger organizations, capable of collecting resources and delivering real benefits to their members, will move these groups, gradually, toward a democratically inclusive politics. The driving force will be the more active members, socialized by their activity. Remember that this has happened before, in the course of ethnic and class conflict. When groups consolidate, the center holds the periphery and turns it into a political constituency. And so union militants, say, begin on the picket line and the strike committee and move on to the school board and the city council. Religious and ethnic activists begin by defending the interests of their own community and end up in political coalitions, fighting for a place on "balanced" tickets, and talking (at least) about the common good. The cohesiveness of the group invigorates its members; the ambition and mobility of the most vigorous members liberalize the group.

I don't mean to sound like the famous Pollyanna. These outcomes won't come about by chance; perhaps they won't come about at all. Everything is harder now—family, class, and community are less cohesive than they once were; local governments and philanthropies command fewer resources; the street world of crime and drugs is more frightening; individual men and women seem more adrift. And there is one further difficulty that we ought to welcome. In the past, organized groups have succeeded in entering the American mainstream only by leaving other groups (and the weakest of their own members) behind. And the men and women left behind commonly accepted their fate or, at least, failed to make much noise about it. Today, as I have been arguing, the level of resignation is considerably lower, and if much of the subsequent noise is incoherent and futile, it serves nonetheless to remind the rest of us that there is a larger social agenda than our own success. Multiculturalism as an ideology is not only the product of, it is also a program for, greater social *and economic* equality.

If we want the mutual reinforcements of community and individuality to work effectively for everyone, we will have to act politically to make them effective. They require certain background or framing conditions that can only be provided by state action. Group life won't rescue individual men and women from dissociation and passivity unless there is a political strategy for mobilizing, organizing, and, if necessary, subsidizing the right sort of groups. And strong-minded individuals won't diversify their commitments and extend their ambitions unless there are opportunities open to them in the larger world: jobs, offices, and responsibilities. The centrifugal forces of culture and selfhood will correct one another only if the correction is planned. It is necessary to aim at a balance of the two—which means that we can never be consistent defenders of multiculturalism or individualism; we can never be communitarians or liberals simply, but now one, now the other, as the balance requires. . . .

SUGGESTIONS FOR FURTHER READING

Bernard Bailyn, *The Peopling of British North America: An Introduction* (New York: Vintage Books, 1988).

Luigi Barzini, *O America, When You and I Were Young* (New York: Harper & Row, 1977).

Nathan Glazer and Daniel Patrick Moynihan, *Beyond the Melting Pot: The Negroes, Puerto Ricans, Jews, Italians, and Irish of New York City*, second edition (Cambridge, MA: Massachusetts Institute of Technology Press, 1970).

Oscar Handlin, *The Uprooted*, second edition (Boston: Little, Brown and Co., 1973).

Higham, John, *Strangers in the Land: Patterns of American Nativism, 1860–1925*, second edition (New Brunswick, NJ: Rutgers University Press, 1988).

Horace M. Kallen, *Cultural Pluralism and the American Idea* (Philadelphia: University of Pennsylvania Press, 1956).

James H. Kettner, *The Development of American Citizenship, 1608–1870* (Chapel Hill: University of North Carolina Press, 1978).

Arthur Mann, *The One and the Many: Reflections on the American Identity* (Chicago: The University of Chicago Press, 1979).

Peter H. Schuck and Rogers S. Smith, *Citizenship Without Consent: Illegal Aliens in the American Polity* (New Haven: Yale University Press, 1985).

Peter Skerry, *Mexican Americans: The Ambivalent Minority* (New York: The Free Press, 1993).

Ronald Takaki, *A Different Mirror: A History of Multicultural America* (Boston: Little, Brown, & Co., 1993).

Ronald Takaki, *Strangers from a Different Shore: A History of Asian Americans* (Boston: Little, Brown and Co., 1989).

Oliver Trager, ed. *America's Minorities and the Multicultural Debate* (New York: Facts on File, 1992).

Howard Zinn, *A People's History of the United States* (New York: Harper & Row, 1980).

PART IV

Race and Politics:
Two Americas or One?

PART IV

Race and Politics:
Two Americas or One?

I still have a dream. It is a dream deeply rooted in the American Dream.

—Dr. Martin Luther King, Jr.

No, I'm not an American. I'm one of 22 million black people who are the victims of Americanism. One of the 22 million black people who are the victims of democracy, nothing but disguised hypocrisy. So, I'm not standing here speaking to you as an American, or a patriot, or a flag saluter, or a flag waver—no, not I. I'm speaking as a victim of this American system. And I see America through the eyes of a victim. I don't see any American dream; I see an American nightmare.[1]

—Malcolm X

The black experience in America is rooted deeply and tragically in slavery. We have not yet nor does it seem that in the foreseeable future we will pull ourselves out of the pit into which slave holding has tossed us. The realization of Dr. King's dream (see the speech in this chapter) seems little closer in the last decade of the twentieth century than it did in 1963 when those famous words were spoken. Race relations continue to be, in Gunnar Myrdal's famous phrase, "an American dilemma."[2] Moreover, because of the legacy of slavery, no matter how multicultural America becomes, black–white relations will remain central to and unique in our experience as Americans.

Dr. Martin Luther King, Jr., and Malcolm X pose stark alternatives for dealing with this dilemma, and both have important predecessors and successors for their views. For Dr. King, racism is a fact of American life

---

[1] Malcolm X, "The Ballot or the Bullet." In George Breitman, ed. *Malcolm X Speaks: Selected Speeches and Statements* (New York: Pathfinder Press, 1989), p. 26.

[2] This is, of course, the title of Gunnar Myrdal's classic study of race relations in America, *An American Dilemma: The Negro Problem and Modern Democracy* (New York: Harper & Brothers Publishers, 1944).

to be overcome. He was not naive and did not think that this would be an easy task. He had spent too many nights in jail and had been beaten and seen his friends and supporters beaten or killed too many times to sustain vain hopes. Moreover, his dream led to tangible results, in fact, to the largest steps toward desegregation since the end of the Civil War. Malcolm X sees in America's future not a dream to be achieved but a nightmare from which he asks African-Americans to awaken. Sadly, he was assassinated in 1965 before having had the opportunity to think through what vision he offered in its place or what steps were needed to get there. Nonetheless, if King represents accomplishment and hope about the future, Malcolm's words represent a pessimism about race relations, also with deep roots in our history.

The words slave or slavery are not explicitly used in the Constitution, though the practice is clearly recognized. In fact, the clause permitting the continued importation of "such Persons as any of the States now existing shall think proper to admit" at least until 1808, is one of only two clauses which is excluded from the amendment process. That the word is not used indicates an unwillingness of some members of the Constitutional Convention (e.g., Gouverneur Morris of Pennsylvania and George Mason of Virginia) to condone the institution by name even as they permitted it to continue in fact. This sort of ambivalence was not unusual in the founding era. Thomas Jefferson, a slave owner who may have had an affair with a slave woman, once wrote regarding slavery that, "I tremble for my country when I reflect that God is just."[3] He could not reconcile the principles of the Declaration of Independence with an institution that denied these principles to so many based on color.

Ironically, the very liberalism Jefferson espoused indirectly encouraged a form of racism. If the Declaration claims that all men are created equal while slavery continues to exist, it must mean that slaves are less than persons and not fit for personal freedom and self-government. The only way to reconcile liberalism with slavery, in other words, was to deny the very humanity of the slaves. However, Jefferson, Washington, and Madison, all founders who owned slaves, could never bring themselves to fully deny the slaves' humanity, nor could they see a way clear of slavery. To paraphrase Jefferson, slavery in America was, to many of the founders, like holding a wolf by the ears. One was afraid to hold on but even more afraid to let go.

Perhaps even more ominously for America's future, Jefferson believed that "the great moral and political evil" of slavery one day must

---

[3] Jefferson, *Notes on Virginia*, query *xviii*. In *The Life and Selected Writings of Thomas Jefferson*. Edited by Adrienne Koch and William Peden. (New York: The Modern Library, 1972), p. 279.

end but, at the same time, he did not believe that blacks and whites could coexist as political equals. "Nothing is more certainly written in the book of fate," he wrote, "than that these people are to be free; nor is it less certain that the two races, equally free, cannot live in the same government."[4] Such prominent white Americans as Jefferson, Madison, and Lincoln in the late eighteenth through the mid nineteenth century expressed views on the prospects of racial equality that were ironically akin to those of later black separatists such as Marcus Garvey and Malcolm X. All favored, at one point or another, recolonization schemes that would repatriate slaves from America to Africa or the Caribbean. Moreover, they sensed that slavery and its legacy had a corrupting influence on masters—in fact, on all whites, slave owners or not— as well as on slaves. The inegalitarian attitudes of dominance and superiority, and the disdain for labor it encouraged, undermined the yeoman virtues on which a republican regime must rest. Benjamin Rush expresses this view most cogently, along with other reasons for opposing slavery, in the piece reproduced here.

The writings in this Part come from diverse perspectives, black and white. The piece by Rush is an impassioned early criticism of slavery that is grounded in liberal, republican, and Christian ideas. As the Civil War approached, there hardened in the South an unapologetic defense of slavery represented here by George Fitzhugh. His argument is rooted in preliberal beliefs about society as an organic hierarchical whole, which those at the top directed and enjoyed thanks to the leisure provided by slave labor.

Abraham Lincoln figures prominently in any discussion of race and slavery in America. We reprint here his Second Inaugural Address and an assessment of Lincoln by one of the giants of the abolitionist cause and one of the central figures of the nineteenth century in his own right, Frederick Douglass. Lincoln was not an egalitarian on racial issues, nor was the end of slavery his highest priority in fighting the Civil War. Preserving the union was. Nonetheless, Lincoln did loathe slavery and did fight a war that ended it. Douglass recognizes this achievement even as he candidly explores Lincoln's limitations as a leader on the race issue. Douglass' piece is an exemplary and judicious assessment of Lincoln, a figure whose complex motivations are disputed by scholars to this day. Yet, it goes beyond this to present a view of race relations that would be worth reading had Lincoln's name never appeared in it.

W. E. B. Du Bois, Marcus Garvey, and Booker T. Washington are three vitally important voices on race relations and racial identity from

---

[4] Jefferson describes slavery as an "evil" in his 1782 work, *Notes on Virginia*. The extended quote is taken from his *Autobiography* of 1821. From *The Life and Selected Works of Thomas Jefferson*, pp. 219 and 51, respectively.

the late nineteenth and early twentieth century. Du Bois lived the longest and underwent the greatest changes in viewpoint, an increasingly pessimistic one, over the course of his life. He is remembered for his role in founding the National Association for the Advancement of Colored People (NAACP) and pressing vigorously a civil rights agenda. Washington, the founder of the Tuskegee Institute, urged blacks to avoid confrontational politics and to learn a trade. His message of self-reliance and economic independence is an important one and perhaps has an even greater viability today when it is no longer presented in opposition to pursuing political avenues of reform at the same time. Garvey is a proponent of black separatism. He was for a decade or so the most popular political figure with black audiences in the country. His message of race pride, his extolling the glories of African history, and his forming a "government-in-exile" to eventually govern former slaves in Africa make him a precursor to the separatist message of Malcolm X and of the Nation of Islam, before and after Malcolm's departure from it. He also points toward the rediscovery/creation of African identity in America, from the dashiki-wearing 1960s to the "Afrocentric" debate of the 1990s. It is ironic that it was Du Bois, one-time civil rights leader, who died a hero in Ghana after essentially giving up on the United States, while Garvey never visited the land he admired so much.

We conclude this Part with the Supreme Court's decision in Brown v. Board of Education and with Martin Luther King's famous "I Have a Dream" speech. The Brown decision was a decisive step in ending legal segregation in this country. King's speech sets out his vision for an integrated America characterized by mutual respect among all peoples. These are, to be sure, not the last words on race in American thought or practice. The themes discussed by Garvey pertaining to separatism and by Du Bois concerning the conflict of identities of African-American people also are alive today in only slightly different forms than those in which they were originally expressed. Race will continue to be an American dilemma, despite the existence of large numbers of people of good will of all races who wish to bridge the divide.

Benjamin Rush,
"An Address to the Inhabitants of the British Settlements in America Upon Slave-Keeping" (1773)

Editor's Introduction: Benjamin Rush (1745–1813), physician, political activist, social reformer, and pamphleteer, was born into a large Pennsylvania Quaker family, though he later converted to Presbyterianism. Rush began his career in medicine as an apprentice and later studied in Edinburgh, Scotland, where he received an M.D. in 1768. He was to become a leading physician of the age, conducting important studies into cholera and other infectious diseases, as well as writing classic texts on chemistry and psychiatry. Rush's political activism and interest in social reform continued throughout his life. He served as a surgeon in the Continental Army, established the first free dispensary in the United States, opposed capital punishment in Pennsylvania, and promoted the establishment of public schools and better education for women. Rush signed the Declaration of Independence as a member of the Second Continental Congress and also served as a delegate to the Constitutional ratifying convention in Pennsylvania as an avid Federalist.

In 1773, Pennsylvania Quakers attempted to pass a bill that would double the importation tax on Africans, making slavery prohibitively expensive. They lacked the Presbyterian votes needed for passage and turned to Rush for his support. Rush must have felt some ambivalence about the request, as he and his mother each owned a slave for periods of their lives. Nonetheless, he agreed to write and publish the following antislavery essay, which develops a number of arguments against slavery rooted in Christian, liberal, and republican ideals.

*   *   *

Delivered in Philadelphia in 1773.

So much hath been said upon the subject of Slave-Keeping, that an Apology may be required for this Address. The only one I shall offer is, that the Evil still continues. This may in part be owing to the great attachment we have to our own Interest, and in part, to the subject not

Source: Charles S. Hyneman and Donald L. Lutz. *American Political Writings during the Founding Era: 1760–1805* (Indianapolis: Liberty Press, 1983). Reprinted with permission of the editors.

being fully exhausted. The design of the following address is to sum up the leading arguments against it, several of which have not been urged by any of those Authors who have written upon it.

Without entering into the History of the facts which relate to the Slave Trade, I shall proceed to combat the principal arguments which are used to support it.

I need hardly say any thing in favour of the Intellects of the Negroes, or of their capacities for virtue and happiness, although these have been supposed, by some, to be inferior to those of the inhabitants of Europe. The accounts which travellers give us of their ingenuity, humanity, and strong attachment to their parents, relations, friends and country, show us that they are equal to the Europeans, when we allow for the diversity of temper and genius which is occasioned by climate. We have many well-attested anecdotes of as sublime and disinterested virtue among them as ever adorned a Roman or a Christian character. But we are to distinguish between an African in his own country, and an African in a state of slavery in America. Slavery is so foreign to the human mind, that the moral faculties, as well as those of the understanding are debased, and rendered torpid by it. All the vices which are charged upon the Negroes in the southern colonies and the West-Indies, such as Idleness, Treachery, Theft, and the like, are the genuine offspring of slavery, and serve as an argument to prove that they were not intended for it.

Nor let it be said, in the present Age, that their black color (as it is commonly called) either subjects them to, or qualifies them for slavery. The vulgar notion of their being descended from Cain, who was supposed to have been marked with this color, is too absurd to need a refutation.— Without enquiring into the Cause of this blackness, I shall only add upon this subject, that so far from being a curse, it subjects the Negroes to no inconveniences, but on the contrary qualifies them for that part of the Globe in which providence has placed them. The ravages of heat, diseases and time, appear less in their faces than in a white one; and when we exclude variety of color from our ideas of Beauty, they may be said to possess every thing necessary to constitute it in common with the white people.

It has been urged by the inhabitants of the Sugar Islands and South Carolina, that it would be impossible to carry on the manufactories of Sugar, Rice, and Indigo, without negro slaves. No manufactory can ever be of consequence enough to society to admit the least violation of the Laws of justice or humanity. But I am far from thinking the arguments used in favour of employing Negroes for the cultivation of these articles, should have any Weight.—M. Le Poivre, late envoy from the king of France, to the king of Cochin-China, and now intendant of the isles of Bourbon and Mauritius, in his observations upon the manners and arts of the various nations in Africa and Asia, speaking of the culture of sugar in Cochin-China, has the following remarks.

[Text omitted]

"Liberty and property form the basis of abundance, and good agriculture: I never observed it to flourish where those rights of mankind were not firmly established. The earth, which multiplies her productions with a kind of profusion, under the hands of the free-born labourer, seems to shrink into barrenness under the sweat of the slave. Such is the will of the great Author of our Nature, who has created man free, and assigned to him the earth, that he might cultivate his possession with the sweat of his brow; but still should enjoy his Liberty." Now if the plantations in the islands and the southern colonies were more limited, and freemen only employed in working them, the general product would be greater, although the profits to individuals would be less,—a circumstance this, which by diminishing opulence in a few, would suppress Luxury and Vice, and promote that equal distribution of property, which appears best calculated to promote the welfare of Society.

[Text omitted]

But there are some who have gone so far as to say that Slavery is not repugnant to the Genius of Christianity, and that it is not forbidden in any part of the Scripture. Natural and Revealed Religion always speak the same things, although the latter delivers its precepts with a louder and more distinct voice than the former. If it could be proved that no testimony was to be found in the Bible against a practice so pregnant with evils of the most destructive tendency to society, it would be sufficient to overthrow its divine Original. We read it is true of Abraham's having slaves born in his house; and we have reason to believe, that part of the riches of the patriarchs consisted in them; but we can no more infer the lawfulness of the practice, from the short account which the Jewish historian gives us of these facts, than we can vindicate telling a lie, because Rahab is not condemned for it in the account which is given of her deceiving the king of Jericho. We read that some of the same men indulged themselves in a plurality of wives, without any strictures being made upon their conduct for it; and yet no one will pretend to say, that this is not forbidden in many parts of the Old Testament. But we are told the Jews kept the Heathens in perpetual bondage. The Design of providence in permitting this evil, was probably to prevent the Jews from marrying amongst strangers, to which their intercourse with them upon any other footing than that of slaves would naturally have inclined them. Had this taken place—their national religion would have been corrupted—they would have contracted all their vices, and the intention of Providence in keeping them a distant people, in order to accomplish the promise made to Abraham, that "in his seed all the nations of the earth should be blessed," would have been defeated; so that the descent of the Messiah from Abraham, could not have been traced, and the divine commission of the Son of God, would have wanted one of its most powerful arguments to support it. But with regard to their own countrymen, it is plain, perpetual slavery was not tolerated. Hence, at the end of seven years or in the year of the jubilee, all the Hebrew slaves were set at liberty, and it was held unlawful to detain them in servitude longer than that time, except by their own Consent. But if, in the partial Revelation which God made, of his will to the Jews, we find such testimonies against slavery, what may we not expect from the Gospel, the Design of which was to abolish all distinctions of name and country. While the Jews thought they complied with the precepts of law, in confining the love of their neighbour "to the children of their own people," Christ commands us to look upon all mankind even our Enemies as our neighbours and brethren, and "in all things, to do unto them whatever we would wish they should do unto us." He tells us further that his "Kingdom is not of this World," and therefore constantly avoids saying any thing that might interfere directly with the Roman or Jewish Governments: and although he does not call upon masters to emancipate their slaves, or slaves to assert that Liberty wherewith God and Nature had made them free, yet there is scarcely a parable or a sermon in the whole history of his life, but what contains the strongest arguments against Slavery. Every prohibition of Covetousness–Intemperance–Pride–Uncleanness–Theft–and Murder, which he delivered;—every lesson of meekness, humility, forbearance, Charity, Self-denial, and brotherly-love, which he taught, are levelled against this evil;—for Slavery, while it includes all the former Vices, necessarily excludes the practice of all the latter Virtues, both from the Master and the Slave.—Let such, therefore, who vindicate the traffic of buying and selling Souls, seek some modern System of Religion to support it, and not presume to sanctify their crimes by attempting to reconcile it to the sublime and perfect Religion of the Great author of Christianity.

There are some amongst us who cannot help allowing the force of our last argument, but plead as a motive for importing and keeping slaves, that they become acquainted with the principles of the religion of our country.—This is like justifying a highway robbery because part of the money acquired in this manner was appropriated to some religious use.— Christianity will never be propagated by any other methods than those employed by Christ and his Apostles. Slavery is an engine as little fitted for that purposed as Fire or the Sword. A Christian Slave is a contradiction in terms. But if we enquire into the methods employed for converting the Negroes to Christianity, we shall find the means suited to the end proposed. In many places Sunday is appropriated to work for themselves, reading and writing are discouraged among them. A belief is even inculcated amongst some, that they have no Souls. In a word,—Every attempt to instruct or convert them, has been constantly opposed by their masters. Nor has the example of their christian masters any tendency to prejudice them in favor of our religion. How often do they betray, in their sudden transports of anger and resentment, (against which there is no restraint provided towards their Negroes) the most violent degrees of passion and fury!—What luxury—what ingratitude to the supreme being—what impiety in their ordinary conversation do some of them discover in the presence of their slaves! I say nothing of the dissolution of marriage vows, or the entire abolition of matrimony, which the frequent sale of them introduces, and which are directly contrary to the laws of nature and the principles of christianity. Would to Heaven I could here conceal the shocking violations of chastity, which some of them are obliged to undergo without daring to complain. Husbands have been forced to prostitute their wives, and mothers their daughters to gratify the brutal lust of a master. This—all—this is practised—Blush—ye impure and hardened wretches, while I repeat it—by men who call themselves christians!

But further—It has been said that we do a kindness to the Negroes by bringing them to America, as we thereby save their lives, which had been forfeited by their being conquered in war. Let such as prefer or inflict slavery rather than Death, disown their being descended from or connected with our mother countries.—But it will be found upon enquiry, that many are stolen or seduced from their friends who have never been conquered; and it is plain, from the testimony of historians and travellers, that wars were uncommon among them, until the christians who began the slave trade, stirred up the different nations to fight against each other. Sooner let them imbrue their hands in each others blood, or condemn one another to perpetual slavery, than the name of one christian, or one American, be stained by the perpetration of such enormous crimes.

Nor let it be urged that by treating slaves well, we render their situation happier in this Country, than it was in their own.—Slavery and Vice are connected together, and the latter is always a source of misery. Besides, by the greatest humanity we can show them, we only lessen, but do not remove the crime, for the injustice of it continues the same. The laws of retribution are so strongly inculcated by the moral governor of the world, that even the ox is entitled to his reward for "treading the Corn." How great then must be the amount of that injustice, which deprives so many of our fellow creatures of the Just reward of their labor.

But it will be asked here, What steps shall we take to remedy this Evil, and what shall we do with those Slaves we have already in this

Country? This is indeed a most difficult question. But let every man contrive to answer it for himself.—

The first thing I would recommend to put a stop to slavery in this country, is to leave off importing slaves. For this purpose let our assemblies unite in petitioning the king and parliament to dissolve the African committee of merchants: It is by them that the trade is chiefly carried on to America. We have the more reason to expect relief from an application at this juncture, as by a late decision in favor of a Virginia slave in Westminster-Hall, the Clamors of the whole nation are raised against them. Let such of our countrymen as engage in the slave trade, be shunned as the greatest enemies to our country, and let the vessels which bring the slaves to us, be avoided as if they bore in them the Seeds of that forbidden fruit, whose baneful taste destroyed both the natural and moral world.—As for the Negroes among us, who, from having acquired all the low vices of slavery, or who from age or infirmities are unfit to be set at liberty, I would propose, for the good of society, that they should continue the property of those with whom they grew old, or from whom they contracted those vices and infirmities. But let the young Negroes be educated in the principles of virtue and religion—let them be taught to read, and write—and afterwards instructed in some business, whereby they may be able to maintain themselves. Let laws be made to limit the time of their servitude, and to entitle them to all the privileges of free-born British subjects. At any rate let Retribution be done to God and to Society.

And now my countrymen, What shall I add more to rouse up your Indignation against Slave-keeping. Consider the many complicated crimes it involves in it. Think of the bloody Wars which are fomented by it, among the African nations, or if these are too common to affect you, think of the pangs which attend the dissolution of the ties of the nature in those who are stolen from their relations. Think of the many thousands who perish by sickness, melancholy, and suicide, in their voyages to America. Pursue the poor devoted victims to one of the West India islands, and see them exposed there to public sale. Hear their cries, and see their looks of tenderness at each other, upon being separated.—Mothers are torn from their Daughters, and Brothers from Brothers, without the liberty of a parting embrace. Their master's name is now marked upon their breasts with a red hot iron. But let us pursue them into a Sugar Field: and behold a scene still more affecting than this—See! the poor wretches with what reluctance they take their instruments of labor into their hands,—Some of them, overcome with heat and sickness, seek to refresh themselves by a little rest.—But, behold an Overseer approaches them—In vain they sue for pity.—He lifts up his Whip, while streams of Blood follow every stroke. Neither age nor sex are spared.—Methinks one of them is woman far advanced in her pregnancy.—At a little distance from these behold a man, who from his countenance and deportment appears as if he was descended from illustrious ancestors.—Yes.—He is the son of a Prince, and was torn by a stratagem, from an amiable wife and two young children.—Mark his sullen looks!—now he bids defiance to the tyranny of his Master, and in an instant—plunges a Knife into his Heart.—But let us return from this Scene, and see the various modes of arbitrary punishments inflicted upon them by their masters. Behold one covered with stripes, into which melted wax is poured—another tied down to a block or a stake—a third suspended in the air by his thumbs—a fourth—I cannot relate it.—Where now is Law or Justice?—Let us fly to them to step in for their relief.—Alas!—The one is silent, and the other denounces more terrible punishment upon them. Let us attend the place appointed for inflicting the penalties of the law. See here one without a limb, whose only crime was an attempt to regain his Liberty,—another led to a Gallows for stealing a morsel of Bread, to which his labor gave him a better title than his master—a third famishing on a gibbet—a fourth, in a flame of Fire! his shrieks pierce the very heavens.—O! God! where is thy Vengeance!—O! Humanity—Justice—Liberty—Religion!—Where,—where are ye fled.—

This is no exaggerated Picture. It is taken from real Life.—Before I conclude I shall take the liberty of addressing several Classes of my countrymen in behalf of our Brethren (for by that name may we now call them) who are in a state of Slavery amongst us.

In the first place let MAGISTRATES both supreme and inferior, exert the authority they are invested with, in suppressing this evil. Let them discountenance it by their example, and show a readiness to concur in every measure proposed to remedy it.

Let LEGISLATORS, reflect upon the trust reposed in them. Let their laws be made after the Spirit of Religion—Liberty—and our most excellent English Constitution. You cannot show your attachment to your King, or your love to your country better, than by suppressing an evil which endangers the dominions of the former, and will in Time destroy the liberty of the latter. Population, and the accession of strangers, in which the Riches of all countries consist, can only flourish in proportion as slavery is discouraged. Extend the privileges we enjoy, to every human creature born amongst us, and let not the Journals of our Assemblies be disgraced with the records of laws, which allow exclusive privileges to men of one color in preference to another.

Ye men of SENSE and VIRTUE—Ye ADVOCATES for American Liberty, rouse up and espouse the cause of Humanity and general Liberty. Bear a testimony against a vice which degrades human nature, and dissolves that universal tie of benevolence which should connect all the children of men together in one great Family.—The plant of liberty is of so tender a Nature, that it cannot thrive long in the neighbourhood of slavery. Remember the eyes of all Europe are fixed upon you, to preserve an asylum for freedom in this country, after the last pillars of it are fallen in every other quarter of the Globe.

But chiefly—ye MINISTERS OF THE GOSPEL, whose dominion over the principles and actions of men is so universally acknowledged and felt,—Ye who estimate the worth of your fellow creatures by their Immortality, and therefore must look upon all mankind as equal,—let your zeal keep pace with your opportunities to put a stop to slavery. While you enforce the duties of "tithe and cummin," neglect not the weightier laws of justice and humanity. Slavery is an Hydra sin, and includes in it every violation of the precepts of the Law and the Gospel. In vain will you command your flocks to offer up the incence of Faith and Charity, while they continue to mingle the Sweat and blood of Negro slaves with their sacrifices.—If the Blood of Able cried aloud for vengeance;—If, under the Jewish dispensation, Cities of refuge could not screen the deliberate murderer—if even manslaughter required sacrifices to expiate it,—and if a single murder so seldom escapes with impunity in any civilized country, what may you not say against that trade, or those manufactures—or Laws, which destroy the lives of so many thousands of our fellow creatures every year?—If in the Old Testament "God swears by his holiness, and by the excellency of Jacob, that the Earth shall tremble and every one mourn that dwelleth therein for the iniquity of those who oppress the poor and crush the needy, who buy the poor with silver, and the needy with a pair of shoes, what judgments may you not denounce upon those who continue to perpetrate these crimes, after the more full discovery which God has made of the law of Equity in the New-Testament. Put them in mind of the Rod which was held over them a few years ago in the Stamp, and Revenue Acts. Remember that national crimes require national punishments, and without declaring what punishment awaits this evil, you may venture to assure them, that it cannot pass with impunity, unless God shall cease to be just or merciful.

THE END.

Henry David Thoreau, "Slavery in Massachusetts" (1854)

Editor's Introduction: Henry David Thoreau (1817–1862) was born in Concord, Massachusetts, and became a proponent of a peculiarly American style of individualism. Thoreau is perhaps most famous as the author of *Walden*, a book born of his experience of withdrawing from society and living for two years on Walden Pond. Thoreau urged a life of simplicity and communion with nature and was very suspicious of government or any large collective enterprises.

During his first year at Walden, Thoreau was arrested for failing to pay a poll tax to protest the Mexican–American War and slavery which, he believed, the war would spread. This gave rise to his famous essay, "Civil Disobedience," which developed the doctrine of nonviolent resistance to immoral governmental laws and policies, a doctrine that was to inspire such later exemplars of civil disobedience as Mahatma Gandhi and Martin Luther King, Jr. In the essay, Thoreau wrote that "any man more right than his neighbors constitutes a majority of one already."

In the following speech, delivered the same year "Civil Disobedience" was published, Thoreau takes his fellow citizens of Massachusetts to task for their complicity in slave-holding through enforcement of the Fugitive Slave Law. This law required northerners to return escaped slaves to their owners. For Thoreau this was a clear example of an unjust law, given the fundamental injustice of slavery, and thus, a law that each person was morally obliged to resist.

*　　　　*　　　　*

I LATELY ATTENDED a meeting of the citizens of Concord, expecting, as one among many, to speak on the subject of slavery in Massachusetts; but I was surprised and disappointed to find that what had called my townsmen together was the destiny of Nebraska, and not of Massachusetts, and that what I had to say would be entirely out of order. I had thought that the house was on fire, and not the prairie; but though several of the citizens of Massachusetts are now in prison for attempting to rescue a slave from her own clutches, not one of the speakers at that meeting expressed regret for it, not one even referred to it. It was only the disposition of some wild lands a thousand miles off which appeared

Source: *The Writings of Henry David Thoreau, Walden Edition* (Boston: Houghton, Mifflin, 1906).

to concern them. The inhabitants of Concord are not prepared to stand by one of their own bridges, but talk only of taking up a position on the highlands beyond the Yellowstone River. Our Buttricks and Davises and Hosmers are retreating thither, and I fear that they will leave no Lexington Common between them and the enemy. There is not one slave in Nebraska; there are perhaps a million slaves in Massachusetts.

They who have been bred in the school of politics fail now and always to face the facts. Their measures are half measures and makeshifts merely. They put off the day of settlement indefinitely, and meanwhile the debt accumulates. Though the Fugitive Slave Law had not been the subject of discussion on that occasion, it was at length faintly resolved by my townsmen, at an adjourned meeting, as I learn, that the compromise compact of 1820 having been repudiated by one of the parties, "Therefore, . . . the Fugitive Slave Law of 1850 must be repealed." But this is not the reason why an iniquitous law should be repealed. The fact which the politician faces is merely that there is less honor among thieves than was supposed, and not the fact that they are thieves.

As I had no opportunity to express my thoughts at that meeting, will you allow me to do so here?

[Text omitted]

The whole military force of the State [of Massachusetts] is at the service of a Mr. Suttle, a slaveholder from Virginia, to enable him to catch a man whom he calls his property; but not a soldier is offered to save a citizen of Massachusetts from being kidnapped! Is this what all these soldiers, all this *training*, have been for these seventy-nine years past? Have they been trained merely to rob Mexico and carry back fugitive slaves to their masters?

These very nights I heard the sound of a drum in our streets. There were men *training* still; and for what? I could with an effort pardon the cockerels of Concord for crowing still, for they, perchance, had not been beaten that morning; but I could not excuse this rub-a-dub of the "trainers." The slave was carried back by exactly such as these; *i.e.*, by the soldier, of whom the best you can say in this connection is that he is a fool made conspicuous by a painted coat.

Three years ago, also, just a week after the authorities of Boston assembled to carry back a perfectly innocent man, and one whom they knew to be innocent, into slavery, the inhabitants of Concord caused the bells to be rung and the cannons to be fired, to celebrate their liberty—and the courage and love of liberty of their ancestors who fought at the bridge. As if *those* three millions had fought for the right to be free themselves, but to hold in slavery three million others. Nowadays, men wear a fool's-cap, and call it a liberty-cap. I do not know but there are some who, if they were tied to a whipping-post, and could but get one hand free, would use it to ring the bells and fire the cannons to celebrate *their* liberty. So some of my townsmen took the liberty to ring and fire. That was the extent of their freedom; and when the sound of the bells died away, their liberty died away also; when the powder was all expended, their liberty went off with the smoke.

The joke could be no broader if the inmates of the prisons were to subscribe for all the powder to be used in such salutes, and hire the jailers to do the firing and ringing for them, while they enjoyed it through the grating.

This is what I thought about my neighbors.

Every humane and intelligent inhabitant of Concord, when he or she heard those bells and those cannons, thought not with pride of the events of the 19th of April, 1775, but with shame of the events of the 12th of April, 1851. But now we have half buried that old shame under a new one.

[Text omitted]

Much has been said about American slavery, but I think that we do not even yet realize what slavery is. If I were seriously to propose to Congress to make mankind into sausages, I have no doubt that most of the members would smile at my proposition, and if any believed me to be in earnest, they would think that I proposed something much worse than Congress had ever done. But if any of them will tell me that to make a man into a sausage would be much worse—would be any worse—than to make him into a slave—than it was to enact the Fugitive Slave Law—I will accuse him of foolishness, of intellectual incapacity, of making a distinction without a difference. The one is just as sensible a proposition as the other.

I hear a good deal said about trampling this law under foot. Why, one need not go out of his way to do that. This law rises not to the level of the head or the reason; its natural habitat is in the dirt. It was born and bred, and has its life, only in the dust and mire, on a level with the feet; and he who walks with freedom, and does not with Hindoo mercy avoid treading on every venomous reptile, will inevitably tread on it, and so trample it under foot—and Webster, its maker, with it, like the dirt-bug and its ball.

Recent events will be valuable as a criticism on the administration of justice in our midst, or, rather, as showing what are the true resources of justice in any community. It has come to this, that the friends of liberty, the friends of the slave, have shuddered when they have understood that his fate was left to the legal tribunals of the country to be decided. Free men have no faith that justice will be awarded in such a case. The judge may decide this way or that; it is a kind of accident, at best. It is evident that he is not a competent authority in so important a case. It is no time, then, to be judging according to his precedents, but to establish a precedent for the future. I would much rather trust to the sentiment of the people. In their vote you would get something of some value, at least, however small; but in the other case, only the trammeled judgment of an individual, of no significance, be it which way it might.

[Text omitted]

The law will never make men free; it is men who have got to make the law free. They are the lovers of law and order who observe the law when the government breaks it.

Among human beings, the judge whose words seal the fate of a man furthest into eternity is not he who merely pronounces the verdict of the law, but he, whoever he may be, who, from a love of truth, and unprejudiced by any custom or enactment of men, utters a true opinion or *sentence* concerning him. He it is that *sentences* him. Whoever can discern truth has received his commission from a higher source than the chiefest justice in the world who can discern only law. He finds himself constituted judge of the judge. Strange that it should be necessary to state such simple truths!

[Text omitted]

I would remind my countrymen that they are to be men first, and Americans only at a late and convenient hour. No matter how valuable law may be to protect your property, even to keep soul and body together, if it do not keep you and humanity together.

I am sorry to say that I doubt if there is a judge in Massachusetts who is prepared to resign his office, and get his living innocently, whenever it is required of him to pass sentence under a law which is merely contrary to the law of God. I am compelled to see that they put themselves, or rather are by character, in this respect, exactly on a level with the marine who discharges his musket in any direction he is ordered to. They are just as much tools, and as little men. Certainly, they are not the more to be respected, because their master enslaves their understandings and consciences, instead of their bodies.

The judges and lawyers—simply as such, I mean—and all men of expediency, try this case by a very low and incompetent standard. They consider, not whether the Fugitive Slave Law is right, but whether it is what they call *constitutional*. Is virtue constitutional, or vice? Is equity constitutional, or iniquity? In important moral and vital questions, like this, it is just as impertinent to ask whether a law is constitutional or not, as to ask whether it is profitable or not. They persist in being the servants of the worst of men, and not the servants of humanity. The question is, not whether you or your grandfather, seventy years ago, did not enter into an agreement to serve the Devil, and that service is not accordingly now due; but whether you will not now, for once and at last, serve God— in spite of your own past recreancy, or that of your ancestor—by obeying that eternal and only just CONSTITUTION, which He, and not any Jefferson or Adams, has written in your being.

The amount of it is, if the majority vote the Devil to be God, the minority will live and behave accordingly, and obey the successful candidate, trusting that, some time or other, by some speaker's casting-vote, perhaps, they may reinstate God. This is the highest principle I can get out or invent for my neighbors. These men act as if they believed that they could safely slide down a hill a little way—or a good way—and would surely come to a place, by and by, where they could begin to slide up again. This is expediency, or choosing that course which offers the slightest obstacles to the feet, that is, a down-hill one. But there is no such thing as accomplishing a righteous reform by the use of "expediency." There is no such thing as sliding up hill. In morals the only sliders are back-sliders.

Thus we steadily worship Mammon, both school and state and church, and on the seventh day curse God with a tintamar from one end of the Union to the other.

Will mankind never learn that policy is not morality—that it never secures any moral right, but considers merely what is expedient? chooses the available candidate—who is invariably the Devil—and what right have his constituents to be surprised, because the Devil does not behave like an angel of light? What is wanted is men, not of policy, but of probity— who recognize a higher law than the Constitution, or the decision of the majority. The fate of the country does not depend on how you vote at the polls—the worst man is as strong as the best at that game; it does not depend on what kind of paper you drop into the ballot-box once a year, but on what kind of man you drop from your chamber into the street every morning.

What should concern Massachusetts is not the Nebraska Bill, nor the Fugitive Slave Bill, but her own slaveholding and servility. Let the State dissolve her union with the slaveholder. She may wriggle and hesitate, and ask leave to read the Constitution once more; but she can find no respectable law or precedent which sanctions the continuance of such a union for an instant.

Let each inhabitant of the State dissolve his union with her, as long as she delays to do her duty.

[Text omitted]

The effect of a good government is to make life more valuable; of a bad one, to make it less valuable. We can afford that railroad and all merely material stock should lose some of its value, for that only compels us to live more simply and economically; but suppose that the value of life itself should be diminished! How can we make a less demand on man and nature, how live more economically in respect to virtue and all noble qualities, than we do? I have lived for the last month—and I think that every man in Massachusetts capable of the sentiment of patriotism must have had a similar experience—with the sense of having suffered a vast and indefinite loss. I did not know at first what ailed me. At last it occurred to me that what I had lost was a country. I had never respected the government near to which I lived, but I had foolishly thought that I might manage to live here, minding my private affairs, and forget it. For my part, my old and worthiest pursuits have lost I cannot say how much of their attraction, and I feel that my investment in life here is worth many per cent less since Massachusetts last deliberately sent back an innocent man, Anthony Burns, to slavery. I dwelt before, perhaps, in the illusion that my life passed somewhere only *between* heaven and hell, but now I cannot persuade myself that I do not dwell *wholly within* hell. The site of that political organization called Massachusetts is to me morally covered with volcanic scoriae and cinders, such as Milton describes in the infernal regions. If there is any hell more unprincipled than our rulers, and we, the ruled, I feel curious to see it. Life itself being worth less, all things with it, which minister to it, are worth less. Suppose you have a small library, with pictures to adorn the walls—a garden laid out around—and contemplate scientific and literary pursuits and discover all at once that your villa, with all its contents is located in hell, and that the justice of the peace has a cloven foot and a forked tail—do not these things suddenly lose their value in your eyes?

I feel that, to some extent, the State has fatally interfered with my lawful business. It has not only interrupted me in my passage through Court Street on errands of trade, but it has interrupted me and every man on his onward and upward path, on which he had trusted soon to leave Court Street far behind. What right had it to remind me of Court Street? I have found that hollow which even I had relied on for solid.

I am surprised to see men going about their business as if nothing had happened. I say to myself, "Unfortunates! they have not heard the news." I am surprised that the man whom I just met on horseback should be so earnest to overtake his newly bought cows running away—since all property is insecure, and if they do not run away again, they may be taken away from him when he gets them. Fool! does he not know that his seed-corn is worth less this year—that all beneficent harvests fail as you approach the empire of hell? No prudent man will build a stone house under these circumstances, or engage in any peaceful enterprise which it requires a long time to accomplish. Art is as long as ever, but life is more interrupted and less available for a man's proper pursuits. It is not an era of repose. We have used up all our inherited freedom. If we would save our lives, we must fight for them.

I walk toward one of our ponds; but what signifies the beauty of nature when men are base? We walk to lakes to see our serenity reflected in them; when we are not serene, we go not to them. Who can be serene in a country where both the rulers and the ruled are without principle? The remembrance of my country spoils my walk. My thoughts are murder to the State, and involuntarily go plotting against her.

But it chanced the other day that I scented a white water-lily, and a season I had waited for had arrived. It is the emblem of purity. It bursts up so pure and fair to the eye, and so sweet to the scent, as if to show us what purity and sweetness reside in, and can be extracted from, the slime and muck of earth. I think I have plucked the first one that has opened for a mile. What confirmation of our hopes is in the fragrance of this flower! I shall not so soon despair of the world for it, notwithstanding slavery, and the cowardice and want of principle of Northern men. It suggests what kind of laws have prevailed longest and widest, and still prevail, and that the time may come when man's deeds will smell as sweet. Such is the odor which the plant emits. If Nature can compound this fragrance still annually, I shall believe her still young and full of vigor, her integrity and genius unimpaired, and that there is virtue even in man, too, who is fitted to perceive and love it. It reminds me that Nature has been partner to no Missouri Compromise. I scent no compromise in the fragrance of the water-lily. It is not a *Nymphaea* DOUGLASII. In it, the sweet, and pure, and innocent are wholly sundered from the obscene and baleful. I do not scent in this the time-serving irresolution of a Massachusetts Governor, nor of a Boston Mayor. So behave that the odor of your actions may enhance the general sweetness of the atmosphere, that when we behold or scent a flower, we may not be reminded how inconsistent your deeds are with it; for all odor is but one form of advertisement of a moral quality, and if fair actions had not been performed, the lily would not smell sweet. The foul slime stands for the sloth and vice of man, the decay of humanity; the fragrant flower that springs from it, for the purity and courage which are immortal.

Slavery and servility have produced no sweet-scented flower annually, to charm the senses of men, for they have no real life: they are merely a decaying and a death, offensive to all healthy nostrils. We do not complain that they *live*, but that they do not *get buried*. Let the living bury them: even they are good for manure.

THE END

George Fitzhugh, "Cannibals All! Or, Slaves Without Masters" (1857)

Editor's Introduction: George Fitzhugh (1806–1881), born in Prince William County, Virginia, is a most unusual figure in the history of American political and social thought. Fitzhugh's parents were not very prosperous small farmers, but his lineage included many owners of large plantations and socially prominent Southerners. He lacked formal education but read widely in history, philosophy, and current events, including the works of Northern abolitionists, whose ideas he despised. Fitzhugh stands squarely outside of the liberal tradition in America, and this alone differentiates him from the vast majority of American political thinkers. He was a steadfast foe to the industrial capitalist society emerging in the North, but not for the reasons Marxists or other socialists offer.

In *Cannibals All*, Fitzhugh argues that all societies are based upon the exploitation of labor. This is as true in what he might sarcastically call the "progressive" North as in the South where slavery existed. In fact, Fitzhugh argues that the "wage slave" of capitalism is worse off than the Southern chattel slave. This is so as the latter's master takes a life-long responsibility for his well-being, while the industrial worker is simply dismissed when he is no longer productive. Fitzhugh also rejects the Jeffersonian premise of natural equality of "all men" and develops a social vision akin to that of the feudal Middle Ages. In his ideal world, a nobility secure in their social station and free from the need to labor would pursue learning, culture, and other high pleasures supported by the labor of politically powerless working-class whites and slaves.

Fitzhugh's position is rather eccentric even for his day, though not entirely unique among the Southern gentry. It represents a hardening of positions over slavery as the abolitionist movement in the North was growing and the institution was increasingly under attack. His defense of slavery shows none of the ambivalence one finds in the writings of such founders as Madison, Jefferson, and Washington, an ambivalence that emerges largely from their inability to square their belief in the liberal principles embodied in the Declaration of Independence with slave ownership—including their own. Rejecting those principles, Fitzhugh does not experience these misgivings.

Source: George Fitzhugh, *Cannibals All! Or, Slaves Without Masters* (Richmond: A. Morris, 1857).

*   *   *

The Universal Trade

We are all, North and South, engaged in the White Slave Trade, and he who succeeds best is esteemed most respectable. It is far more cruel than the Black Slave Trade, because it exacts more of its slaves, and neither protects nor governs them. We boast that it exacts more when we say, "that the *profits* made from employing free labor are greater than those from slave labor." The profits, made from free labor, are the amount of the products of such labor, which the employer, by means of the command which capital or skill gives him, takes away, exacts, or "exploitates" from the free laborer. The profits of slave labor are that portion of the products of such labor which the power of the master enables him to appropriate. These profits are less, because the master allows the slave to retain a larger share of the results of his own labor than do the employers of free labor. But we not only boast that the White Slave Trade is more exacting and fraudulent (in fact, though not in intention) than Black Slavery; but we also boast that it is more cruel, in leaving the laborer to take care of himself and family out of the pittance which skill or capital have allowed him to retain. When the day's labor is ended, he is free, but is overburdened with the cares of family and household, which make his freedom an empty and delusive mockery. But his employer is really free, and may enjoy the profits made by others' labor, without a care, or a trouble, as to their well-being. The negro slave is free too, when the labors of the day are over, and free in mind as well as body; for the master provides food, raiment, house, fuel, and everything else necessary to the physical well-being of himself and family. The master's labors commence just when the slave's end. No wonder men should prefer white slavery to capital, to negro slavery, since it is more profitable, and is free from all the cares and labors of black slave-holding.

Now, reader, if you wish to know yourself—to "descant on your own deformity"—read on. But if you would cherish self-conceit, self-esteem, or self-appreciation, throw down our book; for we will dispel illusions which have promoted your happiness, and show you that what you have considered and practiced as virtue is little better than moral Cannibalism. But you will find yourself in numerous and respectable company; for all good and respectable people are "Cannibals all" who do not labor, or who are successfully trying to live without labor, on the unrequited labor of other people:—Whilst low, bad, and disreputable people, are those who labor to support themselves, and to support said respectable people besides. Throwing the negro slaves out of the account, and society is divided in Christendom into four classes: the rich, or independent respectable people, who live well and labor not at all, the professional and skillful respectable people, who do a little light work, for enormous wages; the poor hard-working people, who support everybody, and starve themselves; and the poor thieves, swindlers, and sturdy beggars, who live like gentlemen, without labor, on the labor of other people. The gentlemen exploitate, which being done on a large scale and requiring a great many victims, is highly respectable—whilst the rogues and beggars take so little from others that they fare little better than those who labor.

But, reader, we do not wish to fire into the flock. "Thou art the man!" You are a Cannibal! and if a successful one, pride yourself on the number of your victims quite as much as any Fiji chieftain, who breakfasts, dines, and sups on human flesh—and your conscience smites you, if you have failed to succeed, quite as much as his, when he returns from an unsuccessful foray.

Probably, you are a lawyer, or a merchant, or a doctor, who has made by your business fifty thousand dollars, and retired to live on your capital. But, mark! not to spend your capital. That would be vulgar, disreputable, criminal. That would be, to live by your own labor; for your capital is your amassed labor. That would be to do as common working men do; for they take the pittance which their employers leave them to live on. They live by labor; for they exchange the results of their own labor for the products of other people's labor. It is, no doubt, an honest, vulgar way of living, but not at all a respectable way. The respectable way of living is to make other people work for you, and to pay them nothing for so doing—and to have no concern about them after their work is done. Hence, white slave-holding is much more respectable than negro slavery—for the master works nearly as hard for the negro as he for the master. But you, my virtuous, respectable leader, exact three thousand dollars per annum from white labor (for your income is the product of white labor) and make not one cent of return in any form. You retain your capital, and never labor, and yet live in luxury on the labor of others. Capital commands labor, as the master does the slave. Neither pays for labor; but the master permits the slave to retain a larger allowance from the proceeds of his own labor, and hence "free labor is cheaper than slave labor." You, with the command over labor which your capital gives you, are a slave owner—a master, without the obligations of a master. They who work for you, who create your income, are slaves, without the rights of slaves. Slaves without a master! Whilst you were engaged in amassing your capital, in seeking to become independent, you were in the White Slave Trade. To become independent is to be able to make other people support you, without being obliged to labor for *them*. Now, what man in society is not seeking to attain this situation?

He who attains it is a slave owner, in the worst sense. He who is in pursuit of it is engaged in the slave trade. You, reader, belong to the one or other class. The men without property, in free society, are theoretically in a worse condition than slaves. Practically, their condition corresponds with this theory, as history and statistics everywhere demonstrate. The capitalists, in free society, live in ten times the luxury and show that Southern masters do, because the slaves to capital work harder and cost less than negro slaves.

The negro slaves of the South are the happiest, and, in some sense, the freest people in the world. The children and the aged and infirm work not at all, and yet have all the comforts and necessaries of life provided for them. They enjoy liberty, because they are oppressed neither by care nor labor. The women do little hard work, and are protected from the despotism of their husbands by their masters. The negro men and stout boys work, on the average, in good weather, not more than nine hours a day. The balance of their time is spent in perfect abandon. Besides, they have their Sabbaths and holidays. White men, with so much of license and liberty, would die of ennui; but negroes luxuriate in corporeal and mental repose. With their faces upturned to the sun, they can sleep at any hour; and quiet sleep is the greatest of human enjoyments. "Blessed be the man who invented sleep." 'Tis happiness in itself—and results from contentment with the present, and confident assurance of the future. We do not know whether free laborers ever sleep. They are fools to do so; for, whilst they sleep, the wily and watchful capitalist is devising means to ensnare and exploitate them. The free laborer must work or starve. He is more of a slave than the negro, because he works longer and harder for less allowance than the slave, and has no holiday, because the cares of life with him begin when its labors end. He has no liberty, and not a single right. We know, 'tis often said, air and water are common property, which all have equal right to participate and enjoy; but this is utterly false. The appropriation of the lands carries with it the appropriation of all on or above the lands, *usque ad coelum, aut ad inferos.*[1] A man cannot breathe the air without a place to breathe it from, and all places are appropriated. All water is private property "to the middle of the stream," except the ocean, and that is not fit to drink.

Free laborers have not a thousandth part of the rights and liberties of negro slaves. Indeed, they have not a single liberty, unless it be the right or liberty to die. But the reader may think that he and other capitalists and employers are freer than negro slaves. Your capital would soon

---

[1] "Even to heaven or to hell."

vanish, if you dared indulge in the liberty and abandon of negroes. You hold your wealth and position by the tenure of constant watchfulness, care, and circumspection. You never labor; but you are never free.

Where a few own the soil, they have unlimited power over the balance of society, until domestic slavery comes in to compel them to permit this balance of society to draw a sufficient and comfortable living from *terra mater*. Free society asserts the right of a few to the earth—slavery maintains that it belongs, in different degrees, to all.

But, reader, well may you follow the slave trade. It is the only trade worth following, and slaves the only property worth owning. All other is worthless, a mere *caput mortuum*,[2] except in so far as it vests the owner with the power to command the labors of others—to enslave them. Give you a palace, ten thousand acres of land, sumptuous clothes, equipage, and every other luxury; and with your artificial wants you are poorer than Robinson Crusoe, or the lowest working man, if you have no slaves to capital, or domestic slaves. Your capital will not bring you an income of a cent, nor supply one of your wants, without labor. Labor is indispensable to give value to property, and if you owned every thing else, and did not own labor, you would be poor. But fifty thousand dollars means, and is, fifty thousand dollars worth of slaves. You can command, without touching on that capital, three thousand dollars' worth of labor per annum. You could do no more were you to buy slaves with it, and then you would be cumbered with the cares of governing and providing for them. You are a slaveholder now, to the amount of fifty thousand dollars, with all the advantages, and none of the cares and responsibilities of a master.

"Property in man" is what all are struggling to obtain. Why should they not be obliged to take care of man, their property, as they do of their horses and their hounds, their cattle and their sheep. Now, under the delusive name of liberty, you work him "from morn to dewy eve"—from infancy to old age—then turn him out to starve. You treat your horses and hounds better. Capital is a cruel master. The free slave trade, the commonest, yet the cruellest of trades. . . .

---

[2] "Worthless residue."

Abraham Lincoln,
"Second Inaugural Address" (1865)

Editor's Introduction: Engraved in the Lincoln Memorial in Washington, D.C. on the wall facing the Gettysburg Address, is Lincoln's Second Inaugural Address. By the time of this speech in March 1865, the outcome of the Civil War was no longer in doubt. General Robert E. Lee's surrender at the Appomattox Courthouse took place just over a month later. In the Address, Lincoln is preparing the grounds for reconciliation with the South after the war. At the same time, he is suggesting in most powerful terms that the terrible costs the nation endured in the war, including some 600,000 dead, are the "righteous judgment" of a just God. Lincoln was not an egalitarian in terms of race. He doubted whether black and white could ever live together in America as social equals, and even stated that, if they could not, he would prefer to see that whites remained in the superior position. Nonetheless, he abhorred slavery and believed that the principles of the Declaration of Independence applied to all men regardless of color. Lincoln's legacy on race in America defies easy summary or categorization. However, Frederick Douglass' judicious speech on Lincoln, also in this collection, is a good place to begin that assessment.

*   *   *

At this second appearing to take the oath of the Presidential office, there is less occasion for an extended address than there was at the first. Then a statement, somewhat in detail, of a course to be pursued, seemed fitting and proper. Now, at the expiration of four years, during which public declarations have been constantly called forth on every point and phase of the great contest which still absorbs the attention and engrosses the energies of the nation, little that is new could be presented. The progress of our arms, upon which all else chiefly depends, is as well known to the public as to myself; and it is, I trust, reasonably satisfactory and encouraging to all. With high hope for the future, no prediction in regard to it is ventured.

On the occasion corresponding to this four years ago, all thoughts were anxiously directed to an impending civil war. All dreaded it—all sought to avert it. While the inaugural address was being delivered from this place, devoted altogether to *saving* the Union without war, insurgent agents were in the city seeking to *destroy* it without war—seeking to dissolve the Union, and divide effects, by negotiation. Both parties deprecated war; but one of them would *make* war rather than let the nation survive; and the other would *accept* war rather than let it perish. And the war came.

One eighth of the whole population were colored slaves, not distributed generally over the Union, but localized in the Southern part of it. These slaves constituted a peculiar and powerful interest. All knew that this interest was, somehow, the cause of the war. To strengthen, perpetuate, and extend this interest was the object for which the insurgents would rend the Union, even by war; while the government claimed no right to do more than to restrict the territorial enlargement of it.

Neither party expected for the war the magnitude, or the duration, which it has already attained. Neither anticipated that the *cause* of the conflict might cease with, or even before, the conflict itself should cease. Each looked for an easier triumph, and a result less fundamental and astounding. Both read the same Bible, and pray to the same God; and each invokes His aid against the other. It may seem strange that any men should dare to ask a just God's assistance in wringing their bread from the sweat of other men's faces; but let us judge not, that we be not judged. The prayers of both could not be answered;—that of neither has been answered fully. The Almighty has His own purposes. "Woe unto the world because of offenses! for it must needs be that offenses come; but woe to that man by whom the offense cometh!" If we shall suppose that American Slavery is one of those offenses which, in the providence of God, must needs come, but which, having continued through His appointed time, He now wills to remove, and that He gives to both North and South this terrible war, as the woe due to those by whom the offense came, shall we discern therein any departure from those divine attributes which the believers in a Living God always ascribe to Him? Fondly do we hope—fervently do we pray—that this mighty scourge of war may speedily pass away. Yet, if God wills that it continue until all the wealth piled by the bondman's two hundred and fifty years of unrequited toil shall be sunk, and until every drop of blood drawn with the lash shall be paid by another drawn with the sword, as was said three thousand years ago, so still it must be said, "The judgments of the Lord are true and righteous altogether."

With malice toward none; with charity for all; with firmness in the right, as God gives us to see the right, let us strive on to finish the work we are in; to bind up the nation's wounds; to care for him who shall have borne the battle, and for his widow, and his orphan—to do all which may achieve and cherish a just and lasting peace among ourselves, and with all nations.

Frederick Douglass,
"Oration in Memory of Abraham Lincoln" (1876)

Editor's Introduction: Frederick Douglass (c. 1817–1895) was born a slave in Tuckahoe, Maryland. He was to become one of the greatest spokespersons and activists for the abolitionist cause. Douglass escaped from slavery in 1838. He gave his first antislavery speech in 1841 and immediately struck a responsive chord, becoming the most sought-after black abolitionist speaker. In 1845 he published the first version of his life story, *Narrative of the Life of Frederick Douglass, An American Slave,* which became a sensation and contributed to Douglass's renown and influence.

Though Douglass worked closely with other abolitionists such as William Lloyd Garrison and Wendell Phillips, he was more militant than they were. Garrison took as his motto the phrase, "No Union with Slaveholders!" Douglass was less concerned with ending this union than with ending slavery and thought that, ultimately, this would only be done through force, a conclusion Garrison for one resisted. That Lincoln was willing to wield the sword (even if his first goal in fighting the Civil War was preservation of the Union and not the end of slavery) is a source of Douglass's admiration for him. Further, he did not question Lincoln's deep hatred of slavery and admired the steps the President took to end it, especially issuing the Emancipation Proclamation, as the Civil War progressed.

On the other hand, Douglass also recognized Lincoln's limitations regarding racial equality. He argues that blacks were at best Lincoln's "stepchildren" while whites were his children. Lincoln shared the prejudices of his day, Douglass writes, but was an historical force for the end of slavery and offered the first glimmers of hope for racial equality in America.

*　　　　*　　　　*

Friends and Fellow-citizens:

[Text omitted]

We stand today at the national center to perform something like a national act—an act which is to go into history; and we are here where

---

Source: *Oration Delivered on the Occasion of the Unveiling of the Freedmen's Monument in Memory of Abraham Lincoln, in Lincoln Park, Washington, D.C., April 14, 1876* (St. Louis, 1876).

269

every pulsation of the national heart can be heard, felt, and reciprocated. A thousand wires, fed with thought and winged with lightning, put us in instantaneous communication with the loyal and true men all over this country.

Few facts could better illustrate the vast and wonderful change which has taken place in our condition as a people than the fact of our assembling here for the purpose we have today. Harmless, beautiful, proper, and praiseworthy as this demonstration is, I cannot forget that no such demonstration would have been tolerated here twenty years ago. The spirit of slavery and barbarism, which still lingers to blight and destroy in some dark and distant parts of our country, would have made our assembling here the signal and excuse for opening upon us all the flood-gates of wrath and violence. That we are here in peace today is a compliment and a credit to American civilization, and a prophecy of still greater national enlightenment and progress in the future. I refer to the past not in malice, for this is no day for malice; but simply to place distinctly in front the gratifying and glorious change which has come both to our white fellow-citizens and ourselves, and to congratulate all upon the contrast between now and then; the new dispensation of freedom with its thousand blessings to both races, and the old dispensation of slavery with its ten thousand evils to both races—white and black. In view, then, of the past, the present, and the future, with the long and dark history of our bondage behind us, and with liberty, progress, and enlightenment before us, I . . . congratulate you upon this auspicious day and hour.

[Text omitted]

The sentiment that brings us here to-day is one of the noblest that can stir and thrill the human heart. It has crowned and made glorious the high places of all civilized nations with the grandest and most enduring works of art, designed to illustrate the characters and perpetuate the memories of great public men. It is the sentiment which from year to year adorns with fragrant and beautiful flowers the graves of our loyal, brave, and patriotic soldiers who fell in defence of the Union and liberty. It is the sentiment of gratitude and appreciation, which often, in the presence of many who hear me, has filled yonder heights of Arlington with the eloquence of eulogy and the sublime enthusiasm of poetry and song; a sentiment which can never die while the Republic lives.

For the first time in the history of our people, and in the history of the whole American people, we join in this high worship, and march conspicuously in the line of this time-honored custom. . . . I commend the fact to notice; let it be told in every part of the Republic; let men of all parties and opinions hear it; let those who despise us, not less than those who respect us, know that now and here, in the spirit of liberty, loyalty, and gratitude, let it be known everywhere, and by everybody who takes an interest in human progress and in the amelioration of the condition of mankind, that, in the presence and with the approval of the members of the American House of Representatives, reflecting the general sentiment of the country; that in the presence of that august body, the American Senate, representing the highest intelligence and the calmest judgment of the country; in the presence of the Supreme Court and Chief Justice of the United States, to whose decisions we all patriotically bow; in the presence and under the steady eye of the honored and trusted President of the United States, with the members of his wise and patriotic Cabinet, we, the colored people, newly emancipated and rejoicing in our blood-bought freedom, near the close of the first century in the life of this Republic, have now and here unveiled, set apart, and dedicated a monument of enduring granite and bronze, in every line, feature, and figure of which the men of this generation may read, and those of after-coming generations may read, something of the exalted character and great works of Abraham Lincoln, the first martyr President of the United States.

Fellow-citizens, in what we have said and done today, and in what we may say and do hereafter, we disclaim everything like arrogance and assumption. We claim for ourselves no superior devotion to the character, history, and memory of the illustrious name whose monument we have here dedicated today. We fully comprehend the relation of Abraham Lincoln both to ourselves and to the white people of the United States. Truth is proper and beautiful at all times and in all places, and it is never more proper and beautiful in any case than when speaking of a great public man whose example is likely to be commended for honor and imitation long after his departure to the solemn shades, the silent continents of eternity. It must be admitted, truth compels me to admit even here in the presence of the monument we have erected to his memory, Abraham Lincoln was not, in the fullest sense of the word, either our man or our model. In his interests, in his associations, in his habits of thought, and in his prejudices, he was a white man.

He was preeminently the white man's President, entirely devoted to the welfare of white men. He was ready and willing at any time during the first years of his administration to deny, postpone, and sacrifice the rights of humanity in the colored people to promote the white people of this country. In all his education and feeling he was American of the Americans. He came into the Presidential chair upon one principle alone, namely, opposition to the extension of slavery. His arguments in further-ance of this policy had their motive and mainspring in his patriotic devo-tion to the interests of his own race. To protect, defend, and perpetuate slavery in the states where it existed Abraham Lincoln was not less ready than any other President to draw the sword of the nation. He was ready to execute all the supposed guarantees of the United States Constitution in favor of the slave system anywhere inside the slave states. He was willing to pursue, recapture, and send back the fugitive slave to his master, and to suppress a slave rising for liberty, though his guilty master were already in arms against the Government. The race to which we belong were not the special objects of his consideration. Knowing this, I concede to you, my white fellow-citizens, a preeminence in this worship at once full and supreme. First, midst, and last, you and yours were the objects of his deepest affection, and his most earnest solicitude. You are the children of Abraham Lincoln. We are at best only his step-children; children by adoption, children by forces of circumstances and necessity. To you it especially belongs to sound his praises, to preserve and perpetuate his memory, to multiply his statues, to hang his pictures high upon your walls, and commend his example, for to you he was a great and glorious friend and benefactor. Instead of supplanting you at his altar, we would exhort you to build high his monuments; let them be of the most costly material, of the most cunning workmanship; let their forms be symmetrical, beautiful, and perfect; let their bases be upon solid rocks, and their summits lean against the unchanging blue, overhanging sky, and let them endure forever! But while in abundance of your wealth, and in the fullness of your just and patriotic devotion, you do all this, we entreat you to despise not the humble offering we this day unveil to view; for while Abraham Lincoln saved for you a country, he delivered us from a bondage, according to Jefferson, one hour of which was worse than ages of the oppression your fathers rose in rebellion to oppose.

Fellow-citizens, ours is no new-born zeal and devotion—merely a thing of this moment. The name of Abraham Lincoln was near and dear to our hearts in the darkest and most perilous hours of the Republic. We were no more ashamed of him when shrouded in clouds of darkness, of doubt, and defeat than when we saw him crowned with victory, honor, and glory. Our faith in him was often taxed and strained to the uttermost, but it never failed. When he tarried long in the mountain; when he strangely told us that we were the cause of the war; when he still more strangely told us that we were to leave the land in which we were born; when he refused to employ our arms in defence of the Union; when, after accepting our services as colored soldiers, he refused to retaliate our murder and torture as colored prisoners; when he told us he would save the Union if he could with slavery; when he revoked the Proclamation of Emancipation of General Fremont; when he refused to remove the popular commander of the Army of the Potomac, in the days of its inaction and defeat, who was more zealous in his efforts to protect slavery than to suppress rebellion; when we saw all this, and more, we were at times grieved, stunned, and greatly bewildered; but our hearts believed while they ached and bled. Nor was this, even at that time, a blind and unreasoning superstition. Despite the mist and haze that surrounded him; despite the tumult, the hurry, and confusion of the hour, we were able to take a comprehensive view of Abraham Lincoln, and to make reasonable allowance for the circumstances of his position. We saw him, measured him, and estimated him; not by stray utterances to injudicious and tedious delegations, who often tried his patience; not by isolated facts torn from their connection; not by any partial and imperfect glimpses, caught at inopportune moments; but by a broad survey, in the light of the stern logic of great events, and in view of that divinity which shapes our ends, rough hew them how we will, we came to the conclusion that the hour and the man of our redemption had somehow met in the person of Abraham Lincoln. It mattered little to us what language he might employ on special occasions; it mattered little to us, when we fully knew him, whether he was swift or slow in his movements; it was enough for us that Abraham Lincoln was at the head of a great movement, and was in living and earnest sympathy with that movement, which, in the nature of things, must go on until slavery should be utterly and forever abolished in the United States.

When, therefore, it shall be asked what we have to do with the memory of Abraham Lincoln, or what Abraham Lincoln had to do with us, the answer is ready, full, and complete. Though he loved Caesar less than Rome, though the Union was more to him than our freedom or our future, under his wise and beneficent rule we saw ourselves gradually lifted from the depths of slavery to the heights of liberty and manhood; under his wise and beneficent rule, and by measures approved and vigorously pressed by him, we saw that the handwriting of ages, in the form of prejudice and proscription, was rapidly fading away from the face of our whole country; under his rule, and in due time, about as soon after all as the country could tolerate the strange spectacle, we saw our brave sons and brothers laying off the rags of bondage, and being clothed all over in the blue uniforms of the soldiers of the United States; under his rule we saw two hundred thousand of our dark and dusky people responding to the call of Abraham Lincoln, and with muskets on their shoulders, and eagles on their buttons, timing their high footsteps to liberty and union under the national flag; under his rule we saw the independence of the black republic of Haiti, the special object of slaveholding aversion and horror, fully recognized, and her minister, a colored gentleman, duly received here in the city of Washington; under his rule we saw the internal slave-trade, which so long disgraced the nation, abolished, and slavery abolished in the District of Columbia; under his rule we saw for the first time the law enforced against the foreign slave trade, and the first slave-trader hanged like any other pirate or murderer; under his rule, assisted by the greatest captain of our age, and his inspiration, we saw the Confederate States, based upon the idea that our race must be slaves, and slaves forever, battered to pieces and scattered to the four winds; under his rule, and in the fullness of time, we saw Abraham Lincoln, after giving the slaveholders three months' grace in which to save their hateful slave system, penning the immortal paper, which, though special in its language, was general in its principles and effect, making slavery forever impossible in the United States. Though we waited long, we saw all this and more.

Can any colored man, or any white man friendly to the freedom of all men, ever forget the night which followed the first day of January, 1863, when the world was to see if Abraham Lincoln would prove to be as good as his word? I shall never forget that memorable night, when in a distant city I waited and watched at a public meeting, with three thousand others not less anxious than myself, for the word of deliverance others not which we have heard read today. Nor shall I ever forget the outburst of joy and thanksgiving that rent the air when the lightning brought to us the emancipation proclamation. In that happy hour we forgot all delay, and forgot all tardiness, forgot that the President had bribed the rebels to lay down their arms by a promise to withhold the bolt which would smite the slave-system with destruction; and we were thenceforward willing to allow the President all the latitude of time, phraseology, and every honorable device that statesmanship might require for the achievement of a great and beneficent measure of liberty and progress.

[Text omitted]

I have said that President Lincoln was a white man, and shared the prejudices common to his countrymen towards the colored race. Looking back to his times and to the condition of his country, we are compelled to admit that this unfriendly feeling on his part may be safely set down as one element of his wonderful success in organizing the loyal American people for the tremendous conflict before them, and bringing them safely through that conflict. His great mission was to accomplish two things; first, to save his country from dismemberment and ruin; and, second, to free his country from the great crime of slavery. To do one or the other, or both, he must have the earnest sympathy and the powerful cooperation of his loyal fellow-countrymen. Without this primary and essential condition to success his efforts must have been vain and utterly fruitless. Had he put the abolition of slavery before the salvation of the Union, he would have inevitably driven from him a powerful class of the American people and rendered resistance to rebellion impossible. Viewed from the genuine abolition ground, Mr. Lincoln seemed tardy, cold, dull, and indifferent; but measuring him by the sentiment of his country, a sentiment he was bound as a statesman to consult, he was swift, zealous, radical, and determined.

Though Mr. Lincoln shared prejudices of his white fellow-countrymen against the Negro, it is hardly necessary to say that in his heart of hearts he loathed and hated slavery. . . .[1] The man who could say, "Fondly do we hope, fervently do we pray, that this mighty scourge of war shall soon pass away, yet if God wills it continue till all the wealth piled by two hundred years of bondage shall have been wasted, and each drop of blood drawn by the lash shall have been paid for by one drawn by the sword, the judgments of the Lord are true and righteous altogether," gives all needed proof of his feeling on the subject of slavery. He was willing, while the South was loyal, that it should have its pound of flesh, because he thought that it was so nominated in the bond; but farther than this no earthly power could make him go.

Fellow-citizens, whatever else in this world may be partial, unjust, and uncertain, time, time! is impartial, just, and certain in its action. . . . The honest and comprehensive statesman, clearly discerning the needs of his country, and earnestly endeavoring to do his whole duty, though covered and blistered with reproaches, may safely leave his course to the silent judgment of time. Few great public men have ever been the victims of fiercer denunciation than Abraham Lincoln was during his administration. . . . He was assailed by Abolitionists; he was assailed by slaveholders; he was assailed by the men who were for peace at any price; he was assailed by those who were for a more vigorous prosecution of the war; he was assailed for not making the war an abolition war; and he was bitterly assailed for making the war an abolition war.

But now behold the change: the judgment of the present hour is, that taking him for all in all, measuring the tremendous magnitude of the work before him, considering the necessary means to ends, and surveying the end from the beginning, infinite wisdom has seldom sent any man into the world better fitted for his mission than Abraham Lincoln. His birth, his training, and his natural endowments, both mental and physical, were strongly in his favor. Born and reared among the lowly, a stranger to wealth and luxury, compelled to grapple single-handed with

---

[1] "I am naturally anti-slavery. If slavery is not wrong, nothing is wrong. I cann' remember when I did not so think and feel."—Letter of Mr. Lincoln to Mr. Hod of Kentucky, April 4, 1864.

the flintiest hardships of life, from tender youth to sturdy manhood, he grew strong in the manly and heroic qualities demanded by the great mission to which he was called by the votes of his countrymen. . . .

All day long he could split heavy rails in the woods, and half the night long he could study his English Grammar by the uncertain flare and glare of the light made by a pine-knot. He was at home on the land with his axe, with his maul, with gluts, and his wedges; and he was equally at home on water, with his oars, with his poles, with his planks, and with his boat-hooks. And whether in his flat-boat on the Mississippi River, or at the fireside of his frontier cabin, he was a man of work. A son of toil himself, he was linked in brotherly sympathy with the sons of toil in every loyal part of the Republic. This very fact gave him tremendous power with the American people, and materially contributed not only to selecting him to the Presidency, but in sustaining his administration of the Government.

Upon his inauguration as President of the United States, an office, even when assumed under the most favorable conditions, fitted to tax and strain the largest abilities, Abraham Lincoln was met by a tremendous crisis. He was called upon not merely to administer the Government, but to decide, in the face of terrible odds, the fate of the Republic.

A formidable rebellion rose in his path before him; the Union was already practically dissolved; his country was torn and rent asunder at the center. Hostile armies were already organized against the Republic, armed with the munitions of war which the Republic had provided for its own defence. The tremendous question for him to decide was whether his country should survive the crisis and flourish, or be dismembered and perish. His predecessor in office had already decided the question in favor of national dismemberment, by denying to it the right of self-defence and self-preservation—a right which belongs to the meanest insect.

Happily for the country, happily for you and for me, the judgement of James Buchanan, the patrician, was not the judgment of Abraham Lincoln, the plebeian. He brought his strong common sense, sharpened 'n the school of adversity, to bear upon the question. He did not hesitate, ''d not doubt, he did not falter; but at once resolved that at whatever whatever cost, the union of the States should be preserved. A ᵒlf, his faith was strong and unwavering in the patriotism of Timid men said before Mr. Lincoln's inauguration, that ' President of the United States. A voice in influential 'ᵀnion slide." Some said that a Union maintained ₃s. Others said a rebellion of 8,000,000 cannot midst of all this tumult and timidity, and against ₁n was clear in his duty, and had an oath in heaven.

He calmly and bravely heard the voice of doubt and fear all around him; but he had an oath in heaven, and there was not power enough on earth to make this honest boatman, backwoodsman, and broad-handed splitter of rails evade or violate that sacred oath. He had not been schooled in the ethics of slavery; his plain life had favored his love of truth. He had not been taught that treason and perjury were the proof of honor and honesty. His moral training was against his saying one thing when he meant another. The trust that Abraham Lincoln had in himself and in the people was surprising and grand, but it was also enlightened and well founded. He knew the American people better than they knew themselves, and his truth was based upon this knowledge.

[Text omitted]

Fellow-citizens, I end, as I began, with congratulations. We have done a good work for our race today. In doing honor to the memory of our friend and liberator, we have been doing highest honors to ourselves and those who come after us; we have been fastening ourselves to a name and fame imperishable and immortal; we have also been defending ourselves from a blighting scandal. When now it shall be said that the colored man is soulless, that he has no appreciation of benefits or benefactors; when the foul reproach of ingratitude is hurled at us, and it is attempted to scourge us beyond the range of human brotherhood, we may calmly point to the monument we have this day erected to the memory of Abraham Lincoln.

W. E. B. Du Bois,
"The Conservation of Races" (1897) and
"On Being Ashamed of Oneself" (1933)

Editor's Introduction: W. E. B. Du Bois (1868–1963) was one of the great leaders in the struggle for social and political equality of African-Americans. He was born in Massachusetts, attended Fisk University, and later received his Ph.D. from Harvard, the first black ever to do so. Du Bois founded the Niagara Movement for racial equality in 1905, a precursor to the National Association for the Advancement of Colored People (NAACP), which he also helped organize in 1909. He served the NAACP in a number of capacities, including as editor of its journal, the *Crisis*, from 1910 to 1934. His *The Souls of Black Folks* (1903) is a beautifully written and poignant statement on African-American identity in the United States and deserves a wide audience even today.

Du Bois engaged in a longstanding dispute with Booker T. Washington (see the following selection) on the goals and strategies for progress toward racial justice in the United States. Du Bois focused much attention on the need for well-educated, highly moral, and politically savvy African-Americans to organize the struggle for civil rights, an idea he developed in his influential essay, "The Talented Tenth," and in his 1897 piece reproduced here.

As Du Bois grew older, his patience with the American racial situation wore thin and his ideas on social equality grew more radical. He became involved in the world peace movement in the 1940s and expressed admiration for the USSR, clearly an unwelcome sentiment in the United States. At the age of 93, Du Bois joined the U.S. Communist party, renounced his U.S. citizenship, and became a citizen of Ghana. He died in Ghana on August 27, 1963. The next day this news was conveyed to the crowd of 250,000 who had participated in the March On Washington for civil rights.

*   *   *

THE CONSERVATION OF RACES (1897)

[Text omitted]

No Negro who has given earnest thought to the situation of his people in America has failed . . . to ask himself at some time: What, after

---

Source: American Negro Academy, *Occasional Papers*, No. 2, 1897.

all, am I? Am I an American or am I a Negro? Can I be both? Or is it my duty to cease to be a Negro as soon as possible and be an American? If I strive as a Negro, am I not perpetuating the very cleft that threatens and separates Black and White America? Is not my only possible practical aim the subduction of all that is Negro in me to the American? Does my black blood place upon me any more obligation to assert my nationality than German, or Irish or Italian blood would?

It is such incessant self-questioning and the hesitation that arises from it, that is making the present period a time of vacillation and contradiction for the American Negro; combined race action is stifled, race responsibility is shirked, race enterprises languish, and the best blood, the best talent, the best energy of the Negro people cannot be marshalled to do the bidding of the race. They stand back to make room for every rascal and demagogue who chooses to cloak his selfish deviltry under the veil of race pride.

Is this right? Is it rational? Is it good policy? Have we in America a distinct mission as a race—a distinct sphere of action and an opportunity for race development, or is self-obliteration the highest end to which Negro blood dare aspire?

If we carefully consider what race prejudice really is, we find it, historically, to be nothing but the friction between different groups of people; it is the difference in aim, in feeling, in ideals of two different races; if, now, this difference exists touching territory, laws, language, or even religion, it is manifest that these people cannot live in the same territory without fatal collision; but if, on the other hand, there is substantial agreement in laws, language and religion; if there is a satisfactory adjustment of economic life, then there is no reason why, in the same country and on the same street, two or three great national ideals might not thrive and develop, that men of different races might not strive together for their race ideals as well, perhaps even better, than in isolation. Here, it seems to me, is the reading of the riddle that puzzles so many of us. We are Americans, not only by birth and by citizenship, but by our political ideals, our language, our religion. Farther than that, our Americanism does not go. At that point, we are Negroes, members of a vast historic race that from the very dawn of creation has slept, but half awakening in the dark forests of its African fatherland. We are the first fruits of this new nation, the harbinger of the black to-morrow which is yet destined to soften the whiteness of the Teutonic to-day. We are that people whose subtle sense of song has given America its only American music, its only American fairy tales, its only touch of pathos and humor amid its mad money-getting plutocracy. As such, it is our duty to conserve our physical powers, our intellectual endowments, our spiritual ideals; as a race we must strive by race organization, by race solidarity, by race unity to the realization of that broader humanity which freely recognizes differences in men, but sternly deprecates inequality in their opportunities of development.

For the accomplishment of these ends we need race organizations: Negro colleges, Negro newspapers, Negro business organizations, a Negro school of literature and art, and an intellectual clearing house, for all these products of the Negro mind, which we may call a Negro Academy. Not only is all this necessary for positive advance, it is absolutely imperative for negative defense. Let us not deceive ourselves at our situation in this country. Weighted with a heritage of moral iniquity from our past history, hard pressed in the economic world by foreign immigrants and native prejudice, hated here, despised there and pitied everywhere; our one haven of refuge is ourselves, and but one means of advance, our own belief in our great destiny, our own implicit trust in our ability and worth. There is no power under God's high heaven that can stop the advance of eight thousand honest, earnest, inspired and united people. But—and here is the rub—they *must* be honest, fearlessly criticising their own faults, zealously correcting them; they must be *earnest.* No people that laughs at itself, and ridicules itself, and wishes to God it was anything but itself ever wrote its name in history; it *must* be inspired with the Divine faith of our black mothers, that out of the blood and dust of battle will march a victorious host, a mighty nation, a peculiar people, to speak to the nations of earth a Divine truth that shall make them free. And such a people must be united; not merely united for the organized theft of political spoils, not united to disgrace religion with whoremongers and ward-heelers; not united merely to protest and pass resolutions, but united to stop the ravages of consumption among the Negro people, united to keep the black boys from loafing, gambling and crime; united to guard the purity of black women and to reduce that vast army of black prostitutes that is today marching to hell; and united in serious organizations, to determine by careful conference and thoughtful interchange of opinion the broad lines of policy and action for the American Negro.

This, is the reason for being which the American Negro Academy has. It aims at once to be the epitome and expression of the intellect of the black-blooded people of America, the exponent of the race ideals of one of the world's great races. As such, the Academy must, if successful, be

(a). Representative in character.
(b). Impartial in conduct.
(c). Firm in leadership.

It must be representative in character; not in that it represents all interests or all factions, but in that it seeks to comprise something of the *best* thought, the most unselfish striving and the highest ideals. There are scattered in forgotten nooks and corners throughout the land, Negroes of some considerable training, of high minds, and high motives, who are unknown to their fellows, who exert far too little influence. These the Negro Academy should strive to bring into touch with each other and to give them a common mouth-piece.

The Academy should be impartial in conduct; while it aims to exalt the people it should aim to do so by truth—not by lies, by honesty—not by flattery. It should continually impress the fact upon the Negro people that they must not expect to have things done for them—they MUST DO FOR THEMSELVES; that they have on their hands a vast work of self-reformation to do, and that a little less complaint and whining, and a little more dogged work and manly striving would do us more credit and benefit than a thousand Force or Civil Rights bills.

Finally, the American Negro Academy must point out a practical path of advance to the Negro people; there lie before every Negro today hundreds of questions of policy and right which must be settled and which each one settles now, not in accordance with any rule, but by impulse or individual preference; for instance: What should be the attitude of Negroes toward the educational qualification for votes? What should be our attitude toward separate schools? How should we meet discriminations on railways and in hotels? Such questions need not so much specific answers for each part as a general expression of policy, and nobody should be better fitted to announce such a policy than a representative honest Negro Academy.

All this, however, must come in time after careful organization and long conference. The immediate work before us should be practical and have direct bearing upon the situation of the Negro. The historical work of collecting the laws of the United States and of the various States of the Union with regard to the Negro is a work of such magnitude and importance that no body but one like this could think of undertaking it. If we could accomplish that one task we would justify our existence.

In the field of Sociology an appalling work lies before us. First, we must unflinchingly and bravely face the truth, not with apologies, but with solemn earnestness. The Negro Academy ought to sound a note of warning that would echo in every black cabin in the land: *Unless we conquer our present vices they will conquer us;* we are diseased, we are developing criminal tendencies, and an alarmingly large percentage of our men and women are sexually impure. The Negro Academy should stand and proclaim this over the housetops, crying with Garrison: *I will not equivocate, I will not retreat a single inch, and I will be heard.* The Academy should seek to gather about it the talented, unselfish men, the pure and noble-minded women, to fight an army of devils that disgraces our manhood and our womanhood. There does not stand today upon God's earth a race more capable in muscle, in intellect, in morals, than the American Negro, if he will bend his energies in the right direction; if he will

> Burst his birth's invidious bar
> And grasp the skirts of happy chance,
> And breast the blows of circumstance,
> And grapple with his evil star.

In science and morals, I have indicated two fields of work for the Academy. Finally, in practical policy, I wish to suggest the following *Academy Creed:*

1. We believe that the Negro people, as a race, have a contribution to make to civilization and humanity, which no other race can make.

2. We believe it the duty of the Americans of Negro descent as a body, to maintain their race identity until this mission of the Negro people is accomplished, and the ideal of human brotherhood has become a practical possibility.

3. We believe that, unless modern civilization is a failure, it is entirely feasible and practicable for two races in such essential political, economic, and religious harmony as the white and colored people of America, to develop side by side in peace and mutual happiness, the peculiar contribution which each has to make to the culture of their common country.

4. As a means to this end we advocate, not such social equality between these races as would disregard human likes and dislikes, but such a social equilibrium as would, throughout all the complicated relations of life, give due and just consideration to culture, ability, and moral worth, whether they be found under white or black skins.

5. We believe that the first and greatest step toward the settlement of the present friction between the races—commonly called the Negro Problem—lies in the correction of the immorality, crime and laziness among the Negroes themselves, which still remains as a heritage from slavery. We believe that only earnest and long continued efforts on our own part can cure these social ills.

6. We believe that the second great step toward a better adjustment of the relations between the races, should be a more impartial selection of ability in the economic and intellectual world, and a greater respect for personal liberty and worth, regardless of race. We believe that only earnest efforts on the part of the white people of this country will bring much needed reform in these matters.

7. On the basis of the foregoing declaration, and firmly believing in our high destiny, we, as American Negroes, are resolved to strive in every

honorable way for the realization of the best and highest aims, for the development of strong manhood and pure womanhood, and for the rearing of a race ideal in America and Africa, to the glory of God and the uplifting of the Negro people.

ON BEING ASHAMED OF ONESELF: An Essay on Race Pride (1933)

My GRANDFATHER left a passage in his diary expressing his indignation at receiving an invitation to a "Negro" picnic. Alexander Du-Bois, born in the Bahamas, son of Dr. James DuBois of the well-known DuBois family of Poughkeepsie, N.Y., had been trained as a gentleman in the Cheshire School of Connecticut, and the implications of a Negro picnic were anathema to his fastidious soul. It meant close association with poverty, ignorance and suppressed and disadvantaged people, dirty and with bad manners.

This was in 1856. Seventy years later, Marcus Garvey discovered that a black skin was in itself a sort of patent to nobility, and that Negroes ought to be proud of themselves and their ancestors, for the same or analogous reasons that made white folk feel superior.

Thus, within the space of three-fourths of a century, the pendulum has swung between race pride and race suicide, between attempts to build up a racial ethos and attempts to escape from ourselves. In the years between emancipation and 1900, the theory of escape was dominant. We were, by birth, law and training, American citizens. We were going to escape into the mass of Americans in the same way that the Irish and Scandinavians and even the Italians were beginning to disappear. The process was going to be slower on account of the badge of color; but then, after all, it was not so much the matter of physical assimilation as of spiritual and psychic amalgamation with the American people.

For this reason, we must oppose all segregation and all racial patriotism; we must salute the American flag and sing "Our Country 'Tis of Thee" with devotion and fervor, and we must fight for our rights with long and carefully planned campaign; uniting for this purpose with all sympathetic people, colored or white.

This is still the dominant philosophy of most American Negroes and it is back of the objection to even using a special designation like "Negro" or even "Afro-American" or any such term.

But there are certain practical difficulties connected with this program which are becoming more and more clear today. First of all comes the fact that we are still ashamed of ourselves and are thus estopped from

---

Source: *The Crisis, September* 1933.

valid objection when white folks are ashamed to call us human. The reasons of course, are not as emphatic as they were in the case of my grandfather. I remember a colored man, now ex-patriate, who made this discovery in my company, some twenty-five years ago. He was a handsome burning brown, tall, straight and well-educated, and he occupied a position which he had won, across and in spite of the color line. He did not believe in Negroes, for himself or his family, and he planned elaborately to escape the trammels of race. Yet, he had responded to a call for a meeting of colored folk which touched his interests, and he came. He found men of his own calibre and training; he found men charming and companionable. He was thoroughly delighted. I know that never before, or I doubt if ever since, he had been in such congenial company. He could not help mentioning his joy continually and reiterating it.

All colored folk had gone through the same experience, for more and more largely in the last twenty-five years, colored America has discovered itself; has discovered groups of people, association with whom is a poignant joy and despite their ideal of American assimilation, in more and more cases and with more and more determined object they seek each other.

That involves, however, a drawing of class lines inside the Negro race, and it means the emergence of a certain social aristocracy, who by reasons of looks and income, education and contact, form the sort of upper social group which the world has long known and helped to manufacture and preserve. The early basis of this Negro group was simply color and a bald imitation of the white environment. Later, it tended, more and more, to be based on wealth and still more recently on education and social position.

This leaves a mass of untrained and uncultured colored folk and even of trained but ill-mannered people and groups of impoverished workers of whom this upper class of colored Americans are ashamed. They are ashamed both directly and indirectly, just as any richer or better sustained group in a nation is ashamed of those less fortunate and withdraws its skirts from touching them. But more than that, because the upper colored group is desperately afraid of being represented before American whites by this lower group, or being mistaken for them, or being treated as though they were part of it, they are pushed to the extreme of effort to avoid contact with the poorest classes of Negroes. This exaggerates, at once, the secret shame of being identified with such people and the anomaly of insisting that the physical characteristics of these folk which the upper class shares, are not the stigmata of degradation.

When, therefore, in offense or defense, the leading group of Negroes must make common cause with the masses of their own race, the embarrassment or hesitation becomes apparent. They are embarrassed and indignant because an educated man should be treated as a Negro, and that no Negroes receive credit for social standing. They are ashamed and embarrassed because of the compulsion of being classed with a mass of people over whom they have no real control and whose action they can influence only with difficulty and compromise and with every risk of defeat.

Especially is all natural control over this group difficult—I mean control of law and police, of economic power, of guiding standards and ideals, of news propaganda. On this comes even greater difficulty because of the incompatibility of any action which looks toward racial integrity and race action with previous ideals. What are we really aiming at? The building of a new nation or the integration of a new group into the old nation? Should it be changed? If we seek new group loyalty, new pride of race, new racial integrity—how, where, and by what method shall these things be attained? A new plan must be built up. It cannot be the mere rhodomontade and fatuous propaganda on which Garveyism was based. It has got to be far-sighted planning. It will involve increased segregation and perhaps migration. It will be pounced upon and aided and encouraged by every "nigger-hater" in the land.

Moreover, in further comment on all this, it may be pointed out that this is not the day for the experiment of new nations or the emphasis of racial lines. This is, or at least we thought it was, the day of the Inter-nation, of Humanity, and the disappearance of "race" from our vocabulary. Are we American Negroes seeking to move against, or into the face of this fine philosophy? Here then is the real problem, the real new dilemma between rights of American citizens and racial pride, which faces American Negroes today and which is not always or often clearly faced.

The situation is this: America, in denying equality of rights, of employment and social recognition to American Negroes, has said in the past that the Negro was so far below the average nation in social position, that he could not be recognized until he had developed further. In the answer to this, the Negro has eliminated five-sixths of his illiteracy according to official figures, and greatly increased the number of colored persons who have received education of the higher sort. They still are poor with a large number of delinquents and dependents. Nevertheless, their average situation in this respect has been greatly improved and, on the other hand, the emergence and accomplishment of colored men of ability has been undoubted. Notwithstanding this, the Negro is still a group apart, with almost no social recognition, subject to insult and discrimination, with income and wage far below the average of the nation and the most deliberately exploited industrial class in America. Even trained Negroes have increasing difficulty in making a living sufficient to sustain a civilized standard of life. Particularly in the recent vast economic changes, color discrimination as it now goes on, is going to make it increasingly difficult for the Negro to remain an integral part of the industrial machine or to increase his participation in accordance with his ability.

[Text omitted]

On the other hand, organized labor is giving Negroes less recognition today than ever. It has practically excluded them from all the higher lines of skilled work, on railroads, in machine-shops, in manufacture and in the basic industries. In agriculture, where the Negro has theoretically the largest opportunity, he is excluded from successful participation, not only by conditions common to all farmers, but by special conditions due to lynching, lawlessness, disfranchisement and social degradation.

[Text omitted]

The next step, then, is certainly one on the part of the Negro and it involves group action. It involves the organization of intelligent and earnest people of Negro descent for their preservation and advancement in America, in the West Indies and in Africa; and no sentimental distaste for racial or national unity can be allowed to hold them back from a step which sheer necessity demands.

A new organized group action along economic lines, guided by intelligence and with the express object of making it possible for Negroes to earn a better living and, therefore, more effectively to support agencies for social uplift, is without the slightest doubt the next step. It will involve no opposition from white America because they do to believe we can accomplish it. They expect always to be able to crush, insult, ignore and exploit 12,000,000 individual Negroes without intelligent organized opposition. This organization is going to involve deliberate propaganda for race pride. That is, it is going to start out by convincing American Negroes that there is no reason for their being ashamed of themselves; that their record is one which should make them proud; that their history in Africa and the world is a history of effort, success and trial, comparable with that of any other people.

Such measured statements can, and will be exaggerated. There will be those who will want to say that the black race is the first and greatest of races, that its accomplishments are most extraordinary, that its desert is most obvious and its mistakes negligible. This is the kind of talk we hear from people with the superiority complex among the white and the yellow race.

We cannot entirely escape it, since it is just as true, and just as false as such statements among other races; but we can use intelligence in modifying and restraining it. We can refuse deliberately to lie about our history, while at the same time taking just pride in Nefertari, Askia, Moshesh, Toussaint and Frederick Douglass, and testing and encouraging belief in our own ability by organized economic and social action.

There is no other way; let us not be deceived. American Negroes will be beaten into submission and degradation if they merely wait unorganized to find some place voluntarily given them in the new reconstruction of the economic world. They must themselves force their race into the new economic set-up and bring with them the millions of West Indians and Africans by peaceful organization for normative action or else drift into greater poverty, greater crime, greater helplessness until there is no resort but the last red alternative of revolt, revenge and war.

Booker T. Washington,
"Democracy and Education" (1896)

Editor's Introduction: Booker T. Washington (1856–1915) was born in Virginia and began working in the coal mines at the age of nine. He attended Hampton Institute, and then taught in the rural South. In 1881 he was appointed president of Tuskegee Institute, an Alabama trade school which began with a mere $2,000 per year granted from the state, a shanty donated by a local church for instruction, and no property. From these humble beginnings, Washington created a center for training in skilled labor which included brickmaking, carpentry, blacksmithing, and agriculture for men, and cooking and sewing for women. By the time of his death, Tuskegee Institute had an endowment of approximately $2 million, and other property assessed at $1.5 million, a good indication of Washington's organizational and political skills. Moreover, the Tuskegee Institute embodied Washington's philosophy of progress toward racial justice in America.

Washington received considerable attention for his ideas on race relations with his speech at the Cotton States and International Exposition held in Atlanta in 1895. He encouraged blacks to stay in the South, to become skilled laborers, and to first attain economic independence before demanding social and political equality, this at a time when few blacks owned the land they farmed or private businesses. This speech was conciliatory toward southern whites and stressed the importance of blacks' economic achievement to the prosperity of the entire South. Due largely to his message of self-help to blacks and his accommodating manner, Washington became well-accepted among both northern and southern whites. In addition, his autobiography, *Up From Slavery*, was widely read by many individuals, such as Andrew Carnegie and Henry H. Rogers of Standard Oil, who would help build Tuskegee Institute through their philanthropy.

Washington would soon come under fire from more militant black intellectuals such as W. E. B. Du Bois and Ida Wells Barnett, and he remains a controversial figure in African-American history. However, while Washington was not a civil rights advocate, neither was he indifferent to the political plight of African-Americans. There is evidence that he worked secretly to sponsor litigation challenging the disenfranchisement

Source: E. Davidson Washington, ed., *Selected Speeches of Booker T. Washington* (Garden City, NY: Doubleday, Doran & Co., 1932).

of blacks and their exclusion from jury service in the South, though usually without success. In the following piece, his political concerns are clearly in evidence as he bemoans the disenfranchisement of blacks through such devices as literacy tests and argues that economic independence and education are essential conditions for political equality.

*   *   *

Delivered Before the Institute of Arts and Sciences, Brooklyn, New York, September 30, 1896

[Text omitted]

—I have referred to industrial education as a means of fitting the millions of my people in the South for the duties of citizenship. Until there is industrial independence it is hardly possible to have a pure ballot. In the country districts of the Gulf states it is safe to say that not more than one black man in twenty owns the land he cultivates. Where so large a proportion of the people are dependent, live in other people's houses, eat other people's food, and wear clothes they have not paid for, it is a pretty hard thing to tell how they are going to vote. My remarks thus have referred mainly to my own race. But there is another side. The longer I live and the more I study the question, the more I am convinced that it is not so much a problem as to what you will do with the Negro as what the Negro will do with you and your civilization. In considering this side of the subject, I thank God that I have grown to the point where I can sympathize with a white man as much as I can sympathize with a black man. I have grown to the point where I can sympathize with a Southern white man as much as I can sympathize with a Northern white man. To me "a man's a man for a' that and a' that." As bearing upon democracy and education, what of your white brethren in the South, those who suffered and are still suffering the consequences of American slavery for which both you and they are responsible? You of the great and prosperous North still owe to your unfortunate brethren of the Caucasian race in the South, not less than to yourselves, a serious and uncompleted duty. What was the task you asked them to perform? Returning to their destitute homes after years of war to face blasted hopes, devastation, a shattered industrial system, you asked them to add to their own burdens that of preparing in education, politics, and economics in a few short years, for citizenship, four millions of former slaves. That the South, staggering under the burden, made blunders, and that in a measure there has been disappointment, no one need be surprised.

The educators, the statesmen, the philanthropists have never comprehended their duty toward the millions of poor whites in the South who were buffeted for two hundred years between slavery and freedom, between civilization and degradation, who were disregarded by both master and slave. It needs no prophet to tell the character of our future civilization when the poor white boy in the country districts of the South receives one dollar's worth of education and your boy twenty dollars' worth, when one never enters a library or reading room and the other has libraries and reading rooms in every ward and town. When one hears lectures and sermons once in two months and the other can hear a lecture or sermon every day in the year. When you help the South you help yourselves. Mere abuse will not bring the remedy. The time has come, it seems to me, when in this matter we should rise above party or race or sectionalism into the region of duty of man to man, citizen to citizen, Christian to Christian, and if the Negro who has been oppressed and denied rights in a Christian land can help you North and South to rise, can be the medium of your rising into this atmosphere of generous Christian brotherhood and self-forgetfulness, he will see in it a recompense for all that he has suffered in the past. Not very long ago a white citizen of the South boastingly expressed himself in public to this effect: "I am now forty-six years of age, but have never polished my own boots, have never saddled my own horse, have never built a fire in my own room, have never hitched a horse." He was asked a short time since by a lame man . to hitch his horse, but refused and told him to get a Negro to do it. Our state law requires that a voter be required to read the constitution before voting, but the last clause of the constitution is in Latin and the Negroes cannot read Latin, and so they are asked to read the Latin clause and are thus disfranchised, while the whites are permitted to read the English portion of the constitution. I do not quote these statements for the purpose of condemning the individual or the South, for though myself a member of a despised and unfortunate race, I pity from the bottom of my heart any of God's creatures whence such a statement can emanate. Evidently here is a man who, as far as mere book training is concerned, is educated, for he boasts of his knowledge of Latin, but, so far as the real purpose of education is concerned—the making of men useful, honest, and lib-eral—this man has never been touched. Here is a citizen in the midst of our republic, clothed in a white skin, with all the technical signs of educa-tion, but who is as little fitted for the highest purpose of life as any creature found in Central Africa. My friends, can we make our education reach down far enough to touch and help this man? Can we so control science, art, and literature as to make them to such an extent a means rather than an end; that the lowest and most unfortunate of God's creatures shall be lifted up, ennobled and glorified; shall be a freeman instead of a slave of narrow sympathies and wrong customs? Some years ago a bright young man of my race succeeded in passing a competitive examination for a cadetship at the United States naval academy at Annapolis. Says the young man, Mr. Henry Baker, in describing his stay at this institution: "I was several times attacked with stones and was forced finally to appeal to the officers, when a marine was detailed to accompany me across the campus and from the mess hall at meal times. My books were mutilated, my clothes were cut and in some instances destroyed, and all the petty annoyances which ingenuity could devise were inflicted upon me daily, and during seamanship practice aboard the *Dale* attempts were often made to do me personal injury while I would be aloft in the rigging. No one ever addressed me by name. I was called the Moke usually, the Nigger for variety. I was shunned as if I were a veritable leper and received curses and blows as the only method my persecutors had of relieving the monotony." Not once during the two years, with one exception, did any one of the more than four hundred cadets enrolled ever come to him with a word of advice, counsel, sympathy, or information, and he never held conversation with any one of them for as much as five minutes during the whole course of his experience at the academy, except on occasions when he was defending himself against their assaults. The one exception where the departure from the rule was made was in the case of a Pennsylvania boy, who stealthily brought him a piece of his birthday cake at twelve o'clock one night. The act so surprised Baker that his suspicions were aroused, but these were dispelled by the donor, who read to him a letter which he had received from his mother, from whom the cake came, in which she requested that a slice be given to the colored cadet who was without friends. I recite this incident not for the purpose merely of condemning the wrong done a member of my race: no, no, not that. I mention the case, not for the one cadet, but for the sake of the four hundred cadets, for the sake of the four hundred American families, the four hundred American communities whose civilization and Christianity these cadets represented. Here were four hundred and more picked young men representing the flower of our country, who has passed through our common schools and were preparing themselves at public expense to defend the honor of our country. And yet, with grammar, reading, and arithmetic in the public schools, and with lessons in the arts of war, the principles of physical courage at Annapolis, both systems seemed to have utterly failed to prepare a single one of these young men for real life, that he could be brave enough, Christian enough, American enough, to take this poor defenseless black boy by the hand in open daylight and let the world know that he was his friend. Education, whether of black man or white man, that gives one physical courage to stand in front of the cannon and fails to give him moral courage to stand up in defense of right and justice is a failure. With all that the Brooklyn Institute of Arts and Sciences stands for in its equipment, its endowment, its wealth and culture, its instructors, can it produce a mother that will produce a boy that will not be ashamed to have the world know that he is a friend to the most unfortunate of God's creatures? Not long ago a mother, a black mother, who lived in one of your Northern states, had heard it whispered around in her community for years that the Negro was lazy, shiftless, and would not work. So when her boy grew to sufficient size, at considerable expense and great self-sacrifice, she had her boy thoroughly taught the machinist's trade. A job was secured in a neighboring shop. With dinner bucket in hand and spurred on by the prayers of the now happy mother, the boy entered the shop to begin his first day's work. What happened? Had any one of the twenty white Americans been so educated that he gave this stranger a welcome into their midst? No, not this. Every one of the twenty white men threw down his tools and deliberately walked out, swearing that he would not give a black man an opportunity to earn an honest living. Another shop was tried, with the same result, and still another and the same. Today this promising and ambitious black man is a wreck— a confirmed drunkard, with no hope, no ambition. My friends, who blasted the life of this young man? On whose hands does his blood rest? Our system of education, or want of education, is responsible. Can our public schools and colleges turn out a set of men that will throw open the doors of industry to all men everywhere, regardless of color, so all shall have the same opportunity to earn a dollar that they now have to spend a dollar? I know a good many species of cowardice and prejudice, but I know none equal to this. I know not who is the worst, the ex-slave-holder who perforce compelled his slave to work without compensation, or the man who perforce compels the Negro to refrain from working for compensation. My friends, we are one in this country. The question of the highest citizenship and the complete education of all concerns nearly ten million of my own people and over sixty million of yours. We rise as you rise; when we fall you fall. When you are strong we are strong; when we are weak you are weak. There is no power that can separate our destiny. The Negro can afford to be wronged; the white man cannot afford to wrong him. Unjust laws or customs that exist in many places regarding the races injure the white man and inconvenience the Negro. No race can wrong another race simply because it has the power to do so without being permanently injured in morals. The Negro can endure the temporary inconvenience, but the injury to the white man is permanent. It is for the white man to save himself from his degradation that I plead. If a white man steals a Negro's ballot it is the white man who is permanently injured. Physical death comes to the one Negro lynched in a country, but death of the morals—death of the soul—comes to the thousands responsible for the lynching. We are a patient, humble people. We can afford to work and wait. There is plenty in this country for us to do. Away up in the atmosphere of goodness, forbearance, patience, long-suffering, and forgiveness the workers are not many or overcrowded. If others would be little we can be great. If others would be mean we can be good. If others would push us down we can help push them up. Character, not circumstances, makes the man. It is more important that we be prepared for voting than that we vote, more important that we be prepared to hold office than that we hold office, more important that we be prepared for the highest recognition than that we be recognized. Those who fought and died on the battlefield performed their duty heroically and well, but a duty remains for you and me. The mere fiat of law could not make an ignorant voter an intelligent voter; could not make one citizen respect another; these results come to the Negro, as to all races, by beginning at the bottom and working up to the highest civilization and accomplishment. In the economy of God, there can be but one standard by which an individual can succeed—there is but one for a race. This country demands that every race measure itself by the American standard. By it a race must rise or fall, succeed or fail, and in the last analysis mere sentiment counts but little. During the next half-century and more my race must continue passing through the severe American crucible.

We are to be tested in our patience, in our forbearance, our power to endure wrong, to withstand temptation, to succeed, to acquire and use skill, our ability to compete, to succeed in commerce; to disregard the superficial for the real, the appearance for the substance; to be great and yet the servant of all. This, this is the passport to all that is best in the life of our republic, and the Negro must possess it or be debarred. In working out our destiny, while the main burden and center of activity must be with us, we shall need in a large measure the help, the encouragement, the guidance that the strong can give the weak. Thus helped, we of both races in the South shall soon throw off the shackles of racial and sectional prejudice and rise above the clouds of ignorance, narrowness, and selfishness into that atmosphere, that pure sunshine, where it will be our highest ambition to serve man, our brother, regardless of race or past conditions.

Marcus Garvey,
"The Negro and his Weakness" (1935) and "Be King of Circumstances" (1935)

Editor's Introduction: Marcus Garvey (1887–1940) was born in Jamaica, where he founded the Universal Negro Improvement Association (UNIA) in 1914. He came to the United States in 1916 and settled in New York City. He organized thirty branches of the UNIA in the United States and several abroad. Garvey advocated racial separation, believing that it was impossible for blacks to gain social justice in a white majority country. In fact, while in America, he set up an African "government-in-exile" with himself as provisional president. Garvey preached a strong message of race pride, as is communicated in the poem reproduced here. His message met with enthusiastic response in Harlem in New York City and elsewhere, and appealed especially to blacks who had migrated recently from rural areas. Garvey was the most popular black leader of his day and attracted hundreds of thousands if not millions of supporters to his cause. His ideas were opposed vociferously by W. E. B. Du Bois, who described Garvey as "bombastic" and his plans as "impracticable."

Garvey founded a newspaper in the United States called *The Black Man*, from which the following pieces are taken. He also attempted to found a shipping company, the Black Star Line, to provide a commercial link and ferry connecting the black peoples of the world; it ultimately failed. In 1925 he was convicted for using the mail to defraud investors in the shipping concern. He was pardoned in 1927 by President Coolidge and deported as an undesirable alien. He died in London without ever visiting Africa. In the African-American community, his separatist ideology has had an influence on such organizations as the Nation of Islam and such thinkers as Malcolm X.

*　　　*　　　*

THE NEGRO AND HIS WEAKNESS (1935)

Hasn't the Negro committed and is still committing a crime against himself? The observant student of racial psychology can come to no other conclusion than that he has and is still doing so. The crime that is being

Source: *The Blackman*, Vol. 1, No. 10, October 1935. Edited by Marcus Garvey, D.C.L., Founder and President-General of the Universal Negro Improvement Association.

committed is that of wholesale racial neglect. Our fathers, in our modern history, did this to an alarming degree, and the present generation is paying the terrible price; but we, to-day, have not changed much from the attitude of our fathers, and so we march on to destiny feeling and suffering from every reverse that is common to a people who have inherited no serious preparation and who of themselves are making none for the solution of their many problems.

Human Efforts

It is an established fact that all human efforts are subject to change. The changes are generally effected through conditions and circumstances as they do occur; hence human institutions and general human actions must be properly planned and systematically carried out so as to have the beneficial effects that may be desired. All this can only come through the preparation of proper leadership. Leadership involves the application of serious thought, calculating thought, thought beforehand, thought that is visionary, but based upon good and substantial reasons. It is this kind of thought that has cleared the way for the stronger, greater and more successful races of the world. It is this thought of leadership that the Negro lacks and has always lacked. This is the monumental crime that we have committed against ourselves—a crime of not thinking sufficiently in one generation so as to be able to bequeath to succeeding ones that which would help them to the maintenance of a better human equilibrium and the finding of their proper place in the social life of man. The Negro has had the same opportunities, the same advantages as all other human beings, to carve his own way out of the environmental circumstances that originally leveled the sphere of man. The scientist has not been able to prove that the Negro sprang from any other ethnic or anthropological source than that of the human being. It is a fact established that he was made or created with mind similar to that of any other human being, and it is an accepted fact that man's mind is his guide. In fact it is his entire being, without it he reaches the level of the brute because he is unable to help himself. If mind, therefore, is a common possession of the human race, there is no reason why one section of the human race should positively fail to use that mind with the objective through reason, of evolving thought consistent with the function of life in the proper sphere according to Nature's gifts and Nature's laws.

Nature's Gifts

The world is Nature's gift to man. The ownership of the world is made possible by utilizing the laws of Nature. To understand the laws and apply them means that we must make our minds function with the profoundest knowledge of these laws. We must, therefore, delve into all the elemental attributes of Nature. We must, after discovering them, summon them to that practical use for which they were originally intended by the Creator. To do all this means as suggested the profundity of thought. Whilst the bulk of a people never think in the higher terms of life, to lead themselves on to any particular destiny, the select few, who are called leaders, never fail to assume their responsibility of guiding the majority toward their desired ends. That is where leadership becomes important—imperatively so—and any race that attempts to go through the journey of life without proper constituted leadership is bound to flounder and ultimately be wrecked on the shores of time.

Almost Wrecked

As we see things to-day, isn't it sad to admit that the Negro is almost wrecked on the shoals of life—wrecked because he lacked leadership in the past, and he lacks it now. We want men of vision, men of character, men of determination, men of real will and force, who will refuse to be distracted or be superinfluenced by the designs of others; but who will look straightforward and solely in the interest of race and lead the people on to their peculiar glory. If we are weak to-day—and we are weak—it is because of the neglects of the past, and the apparent gross neglect of the present.

Our Environments

It is true that our environments are of such as to unmake us, and to wholly distract us in our weakness; but must we succumb to this weakness? Man is a peculiar being, he is a creature who is able to retrieve his lost ground, to recover himself, if he wills. If it were not so, there would have been no human hope. As proof of this we can apply the knowledge of practical experience in our own affairs. No one will suggest positively because his father was of weak character, he himself is supposed to be a weakling in his subsequent career. We have seen imbecilic fathers superseded by brilliant progeny. That proves that mentality, whilst to a certain extent man may be influenced by heritage, he is still somewhat independent in himself, so that it is possible for any man at any period of his life, when he becomes conscious, to restore himself to a state of mind that would be considered of beneficial interest. If it were not so, then everything would be hopeless. Nature intended that man through his own consciousness should establish his own sovereignty over life. The Negro, therefore, has the function of being a sovereign—a sovereign of his career, individual and racial, a sovereign of his circumstances and conditions just like any other man. Out of the environments and circum-stances of life other men and other races have carved their way to glory and to honour, they have built their principalities, their powers, their kingdoms, and their empires, they laid the foundation of their great industries, their commerce and their general institutions. If they can do this, why cannot the Negro realize that this too falls within his province.

Must Not Succumb

We must not succumb to our weakness, that of the past or of the present; we must recover ourselves, and so the appeal is made to the Negroes of America, South and Central, of Canada and of the West Indies, of Africa and elsewhere, to make the determined effort to regain that noble consciousness that our ancient fathers once possessed—that consciousness that led them toward the ideal of Empire, that brought out of them the created civilization which other men inherited. Bow down no longer to the hostile environment of an alien world, but enthrone your own thoughts. Lift them high toward everything that is good, everything that is lofty, everything that is desired by men of the twentieth century. Your scope is the universe, your field of operation is earth. Bring to your command the forces of the Universe and conquer the world of which you were made a lord. When this ideal is firmly fixed in your mind, no Negro will go around the world hat in hand, beggar and suppliant, but every unit of the race will stand up like a real man and play his part as God and Nature intended. Get the vision, the vision true, the vision of man's sovereignty over life, the vision of the man created just a little lower than the angels, whose function is mastery over all within Nature's scope. Between earth and Heaven, between earth and hell, man stands out, and but for the Angels is the nearest creature to God. The creative mind of God has been bequeathed to man in a limited sense, so that man out of his own thoughts may create his place in a world where God originally placed him. Black man, rise to the occasion. Weep no more but stand up in the feelings of your human strength and make your new conquest wherever you are.

BE KING OF CIRCUMSTANCES (1935)

The rise of nations and of men
Record the struggles passed and won,
But none may tell just where and when
The urge did come and thus begun.
It might have been through glorious deeds
Performed by earlier men of fame,
Whose inspiration often leads
To visions that remake a name.

A Constantine, Alexander, too,
A Hannibal and Caesar great
May change the thought of even you
And give a hero to the State.
To read the deeds of men renowned
Will make you choose a given course
That often strikes the note profound,
Revealing thus the man of force.

The deeds we do must make the race
And force the nation to the top,
And when we gain the honour place
We forge ahead and never stop.
Keep winning more and still some more,
And set a pace for fainter heart;
Your deeds shall spread from shore to shore,
And worlds shall know you played your part.

Though black of race you are, my friend,
Your part in life is ever here:
There's work for you; the human trend
Calls for each one to have his share.
Go then and play your part to-day,
And think that you are king of all
Circumstances that come your way.
Before which you must never fall.

Brown v. Board of Education of Topeka, Kansas
347 U.S. 483 (1954)

Editor's Introduction: The Brown decision by a unanimous Supreme Court represents one of the most decisive steps toward racial integration in American history. The issue before the Court was whether the equal protection clause of the Fourteenth Amendment to the Constitution mandated integrated schools.

The most significant precedent the Court overturned was an 1896 case involving railroad transportation, *Plessy v. Ferguson.* In that case, the justices developed the "separate but equal" doctrine holding that rail lines need not integrate if equal facilities were provided to both races. However, under legal segregation, separate facilities for blacks were rarely if ever of equal quality to those for whites. In any case, the Court held in Brown that "(s)eparate educational facilities are inherently unequal" as separation "is usually interpreted as denoting the inferiority of the negro group." In the decision, the Court considers the role public education had come to play in American political and social life and the importance of access to integrated education as a step toward equal citizenship.

The Brown decision met with considerable resistance, giving rise to such incidents as President Eisenhower's sending armed troops to Little Rock, Arkansas, in 1957 to escort young black schoolchildren to class. Brown played a key role in ending *de jure* segregation in education (i.e., segregation by law) but it did not end—nor could any court decision end—*de facto* segregation (i.e., segregation in fact) due to the disparate housing patterns of blacks and whites. Efforts to end *de facto* school segregation were pursued in the 1960s and 1970s through such remedies as court-ordered busing and met with mixed success. Though contributing to integration in some school districts, they, along with other factors, precipitated "white flight" from many large cities, thereby actually increasing *de facto* segregation in others.

*   *   *

MR. CHIEF JUSTICE WARREN delivered the opinion of the Court.

These cases come to us from the States of Kansas, South Carolina, Virginia, and Delaware. They are premised on different facts and different local conditions, but a common legal question justifies their consideration together in this consolidated opinion.

In each of the cases, minors of the Negro race, through their legal representatives, seek the aid of the courts in obtaining admission to the public schools of their community on a nonsegregated basis. In each

299

instance, they had been denied admission to schools attended by white children under laws requiring or permitting segregation according to race. This segregation was alleged to deprive the plaintiffs of the equal protection of the laws under the Fourteenth Amendment. In each of the cases other than the Delaware case, a three-judge federal district court denied relief to the plaintiffs on the so-called "separate but equal" doctrine announced by this Court in *Plessy v. Ferguson*, 163 U.S. 537. Under that doctrine, equality of treatment is accorded when the races are provided substantially equal facilities, even though these facilities be separate. In the Delaware case, the Supreme Court of Delaware adhered to that doctrine, but ordered that the plaintiffs be admitted to the white schools because of their superiority to the Negro schools.

The plaintiffs contend that segregated public schools are not "equal" and cannot be made "equal," and that hence they are deprived of the equal protection of the laws. Because of the obvious importance of the question presented, the Court took jurisdiction. Argument was heard in the 1952 Term, and reargument was heard this Term on certain questions propounded by the Court.

Reargument was largely devoted to the circumstances surrounding the adoption of the Fourteenth Amendment in 1868. It covered exhaustively consideration of the Amendment in Congress, ratification by the states, then existing practices in racial segregation, and the views of proponents and opponents of the Amendment. This discussion and our own investigation convince us that, although these sources cast some light, it is not enough to resolve the problem with which we are faced. At best, they are inconclusive. The most avid proponents of the post-War Amendments undoubtedly intended them to remove all legal distinctions among "all persons born or naturalized in the United States." Their opponents, just as certainly, were antagonistic to both the letter and the spirit of the Amendments and wished them to have the most limited effect. What others in Congress and the state legislatures had in mind cannot be determined with any degree of certainty.

An additional reason for the inconclusive nature of the Amendment's history, with respect to segregated schools, is the status of public education at that time. In the South, the movement toward free common schools, supported by general taxation, had not yet taken hold. Education of white children was largely in the hands of private groups. Education of Negroes was almost nonexistent, and practically all of the race were illiterate. In fact, any education of Negroes was forbidden by law in some states. Today, in contrast, many Negroes have achieved outstanding success in the arts and sciences as well as in the business and professional world. It is true that public school education at the time of the Amendment had advanced further in the North, but the effect of the Amendment on

Northern States was generally ignored in the congressional debates. Even in the North, the conditions of public education did not approximate those existing today. The curriculum was usually rudimentary; ungraded schools were common in rural areas; the school term was but three months a year in many states; and compulsory school attendance was virtually unknown. As a consequence, it is not surprising that there should be so little in the history of the Fourteenth Amendment relating to its intended effect on public education.

In the first cases in this Court construing the Fourteenth Amendment, decided shortly after its adoption, the Court interpreted it as proscribing all state-imposed discriminations against the Negro race. The doctrine of "separate but equal" did not make its appearance in this Court until 1896 in the case of Plessy v. Ferguson . . . involving not education but transportation. American courts have since labored with the doctrine for over half a century. In this Court, there have been six cases involving the "separate but equal" doctrine in the field of public education. In *Cumming v. County Board of Education*, 175 U.S. 528, and *Gong Lum v. Rice*, 275 U.S. 78, the validity of the doctrine itself was not challenged. In more recent cases, all on the graduate school level, inequality was found in that specific benefits enjoyed by white students were denied to Negro students of the same educational qualifications. . . . In none of these cases was it necessary to re-examine the doctrine to grant relief to the Negro plaintiff. And in *Sweatt v. Painter*, supra, the Court expressly reserved decision on the question whether *Plessy v. Ferguson* should be held inapplicable to public education.

In the instant cases, that question is directly presented. Here, unlike *Sweatt v. Painter*, there are findings below that the Negro and white schools involved have been equalized, or are being equalized, with respect to buildings, curricula, qualifications and salaries of teachers, and other "tangible" factors. Our decision, therefore, cannot turn on merely a comparison of these tangible factors in the Negro and white schools involved in each of the cases. We must look instead to the effect of segregation itself on public education.

In approaching this problem, we cannot turn the clock back to 1868 when the Amendment was adopted, or even to 1896 when *Plessy v. Ferguson* was written. We must consider public education in the light of its full development and its present place in American life throughout the Nation. Only in this way can it be determined if segregation in public schools deprives these plaintiffs of the equal protection of the laws.

Today, education is perhaps the most important function of state and local governments. Compulsory school attendance laws and the great expenditures for education both demonstrate our recognition of the importance of education to our democratic society. It is required in the performance of our most basic public responsibilities, even service in the armed forces. It is the very foundation of good citizenship. Today it is a principal instrument in awakening the child to cultural values, in preparing him for later professional training, and in helping him to adjust normally to his environment. In these days, it is doubtful that any child may reasonably be expected to succeed in life if he is denied the opportunity of an education. Such an opportunity, where the state has undertaken to provide it, is a right which must be made available to all on equal terms.

We come then to the question presented: Does segregation of children in public schools solely on the basis of race, even though the physical facilities and other "tangible" factors may be equal, deprive the children of the minority group of equal educational opportunities? We believe that it does.

In *Sweatt v. Painter* . . . , in finding that a segregated law school for Negroes could not provide them equal educational opportunities, this Court relied in large part on "those qualities which are incapable of objective measurement but which make for greatness in a law school." In *McLaurin v. Oklahoma State Regents,* . . . the Court, in requiring that a Negro admitted to a white graduate school be treated like all other students, again resorted to intangible considerations: ". . . his ability to study, to engage in discussions and exchange views with other students, and, in general, to learn his profession." Such considerations apply with added force to children in grade and high schools. To separate them from others of similar age and qualifications solely because of their race generates a feeling of inferiority as to their status in the community that may affect their hearts and minds in a way unlikely ever to be undone. The effect of this separation on their educational opportunities was well stated by a finding in the Kansas case by a court which nevertheless felt compelled to rule against the Negro plaintiffs:

"Segregation of white and colored children in public schools has a detrimental effect upon the colored children. The impact is greater when it has the sanction of the law; for the policy of separating the races is usually interpreted as denoting the inferiority of the negro group. A sense of inferiority affects the motivation of a child to learn. Segregation with the sanction of law, therefore, has a tendency to [retard] the educational and mental development of negro children and to deprive them of some of the benefits they would receive in a racial[ly] integrated school system."

Whatever may have been the extent of psychological knowledge at the time of *Plessy v. Ferguson,* this finding is amply supported by modern authority. Any language in *Plessy v. Ferguson* contrary to this finding is rejected.

We conclude that in the field of public education the doctrine of "separate but equal" has no place. Separate educational facilities are inherently unequal. Therefore, we hold that the plaintiffs and others similarly situated for whom the actions have been brought are, by reason of the segregation complained of, deprived of the equal protection of the laws guaranteed by the Fourteenth Amendment. This disposition makes unnecessary any discussion whether such segregation also violates the Due Process Clause of the Fourteenth Amendment.

Because these are class actions, because of the wide applicability of this decision, and because of the great variety of local conditions, the formulation of decrees in these cases presents problems of considerable complexity. On reargument, the consideration of appropriate relief was necessarily subordinated to the primary question—the constitutionality of segregation in public education. We have now announced that such segregation is a denial of the equal protection of the laws. In order that we may have the full assistance of the parties in formulating decrees, the cases will be restored to the docket, and the parties are requested to present further argument on Questions 4 and 5 previously propounded by the Court for the reargument this Term. The Attorney General of the United States is again invited to participate. The Attorneys General of the states requiring or permitting segregation in public education will also be permitted to appear as amici curiae upon request to do so by September 15, 1954, and submission of briefs by October 1, 1954.
It is so ordered.

Dr. Martin Luther King, Jr.
"I Have A Dream," (1963)

Editor's Introduction: Dr. Martin Luther King, Jr. (1929–1968) was born in Atlanta, Georgia, and went on to become the leading activist, theorist, and symbol of the civil rights movement. After receiving a doctorate in theology, he became a Baptist minister in Montgomery, Alabama. He and several other black religious leaders founded the Southern Christian Leadership Conference in 1957, which, under King's leadership, was a leading civil rights organization for many years. An early success for King was to lead a boycott that forced the desegregation of the city bus lines in Montgomery Alabama in 1955–1956. King went on to lead a great many protests that directed national attention toward racial prejudice and injustice and paved the way for the passage of the Civil Rights Act in 1964 and the Voting Rights Act in 1965.

He also developed the theory of "nonviolent direct action" to guide his political undertakings. This theory developed the notion of civil disobedience as earlier formulated by Thoreau and put into practice by Gandhi in India. King believed that people had a duty to resist unjust law but must do so nonviolently, showing respect for the rule of law in the process.

The following speech was delivered to some 250,000 during the 1963 "March on Washington." King's speech culminated a long successful day and captured the mood and goals of the civil rights movement with his inimitable passion and moving oratory. King's dream, "deeply rooted in the American dream," was that one day his children would "live in a nation where they will not be judged by the color of their skin but by the content of their character." King was assassinated in 1968 as he was beginning to organize a multiracial coalition of poor people and as he also was becoming a more vocal opponent of the Vietnam War.

*   *   *

I am happy to join with you today in what will go down in history as the greatest demonstration for freedom in the history of our nation.

Fivescore years ago, a great American, in whose symbolic shadow we stand today, signed the Emancipation Proclamation. This momentous decree came as a great beacon light of hope to millions of Negro slaves

Source: Prepared by Gerald Murphy (The Cleveland Free-Net - aa300). Distributed by the Cybercasting Services Division of the National Public Telecomputing Network (NPTN).

who had been seared in the flames of whithering injustice. It came as a joyous daybreak to end the long night of their captivity.

But one hundred years later, the Negro still is not free; one hundred years later, the life of the Negro is still sadly crippled by the manacles of segregation and the chains of discrimination; one hundred years later, the Negro lives on a lonely island of poverty in the midst of a vast ocean of material prosperity; one hundred years later, the Negro is still languished in the corners of American society and finds himself in exile in his own land. So we have come here today to dramatize a shameful condition. In a sense we have come to our Nation's Capital to cash a check. When the architects of our republic wrote the magnificent words of the Constitution and the Declaration of Independence, they were signing a promissory note to which every American was to fall heir. This note was a promise that all men, yes, black men as well as white men, would be guaranteed the inalienable rights of life, liberty, and the pursuit of happiness.

It is obvious today that America has defaulted on this promissory note insofar as her citizens of color are concerned. Instead of honoring this sacred obligation, America has given the Negro a bad check; a check which has come back marked "insufficient funds." We refuse to believe that there are insufficient funds in the great vaults of opportunity of this nation. And so we've have come to cash this check, a check that will give us upon demand the riches of freedom and security of justice.

We have also come to this hallowed spot to remind America of the fierce urgency of now. This is no time to engage in the luxury of cooling off or to take the tranquilizing drug of gradualism. Now is the time to make real the promise of democracy; now is the time to rise from the dark and desolate valley of segregation to the sunlit path of racial justice; now is the time to lift our nation from the quicksands of racial injustice to the solid rock of brotherhood; now is the time to make justice a reality to all of God's children. It would be fatal for the nation to overlook the urgency of the moment. This sweltering summer of the Negro's legitimate discontent will not pass until there is an invigorating autumn of freedom and equality.

Nineteen sixty-three is not an end, but a beginning. And those who hope that the Negroes needed to blow off steam and will now be content, will have a rude awakening if the nation returns to business as usual.

There will be neither rest nor tranquility in America until the Negro is granted his citizenship rights. The whirlwinds of revolt will continue to shake the foundations of our nation until the bright day of justice emerges.

But there is something that I must say to my people who stand on the warm threshold which leads into the palace of justice. In the process of gaining our rightful place we must not be guilty of wrongful deeds.

Let us not seek to satisfy our thirst for freedom by drinking from the cup of bitterness and hatred. We must forever conduct our struggle on the high plain of dignity and discipline. We must not allow our creative protest to degenerate into physical violence. Again and again we must rise to the majestic heights of meeting physical force with soul force.

The marvelous new militancy which has engulfed the Negro community must not lead us to distrust of all white people, for many of our white brothers, as evidenced by their presence here today, have come to realize that their destiny is tied up with our destiny and have come to realize that their freedom is inextricably bound to our freedom. This offense we share mounted to storm the battlements of injustice must be carried forth by a biracial army. We cannot walk alone.

And as we walk, we must make the pledge that we shall always march ahead. We cannot turn back. There are those who are asking the devotees of civil rights, "When will you be satisfied?" We can never be satisfied as long as the Negro is the victim of the unspeakable horrors of police brutality.

We can never be satisfied as long as our bodies, heavy with the fatigue of travel, cannot gain lodging in the motels of the highways and the hotels of the cities. We cannot be satisfied as long as the Negro's basic mobility is from a smaller ghetto to a larger one.

We can never be satisfied as long as our children are stripped of their selfhood and robbed of their dignity by signs stating "for whites only." We cannot be satisfied as long as a Negro in Mississippi cannot vote and a Negro in New York believes he has nothing for which to vote. No, we are not satisfied, and we will not be satisfied until justice rolls down like waters and righteousness like a mighty stream.

I am not unmindful that some of you have come here out of excessive trials and tribulation. Some of you have come from narrow jail cells. Some of you have come from areas where your quest for freedom left you battered by storms of persecutions and staggered by the winds of police brutality. You have been the veterans of creative suffering. Continue to work with the faith that unearned suffering is redemptive.

Go back to Mississippi; go back to Alabama; go back to South Carolina; go back to Georgia; go back to Louisiana; go back to the slums and ghettos of the northern cities, knowing that somehow this situation can, and will be changed. Let us not wallow in the valley of despair.

I say to you, my friends, that even though we have to face the difficulties of today and tomorrow, I still have a dream. It is a dream deeply rooted in the American dream, that one day this nation will rise up and live out the true meaning of its creed,—we hold this truth to be self-evident that all men are created equal.

I have a dream that one day on the red hills of Georgia, the sons of former slaves and sons of former slave owners will be able to sit down together at the table of brotherhood.

I have a dream that one day, even the state of Mississippi, a state sweltering with the heat of injustice, sweltering with the heat of oppression, will be transformed into an oasis of freedom and justice.

I have a dream that my four little children will one day live in a nation where they will not be judged by the color of their skin but by the content of their character. I have a dream today!

I have a dream that one day, down in Alabama, with its vicious racists, with its governor having his lips dripping with the words of interposition and nullification, that one day, right down in Alabama, little black boys and black girls will be able to join hands with little white boys and white girls as sisters and brothers. I have a dream today!

I have a dream that one day every valley shall be exalted, every hill and mountain shall be made low, the rough places will be made plains, and the crooked places shall be made straight and the glory of the Lord will be revealed and all flesh shall see it together.

This is our hope. This is the faith that I go back to the South with.

With this faith we will be able to hear out of the mountain of despair a tone of hope. With this faith we will be able to transform the jangling discords of our nation into a beautiful symphony of brotherhood.

With this faith we will be able to work together, to pray together, to struggle together, to go to jail together, to climb up for freedom together, knowing that we will be free one day. This will be the day when all of God's children will be able to sing with new meaning—"my country 'this of thee; sweet land of liberty; of thee I sing; land where my fathers died, land of the Pilgrim's pride; from every mountainside, let freedom ring"—and if America is to be a great nation, this must become true.

So let freedom ring from the hilltops of New Hampshire.
Let freedom ring from the mighty mountains of New York.
Let freedom ring from the heightening Alleghenies of Pennsylvania.
Let freedom ring from the snow-capped Rockies of Colorado.
Let freedom ring from the curvaceous slopes of California.
But not only that.
Let freedom ring from Stone Mountain of Georgia.
Let freedom ring from Lookout Mountain of Tennessee.
Let freedom ring from every hill and molehill of Mississippi, from every mountainside, let freedom ring.

And when we allow freedom to ring, when we let it ring from every village and every hamlet, from every state and every city, we will be able to speed up that day when all of God's children—black men and white men, Jews and Gentiles, Catholics and Protestants—will be able to join hands and sing in the words of the old Negro spiritual, "Free at last, free at last; thank God Almighty, we are free at last."

Malcolm X,
"The Ballot or the Bullet" (1964)

Editor's Introduction: Malcolm X (1925–1965) was born Malcolm Little in Omaha, Nebraska. His father had been a follower of Marcus Garvey, and Malcolm was exposed to Garvey's teachings as a child. Malcolm moved to Boston as a teenager and became involved in numerous criminal activities, which he describes in his autobiography. While serving a sentence for burglary he became aware of the teachings of the Honorable Elijah Muhammad and converted to the Nation of Islam, on whose behalf he was to emerge as a principle spokesman after his release. Malcolm broke with the Nation of Islam in 1964, claiming that he had recently become aware that Elijah Muhammad had fathered illegitimate children with his secretary. There is evidence, however, that Malcolm was aware of his leader's affairs before this time and that he really left because of growing impatience with the political and religious direction of the Nation. He was more militant politically than Elijah Muhammad desired and also began to question the Nation's religious tenets after taking a 1964 pilgrimage to Mecca, where he worshiped with other Moslems of all races. Upon his return from Mecca, Malcolm had lost none of his militancy but was more open to interracial cooperation and had come to see that the Nation's teachings were not true to the Islamic faith.

From that point up to his assassination in February 1965 at the hands of several followers of Elijah Muhammad, Malcolm worked to form a new organization and philosophy to promote black nationalism. Though Malcolm was still struggling to find a new direction at the point of his death, the following speech gives a good sense of his ideas at the time. His appeal to solidarity with other nonwhite people throughout the world and to the United Nations as a forum for addressing human rights abuses in the United States, his call for economic self-reliance, and his willingness to work with any political organization, whether African-American or multiracial, are key elements of Malcolm's evolving philosophy.

Though Malcolm was a poor political prognosticator in the speech (just months after it, the United States Congress, led by President Lyndon B. Johnson, passed the most sweeping civil rights and voting rights legislation in our history—just what Malcolm said it would not do), his call for

Source: George Breitman, ed. *Malcolm X Speaks: Selected Speeches and Statements* (New York: Pathfinder Press, 1989). Reprinted with permission of Betty Shabazz and Pathfinder Press.

black nationalism, his internationalism, and his stress on self-help in the African-American community strike themes that became central to the Black Power movement in the 1960s and still have resonance today.

*   *   *

Mr. Moderator, Brother Lomax, brothers and sisters, friends and enemies: I just can't believe everyone in here is a friend and I don't want to leave anybody out. The question tonight, as I understand it, is "The Negro Revolt, and Where Do We Go From Here?" or "What Next?" In my little humble way of understanding it, it points toward either the ballot or the bullet.

Before we try and explain what is meant by the ballot or the bullet, I would like to clarify something concerning myself. I'm still a Muslim, my religion is still Islam. That's my personal belief. Just as Adam Clayton Powell is a Christian minister who heads the Abyssinian Baptist Church in New York, but at the same time takes part in the political struggles to try and bring about rights to the black people in this country; and Dr. Martin Luther King is a Christian minister down in Atlanta, Georgia, who heads another organization fighting for the civil rights of black people in this country; . . . well, I myself am a minister, not a Christian minister, but a Muslim minister; and I believe in action on all fronts by whatever means necessary.

Although I'm still a Muslim, I'm not here tonight to discuss my religion. I'm not here to try and change your religion. I'm not here to argue or discuss anything that we differ about, because it's time for us to submerge our differences and realize that it is best for us to first see that we have the same problem, a common problem—a problem that will make you catch hell whether you're a Baptist, or a Methodist, or a Muslim, or a nationalist. Whether you're educated or illiterate, whether you live on the boulevard or in the alley, you're going to catch hell just like I am. We're all in the same boat and we all are going to catch the same hell from the same man. He just happens to be a white man. All of us have suffered here, in this country, political oppression at the hands of the white man, economic exploitation at the hands of the white man, and social degradation at the hands of the white man.

Now in speaking like this, it doesn't mean that we're anti-white, but it does mean we're anti-exploitation, we're anti-degradation, we're anti-oppression. And if the white man doesn't want us to be anti-him, let him stop oppressing and exploiting and degrading us. Whether we are Christians or Muslims or nationalists or agnostics or atheists, we must first learn to forget our differences. If we have differences, let us differ in the closet; when we come out in front, let us not have anything to argue about until we get finished arguing with the man. . . .

[Text omitted]

I'm not a politician, not even a student of politics; in fact, I'm not a student of much of anything. I'm not a Democrat, I'm not a Republican, and I don't even consider myself an American. If you and I were Americans, there'd be no problem. Those Hunkies that just got off the boat, they're already Americans. Everything that came out of Europe, every blue-eyed thing, is already an American. And as long as you and I have been over here, we aren't Americans yet.

. . . . Being here in America doesn't make you an American. Why, if birth made you American, you wouldn't need any legislation, you wouldn't need any amendments to the Constitution, you wouldn't be faced with civil-rights filibustering in Washington, D.C., right now. They don't have to pass civil-rights legislation to make a Polack an American.

No, I'm not an American. I'm one of the 22 million black people who are the victims of Americanism. One of the 22 million black people who are the victims of democracy, nothing but disguised hypocrisy. So, I'm not standing here speaking to you as an American, or a patriot, or a flag-saluter, or a flag-waver—no, not I. I'm speaking as a victim of this American system. And I see America through the eyes of the victim. I don't see any American dream; I see an American nightmare.

These 22 million victims are waking up. Their eyes are coming open. They're beginning to see what they used to only look at. They're becoming politically mature. They are realizing that there are new political trends from coast to coast. As they see these new political trends, it's possible for them to see that every time there's an election the races are so close that they have to have a recount. . . . Well, what does this mean? It means that when white people are evenly divided, and black people have a bloc of votes of their own, it is left up to them to determine who's going to sit in the White House and who's going to be in the dog house.

It was the black man's vote that put the present administration in Washington, D.C. Your vote, your dumb vote, your ignorant vote, your wasted vote put in an administration in Washington, D.C., that has seen fit to pass every kind of legislation imaginable, saving you until last, then filibustering on top of that. And your and my leaders have the audacity to run around clapping their hands and talk about how much progress we're making. And what a good president we have. If he wasn't good in Texas, he sure can't be good in Washington, D.C. Because Texas is a lynch state. It is in the same breath as Mississippi, no different; only they lynch you in Texas with a Texas accent and lynch you in Mississippi with a Mississippi accent. . . .

In this present administration they have in the House of Representatives 257 Democrats to only 177 Republicans. They control two-thirds of the House vote. Why can't they pass something that will help you and me? In the Senate there are 67 senators who are of the Democratic Party. Only 33 of them are Republicans. Why, the Democrats have got the government sewed up, and you're the one who sewed it up for them. And what have they given you for it? Four years in office, and just now getting around to some civil-rights legislation. Just now, after everything else is gone, out of the way, they're going to sit down now and play with you all summer long—the same old giant con game that they call filibuster. All those are in cahoots together. . . .

So it's time in 1964 to wake up. And when you see them coming up with that kind of conspiracy, let them know your eyes are open. And let them know you got something else that's wide open too. It's got to be the ballot or the bullet. The ballot or the bullet. If you're afraid to use an expression like that, you should get on out of the country, you should get back in the cotton patch, you should get back in the alley. They get all the Negro vote, and after they get it, the Negro gets nothing in return. All they did when they got to Washington was give a few big Negroes big jobs. Those big Negroes didn't need big jobs, they already had jobs. That's camouflage, that's trickery, that's treachery, window-dressing. I'm not trying to knock out the Democrats for the Republicans, we'll get to them in a minute. But it is true—you put the Democrats first and the Democrats put you last.

Look at it the way it is. What alibis do they use, since they control Congress and the Senate? What alibi do they use when you and I ask, "Well, when are you going to keep your promise?" They blame the Dixiecrats. What is a Dixiecrat? A Democrat. A Dixiecrat is nothing but a Democrat in disguise. . . . But the Northern Democrats have never put the Dixiecrats down. No, look at that thing the way it is. They have got a con game going on, a political con game, and you and I are in the middle. It's time for you and me to wake up and start looking at it like it is, and trying to understand it like it is; and then we can deal with it like it is.

[Text omitted]

I say again, I'm not anti-Democrat, I'm not anti-Republican, I'm not anti-anything. I'm just questioning their sincerity, and some of the strategy that they've been using on our people by promising them promises that they don't intend to keep. When you keep the Democrats in power you're keeping the Dixiecrats in power. . . . In the North they do it a different way. They have a system that's known as gerrymandering, whatever that means. It means when Negroes become too heavily concentrated in a certain area, and begin to gain too much political power, the white man comes along and changes the district line. . . .

[Text omitted]

So, where do we go from here? First, we need some friends. We need some new allies. The entire civil-rights struggle needs a new interpretation, a broader interpretation. . . . To those of us whose philosophy is black nationalism, the only way you can get involved in the civil-rights struggle is give it a new interpretation. That old interpretation excluded us. . . . So, we're giving . . . to the civil-rights struggle, an interpretation that will enable us to come into it, take part in it. And these handkerchief-heads who have been dillydallying and pussyfooting and compromising—we don't intend to let them pussyfoot and dillydally and compromise any longer.

[Text omitted]

And now you're facing a situation where the young Negro's coming up. They don't want to hear that "turn-the-other-cheek" stuff, no. In Jacksonville, those were teenagers, they were throwing Molotov cocktails. Negroes have never done that before. But it shows you there's a new deal coming in. There's new thinking coming in. There's new strategy coming in. It'll be Molotov cocktails this month, hand grenades next month, and something else next month. It'll be ballots, or it'll be bullets. It'll be liberty, or it will be death. The only difference about this kind of death—it'll be reciprocal. . . .

The black nationalists, those whose philosophy is black nationalism, in bringing about this new interpretation of the entire meaning of civil rights, look upon it as meaning . . . equality of opportunity. Well, we're justified in seeking civil rights, if it means equality of opportunity, because all we're doing there is trying to collect for our investment. Our mothers and fathers invested sweat and blood. Three hundred and ten years we worked in this country without a dime in return—I mean without a *dime* in return. You let the white man walk around here talking about how rich this country is, but you never stop to think how it got rich so quick. It got rich because you made it rich.

[Text omitted]

This is our investment. This is our contribution—our blood. Not only did we give of our free labor, we gave of our blood. Every time he had a call to arms, we were the first ones in uniform. We died on every battlefield the white man had. We have made a greater sacrifice than anybody who's standing up in American today. We have made a greater contribution and have collected less. Civil rights, for those of us whose philosophy is black nationalism means, "Give it to us now. Don't wait for next year. Give it to us yesterday, and that's not fast enough."

[Text omitted]

If you don't take this kind of stand, your little children will grow up and look at you and think "shame." If you don't take an uncompromising stand—I don't mean go out and get violent; but at the same time you should never be nonviolent unless you run into some nonviolence. I'm nonviolent with those who are nonviolent with me. But when you drop that violence on me, then you've made me go insane, and I'm not responsible for what I do. And that's the way every Negro should get. Any time you know you're within the law, within your legal rights, within your moral rights, in accord with justice, then die for what you believe in. But don't die alone. Let your dying be reciprocal. That is what is meant by equality. What's good for the goose is good for the gander.

When we begin to get in this area, we need new friends, we need new allies. We need to expand the civil-rights struggle to a higher level—to the level of human rights. Whenever you are in a civil-rights struggle, whether you know it or not, you are confining yourself to the jurisdiction of Uncle Sam. . . . All of our African brothers and our Asian brothers and our Latin-American brothers cannot open their mouths and interfere in the domestic affairs of the United States. And as long as it's civil rights, this comes under the jurisdiction of Uncle Sam.

But the United Nations has what's known as the charter of human rights, it has a committee that deals in human rights. . . . When you expand the civil-rights struggle to the level of human rights, you can then take the case of the black man in this country before the nations in the UN. . . . But the only level you can do it on is the level of human rights. Civil rights keeps you under his restrictions, under his jurisdiction. . . . Human rights are the rights that are recognized by all nations of this earth. And any time any one violates your human rights, you can take them to the world court. Uncle Sam's hands are dripping with blood, dripping with the blood of the black man in this country. . . . Let the world know how bloody his hands are. Let the world know the hypocrisy that's practiced over here. Let it be the ballot or the bullet. Let him know that it must be the ballot or the bullet.

[Text omitted]

Right now, in this country, if you and I, 22 million African-Americans—that's what we are—Africans who are in America. You're nothing but Africans. Nothing but Africans. In fact, you'd get farther calling yourself African instead of Negro. Africans don't catch hell. You're the only one catching hell. They don't have to pass civil-rights bills for Africans. An African can go anywhere he wants right now. All you've got to do is tie your head up. That's right, go anywhere you want. Just stop being a Negro. Change you name to Hoogagagooba. That'll show you how silly the white man is. You're dealing with a silly man. A friend of mine who's very dark put a turban on his head and went into a restaurant in Atlanta before they called themselves desegregated. He went into a white restaurant, he sat down, they served him, and he said, "What would happen if a Negro came in here?" And there he's sitting, black as night, but because he had his head wrapped up the waitress looked back at him and says, "Why, there wouldn't no nigger dare come in here."

So, your dealing with a man whose bias and prejudice are making him lose his mind, his intelligence, every day. He's frightened. He looks around and sees what's taking place on this earth, and he sees that the pendulum of time is swinging in your direction. The dark people are waking up. They're losing their fear of the white man. No place where he's fighting right now is he winning. Everywhere he's fighting someone your and my complexion. And they're beating him. He can't win any more. He's won his last battle. He failed to win the Korean War. He couldn't win it. He had to sign a truce. That's a loss. Any time Uncle Sam, with all his machinery for warfare, is held to a draw by some rice-eaters, he's lost the battle. . . . America's not supposed to sign a truce. She's supposed to be bad. But she's not bad any more. . . . The black man knows it, the brown man knows it, the red man knows it, and the yellow man knows it. So they engage him in guerrilla warfare. That's not his style. You've got to have heart to be a guerrilla warrior, and he hasn't got any heart. . . .

I would like say in closing, a few things concerning the Muslim Mosque, Inc., which we established recently in New York City. Its true we're Muslims and our religion is Islam, but we don't mix our religion with our politics and our economics and our social and civil activities— not any more. . . . After our religious services are over, then as Muslims we become involved in political action, economic action and social and civic action. We become involved with anybody, anywhere, any time and in any manner that's designed to eliminate the evils, the political, economic, and social evils that are afflicting the people of our community.

The political philosophy of black nationalism means that the black man should control the politics and the politicians in his own community; no more. The black man in the black community has to be re-educated into the science of politics so he will know what politics is supposed to bring him in return. Don't be throwing out any ballots. A ballot is like a bullet. You don't throw your ballots until you see a target, and if that target is not within your reach, keep your ballot in your pocket. The political philosophy of black nationalism is being taught in the Christian church. It's being taught in SNCC [Student Nonviolent Coordinating Committee] meetings. It's being taught in Muslim meetings. . . . It's being taught everywhere. Black people are fed up with the dillydallying, pussy-footing, compromising approach that we've been using toward getting our freedom. We want freedom *now*, but we're not going to get it saying "We Shall Overcome." We've got to fight until we overcome.

The economic philosophy of black nationalism is pure and simple. It only means that we should control the economy of our community. Why should white people be running all the stores in our community? Why should white people be running the banks of our community? Why should the economy of our community be in the hands of the white man? Why? If a black man can't move his store into a white community, you tell me why a white man should move his store into a black community. The philosophy of black nationalism involves a re-education program in the black community in regards to economics. Our people have to be made to see that any time you take your dollar out of your community and spend it in a community where you don't live, the community where you live will get poorer and poorer, and the community where you spend your money will get richer and richer. Then you wonder why where you live is always a ghetto or a slum area. And where you and I are concerned, not only do we lose it when we spend it out of the community, but the white man has got all our stores in the community tied up; so that though we spend it in the community, at sundown the man who runs the store takes it over across town somewhere. He's got us in his vise. . . . Once you gain control of the economy of your own community, then you don't have to picket and boycott and beg some cracker downtown for a job in his business.

The social philosophy of black nationalism only means that we have to get together and remove the evils, the vices, alcoholism, drug addiction, and other evils that are destroying the moral fiber of our community. We ourselves have to lift the level of our community, the standard of our community to a higher level, make our own society beautiful so that we will be satisfied in our own social circles and won't be running around here trying to knock our way into a social circle where we're not wanted.

So I say, in spreading a gospel such as black nationalism, it is not designed to make the black man re-evaluate the white man—you know him already—but to make the black man re-evaluate himself. Don't change the white man's mind—you can't change his mind, and that whole thing about appealing to the moral conscience of America—America's conscience is bankrupt. She lost all conscience a long time ago. . . . So it is not necessary to change the white man's mind. We have to change our own mind. . . . We have to see each other as brothers and sisters. We have to come together with warmth so we can develop unity and harmony that's necessary to get this problem solved ourselves. How can we do this? How can we avoid jealousy? How can we avoid the suspicion and the divisions that exist in the community? I'll tell you now.

[Text omitted]

Our gospel is black nationalism. We're not trying to threaten the existence of any organization, but we're spreading the gospel of black nationalism. Anywhere there's a church that is also preaching and practicing the gospel of black nationalism, join that church. If the NAACP is preaching and practicing the gospel of black nationalism, join the NAACP. If CORE is spreading and practicing the gospel of black nationalism, join CORE. Join any organization that has a gospel that's for the uplift of the black man. And when you get into it and see them pussyfooting or compromising, pull out of it because that's not black nationalism. We'll find another one.

[Text omitted]

We will work with anybody, anywhere, at any time, who is genuinely interested in tackling the problem head-on, nonviolently as long as the enemy is nonviolent, but violent when the enemy gets violent. We'll work with you on the voter-registration drive, . . . on rent strikes, . . . on school boycotts—I don't believe in any kind of integration; I'm not even worried about it because I know you're not going to get it anyway; you're not going to get it because you're afraid to die; you've got to be ready to die if you try and force yourself on the white man. . . . But we will still work with you on the school boycotts because we're against a segregated school system. A segregated school system produces children who, when they graduate, graduate with crippled minds. But this does not mean that a school is segregated because it's all black. A segregated school means a school that is controlled by people who have no real interest in it whatsoever.

. . . A segregated district or community is [one in which] outsiders control the politics and the economy of that community. They never refer to the white section as a segregated community. It's the all-Negro section that's a segregated community. Why? The white man controls his own school, his own bank, his own economy, his own politics, his own everything, his own community—but he also controls yours. When you're under someone else's control, you're segregated. . . . You've got to *control* your own. Just like the white man has control of his, you need control of yours.

You know the best way to get rid of segregation? The white man is more afraid of separation than he is of integration. Segregation means that he puts you away from him, but not far enough for you to be out of his jurisdiction; separation means you're gone. So we will work with you against the segregated school system because it's criminal, because it is absolutely destructive, in every way imaginable, to the minds of the children who have to be exposed to that type of crippling education.

Last but not least, I must say this concerning the great controversy over rifles and shot guns. The only thing that I've ever said is that in areas where the government has proven itself either unwilling or unable to defend the lives and the property of Negroes, it's time for Negroes to defend themselves. Article number two of the constitutional amendments provides you and me the right to own a rifle or a shotgun. It is constitutionally legal to own a shotgun or a rifle. This doesn't mean you're going to get a rifle and form battalions and go out looking for white folks, although you'd be within your rights—I mean, you'd be justified; but that would be illegal and we don't do anything illegal. If the white man doesn't want the black man buying rifles and shotguns, then let the government do its job. That's all. . . .

[Text omitted]

. . . The black nationalists aren't going to wait. Lyndon B. Johnson is the head of the Democratic Party. If he's for civil rights, let him go into the Senate next week and declare himself. Let him go in there right now and declare himself. Let him go in there and denounce the Southern branch of his party. Let him go in there right now and take a moral stand—right now, not later. Tell him, don't wait until election time. If he waits too long, brothers and sisters, he will be responsible for letting a condition develop in this country which will create a climate that will bring seeds up out of the ground with vegetation on the end of them looking like something these people never dreamed of. In 1964, its the ballot or the bullet. Thank you.

SUGGESTIONS FOR FURTHER READING

James Baldwin, *Notes of a Native Son* (Boston: Bacon Press, 1955).

Taylor Branch, *Parting the Waters: America in the King Years, 1954–1963* (New York: Simon & Schuster, 1988).

W. E. B. Du Bois, *The Souls of Black Folk* (New York: Vintage Books/Library of America, 1990).

Frederick Douglass, *Narrative of the Life of Frederick Douglass*, edited and introduction by Harold Bloom (New York: Chelsea House, 1988).

Eugene D. Genovese, *Roll, Jordan, Roll: The World the Slaves Made* (New York: Vintage Books, 1974).

Alex Haley, *The Autobiography of Malcolm X* (New York: Ballantine Books, 1965).

hooks, bell, *Black Looks: Race and Representation* (Boston: Beacon Press, 1992).

Harry V. Jaffa, *Crisis of the House Divided: An Interpretation of the Issues in the Lincoln–Douglass Debates* (Garden City, NY: Doubleday & Co., Inc., 1959).

David Levering Lewis, *W. E. B. Du Bois: Biography of a Race* (New York: Henry Holt and Company, 1993).

Gunnar Myrdal, *An American Dilemma: The Negro Problem and Modern Democracy* (New York: Harper & Row, 1969).

Harriet Beecher Stowe, *Uncle Tom's Cabin* (New York: Macmillan Publishing Co., 1994).

Clarence E. Walker, *Deromanticizing Black History: Critical Essays and Reappraisals* (Knoxville, TN: University of Tennessee Press, 1991).

Cornel West, *Race Matters* (New York: Vintage Books, 1993).

PART V

Religion and Politics: Pluralism and Common Bonds

PART V

Religion and Politics:
Pluralism and Common Bonds

Our government makes no sense unless it is founded in a deeply felt religious faith—and I don't care what it is.[1]

—DWIGHT DAVID EISENHOWER

Is uniformity attainable? Millions of innocent men, women and children, since the introduction of Christianity, have been burnt, tortured, fined, imprisoned; yet we have not advanced one inch towards uniformity. What has been the effect of coercion? To make one half the world fools, and the other half hypocrites. To support roguery and error all over the earth.[2]

—THOMAS JEFFERSON

The relation between religion and politics in America is filled with paradoxes. Consider the remark attributed to President Eisenhower. "Deeply felt" religious faith is essential, he suggests, to good democratic government. Yet, at the same time, he believes that the content of the faith is of little importance. Think how strange this statement would appear in so many places in the world or at so many times throughout history when religious beliefs and passions have sparked so much strife and bloodshed. In such times and places, whether we look to the Ayatollah's Iran or medieval Europe, or even John Winthrop's Massachusetts, the content of the faith is all. It is important, Eisenhower suggests, that Americans be religious, but not "too" religious if the latter leads one to be doctrinaire and intolerant toward other faiths.

There is ample evidence that most Americans are and long have been religious in the rather undoctrinaire way that President Eisenhower

---

[1] Quoted in Robert N. Bellah, "Civil Religion in America." In Bellah, *Beyond Belief: Essays on Religion in a Post-Traditional World* (New York: Harper & Row, 1970), p. 170.

[2] Jefferson, *Notes on Virginia*, Query XVII. In *Life and Selected Writings*, p. 276.

saw as beneficial for democracy. Indeed, contemporary America ranks highest among developed nations in percentage of people professing a belief in God, as well as in church membership and attendance. In fact, using church membership as one's indicator, Americans today are far more religious than at the time of the founding and more so than at any point in our history.[3] At the same time, Americans probably have never been less biblically literate or known less of the particulars of religious doctrine. This illiteracy may pose its own dangers, but doctrinal warfare is not among them.

In any case, in observing Christian sects in America in the 1830s, Alexis de Tocqueville observed that though sects differed in how they worshiped God, the moral codes they preached in the name of God were pretty much the same—and were harmonious with liberal democracy. He further observed, in a vein similar to that of Eisenhower, that

> (i)f it be of the highest importance to man, as an individual, that his religion should be true, it is not so to society. Society has no future life to hope for or to fear; and provided the citizens profess a religion, the peculiar tenets of that religion are of very little importance to its interests.[4]

Religion is useful in promoting the virtuous conduct which democratic citizenship requires for reasons Tocqueville discusses in the excerpt here. "True religion" is not.

Americans of the founding generation were, of course, overwhelmingly Protestant, though of a number of different denominations. This was fortunate in one regard. Men like Madison and Jefferson were able to work out principles of religious toleration and such principles were able to gain some currency at a time when the burdens of tolerance were lower than they were to become. Though tolerance is never easily achieved or maintained, it is *easier*, at least at first, to tolerate those who are not *too* unlike oneself. Once the belief in the virtue takes hold, it can be extended more readily to a greater diversity of faiths and denominations, and even to nonbelievers.

Of course, the United States has not always been a shining beacon of religious tolerance. As we have seen already, anti-Catholic sentiment

---

[3] Estimates of church membership are provided in Roger Finke and Rodney Stark, *The Churching of America: Winners and Losers in Our Religious Economy* (New Brunswick, NJ: Rutgers University Press, 1992), p. 16.

[4] Alexis de Tocqueville, *Democracy in America*. Abridged and Introduction by Thomas Bender (New York: The Modern Library, 1981), p. 182.

has been rife at many points in our history, usually connected with nativist responses to immigrants. Bias against Jews, Moslems (as recently as during the Gulf War), and minority Christian sects has been common. And as the piece by Red Jacket reminds us, the religions of Native Americans were dismissed as so much superstition and the "civilizing" of the indigenous peoples was generally thought by whites to require their conversion to Christianity. Nonetheless, neither has the United States witnessed the deep-seated and persistent religious hostilities among sects that have led to the bloodshed witnessed in this century in so many other parts of the world.

One reason for this is that our political system has been reasonably successful in separating church from state. Indeed, this separation explains at least in part why religion has and continues to flourish in America. This latter argument might seem strange, but it really is not. The anti-establishment and free exercise clauses of the First Amendment to the Constitution serve to *depoliticize* religious disagreements. The right I have to worship as I choose and the restraints on government in establishing religion allow me a sense of security regarding my faith. I have less to fear from those of other faiths when the exercise of political power in matters of faith is foreclosed to them—as it is to me. It is largely because of this that we have not witnessed the anticlericalism in the United States that has been a theme of French politics, for example, since their 1789 revolution. Religion and politics have always intermingled in the United States. Yet the constraints the Constitution provides limit the opportunities to impose religion by state power—to the benefit of both church and state.

Drawing the lines between church and state is a recurrent theme in the American constitutional law of this century. Do the religious clauses of the First Amendment forbid, for example, placing a creche on the lawn outside of City Hall during Christmas season? Or do they, as *Lemon v. Kurtzman* addresses, allow for public aid to parochial schools if such aid is used to teach secular subjects such as math and science? Finally, does protection of religious freedom allow a Christian Scientist mother to treat her child, ill with meningitis, by prayer alone, an issue addressed in *Walker v. Superior Court of Sacramento*? These are hard cases, but they occur in a gray area surrounded by a larger space of fairly well-settled principle.

To separate church from state as the First Amendment requires is not, however, to sever religion from politics. It was quite common in early America for citizens to receive lessons in political theory and practice from the pulpit, as witnessed in Samuel Kendal's 1804 election day sermon. Further, many of our most significant social movements, from that for abolition in the nineteenth century to the civil rights and antiabortion movements of this century, have been largely religious in inspiration and organization. And it seems that many Americans today, including Ralph

Reed, the executive director of the Christian Coalition, reject the once more prevalent notion that one must leave one's religious convictions at the gate when entering the political arena. John F. Kennedy, in a speech on the "religious question" during the 1960 presidential election campaign, essentially says that he would do just this if elected president. His Catholicism, he claims, would not determine his views even on such issues as birth control or divorce. Moreover, he contends that that is how it should be. Reed in his speech reproduced here, and also the U.S. Conference of Catholic Bishops, endorse the principle of separation of church and state, but suggest that the sensibilities of religious people should be expressed without hesitation in the public square. In a recent statement on political responsibility, the bishops' write the following:

> The religious community has important responsibilities in political life. We believe our nation is enriched and our traditions of pluralism enhanced when religious groups join with others in the debate over the policies and vision that ought to guide our nation. Our constitution protects the right of religious bodies to speak out without governmental interference, endorsement, or sanction. Religious groups should expect neither favoritism nor discrimination in their public roles. The national debate is not enhanced by ignoring or ruling out the contributions of citizens because their convictions are grounded in religious belief.[5]

In addition, the Supreme Court seems to be moving toward the view that the Constitution can be interpreted to accommodate religion so long as laws pertaining to it do not give preference to one sect over another. This "nonpreferentialist" reading of the First Amendment is challenging the notion that there should be a strict "wall of separation" between church and state. An early indication of this direction of the Court is found in the dissent to the Lemon opinion in this volume.

In a country that is both as secular in its political principles and as deeply and diversely religious as the United States, we should expect that a certain tension between religion and politics will long persist. We are in a period in our history when this tension is quite pronounced, as we see in debates over such issues as abortion, birth control, decency in arts and entertainment, school prayer, creationism, care for the poor, and so many more. The readings in this section deal largely with issues of

---

[5] United States Catholic Conference Administrative Board. "Political Responsibility: Revitalizing American Democracy." (Washington, D.C.: United States Catholic Conference, Inc., 1991).

church and state and some hard cases where their separation is called into question. They deal also with the role and form religious convictions can and should play in public debates, where citizens must be cognizant of the "two hats" they are asked to wear as liberal citizens. They are on the one hand people of a particular faith (or lack thereof), whether Protestant, Catholic, Moslem, or Jew, and increasingly, of less established fundamentalist or evangelical churches.[6] On the other hand, they are members of a pluralistic political community which has long accepted that it is wrong to use state power to coerce others to support a faith they cannot by conscience accept. Harmonizing these two roles is one of the great challenges of liberal citizenship and never more so than for people of deep religious faith.

---

[6] In recent years, newly formed evangelical and fundamentalist churches have been growing more rapidly than "mainline" denominations, a trend that is particularly strong among recent immigrants. See Finke and Stark, Chapter 7.

Roger Williams,
"The Bloudy Tenent of Persecution for Cause of Conscience" (1644)

Editor's Introduction: Roger Williams (1603–1683) was born in London, educated at Cambridge, and took holy orders in the Church of England. He converted to Puritanism and moved to the Massachusetts Bay Colony in 1631. Williams soon became an outcast, however, for challenging the attempts of the Puritan leadership to create a theocratic state. He was banished from the Massachusetts Bay Colony in 1636 and founded Providence, the first settlement in Rhode Island. Jews, Quakers, and other religious minorities were welcome in Providence, and Williams came to renounce ties to any known religious sect, claiming to be simply a Christian seeking the truth. He is rightly remembered as an early proponent of religious tolerance in the New World, believing that government should not attempt to dictate religious worship in any form, as it is a matter of individual conscience. Williams urges that there should be a "wall of separation between the garden of the church and the wilderness of this world."[1] We find this metaphor of a wall of separation between church and state repeated by Jefferson in his letter to the Danbury Baptists and again in *Lemon v. Kurtzman*, both reproduced in this Part. It is worth noting, however, that Williams was far more concerned about the role political power could play in corrupting religious faith than about the dangers religion posed to politics. The following selection on religious persecution is in the form of a dialogue between Peace and Truth, with Truth representing Williams' views.

* * *

Chapter LXXII

Peace. Brentius (whom you next quote, saith he) speaketh not to your cause. Wee willingly grant you, that man hath no *power* to make *Lawes* to binde *conscience*, but this hinders not, but men may see the *Lawes* of God observed which doe binde *conscience*.

Source: Roger Williams, *The Bloudy Tenent of Persecution for Cause of Conscience* (London: 1644).

[1] Quote from *Mr. Cotton's Letter Lately Printed, Examined and Answered* in *The Complete Writings of Roger Williams*, vol. I. (New York: Russell and Russell, Inc., 1967).

Truth. I answer, In granting with *Brentius* that man hath not power to make *Lawes* to binde *conscience*, hee overthrowes such his *tenet* and *practice* as *restraine* men from their *Worship*, according to their Conscience and beleefe, and constraine them to such *worships* (though it bee out of a pretence that they are convinced) which their owne *soules* tell them they have no *satisfaction* nor *faith* in.

Secondly, whereas he affirmeth that men may make *Lawes* to see the *Lawes* of *God* observed.

I answer, as *God* needeth not the helpe of a materiall *sword* of *steele* to assist the *sword* of the *Spirit* in the affaires of *conscience*, so those men, those *Magistrates*, yea that *Commonwealth* which makes such *Magistrates*, must needs have power and authority from *Christ Jesus* to sit *Judge* and to determine in all the great controversies concerning *doctrine, discipline, government, &c.*

And then I aske, whether upon this ground it must not evidently follow, that

Either there is no lawfull *Commonwealth* nor *civill State* of men in the world, which is not qualified with this spiritual *discerning*: (and then also that the very *Commonweale* hath more *light* concerning the *Church of Christ*, then the *Church* it selfe.)

Or, that the *Commonweale* and *Magistrates* thereof must judge and punish as they are perswaded in their owne *beleefe* and *conscience*, (be their *conscience Paganish, Turkish*, or *Antichristian*) what is this but to confound *Heaven* and *Earth* together, and not onely to take away the *being* of *Christianity* out of the World, but to take away all *civility*, and the *world* out of the *world*, and to lay all upon heapes of *confusion*?

Chapter LXXIII·

Peace. The like answer (saith he) may bee returned to *Luther*, whom you next alledge.

First, that the *government* of the *civill Magistrate* extendeth no further then over the *bodies* and *goods* of their *subjects*, not over their *soules*, and therefore they may not undertake to give *Lawes* unto the *soules* and con-sciences of men.

Secondly, that the *Church* of *Christ* doth not use the Arme of *secular* power to compell men to the true profession of the *truth*, for this is to be done with *spirituall weapons*, whereby *Christians* are to be exhorted, not compelled. "But this (saith hee) hindreth not that *Christians* sinning against *light* of *faith* and *conscience*, may justly be censured by the *Church* with *excommunication*, and by the *civill sword* also, in case they shall corrupt others to the perdition of their soules."

Truth. I answer, in this joynt *confession* of the *Answerer* with *Luther*, to wit, that the *government* of the *civill Magistrate* extendeth no further then over the *bodies* and *goods* of the subjects, not over their *soules:* who sees not what a cleare *testimony* from his own mouth and pen is given, to wit, that either the *Spirituall* and *Church* estate, the preaching of the *Word*, and the gathering of the *Church*, the *Baptisme* of it, the *Ministry*, *Government* and *Administrations* thereof belong to the *civill body* of the *Commonweale?* That is, to the *bodies* and *goods* of men, which seemes monstrous to imagine: Or else that the *civill Magistrate* cannot (without exceeding the bounds of his office) meddle with those spirituall affaires.

Againe, necessarily must it follow, that these two are contradictory to themselves: to wit,

The *Magistrates* power extends no further then the *bodies* and *goods* of the subject, and yet

The *Magistrate* must punish *Christians* for sinning against the *light* of *faith* and *conscience*, and for *corrupting* the *soules* of men.

The Father of *Lights* make this worthy *Answerer* and all that feare him to see their wandring in this case, not only from his *feare*, but also from the light of *Reason* it selfe, their owne *convictions* and *confessions*.

Secondly, in his joint confession with *Luther*, that the *Church* doth not use the secular power to compell men to the Faith and Profession of the *truth*, he condemneth (as before I have observed)

First, his former *Implication, viz.* that they may bee compelled when they are convinced of the *truth* of it.

Secondly, their owne *practice*, who suffer no man of any different *conscience* and *worship* to live in their jurisdiction, except that he depart from his owne *exercise* of *Religion* and *Worship* differing from the *worship* allowed of in the *civill State*, yea and also actually submit to come to their *Church*.

Which howsoever it is coloured over with this varnish, *viz.* that men are *compelled* no further then unto the hearing of the *Word*, unto which all men are bound: yet it will appeare that *teaching* and being taught in a *Church* estate is a *Church* worship, as true and proper a *Church worship* as the Supper of the Lord, *Act.* 2. 46.

Secondly, all persons (*Papist* and *Protestant*) that are conscientious, have alwayes suffered upon this ground especially, that they have refused to come to each *others Church* or *Meeting.*

John Winthrop,
"A Little Speech on Liberty" (1645)

Editor's Introduction: John Winthrop (1588–1649) was born in Suffolk, England, and sailed to New England in 1630 on the ship *Arabella*. He was elected first governor of the Massachusetts Bay Colony in 1629, before his arrival in the New World, and served several terms thereafter. While aboard the *Arabella*, Winthrop delivered an address which encouraged his fellow Puritans to create a "City upon a Hill" (Matthew 5:14) that would stand as a shining example to the world.

Many American political leaders have applied this phrase to the nation as a whole and it has contributed to the development of "American exceptionalism," i.e., the view that America has a unique moral mission in the world. We hear echoes of Winthrop in Lincoln's Gettysburg Address and in the speeches of such political figures as Ronald Reagan, who adopted the "shining city on a hill" metaphor in his first presidential campaign.

In the following speech, Winthrop addresses the issue of freedom, religious and otherwise. In it, he distinguishes between natural liberty, which is license to do as one wishes, and what he calls "civil," "federal," or "moral" liberty. Civil liberty "is maintained and exercised in a way of subjection to authority; it is of the same kind of liberty wherewith Christ hath made us free." Thus, in Winthrop's view, civil freedom is compatible with authority that directs a community in ecclesiastical and political affairs. Such a view clearly places Winthrop at odds with Roger Williams' understanding of religious freedom and also with the "Antinomianism" (in simplest form, a doctrine reliant on individual faith rather than "works" as a means to salvation) of Anne Hutchinson, whom he banished from the Massachusetts Bay Colony in 1638.

*   *   *

I suppose something may be expected from me, upon this charge that is befallen me, which moves me to speak now to you; yet I intend not to intermeddle in the proceedings of the court, or with any of the persons concerned therein. Only I bless God, that I see an issue of this troublesome business. I also acknowledge the justice of the court, and, for mine own part, I am well satisfied, I was publicly charged, and I am

Source: Hosmer, James Kendall, ed., *Winthrop's Journal: "History of New England,"* Vol. 2 (New York: Charles Scribner's Sons, 1908).

publicly and legally acquitted, which is all I did expect or desire. And though this be sufficient for my justification before men, yet not so before the God, who hath seen so much amiss in my dispensations (and even in this affair) as calls me to be humble. For to be publicly and criminally charged in this court, is matter of humiliation, (and I desire to make a right use of it), notwithstanding I be thus acquitted. If her father had spit in her face, (saith the Lord concerning Miriam), should she not have been ashamed seven days? Shame had lien upon her, whatever the occasion had been. I am unwilling to stay you from your urgent affairs, yet give me leave (upon this special occasion) to speak a little more to this assembly. It may be of some good use, to inform and rectify the judgments of some of the people, and may prevent such distempers as have arisen amongst us. The great questions that have troubled the country are about the authority of the magistrates and the liberty of the people. It is yourselves who have called us to this office; and being called by you, we have our authority from God, in way of an ordinance, such as hath the image of God eminently stamped upon it, the contempt and violation whereof hath been vindicated with examples of divine vengeance. I entreat you to consider that when you choose magistrates, you take them from among yourselves, men subject to like passions as you are. Therefore, when you see infirmities in us, you should reflect upon your own; and that would make you bear the more with us, and not be severe censurers of the failings of your magistrates, when you have continual experience of the like infirmities in yourselves and others. We account him a good servant who breaks not his covenant. The covenant between you and us is the oath you have taken of us, which is to this purpose, that we shall govern you and judge your causes by the rules of God's laws and our own, according to our best skill. When you agree with a workman to build you a ship or house, etc., he undertakes as well for his skill as for his faithfulness, for it is his profession, and you pay him for both. But when you call one to be a magistrate, he doth not profess nor undertake to have sufficient skill for that office, nor can you furnish him with gifts, etc.; therefore you must run the hazard of his skill and ability. But if he fail in faithfulness, which by his oath he is bound unto, that he must answer for. If it fall out that the case be clear to common apprehension, and the rule clear also, if he transgress here, the error is not in the skill, but in the evil of the will: it must be required of him. But if the case be doubtful, or the rule doubtful, to men of such understanding and parts as your magistrates are, if your magistrates should err here, yourselves must bear it.

For the other point concerning liberty, I observe a great mistake in the country about that. There is a twofold liberty—natural (I mean as our nature is now corrupt), and civil or federal. The first is common to man with beasts and other creatures. By this, man, as he stands in relation to man simply, hath liberty to do what he lists; it is a liberty to evil as well as to good. This liberty is incompatible and inconsistent with authority, and cannot endure the least restraint of the most just authority. The exercise and maintaining of this liberty makes men grow more evil, and in time to be worse than brute beasts: *omnes sumus licentia deteriores*. This is that great enemy of truth and peace, that wild beast, which all the ordinances of God are bent against, to restrain and subdue it.

The other kind of liberty I call civil or federal; it may also be termed moral, in reference to the covenant between God and man in the moral law, and the politic covenants and constitutions amongst men themselves. This liberty is the proper end and object of authority, and cannot subsist without it; and it is a liberty to that only which is good, just, and honest. This liberty you are to stand for, with the hazard (not only of your goods, but) of your lives, if need be. Whatsoever crosseth this, is not authority, but a distemper thereof. This liberty is maintained and exercised in a way of subjection to authority; it is of the same kind of liberty wherewith Christ hath made us free. The woman's own choice makes such a man her husband; yet being so chosen, he is her lord, and she is to be subject to him, yet in a way of liberty, not of bondage; and a true wife accounts her subjection her honor and freedom, and would not think her condition safe and free but in her subjection to her husband's authority. Such is the liberty of the church under the authority of Christ, her king and husband; his yoke is so easy and sweet to her as a bride's ornaments; and if through forwardness or wantonness, etc., she shake it off at any time, she is at no rest in her spirit until she take it up again; and whether her lord smiles upon her and embraceth her in his arms, or whether he frowns or rebukes, or smites her, she apprehends the sweetness of his love in all, and is refreshed, supported, and instructed by every such dispensation of his authority over her. On the other side, ye know who they are that complain of this yoke and say, let us break their bands, etc., we will not have this man to rule over us.

Even so, brethren, it will be between you and your magistrates. If you stand for your natural corrupt liberties and will do what is good in your own eyes, you will not endure the least weight of authority, but will murmur, and oppose, and be always striving to shake off that yoke; but if you will be satisfied to enjoy such civil and lawful liberties, such as Christ allows you, then will you quietly and cheerfully submit unto that authority which is set over you, in all the administrations of it, for your good. Wherein, if we fail at any time, we hope we shall be willing (by God's assistance) to hearken to good advice from any of you, or in any other way of God. So shall your liberties be preserved, in upholding the honor and power of authority amongst you.

James Madison et al., "Memorial and Remonstrance Against Religious Assessments" (1785)

Editor's Introduction: We have encountered James Madison (1749–1836) before as a key contributor to the drafting of the Constitution, as the most thorough record-keeper of the Constitutional Convention, as one author of *The Federalist Papers*, as a sponsor of the Bill of Rights in the first Congress, and as an opponent of the Alien and Sedition Acts. In the following piece, Madison takes up the issue of religious liberty.

The Memorial and Remonstrance addresses a bill introduced in the Virginia legislature in the 1784–1785 session that would have levied a tax on property holders to support the teaching of religion. The bill, which was withdrawn prior to a vote, would have provided a state subsidy to clergymen in the Episcopal Church. Madison opposes this sort of subsidy vehemently, arguing that citizens should not be coerced into supporting a religion that they could not accept in conscience. He appeals to the notion of unalienable natural rights, arguing that "what is here a right towards men, is a duty towards the Creator." Further, this duty to render homage to the Creator as one's conscience dictates takes precedence over the duties of citizenship. It is a natural right that all people retain in civil society. Madison's arguments are similar to those found in John Locke's famous "A Letter Concerning Toleration," and represent an important exposition of and contribution to liberal political thought.

*   *   *

We, the subscribers, citizens of the said Commonwealth, having taken into serious consideration, a Bill printed by order of the last Session of General Assembly, entitled "A Bill establishing a provision for Teachers of the Christian Religion," and conceiving that the same, if finally armed with the sanctions of a law, will be a dangerous abuse of power, are bound as faithful members of a free State, to remonstrate against it, and to declare the reasons by which we are determined. We remonstrate against the said Bill,

1. Because we hold it for fundamental and undeniable truth, "that religion or the duty which we owe to our Creator and the manner of discharging it, can be directed only by reason and conviction, not by force

Source: Gaillard Hunt, ed., *The Writings of James Madison* (New York: G. P. Putnam's Sons, 1906).

or violence." The religion then of every man must be left to the conviction and conscience of every man, and it is the right of every man to exercise it as these may dictate. This right is in its nature an unalienable right. It is unalienable because the opinions of men, depending only on the evidence contemplated by their own minds, cannot follow the dictates of other men. It is unalienable also because what is here a right towards men, is a duty towards the Creator. It is the duty of every man to render to the Creator such homage, and such only, as he believes to be acceptable to him. This duty is precedent, both in order of time and degree of obligation, to the claims of Civil Society. Before any man can be considered as a member of Civil Society, he must be considered as a subject of the Governor of the Universe. And if a member of Civil Society, who enters into any subordinate association, must always do it with a reservation of his duty to the general authority, much more must every man who becomes a member of any particular Civil Society do it with a saving of his allegiance to the Universal Sovereign. We maintain therefore that in matters of religion no man's right is abridged by the institution of Civil Society, and that religion is wholly exempt from its cognizance. True it is that no other rule exists, by which any question which may divide a society can be ultimately determined, but the will of the majority; but it is also true, that the majority may trespass on the rights of the minority.

2. Because if religion be exempt from the authority of the society at large, still less can it be subject to that of the Legislative Body. The latter are but the creatures and vicegerents of the former. Their jurisdiction is both derivative and limited. It is limited with regard to the co-ordinate departments; more necessarily is it limited with regard to the constituents. The preservation of a free government requires not merely that the metes and bounds which separate each department of power may be invariably maintained, but more especially that neither of them be suffered to overleap the great barrier which defends the rights of the people. The rulers who are guilty of such an encroachment, exceed the commission from which they derive their authority, and are tyrants. The People who submit to it are governed by laws made neither by themselves nor by an authority derived from them, and are slaves.

3. Because it is proper to take alarm at the first experiment on our liberties. We hold this prudent jealousy to be the first duty of citizens, and one of [the] noblest characteristics of the late Revolution. The freemen of America did not wait till usurped power had strengthened itself by exercise and entangled the question in precedents. They saw all the consequences in the principle, and they avoided the consequences by denying the principle. We revere this lesson too much, soon to forget it. Who does not see that the same authority which can establish Christianity in exclusion of all other religions, may establish with the same ease any

particular sect of Christians in exclusion of all other sects? That the same authority which can force a citizen to contribute three pence only of his property for the support of any one establishment, may force him to conform to any other establishment in all cases whatsoever?

4. Because the bill violates that equality which ought to be the basis of every law. . . . If "all men are by nature equally free and independent," [then] all men are to be considered as entering into Society on equal conditions, as relinquishing no more and therefore retaining no less, one than another, of their natural rights. Above all are they to be considered as retaining an *"equal* title to the free exercise of religion according to the dictates of conscience." Whilst we assert for ourselves a freedom to embrace, to profess, and to observe the religion which we believe to be of divine origin, we cannot deny an equal freedom to those whose minds have not yielded to the evidence which has convinced us. If this freedom be abused, it is an offence against God, not against man. To God therefore, not to men, must an account of it be rendered. As the Bill violates equality by subjecting some to peculiar burdens, so it violates the same principle by granting to other[s] peculiar exemptions. Are the Quakers and Menonists [to whom exemptions are granted] the only sects who think a compulsive support of their religions unnecessary and unwarantable? Can their piety alone be intrusted with the care of public worship? Ought their religions to be endowed above all others with extraordinary privileges by which proselytes may be enticed from all others? We think too favorably of the justice and good sense of these denominations to believe that they either covet pre-eminencies over their fellow citizens, or that they will be seduced by them from the common opposition to the measure.

5. Because the bill implies either that the Civil Magistrate is a competent judge of religious truth, or that he may employ religion as an engine of civil policy. The first is an arrogant pretension falsified by the contradictory opinions of rulers in all ages and throughout the world; the second an unhallowed perversion of the means of salvation.

6. Because the establishment proposed by the Bill is not requisite for the support of the Christian religion. To say that it is, is a contradiction to the Christian religion itself; for every page of it disavows a dependence on the powers of this world. It is a contradiction to fact, for it is known that this religion both existed and flourished, not only without the support of human laws, but in spite of every opposition from them; and not only during the period of miraculous aid, but long after it had been left to its own evidence and the ordinary care of Providence. Nay, it is a contradiction in terms, for a religion not invented by human policy must have pre-existed and been supported before it was established by human policy. It is moreover to weaken in those who profess this religion a pious confidence in its innate excellence and the patronage of its Author and to foster

in those who still reject it, a suspicion that its friends are too conscious of its fallacies to trust it to its own merits.

7. Because experience witnesseth that ecclesiastical establishments, instead of maintaining the purity and efficacy of religion, have had a contrary operation. During almost fifteen centuries has the legal establishment of Christianity been on trial. What have been its fruits? More or less in all places, pride and indolence in the Clergy [and] ignorance and servility in the laity; in both, superstition, bigotry, and persecution. Enquire of the teachers of Christianity for the ages in which it appeared in its greatest luster; those of every sect point to the ages prior to its incorporation with Civil policy. Propose a restoration of this primitive state in which its teachers depended on the voluntary rewards of their flocks; many of them predict its downfall. On which side ought their testimony to have greatest weight, when for or when against their interest?

8. Because the establishment in question is not necessary for the support of Civil Government. If it be urged as necessary for the support of Civil Government only as it is a means of supporting religion, and it be not necessary for the latter purpose, it cannot be necessary for the former. If religion be not within [the] cognizance of Civil Government, how can its legal establishment be said to be necessary to civil Government? What influence in fact have ecclesiastical establishments had on Civil Society? In some instances they have been seen to erect a spiritual tyranny on the ruins of Civil authority; in many instances they have seen upholding the thrones of political tyranny; in no instance have they been seen the guardians of the liberties of the people. Rulers who wished to subvert the public liberty may have found an established clergy convenient auxiliaries. A just government, instituted to secure and perpetuate it, needs them not. Such a government will be best supported by protecting every citizen in the enjoyment of his religion with the same equal hand which protects his person and his property; by neither invading the equal rights of any Sect nor suffering any Sect to invade those of another.

9. Because the proposed establishment is a departure from that generous policy which, offering an asylum to the persecuted and oppressed of every nation and religion, promised a lustre to our country and an accession to the number of its citizens. What a melancholy mark is the Bill of sudden degeneracy? Instead of holding forth an asylum to the persecuted, it is itself a signal of persecution. It degrades from the equal rank of citizens all those whose opinions in religion do not bend to those of the legislative authority. Distant as it may be, in its present form, from the Inquisition it differs from it only in degree. The one is the first step, the other the last in the career of intolerance. The magnanimous sufferer under the cruel scourge in foreign regions, must view the Bill as

a beacon on our coast, warning him to seek some other haven where liberty and philanthropy in their due extent may offer a more certain repose from his troubles.

10. Because it will have a like tendency to banish our citizens. The allurements presented by other situations are every day thinning their number. To superadd a fresh motive to emigration, by revoking the liberty which they now enjoy, would be the same species of folly which has dishonoured and depopulated flourishing kingdoms.

11. Because it will destroy that moderation and harmony which the forbearance of our laws to intermeddle with religion has produced amongst its several sects. Torrents of blood have been spilt in the old world by vain attempts of the secular arm to extinguish religious discord by proscribing all difference in religious opinions. Time has at length revealed the true remedy. Every relaxation of narrow and rigorous policy, wherever it has been tried, has been found to assuage the disease. The American theatre has exhibited proofs that equal and complete liberty, if it does not wholly eradicate it, sufficiently destroys its malignant influence on the health and prosperity of the State. If, with the salutary effects of this system under our own eyes, we begin to contract the bonds of religious freedom, we know no name that will too severely reproach our folly. At least let warning be taken at the first fruits of the threatened innovation. The very appearance of the Bill has transformed that "Christian forbearance, love and charity," which of late mutually prevailed, into animosities and jealousies which may not soon be appeased. What mischiefs may not be dreaded should this enemy to the public quiet be armed with the force of a law?

12. Because the policy of the bill is adverse to the diffusion of the light of Christianity. The first wish of those who enjoy this precious gift ought to be that it may be imparted to the whole race of mankind. Compare the number of those who have as yet received it with the number still remaining under the dominion of false religions, and how small is the former! Does the policy of the Bill tend to lessen the disproportion? No; it at once discourages those who are strangers to the light of [revelation] from coming into the region of it; and [it] countenances, by example, the nations who continue in darkness in shutting out those who might convey it to them. . . .

13. Because attempts to enforce, by legal sanctions, acts obnoxious to so great a proportion of Citizens tend to enervate the laws in general and to slacken the bands of Society. If it be difficult to execute any law which is not generally deemed necessary or salutary, what must be the case where [the law] is deemed invalid and dangerous? And what may be the effect of so striking an example of impotency in the Government, on its general authority.

14. Because a measure of such singular magnitude and delicacy ought not to be imposed, without the clearest evidence that it is called for by a majority of citizens; and no satisfactory method is yet proposed by which the voice of the majority in this case may be determined, or its influence secured. "The people of the respective counties are indeed requested to signify their opinion respecting the adoption of the Bill to the next Session of Assembly." But the representation must be made equal before the voice either of the Representatives or of the Counties, will be that of the people. Our hope is that neither of the former will, after due consideration, espouse the dangerous principle of the Bill. Should the event disappoint us, it will still leave us in full confidence that a fair appeal to the latter will reverse the sentence against our liberties.

15. Because, finally, "the equal right of every citizen to the free exercise of his Religion according to the dictates of conscience" is held by the same tenure with all our other rights. If we recur to its origin, it is equally the gift of nature. If we weigh its importance, it cannot be less dear to us. If we consult the Declaration of those rights which pertain to the good people of Virginia as the "basis and foundation of Government," it is enumerated with equal solemnity, or rather studied emphasis. Either, then, we must say that the will of the Legislature is the only measure of their authority, and that in the plenitude of this authority, they may sweep away all our fundamental rights; or, that they are bound to leave this particular right untouched and sacred. Either we must say that they may controul the freedom of the press, may abolish the trial by jury, may swallow up the Executive and Judiciary powers of the State—nay that they may despoil us of our very right of suffrage and erect themselves into an independent and hereditary assembly—or we must say that they have no authority to enact into law the Bill under consideration. We the subscribers say, that the General Assembly of this Commonwealth have no such authority. And that no effort may be omitted on our part against so dangerous an usurpation, we oppose to it this remonstrance, earnestly praying, as we are in duty bound, that the Supreme Lawgiver of the Universe, by illuminating those to whom it is addressed, may on the one hand turn their councils from every act which would affront his holy prerogative or violate the trust committed to them, and on the other, guide them into every measure which may be worthy of his [blessing, may re]dound to their own praise, and may establish more firmly the liberties, the prosperity, and the happiness of the Commonwealth.

Red Jacket,
"Brother, the Great Spirit Has Made Us All"
(1792)

Editor's Introduction: Red Jacket (c. 1752–1830) was born in New York, a member of the Seneca tribe. He was a great orator and spokesman for Indian causes. He acquired his Anglophone name from persistently wearing a red military jacket given to him by a British officer and veteran of the Revolutionary War. In 1792, Red Jacket was invited to the nation's capital, then Philadelphia, by President Washington and addressed the United States Senate on relations between whites and Native Americans. During the same visit, he spoke at a conference where other Native American chiefs were present and gave the following speech on efforts by whites to convert Native Americans to Christianity. Red Jacket preaches a doctrine of toleration that few whites at the time were prepared to extend to Native Americans.

*　　*　　*

Friend and Brother! It was the will of the Great Spirit that we should meet together this day. He orders all things, and he has given us a fine day for our council. He has taken his garment from before the sun and has caused the bright orb to shine with brightness upon us. Our eyes are opened so that we see clearly. Our ears are unstopped so that we have been able to distinctly hear the words which you have spoken. For all these favors we thank the Great Spirit and him only.

Brother! This council fire was kindled by you. It was at your request that we came together at this time. We have listened with attention to what you have said. You have requested us to speak our minds freely. This gives us great joy, for we now consider that we stand upright before you, and can speak what we think. All have heard your voice and all speak to you as one man. Our minds are agreed. . . .

Brother! Listen to what we say. There was a time when our forefathers owned this great island (meaning the continent of North America—a common belief among the Indians). Their seats extended from the rising to the setting of the sun. The Great Spirit had made it for the use of Indians. He had created the buffalo, the deer, and other animals for food. He made the bear and the deer, and their skins served us for clothing.

Source: William Stone, ed., *The Life and Times of Red Jacket, or Sa-Go-Ye-Wat-Ha* (New York: Wiley and Putnam, 1841).

He had scattered them over the country, and had taught us how to take them. He had caused the earth to produce corn for bread. All this he had done for his red children because he loved them. If we had any disputes about hunting grounds, they were generally settled without the shedding of much blood. But an evil day came upon us. Your forefathers crossed the great waters and landed on this island. Their numbers were small. They found friends and not enemies. They told us they had fled from their own country for fear of wicked men, and had come here to enjoy their religion. They asked for a small seat. We took pity on them, granted their request and they sat down amongst us. We gave them corn and meat. They gave us poison (spiritous liquor) in return. The white people had now found our country. Tidings were carried back and more came amongst us. Yet we did not fear them. We took them to be friends. They called us brothers. We believed them and gave them a large seat. At length their numbers had greatly increased. They wanted more land. They wanted our country. Our eyes were opened, and our minds became uneasy. Wars took place. Indians were hired to fight against Indians, and many of our people were destroyed. They also brought strong liquours among us. It strong and powerful and has slain thousands.

Brother! Our seats were once large, and yours were very small. You have now become a great people, and we have scarcely a place left to spread our blankets. You have got our country, but you are not satisfied. You want to force your religion upon us.

Brother! Continue to listen. You say that you are sent to instruct us how to worship the Great Spirit agreeably to his mind: and if we do not take hold of the religion which you white people teach we shall be unhappy hereafter. You say that you are right, and we are lost. How do you know this to be true? We understand that your religion is written in a book. If it was intended for us as well as for you, why has not the Great Spirit given it to us; and not only to us, but why did he not give to our forefathers the knowledge of that book, with the means of understanding it rightly? We only know that you tell us about it. How shall we know when to believe, being so often deceived by the white people?

Brother! You say there is but one way to worship and serve the Great Spirit. If there is but one religion, why do you white people differ so much about it? Why not all agree, as you can all read the book?

Brother! We do not understand these things. We are told that your religion was given to your forefathers and has been handed down, father to son. We also have a religion which was given to our forefathers, and has been handed down to us, their children. We worship that way. It teaches us to be thankful for all the favors we received, to love each other, and to be united. We never quarrel about religion.

Brother! The Great Spirit has made us all. But he has made a great difference between his white and red children. He has given us a different complexion and different customs. To you he has given the arts; to these he has not opened our eyes. We know these things to be true. Since he has made so great a difference between us in other things, why may not we conclude that he has given us a different religion, according to our understanding? The Great Spirit does right. He knows what is best for his children. We are satisfied.

Brother! We do not wish to destroy your religion, or to take it from you. We only want to enjoy our own.

Brother! You say you have not come to get our land or our money, but to enlighten our minds. I will now tell you that I have been at your meetings and saw you collecting money from the meeting. I cannot tell what this money was intended for, but suppose it was for your minister; and if we should conform to your way of thinking, perhaps you may want some from us.

Brother! We are told that you have been preaching to the white people in this place. These people are our neighbors. We are acquainted with them. We will wait a little while, and see what effect your preaching has upon them. If we find it does them good and makes them honest and less disposed to cheat Indians, we will then consider again what you have said.

Brother! You have now heard our answer to your talk, and this is all we have to say at present. As we are going to part, we will come and take you by the hand, and hope the Great Spirit will protect you on your journey, and return you safe to your friends.

Thomas Jefferson,
"Letter to the Danbury Baptists" (1802)

Editor's Introduction: In his later years, Thomas Jefferson (1743–1826) began to contemplate how he wished to be remembered. In fact, he designed his tombstone to list what he saw as his three greatest accomplishments. These were being author of the Declaration of Independence, father of the University of Virginia, and author of the Statute of Virginia for Religious Freedom. That the last of these was singled out among so many accomplishments gives a sense of just how important religious liberty was to Jefferson.

His own religious convictions are in doubt but he is generally described as a "deist," or one who recognizes a higher power who sets the universe in motion and then recedes from the scene. This Creator, to use a familiar Enlightenment metaphor, is a great clock maker, and the workings of the clock are knowable to man through the exercise of reason. Characteristic of this attitude is advice the Sage of Monticello once offered to his nephew, Peter Carr. "Question with boldness even the existence of a God," he told Carr, "because, if there be one, he must more approve of the homage of reason than that of blindfolded fear."[1] In the moral sphere, Jefferson believed in the basic ethical teachings in the gospels of Christ. In fact, in several writings he attempts to extract these teachings from what he sees as the misuse of Christianity by many doctrinaire and contentious sects.

Jefferson was very aware of the political havoc religious divisions had caused in human history and, because of this, he sought to isolate religion from politics, as is evident in the following letter written to a congregation of Baptist supporters. The Danbury Baptist Association wrote Jefferson after his election to the presidency asking him to set aside a day of fasting and prayer for thanksgiving. Jefferson declined for reasons stated in the letter, which includes the famous "wall of separation" metaphor we have already encountered in the writings of Roger Williams.

* * *

MESSRS. NEHEMIAH DODGE, EPHRAIM ROBBINS, AND STEPHEN S. NELSON, A COMMITTEE OF THE DANBURY BAPTIST ASSOCIATION, IN THE STATE OF CONNECTICUT.

Source: Manuscript collection, Library of Congress.

[1] *Life and Selected Writings of Thomas Jefferson*, p. 431.

January 1, 1802.

Gentlemen—The affectionate sentiments of esteem and approbation which you are so good as to express towards me, on behalf of the Danbury Baptist Association, give me the highest satisfaction. My duties dictate a faithful and zealous pursuit of the interests of my constituents, and in proportion as they are persuaded of my fidelity to those duties, the discharge of them becomes more and more pleasing.

Believing with you that religion is a matter which lies solely between man and his God, that he owes account to none other for his faith or his worship, that the legislative powers of government reach actions only, and not opinions, I contemplate with sovereign reverence that act of the whole American people which declared that their legislature should "make no law respecting an establishment of religion, or prohibiting the free exercise thereof," thus building a wall of separation between church and State. Adhering to this expression of the supreme will of the nation in behalf of the rights of conscience, I shall see with sincere satisfaction the progress of those sentiments which tend to restore to man all his natural rights, convinced he has no natural right in opposition to his social duties.*

I reciprocate your kind prayers for the protection and blessing of the common Father and Creator of man, and tender you for yourselves and your religious association, assurances of my high respect and esteem.

---

* The first draft of this letter contained the following paragraph. In it, he argues that not only Congress but the executive as well should refrain from religious ceremonies and professions. He includes in this prohibition any public support for Thanksgiving by the executive, a practice he did not wish the state to support, given its religious overtones.

> "Congress thus inhibited from acts respecting religion, and the Executive authorities only to execute their acts, I have refrained from presenting even occasional performances of devotion, presented indeed legally, where an Executive is the legal head of Church, but subject here, as religious exercises only to the voluntary regulations and discipline of each respective sect."

In a marginal comment, Jefferson says he omits this passage so as not to offend "republican friends in the eastern states" where the "antient" practice of thanksgiving has existed, though he clearly disagrees with the practice.

Samuel Kendal,
"An Election Sermon: Religion the Only Sure Basis of Free Government" (1804)

Editor's Introduction: Samuel Kendal (1753–1814) was a Congregationalist pastor in Massachusetts, many of whose sermons were published in his day. Clergymen in early America played a vital role in transmitting political ideas to the populace, and elections were common occasions for linking religion and politics.

The gist of Kendal's sermon is clear. Civil government is necessary for human happiness. Free government is sustained only if the people are sufficiently virtuous, and religion is the "only sure basis" for virtue. Kendal states in the sermon that religion is vital for salvation of individual souls, but his main focus is on its instrumental role in sustaining political community. Kendal believes that, though people have reason to be good citizens, and office holders to be good rulers, these reasons will often be overshadowed by narrow, egoistic passions and interests if people do not believe in "some higher authority" to whom they are ultimately accountable.

Though Kendal favors a greater "entanglement" of church and state than Jefferson or Madison would condone, he is by no means arguing for any sort of theocracy. The core tenets of faith he sees as necessary for communal well-being are rather undoctrinaire. Further, he argues that governmental actions should not favor one Christian sect over another, though he approves of government support for Christian religion generally.

*   *   *

DEUTERONOMY, XXXII. 46, 47.

SET YOUR HEARTS UNTO ALL THE WORDS WHICH I TESTIFY AMONG YOU THIS DAY, WHICH YE SHALL COMMAND YOUR CHILDREN TO OBSERVE AND DO, ALL THE WORDS OF THIS LAW.

FOR IT IS NOT A VAIN THING FOR YOU; BECAUSE IT IS YOUR LIFE; AND THROUGH THIS THING YE SHALL PROLONG YOUR DAYS IN THE LAND WITHER YE GO OVER JORDAN TO POSSES IT.

Source: Collections of the American Antiquarian Society.

This important advice was given by the Jewish Legislator, just before his death, to the whole congregation of Israel. Moses had exhibited to his nation unequivocal proof of his attachment to their interest, freedom and happiness. Although acknowledged as the son of Pharaoh's daughter, educated at Egypt's court, and assured of the honors and offices which commonly gratify the ambition of men, he disclaimed kindred and alliance with the oppressors of his people, and boldly demanded their release from servitude. By a series of wonders, wrought in the name of Jehovah, he effected their emancipation, and conducted them to the land promised to their fathers.

To form and carry into operation a system of government, and habituate a newly emancipated people to rule and order were important objects to be accomplished. In these, as in the deliverance of the Hebrews, Moses was under the immediate supernatural direction of Heaven. The government was a theocracy; religion the basis on which the whole structure rested. Their institutions, civil and religious, happily combined to improve the nation, and to guard it against being corrupted by admitting strangers to an equal participation of all its privileges. In its advancement from bondage to an independent rank among the nations of the earth, the people were led by the hand of Moses and Aaron; by the civil magistrate and the minister of religion. Each was a chosen instrument to carry on the merciful designs of Providence in respect to ancient Israel; and each the world hath ever found necessary to promote the peace, order and improvement of society.

Arrived at the borders of the promised land, and apprized that he should not be permitted to pass Jordan, Moses gave the people a new edition of the law in the book before us; and, to aid their memory, rehearsed the mercies and judgments of God, and the duties and dangers of Israel, in a divine song; in which, with an eloquence worthy of his subjects, he celebrated the praises of Jehovah, and warned the nation against departing from the statutes he had appointed unto them.

Having concluded his song, the prophet said to the congregation, assembled to hear his last instruction, "Set your hearts unto all the words which I testify among you this day; which ye shall command your children to observe and do, all the words of this law."

The two great commandments in this law, on which all the rest depend, according to our Savior, are to love the Lord our God with all the heart, and our neighbor as ourselves. It therefore related to religious, moral and social duty. In this view of it the people were directed by their great deliverer, whose character and achievements, situation and prospects, gave weight to his counsel, sincerely to regard its rules and precepts, and to teach and command their children to observe them. The reason assigned for the injunction we have in these words: "For it is not a vain thing for you; because it is your life; and through this thing ye shall prolong your days in the land whither ye go over Jordan to posses it."

By the life of a community we understand its political existence, independence, freedom and happiness. In the preservation, or loss, of these, whatever may be ascribed to natural causes, we often observe the powerful effect of moral causes. To show the influence of these upon national freedom and prosperity is more particularly the duty of the ministers of religion. To this the subject directs our attention. The importance of the injunction in the text will appear from the truth and weight of the reason by which it is enforced. Our main object, therefore, will be to illustrate this general truth, viz.

That religion, and the moral and social virtues, of which *that* is the great spring, are, under God, the life and security of a free people.

In attempting this, the speaker must rely on the candor of our civil fathers, and of this numerous and respectable assembly. What he proposes is, briefly to hint at the necessity and end of civil government; then show that religion is the only sure basis of good government; that its influence upon communities is salutary; that it is the only rational ground of mutual confidence; and that the Christian system is most favorable to liberty and social order.

The necessity, or at least the expediency, of civil government might be inferred from the universal adoption of it among all nations whose history is known. But we perceive for ourselves that it is impossible for society to exist without it; and conclude, as man is a social being, the Creator designed he should be a subject of law and government.

The end of government is the protection, improvement and happiness of the community. To accomplish this end, as in the natural, so in the political body, there must be a head, or governing power, which shall direct the operations of the members, combine their strength for the common defence, and unite their exertions for the public good.

That is the best government which most effectually restrains the dissocial passions, prevents crimes, and, with the least restriction of natural liberty, preserves order, dispenses justice, and procures to the whole the greatest happiness. To these ends the fundamental principles of every government, and all the laws of the state, should be adapted. The government, whose object or tendency is any other than the public good, or whose administration is guided by other motives than the general interest, neither comports with the design of Heaven, nor merits the esteem and confidence of men.

But such is the imperfection of man, that nothing depending on human authority only is adequate to the proposed end of civil government. The language of experience is, that to control the passions, and habituate men to the love of order, and to act for the public good, some higher authority than that which is merely human must influence their minds. Their views are often too limited to comprehend the reasonableness of yielding private interest and inclination to public utility, or the connexion between surrendering a portion of their natural liberty, and enjoying civil liberty, under the protection of law. The institution of government many seem to imagine designed, not for their own, but the benefit of a chosen few; and though they may dread the sanctions of the law, and the power of the magistrate; yet, feeling no moral obligation to obey, and hoping to evade legal justice, they have but slender motives to obedience while unrestrained passion, or personal interest, impels them to counteract the established system of rule and order; or, if they have correct notions of the general design and tendency of good government, yet viewing it merely as an ordinance of man, and reflecting on the imperfection of legislators, they have but a feeble sense of obligation to observe laws, which oppose their immediate advantage. Fond of self government, they reluctantly delegate the necessary power to others; and when they have consented to it, a jealousy of their rulers often renders them hostile to their administration. Some higher and better established principle of action, than a view to public interest and convenience, must operate on the minds of most men, to render them good members of a civil community.

But what must this higher principle be? The ideas of some seem to have been that there must be a system of political morality established, whose object shall be to fix certain rules of social duty, to the observance of which all shall be obliged by the authority of the state. But if such system is to rest solely on the authority of human laws, and to be the result of human wisdom only, its fitness will be always liable to doubts, and a violation of its principles and rules thought no great crime. It being, as I think it must be, conceded that morality is essential to the support and due administration of government, let it be considered whether the laws of morality must not have some higher origin than the consent of political bodies, and be enforced by other authority than that to whose aid they are deemed necessary. Nothing is gained if they are not supposed to proceed from some superior power, to which human beings are amenable. This can be no other than God. Religious faith, or sentiment, must then be called in to the support of that morality, which is essential to the order and well-being of society; and is, therefore, the basis on which good government ultimately rests.

[Text omitted]

Moses provided able men, such as feared God, men of truth, hating covetousness, to be rulers of thousands, of hundreds, of fifties, and of tens; a clear indication that in every department men should be placed, who will act in the fear of God. Destitute of this, their influence and example will tend to subvert the foundations of social order, to weaken the springs of political life, and to corrupt the whole system.

But must our civil rulers be Christians? It certainly cannot be less important to the general interest that they should be, than that other members of the community should be under the influence of this religion; and the constitution of this commonwealth requires of them, previous to their entering on the duties of their office, a declaration of their belief in the Christian religion, and full persuasion of its truth. As that does not contemplate evasion, an unbeliever, whatever he might be tempted to affirm, would not posses the qualification which the constitution makes requisite. As an expression of the public sentiment this provision has merit; but religious tests are feeble barriers against unprincipled men. They take no hold on the conscience of one who mentally consigns himself to an everlasting sleep, and never acts with reference to a judgment to come. It ought, however, to be presumed, unless there should be decisive proof to the contrary, that no man will ever hazard his reputation for veracity, and the confidence of his fellow-men, so much, as to make the declaration in opposition to his inward conviction, and common profession. We may feel assured, at least, that he would not, after such a declaration, place himself in the ranks of the avowed enemies of Christianity. Should this happen, what ground of confidence would be left? The speaker feels almost constrained to apologize for a suggestion so dishonorable to human nature. A possible case only is supposed. Should it ever exist, no apology would be due.

If Christianity tend to enrich the heart with every amiable and beneficial virtue, and highly to improve the present condition of man, it is of vast importance that rulers should feel its influence, and reflect the light of it on every beholder.

[Text omitted]

The opinion of some, that government ought to take no notice of religion, that it is the exclusive concern of the Deity to preserve the worship of himself in the world, and that it would be presumption in legislators to enact any laws relating to it, is not correct, nor consistent with the practice under the freest governments. Improper it would be, and what it is to be hoped we shall never see in our country, to enact "laws to dictate what articles of faith men shall believe, what mode of worship they shall adopt, or to raise and establish one mode of worship, or denomination of Christians above, or in preference to another." In these respects let the mind be perfectly free, and all denominations equally under the protection and countenance of the law. But the support of institutions calculated to promote religious knowledge in general, give efficacy to precepts of the gospel, instil the principles of morality, and improve the social affections, may be a proper subject of legislation.

[Text omitted]

Venerable Fathers in each department, to your care the people of this respectable commonwealth have committed their dearest civil interests. By calling you to your respective stations they have expressed a confidence that you will be watchful and faithful. You have every rational motive to be so; but the highest must be a sense of accountability to that God, by whom actions are witnessed and weighed, and from whom all will receive a just reward. Though ye are called gods on earth, you must all die like men, and, with those over whom you now bear rule, appear in judgment, to receive according to your works.

In contemplating the happy influence of religion upon the state and government of society, it is not intended to diminish its importance in a personal view, and in respect to the solemn period when all civil societies shall be disbanded, secular honors and distinctions known no more, and the whole world arraigned at Jehovah's awful tribunal. In this August event we have the highest personal concern; and from the individual anticipation of it, society derives peculiar advantage. What the public good requires, your own particular happiness more strongly demands. In your honorable stations, and in the private walks of life, may you ever be actuated by the great principles of our holy religion, enjoy its consolations, exemplify its duties, and extend its benign influence; that you may at last share its richest rewards.

Fellow-Citizens of this numerous assembly, you doubtless feel a lively interest in the freedom, prosperity and glory of our common country; and in guarding and transmitting to posterity the fair inheritance we have received from our fathers. Like them, then, fear God, and keep his commandments. We have risen up, and call them blessed. But if we abandon their principles, despise their attention to religion and its institutions, and refuse to follow their virtuous examples, our posterity, denied what we inherit, will have reason to execrate our folly.

Personal salvation, public safety, and the happiness of generations to come, impose on us a sacred obligation to set our hearts unto all the words of the divine law, and to command our children to observe them. The man of religion and virtue is a public benefactor. By teaching his children to follow the example, he increases the benefit; and by exciting others to imitation enhances the obligation. In proportion to the sphere of your influence, you all possess means of your own security, and of promoting our national prosperity and glory. Let this consideration, as well as the still more animating one, that by it you may prepare yourselves and others for a state of endless felicity, be a motive to employ all your influence in the cause of religion and virtue. To these God hath promised his protection and blessing. They will be our life, and the lengthening out of our tranquility. "The work of righteousness shall be peace, and the effect of righteousness, quietness and assurance forever."

Alexis de Tocqueville,
"Indirect Influence of Religious Opinions Upon Political Society in the United States" (1835)

Editor's Introduction: Alexis de Tocqueville (1805–1859) is widely and properly regarded as one of the most profound observers of American politics and culture. A French aristocrat, Tocqueville came to the United States in 1831 to study its penitentiaries. He stayed for several years and pursued a much broader project. Tocqueville traveled widely and spoke to many Americans from all walks of life. The product of his trip was the classic published in 1835, *Democracy in America*, a study of American political institutions and mores.

Few aspects of American life are left unexplored in the work. Everything from constitutions and electoral politics, to religion, the family, the role of women, race relations, industry, arts and literature, and we could go on, is discussed with considerable insight. Tocqueville believed that the American experience with democracy had much to teach European nations like his own. Democratic equality was the wave of the future, and Tocqueville greeted its onset with a sort of "dread." Nonetheless, he saw much to admire in America, especially compared to Europe, which was torn by class envy and civil strife.

In the following passage, Tocqueville observes widespread religious faith in the United States and thinks that it is especially salutary that a democratic people have a belief in God. In democracies, the tyranny of the majority is always a threat to liberty and diversity of views. However, religious faith of the rather undoctrinaire sort found in America militates against this great danger. In his own words, "whilst the law permits the Americans to do what they please, religion prevents them from conceiving, and forbids them to commit, what is rash and unjust."

*   *   *

I have just shown what the direct influence of religion upon politics is in the United States, but its indirect influence appears to me to be still more considerable, and it never instructs the Americans more fully in the art of being free than when it says nothing of freedom.

The sects which exist in the United States are innumerable. They all differ in respect to the worship which is due from man to his Creator,

---

Source: Alexis de Tocqueville, *Democracy in America*, translated by Henry Reeve (New York: The Colonial Press, 1899).

but they all agree in respect to the duties which are due from man to man. Each sect adores the Deity in its own peculiar manner, but all the sects preach the same moral law in the name of God. If it be of the highest importance to man, as an individual, that his religion should be true, the case of society is not the same. Society has no future life to hope for or to fear; and provided the citizens profess a religion, the peculiar tenets of that religion are of very little importance to its interests. Moreover, almost all the sects of the United States are comprised within the great unity of Christianity, and Christian morality is everywhere the same.

It may be believed without unfairness that a certain number of Americans pursue a peculiar form of worship, from habit more than from conviction. In the United States the sovereign authority is religious, and consequently hypocrisy must be common; but there is no country in the whole world in which the Christian religion retains a greater influence over the souls of men than in America; and there can be no greater proof of its unity, and of its conformity to human nature, than that its influence is most powerfully felt over the most enlightened and free nation of the earth.

I have remarked that the members of the American clergy in general, without even excepting those who do not admit religious liberty, are all in favor of civil freedom; but they do not support any particular political system. They keep aloof from parties and from public affairs. In the United States religion exercises but little influence upon the laws and upon the details of public opinion, but it directs the manners of the community, and by regulating domestic life it regulates the State.

I do not question that the great austerity of manners which is observable in the United States, arises, in the first instance, from religious faith. Religion is often unable to restrain man from the numberless temptations of fortune; nor can it check that passion for gain which every incident of his life contributes to arouse, but its influence over the mind of woman is supreme, and women are the protectors of morals. There is certainly no country in the world where the tie of marriage is so much respected as in America, or where conjugal happiness is more highly or worthily appreciated. In Europe almost all the disturbances of society arise from the irregularities of domestic life. To despise the natural bonds and legitimate pleasures of home, is to contract a taste for excesses, a restlessness of heart, and the evil of fluctuating desires. Agitated by the tumultuous passions which frequently disturb his dwelling, the European is galled by the obedience which the legislative powers of the State exact. But when the American retires from the turmoil of public life to the bosom of his family, he finds in it the image of order and of peace. There his pleasures are simple and natural, his joys are innocent and calm; and as he finds that an orderly life is the surest path to happiness, he accustoms himself without difficulty to moderate his opinions as well as his tastes. Whilst the European endeavors to forget his domestic troubles by agitating society, the American derives from his own home that love of order which he afterward carries with him into public affairs.

In the United States the influence of religion is not confined to the manners, but it extends to the intelligence of the people. Amongst the Anglo-Americans, there are some who profess the doctrines of Christianity from a sincere belief in them, and others who do the same because they are afraid to be suspected of unbelief. Christianity, therefore, reigns without any obstacle, by universal consent; the consequence is, as I have before observed, that every principle of the moral world is fixed and determinate, although the political world is abandoned to the debates and the experiments of men. Thus the human mind is never left to wander across a boundless field; and, whatever may be its pretensions, it is checked from time to time by barriers which it cannot surmount. Before it can perpetrate innovation, certain primal and immutable principles are laid down, and the boldest conceptions of human device are subjected to certain forms which retard and stop their completion.

The imagination of the Americans, even in its greatest flights, is circumspect and undecided; its impulses are checked, and its works unfinished. These habits of restraint recur in political society, and are singularly favorable both to the tranquillity of the people and to the durability of the institutions it has established. Nature and circumstances concurred to make the inhabitants of the United States bold men, as is sufficiently attested by the enterprising spirit with which they seek for fortune. If the mind of the Americans were free from all trammels, they would very shortly become the most daring innovators and the most implacable disputants in the world. But the revolutionists of America are obliged to profess an ostensible respect for Christian morality and equity, which does not easily permit them to violate the laws that oppose their designs; nor would they find it easy to surmount the scruples of their partisans, even if they were able to get over their own. Hitherto no one in the United States has dared to advance the maxim, that everything is permissible with a view to the interests of society; an impious adage which seems to have been invented in an age of freedom to shelter all the tyrants of future ages. Thus whilst the law permits the Americans to do what they please, religion prevents them from conceiving, and forbids them to commit, what is rash or unjust.

Religion in America takes no direct part in the government of society, but it must nevertheless be regarded as the foremost of the political institutions of that country; for if it does not impart a taste for freedom, it facilitates the use of free institutions. Indeed, it is in this same point of view that the inhabitants of the United States themselves look upon religious belief. I do not know whether all the Americans have a sincere faith in their religion, for who can search the human heart? but I am certain that they hold it to be indispensable to the maintenance of republican institutions. This opinion is not peculiar to a class of citizens or to a party, but it belongs to the whole nation, and to every rank of society.

In the United States, if a political character attacks a sect, this may not prevent even the partisans of that very sect from supporting him; but if he attacks all the sects together, everyone abandons him, and he remains alone.

Whilst I was in America, a witness, who happened to be called at the assizes of the county of Chester (State of New York), declared that he did not believe in the existence of God, or in the immortality of the soul. The judge refused to admit his evidence, on the ground that the witness had destroyed beforehand all the confidence of the Court in what he was about to say. The newspapers related the fact without any further comment.

The Americans combine the notions of Christianity and of liberty so intimately in their minds, that it is impossible to make them conceive the one without the other; and with them this conviction does not spring from that barren traditionary faith which seems to vegetate in the soul rather than to live.

I have known of societies formed by the Americans to send out ministers of the Gospel into the new Western States to found schools and churches there, lest religion should be suffered to die away in those remote settlements, and the rising States be less fitted to enjoy free institutions than the people from which they emanated. I met with wealthy New Englanders who abandoned the country in which they were born in order to lay the foundations of Christianity and of freedom on the banks of the Missouri, or in the prairies of Illinois. Thus religious zeal is perpetually stimulated in the United States by the duties of patriotism. These men do not act from an exclusive consideration of the promises of a future life; eternity is only one motive of their devotion to the cause; and if you converse with these missionaries of Christian civilization, you will be surprised to find how much value they set upon the goods of this world, and that you meet with a politician where you expect to find a priest. They will tell you that "all the American republics are collectively involved with each other; if the republics of the West were to fall into anarchy, or to be mastered by a despot, the republican institutions which now flourish upon the shores of the Atlantic Ocean would be in great peril. It is, therefore, our interest that the new States should be religious, in order to maintain our liberties."

Such are the opinions of the Americans, and if any hold that the religious spirit which I admire is the very thing most amiss in America, and that the only element wanting to the freedom and happiness of the human race is to believe in some blind cosmogony, or to assert with Cabanis the secretion of thought by the brain, I can only reply that those who hold this language have never been in America, and that they have never seen a religious or a free nation. When they return from their expedition, we shall hear what they have to say.

There are persons in France who look upon republican institutions as a temporary means of power, of wealth, and distinction; men who are the *condottieri* of liberty, and who fight for their own advantage, whatever be the colors they wear: it is not to these that I address myself. But there are others who look forward to the republican form of government as a tranquil and lasting state, towards which modern society is daily impelled by the ideas and manners of the time, and who sincerely desire to prepare men to be free. When these men attack religious opinions, they obey the dictates of their passions to the prejudice of their interests. Despotism may govern without faith, but liberty cannot. Religion is much more necessary in the republic which they set forth in glowing colors than in the monarchy which they attack; and it is more needed in democratic republics than in any others. How is it possible that society should escape destruction if the moral tie be not strengthened in proportion as the political tie is relaxed? and what can be done with a people which is its own master, if it be not submissive to the Divinity?

Mary Baker Eddy, "The Great Revelation" (1903) Mark Twain, "Christian Science" (1906), and Walker v. Superior Court of Sacramento Cty. 47 Cal. 3d 112 (1988)

Editor's Introduction: While Christian Science is a small and shrinking religious sect with no more than 100,000 members, its teachings raise certain fundamental questions regarding relations of church and state in the United States. The Church of Christ, Scientist was founded by Mary Baker Eddy (1821–1910). Eddy and her followers believe that sicknesses of the body are manifestations of spiritual shortcomings and that the body can be cured by prayer rather than by medical treatment. Though Christian Scientists including Eddy have on occasion undergone medical treatment, and it is doctrinally acceptable to do so in certain circumstances (e.g., when pain is too great to allow for concentration on prayer), spiritual healing even in cases of life-threatening illnesses generally is accepted as the proper course of treatment. Eddy's piece here defining the tenets of the faith and Mark Twain's satirical response set the stage for consideration of the political issue that is directly of concern to us: How far does freedom of religion extend, particularly when religious practice conflicts with certain universal duties and obligations of citizens? This issue is raised directly in *Walker v. Superior Court of Sacramento*.

Laurie Walker is a Christian Scientist whose four-year-old daughter became ill with flu-like symptoms in 1984. Ms. Walker, true to her faith, did not seek medical treatment but sought to remedy the ailment through prayer. Regrettably, the child had meningitis and died from the disease shortly after the onset of symptoms. Ms. Walker was charged with involuntary manslaughter and felony child endangerment under California state laws. In the following case the California Supreme Court was asked to decide whether the trial based on these charges could go forward.

The Walkers' attorney claimed that such a prosecution would violate the free exercise clause of the California and federal Constitutions. To complicate matters further, another law under the state's penal code, one to protect children, came into question. This law stipulates that "If a parent of a minor child willfully omits, without lawful excuse, to furnish necessary clothing, food, shelter or medical attendance, or other remedial care for his or her child, he or she is guilty of a misdemeanor." Moreover, the law included under other remedial care "treatment by spiritual means through prayer alone in accordance with the tenets and practices of a recognized church or religious denomination, by a duly accredited practitioner thereof." Christian Scientists have been instrumental in getting spiritual treatment provisions into many such state laws around the nation.

The Court held that while Ms. Walker was exempt from prosecution under this law, she was still subject to prosecution under manslaughter and felony endangerment statutes. The case was therefore returned to the trial court, where Ms. Walker eventually pleaded guilty to a reduced sentence. She later appealed the sentence to the U.S. Supreme Court which, however, did not agree to hear the case. The following excerpt of the California Supreme Court opinion focuses on the constitutional issues raised: Does the free exercise clause exempt Ms. Walker from manslaughter charges for denying her child medical treatment in addition to prayer? In determining that it does not, the court draws an important distinction between what an adult can do on his or her own behalf and the obligations he or she has toward a child prior to the age of consent. "Parents have no right to free exercise of religion at the price of a child's life," the court concludes.

*   *   *

MARY BAKER EDDY, "THE GREAT REVELATION" (1903)

CHRISTIAN Science reveals the grand verity, that to believe man has a finite and erring mind, and consequently a mortal mind and soul and life, is error. Scientific terms have no contradictory significations.

In Science, Life is not temporal, but eternal, without beginning or ending. The word *Life* never means that which is the source of death, and of good and evil. Such an inference is unscientific. It is like saying that addition means subtraction in one instance, and addition in another, and then applying this rule to a demonstration of the science of numbers; even as mortals apply finite terms to God, in demonstration of Infinity. *Life* is a term used to indicate Deity; and every other name for the Supreme Being, if properly employed, has the signification of Life. Whatever errs is mortal, and is the antipodes of Life, or God, and of health and holiness, both in idea and demonstration.

Christian Science reveals Mind, the only living and true God, and all that is made by Him, Mind, as harmonious, immortal, and spiritual: the five material senses defined Mind and matter as distinct, but mutually dependent, each on the other, for intelligence and existence. Science defines Man as immortal, as coexistent and coeternal with God, as made in His own image and likeness; material sense defines life as something

Source: Mary Baker Eddy, *Retrospection and Introspection* (Boston, MA: Joseph Armstrong, Publisher, 1903).

apart from God, beginning and ending, and man as very far from the divine likeness. Science reveals Life as a complete sphere, as eternal self-existent Mind; material sense defines life as a broken sphere, as organized matter, and mind as something separate from God. Science reveals Spirit as all, averring that there is nothing beside God; material sense says that matter, His antipodes, is something besides God. Material sense adds that the divine Spirit created matter, and that matter and evil are as real as Spirit and Good.

Christian Science reveals God and His idea as the all and only. It declares that evil is the absence of Good; whereas, Good is God everpresent, and therefore evil is unreal, and Good is all that is real. Christian Science saith to the wave and storm, "Be still," and there is a great calm. Material sense asks, in its ignorance of Science, "When will the raging of the material elements cease?" Science saith to all manner of disease: "Know that God is all-power and all-presence, and there is nothing beside Him," and the sick are healed. Material sense saith: "Oh, when will my sufferings cease? Where is God? Sickness is something besides Him, which He cannot, or does not, heal."

Christian Science is the only sure basis of harmony. Material sense contradicts Science, for matter, and its so-called organizations, take no cognizance of the spiritual facts of the universe, or of the real man and God. Christian Science declares that there is but one Truth, Life, Love, but one Spirit, Mind, Soul. Any attempt to divide these arises from the fallibility of sense, from mortal man's ignorance, from enmity to God and Divine Science.

Christian Science declares that sickness is a belief, a latent fear, made manifest on the body in different forms of fear, or disease. This fear is formed unconsciously in the silent thought, as when you awaken from sleep and feel ill, experiencing the effect of a fear whose existence you do not realize; but if you fall asleep, actually conscious of the Truth of Christian Science,—namely, that man's harmony is no more to be invaded than the rhythm of the universe,—you cannot awake in fear or suffering of any sort.

Science saith to Fear: "You are the cause of all sickness; but you are a self-constituted falsity,—you are darkness, nothingness. You are without 'hope and without God in the world.' You do not exist, and have no right to exist, for 'perfect Love casteth out fear.' "

God is everywhere. "There is no speech nor language, where His voice is not heard"; and this voice is Truth that destroys error, and Love that casts out fear.

Christian Science reveals the fact, that if suffering exists it is in the mortal mind only, for matter has no sensation and cannot suffer.

If you rule out every sense of disease and suffering from mortal mind, it cannot be found in the body.

Posterity will have the right to demand that Christian Science be stated and demonstrated in its godliness and grandeur,—that however little be taught or learned, that little shall be right. Let there be milk for babes, but let not the milk be adulterated. Unless this method be pursued, the Science of Christian Healing will again be lost, and human suffering will increase.

Test Christian Science by its effect on society, and you will find that the views here set forth—as to the illusion of sin, sickness, and death— bring forth better fruits of health, righteousness, and Life, than *a belief in their reality has ever done.* A demonstration of the *unreality* of evil destroys evil.

MARK TWAIN, "CHRISTIAN SCIENCE" (1906)

No one doubts—certainly not I—that the mind exercises a powerful influence over the body. From the beginning of time, the sorcerer, the interpreter of dreams, the fortune-teller, the charlatan, the quack, the wild medicine-man, the educated physician, the mesmerist, and the hypnotist have made use of the client's *imagination* to help them in their work. They have all recognized the potency and availability of that force. Physicians cure many patients with a bread pill; they know that where the disease is only a fancy, the patient's confidence in the doctor will make the bread pill effective.

Faith in the doctor. Perhaps that is the entire thing. It seems to look like it. In old times the King cured the king's evil by the touch of the royal hand. He frequently made extraordinary cures. Could his footman have done it? No—not in his own clothes. Disguised as the King, could he have done it? I think we may not doubt it. I think we may feel sure that it was not the King's touch that made the cure in any instance, but the patient's faith in the efficacy of a King's touch. Genuine and remarkable cures have been achieved through contact with the relics of a saint. Is it not likely that any other bones would have done as well if the substitution had been concealed from the patient? When I was a boy a farmer's wife who lived five miles from our village had great fame as a faith-doctor— that was what she called herself. Sufferers came to her from all around, and she laid her hand upon them and said, "Have faith—it is all that is

Source: Mark Twain, *Christian Science: With Notes Containing Corrections to Date* (New York: Harper & Brothers Publishers, 1906).

necessary," and they went away well of their ailments. She was not a religious woman, and pretended to no occult powers. She said that the patient's faith in her did the work. Several times I saw her make immediate cures of severe toothaches. My mother was the patient. In Austria there is a peasant who drives a great trade in this sort of industry, and has both the high and the low for patients. He gets into prison every now and then for practising without a diploma, but his business is as brisk as ever when he gets out, for his work is unquestionably successful and keeps his reputation high. In Bavaria there is a man who performed so many great cures that he had to retire from his profession of stage-carpentering in order to meet the demand of his constantly increasing body of customers. He goes on from year to year doing his miracles, and has become very rich. He pretends to no religious helps, no supernatural aids, but thinks there is something in his make-up which inspires the confidence of his patients, and that it is this confidence which does the work, and not some mysterious power issuing from himself.[1]

Within the last quarter of a century, in America, several sects of curers have appeared under various names and have done notable things in the way of healing ailments without the use of medicines. There are the Mind Cure, the Faith Cure, the Prayer Cure, the Mental-Science Cure, and the Christian-Science Cure; and apparently they all do their miracles with the same old, powerful instrument—*the patient's imagination*. Differing names, but no difference in the process. But they do not give that instrument the credit; each sect claims that its way differs from the ways of the others.

They all achieve some cures, there is no question about it; and the Faith Cure and the Prayer Cure probably do no harm when they do no good, since they do not forbid the patient to help out the cure with medicines if he wants to; but the others bar medicines, and claim ability to cure every conceivable human ailment through the application of their mental forces alone. There would seem to be an element of danger here. It has the look of claiming too much, I think. Public confidence would probably be increased if less were claimed.

The Christian Scientist was not able to cure my stomach-ache and my cold; but the horse-doctor did it. This convinces me that Christian

[1] [1 January, 1903. I have personal and intimate knowledge of the "miraculous" cure of a case of paralysis which had kept the patient helpless in bed during two years, in spite of all that the best medical science of New York could do. The traveling "quack" (that is what they called him), came on two successive mornings and lifted the patient out of bed and said "Walk!" and the patient walked. That was the end of it. It was forty-one years ago. The patient has walked ever since. M.T]

Science claims too much. In my opinion it ought to let diseases alone and confine itself to surgery. There it would have everything its own way.

The horse-doctor charged me thirty kreutzers, and I paid him; in fact, I doubled it and gave him a shilling. Mrs. Fuller brought in an itemized bill for a crate of broken bones mended in two hundred and thirty-four places—one dollar per fracture.

"Nothing exists but Mind?"

"Nothing," she answered. "All else is substanceless, all else is imaginary."

I gave her an imaginary check, and now she is suing me for substantial dollars. It looks inconsistent.

WALKER V. SUPERIOR COURT OF SACRAMENTO CTY., 47 CAL. 3d 112 (1988)

II. Constitutional Defenses

A. Free exercise under the First Amendment

In the absence of a statutory basis to bar defendant's prosecution, we necessarily reach her constitutional claims. Defendant and the Church first contend that her conduct is absolutely protected from criminal liability by the First Amendment to the United States Constitution and article I, section 4, of the California Constitution. We do not agree.

The First Amendment bars government from "prohibiting the free exercise" of religion. Although the clause absolutely protects religious belief, religiously motivated conduct "remains subject to regulation for the protection of society." (*Cantwell v. Connecticut* (1940) 310 U.S. 296, 303–304. . . .) To determine whether governmental regulation of religious conduct is violative of the First Amendment, the gravity of the state's interest must be balanced against the severity of the religious imposition. (*Wisconsin v. Yoder* (1972) 406 U.S. 205, 221 . . .). If the regulation is justified in view of the balanced interests at stake, the free exercise clause requires that the policy additionally represent the least restrictive alternative available to adequately advance the state's objectives. . . .

Defendant does not dispute the gravity of the governmental interest involved in this case, as well she should not. Imposition of felony liability for endangering or killing an ill child by failing to provide medical care furthers an interest of unparalleled significance: the protection of the very lives of California's children, upon whose "healthy, well-rounded growth . . . into full maturity as citizens" our "democratic society rests, for its continuance . . . ." (*Prince v. Massachusetts* (1944) 321 U.S. 158, 168). . . . Balanced against this interest is a religious infringement of significant dimensions. Defendant unquestionably relied on prayer treatment as an article of genuine faith, the restriction of which would seriously impinge on the practice of her religion. We note, however, that resort to medicine does not constitute "sin" for a Christian Scientist . . ., does not subject a church member to stigmatization . . . , does not result in divine retribution . . . , and, according to the Church's amicus curiae brief, is not a matter of church compulsion.

Regardless of the severity of the religious imposition, the governmental interest is plainly adequate to justify its restrictive effect. As the United States Supreme Court stated in *Prince v. Massachusetts,* . . . "Parents may be free to become martyrs themselves. But it does not follow they are free, in identical circumstances, to make martyrs of their children before they have reached the age of full legal discretion when they can make that choice for themselves." The court in Prince considered a free-exercise claim asserted by parents whose religious beliefs required that their children sell religious tracts in violation of child labor laws. If parents are not at liberty to "martyr" children by taking their labor, it follows a fortiori that they are not at liberty to martyr children by taking their very lives. As the court explained, "The right to practice religion freely does not include liberty to expose the community or child to communicable disease or the latter to ill health or death."

In an attempt to avoid this inexorable conclusion, the Church argues at length over the purportedly pivotal distinction between the governmental compulsion of a religiously objectionable act and the governmental prohibition of a religiously motivated act. Accepting arguendo the force of the distinction, we find that it has no relevance in a case involving an interest of this magnitude. As the court in Prince recognized, parents have no right to free exercise of religion at the price of a child's life, regardless of the prohibitive or compulsive nature of the governmental infringement. Furthermore, the United States Supreme Court has specifically sustained the compulsion of religiously prohibited conduct for interests no more compelling than here implicated. In *Jacobson v. Massachusetts* (1905) 197 U.S. 11, 39 . . . , the court upheld a law compelling the vaccination of children for communicable diseases in the face of parental religious objections. In *United States v. Lee* (1982) 455 U.S. 252, 261 . . . , the court upheld a law requiring that the Amish violate the tenets of their faith by participating in the Social Security system. And in *Gillette v. United States* (1971) 401 U.S. 437, 462 . . . , the court upheld the government's right to compel certain conscientious objectors to make war despite the religious character of their objections. We see no basis in these precedents for the conclusion that parents may constitutionally insulate themselves from state compulsion so long as their life-threatening religious conduct takes the form of an omission rather than an act.

The imposition of felony liability for failure to seek medical care for a seriously ill child is thus justified by a compelling state interest. To survive a First Amendment challenge, however, the policy must also represent the least restrictive alternative available to the state. Defendant and the Church argue that civil dependency proceedings advance the governmental interest in a far less intrusive manner. This is not evident. First, we have already observed the profoundly intrusive nature of such proceedings; it is not clear that parents would prefer to lose custody of their children pursuant to a disruptive and invasive judicial inquiry than to face privately the prospect of criminal liability. Second, child dependency proceedings advance the governmental interest only when the state learns of a child's illness in time to take protective measures, which quite likely will be the exception rather than the rule: "Under ordinary circumstances, . . . the case of a true believer in faith healing will not even come to the attention of the authorities, unless and until someone dies." (Comment, Religious Beliefs and the Criminal Justice System: Some Problems of the Faith Healer, supra, 8 Loyola L.A. L.Rev. at pp. 403–404.) Finally, the imposition of criminal liability is reserved for the actual loss or endangerment of a child's life and thus is narrowly tailored to those instances when governmental intrusion is absolutely compelled.

We conclude that an adequately effective and less restrictive alternative is not available to further the state's compelling interest in assuring the provision of medical care to gravely ill children whose parents refuse such treatment on religious grounds. Accordingly, the First Amendment and its California equivalent do not bar defendant's criminal prosecution. . . .

John F. Kennedy,
"Remarks on Church and State" (1960)

Editor's Introduction: John F. Kennedy (1917–1963) was the first Catholic elected to the presidency and only the second Catholic to run for our highest office, the first being Al Smith in 1928. By 1960, anti-Catholic and nativist sentiments were not as strong as they were during Smith's campaign. Nonetheless, Kennedy decided to confront the "religious question" head on, in particular, the fear of many American Protestants that a Catholic president would allow the pope to exert an influence on American politics and policy. The following remarks were presented to the Ministerial Association in Houston during the 1960 campaign. Kennedy takes what we might call a "Jeffersonian" view of the relations of church and state. Religion, he argues, is a private matter, and there should be an "absolute" separation of church and state. He claims that even on such "hot button" issues as birth control, divorce, gambling, etc., his decisions in office will be based on his perception of national interest and not on religious grounds.

*   *   *

I am grateful for your generous invitation to state my views.

While the so-called religious issue is necessarily and properly the chief topic here tonight, I want to emphasize from the outset that I believe that we have far more critical issues in the 1960 election: the spread of Communist influence, until it now festers only ninety miles off the coast of Florida—the humiliating treatment of our President and Vice-President by those who no longer respect our power—the hungry children I saw in West Virginia, the old people who cannot pay their doctor's bills, the families forced to give up their farms—an America with too many slums, with too few schools, and too late to the moon and outer space.

These are the real issues which should decide this campaign. And they are not religious issues—for war and hunger and ignorance and despair know no religious barrier.

But because I am a Catholic, and no Catholic has ever been elected President, the real issues in this campaign have been obscured—perhaps deliberately in some quarters less responsible than this. So it is apparently necessary for me to state once again—not what kind of church I believe in, for that should be important only to me, but what kind of America I believe in.

Source: The *New York Times.* September 13, 1960. Reprinted with permission.

I believe in an America where the separation of church and state is absolute—where no Catholic prelate would tell the President (should he be a Catholic) how to act and no Protestant minister would tell his parishioners for whom to vote—where no church or church school is granted any public funds or political preference—and where no man is denied public office merely because his religion differs from the President who might appoint him or the people who might elect him.

I believe in an America that is officially neither Catholic, Protestant nor Jewish—where no public official either requests or accepts instructions on public policy from the Pope, the National Council of Churches or any other ecclesiastical source—where no religious body seeks to impose its will directly or indirectly upon the general populace or the public acts of its officials—and where religious liberty is so indivisible that an act against one church is treated as an act against all.

For while this year it may be a Catholic against whom the finger of suspicion is pointed, in other years it has been, and may someday be again, a Jew—or a Quaker—or a Unitarian—or a Baptist. It was Virginia's harassment of Baptist preachers, for example, that led to Jefferson's statute of religious freedom. Today, I may be the victim—but tomorrow it may be you—until the whole fabric of our harmonious society is ripped apart at a time of great national peril.

Finally, I believe in an America where religious intolerance will someday end—where all men and all churches are treated as equal—where every man has the same right to attend or not attend the church of his choice—where there is no Catholic vote, no anti-Catholic vote, no bloc voting of any kind—and where Catholics, Protestants and Jews, both the lay and the pastoral level, will refrain from those attitudes of disdain and division which have so often marred their works in the past, and promote instead the American ideal of brotherhood.

That is the kind of America in which I believe. And it represents the kind of Presidency in which I believe—a great office that must be neither humbled by making it the instrument of any religious group, nor tarnished by arbitrarily withholding it, its occupancy, from the members of any religious group. I believe in a President whose views of religion are his own private affair, neither imposed by him upon the nation or imposed by the nation upon him as an condition to holding that office.

I would not look with favor upon a President working to subvert the First Amendment's guarantees of religious liberty (nor would our system of checks and balances permit him to do so). And neither do I look with favor upon those who would work to subvert Article VI of the Constitution by requiring a religious test—even by indirection—for if they disagree with that safeguard, they should be openly working to repeal it.

I want a Chief Executive whose public acts are responsible to all and obligated to none—who can attend any ceremony, service or dinner his office may appropriately require him to fulfill—and whose fulfillment of his Presidential office is not limited or conditioned by any religious oath, ritual or obligation.

This is the kind of America I believe in—and this is the kind of America I fought for in the South Pacific and the kind my brother died for in Europe. No one suggested then that we might have a "divided loyalty," that we did "not believe in liberty" or that we belonged to a disloyal group that threatened "the freedoms for which our forefathers died."

And in fact this is the kind of America for which our forefathers did die when they fled here to escape religious test oaths, that denied office to members of less favored churches, when they fought for the Constitution, the Bill of Rights, the Virginia Statute of Religious Freedom—and when they fought at the shrine I visited today—the Alamo. For side by side with Bowie and Crockett died Fuentes and McCafferty and Bailey and Bedillio and Carey—but no one knows whether they were Catholics or not. For there was no religious test there.

I ask you tonight to follow in that tradition, to judge me on the basis of fourteen years in the Congress—on my declared stands against unconstitutional aid to parochial schools, and against any boycott of the public schools (which I attended myself)—instead of judging me on the basis of these pamphlets and publications we have all seen that carefully select quotations out of context from the statements of Catholic Church leaders, usually in other countries, frequently in other centuries, and rarely relevant to any situation here—and always omitting, of course, that statement of the American bishops in 1948 which strongly endorsed church–state separation.

I do not consider these other quotations binding upon my public acts—why should you? But let me say, with respect to other countries, that I am wholly opposed to the state being used by any religious group, Catholic or Protestant, to compel, prohibit or persecute the free exercise of any other religion. And that goes for any persecution at any time, by anyone, in any country.

And I hope that you and I condemn with equal fervor those nations which deny their Presidency to Protestants and those which deny it to Catholics. And rather than cite the misdeeds of those who differ, I would also cite the record of the Catholic Church in such nations as France and Ireland—and the independence of such statesmen as de Gaulle and Adenauer.

But let me stress again that these are my views—for, contrary to common newspaper usage, I am not the Catholic candidate for President.

I am the Democratic Party's candidate for President, who happens also to be a Catholic.

I do not speak for my church on public matters—and the church does not speak for me.

Whatever issue may come before me as President, if I should be elected—on birth control, divorce, censorship, gambling, or any other subject—I will make my decision in accordance with these views, in accordance with what my conscience tells me to be in the national interest, and without regard to outside religious pressure or dictate. And no power or threat or punishment could cause me to decide otherwise.

But if the time should ever come—and I do not concede any conflict to be remotely possible—when my office would require me to either violate my conscience, or violate the national interest, then I would resign the office, and I hope any other conscientious public servant would do likewise.

But I do not intend to apologize for these views to my critics of either Catholic or Protestant faith, nor do I intend to disavow either my views or my church in order to win this election. If I should lose on the real issues, I shall return to my seat in the Senate, satisfied that I tried my best and was fairly judged.

But if this election is decided on the basis that 40,000,000 Americans lost their chance of being President on the day they were baptized, then it is the whole nation that will be the loser in the eyes of Catholics and non-Catholics around the world, in the eyes of history, and in the eyes of our own people.

But if, on the other hand, I should win this election, I shall devote every effort of mind and spirit to fulfilling the oath of the Presidency— practically identical, I might add, with the oath I have taken for fourteen years in Congress. For, without reservation, I can, and I quote, "solemnly swear that I will faithfully execute the office of President of the United States and will to the best of my ability preserve, protect and defend the Constitution, so help me God."

Lemon v. Kurtzman et al., 403 U.S. 602 (1971)

Editor's Introduction: The following case calls upon the Supreme Court to consider church–state relations in the fields of primary and secondary education. At issue were statutes passed by the Pennsylvania and Rhode Island legislatures. The Pennsylvania law, passed in 1968, allowed the state superintendent of schools to "purchase" certain educational services from private schools, including religious ones. This meant, in effect, that the state would reimburse parochial schools for the purchase of textbooks and other instructional materials and for teacher salaries. The law specified that state subsidies could be used only for courses with clearly secular goals and not for religious instruction. The Rhode Island statue was similar in that it allowed the state to provide a 15% supplement of teachers' salaries at private schools with low per pupil expenditures. It also specified that teachers eligible for the supplement must be teaching courses offered in public schools and could not teach religion.

It was the intent of both statutes that public funds would not be used for religious purposes. Nonetheless, the Supreme Court held that they led to "excessive entanglement" between church and state and therefore violated the free exercise and establishment clauses of the First Amendment. In the majority opinion, Chief Justice Burger sets out criteria by which it could be determined when the religious provisions of the First Amendment had been violated. His criteria, widely referred to as the "Lemon test" have been employed in many subsequent court decisions. In his dissent of the decision regarding the Rhode Island law, Justice White rejects the view that these statutes overly involve the state in religious affairs. He takes an "accommodationist" position, as opposed to one of strict separation of church and state. That is, he argues that state funding for secular purposes can be filtered through religious institutions without violating the constitution. Justice White does not appear to disagree with the criteria set forth in the majority opinion. Rather, he believes that "excessive entanglement" has not been shown to have actually occurred as a consequence of the statute in question.

*   *   *

MR. CHIEF JUSTICE BURGER delivered the opinion of the Court.

These two appeals raise questions as to Pennsylvania and Rhode Island statutes providing state aid to church-related elementary and secondary schools. Both statutes are challenged as violative of the Establishment and Free Exercise Clauses of the First Amendment and the Due Process Clause of the Fourteenth Amendment.

[Text omitted]

In *Everson v. Board of Education*, 330 U.S. 1 (1947), this Court upheld a state statute that reimbursed the parents of parochial school children for bus transportation expenses. There MR. JUSTICE BLACK, writing for the majority, suggested that the decision carried to "the verge" of forbidden territory under the Religion Clauses. Candor compels acknowledgment, moreover, that we can only dimly perceive the lines of demarcation in this extraordinarily sensitive area of constitutional law.

The language of the Religion Clauses of the First Amendment is at best opaque, particularly when compared with other portions of the Amendment. Its authors did not simply prohibit the establishment of a state church or a state religion, an area history shows they regarded as very important and fraught with great dangers. Instead they commanded that there should be "no law respecting an establishment of religion." A law may be one "respecting" the forbidden objective while falling short of its total realization. A law "respecting" the proscribed result, that is, the establishment of religion, is not always easily identifiable as one violative of the Clause. A given law might not establish a state religion but nevertheless be one "respecting" that end in the sense of being a step that could lead to such establishment and hence offend the First Amendment.   In the absence of precisely stated constitutional prohibitions, we must draw lines with reference to the three main evils against which the Establishment Clause was intended to afford protection: "sponsorship, financial support, and active involvement of the sovereign in religious activity." *Walz v. Tax Commission*, 397 U.S. 664, 668 (1970).

Every analysis in this area must begin with consideration of the cumulative criteria developed by the Court over many years. Three such tests may be gleaned from our cases. First, the statute must have a secular legislative purpose; second, its principal or primary effect must be one that neither advances nor inhibits religion, *Board of Education v. Allen*, 392 U.S. 236, 243 (1968); finally, the statute must not foster "an excessive government entanglement with religion." *Walz*, supra, at 674.

Inquiry into the legislative purposes of the Pennsylvania and Rhode Island statutes affords no basis for a conclusion that the legislative intent was to advance religion. On the contrary, the statutes themselves clearly state that they are intended to enhance the quality of the secular education in all schools covered by the compulsory attendance laws. There is no reason to believe the legislatures meant anything else. A State always has a legitimate concern for maintaining minimum standards in all schools it allows to operate. As in *Allen*, we find nothing here that undermines the stated legislative intent; it must therefore be accorded appropriate deference.

In *Allen* the Court acknowledged that secular and religious teachings were not necessarily so intertwined that secular textbooks furnished to students by the State were in fact instrumental in the teaching of religion. 392 U.S., at 248. The legislatures of Rhode Island and Pennsylvania have concluded that secular and religious education are identifiable and separable. In the abstract we have no quarrel with this conclusion.

The two legislatures, however, have also recognized that church-related elementary and secondary schools have a significant religious mission and that a substantial portion of their activities is religiously oriented. They have therefore sought to create statutory restrictions designed to guarantee the separation between secular and religious educational functions and to ensure that State financial aid supports only the former. All these provisions are precautions taken in candid recognition that these programs approached, even if they did not intrude upon, the forbidden areas under the Religion Clauses. We need not decide whether these legislative precautions restrict the principal or primary effect of the programs to the point where they do not offend the Religion Clauses, for we conclude that the cumulative impact of the entire relationship arising under the statutes in each State involves excessive entanglement between government and religion.

In *Walz v. Tax Commission,* supra, the Court upheld state tax exemptions for real property owned by religious organizations and used for religious worship. That holding, however, tended to confine rather than enlarge the area of permissible state involvement with religious institutions by calling for close scrutiny of the degree of entanglement involved in the relationship. The objective is to prevent, as far as possible, the intrusion of either into the precincts of the other.

Our prior holdings do not call for total separation between church and state; total separation is not possible in an absolute sense. Some relationship between government and religious organizations is inevitable. . . . Fire inspections, building and zoning regulations, and state requirements under compulsory school-attendance laws are examples of necessary and permissible contacts. Indeed, under the statutory exemption before us in *Walz*, the State had a continuing burden to ascertain that the exempt property was in fact being used for religious worship. Judicial caveats against entanglement must recognize that the line of separation, far from being a "wall," is a blurred, indistinct, and variable barrier depending on all the circumstances of a particular relationship.

[Text omitted]

In order to determine whether the government entanglement with religion is excessive, we must examine the character and purposes of the institutions that are benefited, the nature of the aid that the State provides, and the resulting relationship between the government and the religious authority. . . .

[Text omitted]

The substantial religious character of these church-related schools gives rise to entangling church–state relationships of the kind the Religion Clauses sought to avoid. Although the District Court found that concern for religious values did not inevitably or necessarily intrude into the content of secular subjects, the considerable religious activities of these schools led the legislature to provide for careful governmental controls and surveillance by state authorities in order to ensure that state aid supports only secular education.

The dangers and corresponding entanglements are enhanced by the particular form of aid that the Rhode Island Act provides. Our decisions from *Everson* to *Allen* have permitted the States to provide church-related schools with secular, neutral, or nonideological services, facilities, or materials. Bus transportation, school lunches, public health services, and secular textbooks supplied in common to all students were not thought to offend the Establishment Clause. We note that the dissenters in *Allen* seemed chiefly concerned with the pragmatic difficulties involved in ensuring the truly secular content of the textbooks provided at state expense.

In *Allen* the Court refused to make assumptions, on a meager record, about the religious content of the textbooks that the State would be asked to provide. We cannot, however, refuse here to recognize that teachers have a substantially different ideological character from books. In terms of potential for involving some aspect of faith or morals in secular subjects, a textbook's content is ascertainable, but a teacher's handling of a subject is not. We cannot ignore the danger that a teacher under religious control and discipline poses to the separation of the religious from the purely secular aspects of pre-college education. The conflict of functions inheres in the situation.

In our view the record shows these dangers are present to a substantial degree. The Rhode Island Roman Catholic elementary schools are under the general supervision of the Bishop of Providence and his appointed representative, the Diocesan Superintendent of Schools. . . . Religious authority necessarily pervades the school system.

[Text omitted]

We need not and do not assume that teachers in parochial schools will be guilty of bad faith or any conscious design to evade the limitations imposed by the statute and the First Amendment. We simply recognize that a dedicated religious person, teaching in a school affiliated with his or her faith and operated to inculcate its tenets, will inevitably experience great difficulty in remaining religiously neutral. Doctrines and faith are not inculcated or advanced by neutrals. With the best of intentions such a teacher would find it hard to make a total separation between secular teaching and religious doctrine. What would appear to some to be essential to good citizenship might well for others border on or constitute instruction in religion. Further difficulties are inherent in the combination of religious discipline and the possibility of disagreement between teacher and religious authorities over the meaning of the statutory restrictions.

We do not assume, however, that parochial school teachers will be unsuccessful in their attempts to segregate their religious beliefs from their secular educational responsibilities. But the potential for impermissible fostering of religion is present. The Rhode Island Legislature has not, and could not, provide state aid on the basis of a mere assumption that secular teachers under religious discipline can avoid conflicts. The State must be certain, given the Religion Clauses, that subsidized teachers do not inculcate religion—indeed the State here has undertaken to do so. To ensure that no trespass occurs, the State has therefore carefully conditioned its aid with pervasive restrictions. . . .

A comprehensive, discriminating, and continuing state surveillance will inevitably be required to ensure that these restrictions are obeyed and the First Amendment otherwise respected. Unlike a book, a teacher cannot be inspected once so as to determine the extent and intent of his or her personal beliefs and subjective acceptance of the limitations imposed by the First Amendment. These prophylactic contacts will involve excessive and enduring entanglement between state and church.

[Text omitted]

In *Walz* it was argued that a tax exemption for places of religious worship would prove to be the first step in an inevitable progression leading to the establishment of state churches and state religion. That claim could not stand up against more than 200 years of virtually universal practice imbedded in our colonial experience and continuing into the present.

The progression argument, however, is more persuasive here. We have no long history of state aid to church-related educational institutions comparable to 200 years of tax exemption for churches. Indeed, the state programs before us today represent something of an innovation. We have already noted that modern governmental programs have self-perpetuating and self-expanding propensities. These internal pressures are only enhanced when the schemes involve institutions whose legitimate needs are growing and whose interests have substantial political support. Nor can we fail to see that in constitutional adjudication some steps, which when taken were thought to approach "the verge," have become the platform for yet further steps. A certain momentum develops in constitutional theory and it can be a "downhill thrust" easily set in motion but difficult to retard or stop. . . . The dangers are increased by the difficulty of perceiving in advance exactly where the "verge" of the precipice lies. As well as constituting an independent evil against which the Religion Clauses were intended to protect, involvement or entanglement between government and religion serves as a warning signal.

Finally, nothing we have said can be construed to disparage the role of church-related elementary and secondary schools in our national life. Their contribution has been and is enormous. . . . The merit and benefits of these schools, however, are not the issue before us in these cases. The sole question is whether state aid to these schools can be squared with the dictates of the Religion Clauses. Under our system the choice has been made that government is to be entirely excluded from the area of religious instruction and churches excluded from the affairs of government. The Constitution decrees that religion must be a private matter for the individual, the family, and the institutions of private choice, and that while some involvement and entanglement are inevitable, lines must be drawn.

[Text omitted]

DISSENT: MR. JUSTICE WHITE.

It is our good fortune that the States of this country long ago recognized that instruction of the young and old ranks high on the scale of proper governmental functions and not only undertook secular education as a public responsibility but also required compulsory attendance at school by their young. Having recognized the value of educated citizens and assumed the task of educating them, the States now before us assert a right to provide for the secular education of children whether they attend public schools or choose to enter private institutions, even when those institutions are church-related. The Federal Government also asserts that it is entitled, where requested, to contribute to the cost of secular education by furnishing buildings and facilities to all institutions of higher learning, public and private alike. Both the United States and the States urge that if parents choose to have their children receive instruction in the required secular subjects in a school where religion is also taught and a religious atmosphere may prevail, part or all of the cost of such secular instruction may be paid for by governmental grants to the religious institution conducting the school and seeking the grant. Those who challenge this position would bar official contributions to secular education where the family prefers the parochial to both the public and nonsectarian private school.

The issue is fairly joined. It is precisely the kind of issue the Constitution contemplates this Court must ultimately decide. This is true although neither affirmance nor reversal of any of these cases follows automatically from the spare language of the First Amendment, from its history, or from the cases of this Court construing it and even though reasonable men can very easily and sensibly differ over the import of that language.

. . . [T]he Court is surely quite wrong in overturning the Pennsylvania and Rhode Island statutes on the ground that they amount to an establishment of religion forbidden by the First Amendment.

No one in these cases questions the constitutional right of parents to satisfy their state-imposed obligation to educate their children by sending them to private schools, sectarian or otherwise, as long as those schools meet minimum standards established for secular instruction. The States are not only permitted, but required by the Constitution, to free students attending private schools from any public school attendance obligation. . . .

[Text omitted]

Our prior cases have recognized the dual role of parochial schools in American society: they perform both religious and secular functions. . . . Our cases also recognize that legislation having a secular purpose and extending governmental assistance to sectarian schools in the performance of their secular functions does not constitute "law[s] respecting an establishment of religion" forbidden by the First Amendment merely because a secular program may incidentally benefit a church in fulfilling its religious mission. That religion may indirectly benefit from governmental aid to the secular activities of churches does not convert that aid into an impermissible establishment of religion. . . .

It is enough for me that the States and the Federal Government are financing a separable secular function of overriding importance in order to sustain the legislation here challenged. That religion and private interests other than education may substantially benefit does not convert these laws into impermissible establishments of religion.

It is unnecessary, therefore, to urge that the Free Exercise Clause of the First Amendment at least permits government in some respects to modify and mold its secular programs out of express concern for free-exercise values. See *Walz v. Tax Commission,* . . . (tax exemption for religious properties; "the limits of permissible state accommodation to religion are by no means coextensive with the noninterference mandated by the Free Exercise Clause. To equate the two would be to deny a national heritage with roots in the Revolution itself"); *Sherbert v. Verner,* 374 U.S. 398 (1963). . . . ; *Zorach v. Clauson,* supra, at 313–314 (students excused from regular public school routine to obtain religious instruction; "when the state encourages religious instruction . . . it follows the best of our traditions. For it then respects the religious nature of our people and accommodates the public service to their spiritual needs"). . . . The Establishment Clause, however, coexists in the First Amendment with the Free Exercise Clause and the latter is surely relevant in cases such as these. Where a state program seeks to ensure the proper education of its young, in private as well as public schools, free exercise considerations at least counsel against refusing support for students attending parochial schools simply because in that setting they are also being instructed in the tenets of the faith they are constitutionally free to practice.

I would sustain both the federal and the Rhode Island programs at issue in these cases, and I therefore concur in the judgment in No. 153 and dissent from the judgments in Nos. 569 and 570. Although I would also reject the facial challenge to the Pennsylvania statute, I concur in the judgment in No. 89 for the reasons given below.

The Court strikes down the Rhode Island statute on its face. No fault is found with the secular purpose of the program. . . . Nor does the Court find that the primary effect of the program is to aid religion rather than to implement secular goals. The Court nevertheless finds that impermissible "entanglement" will result from administration of the program. The reasoning is a curious and mystifying blend, but a critical factor appears to be an unwillingness to accept the District Court's express findings that on the evidence before it none of the teachers here involved mixed religious and secular instruction. . . .

[Text omitted]

The Court thus creates an insoluble paradox for the State and the parochial schools. The State cannot finance secular instruction if it permits religion to be taught in the same classroom; but if it exacts a promise that religion not be so taught—a promise the school and its teachers are quite willing and on this record able to give—and enforces it, it is then entangled in the "no entanglement" aspect of the Court's Establishment Clause jurisprudence.

[Text omitted]

With respect to Pennsylvania, the Court, accepting as true the factual allegations of the complaint, as it must for purposes of a motion to dismiss, would reverse the dismissal of the complaint and invalidate the legislation. The critical allegations, as paraphrased by the Court, are that "the church-related elementary and secondary schools are controlled by religious organizations, have the purpose of propagating and promoting a particular religious faith, and conduct their operations to fulfill that purpose." . . . From these allegations the Court concludes that forbidden entanglements would follow from enforcing compliance with the secular purpose for which the state money is being paid.

I disagree. There is no specific allegation in the complaint that sectarian teaching does or would invade secular classes supported by state funds. That the schools are operated to promote a particular religion is quite consistent with the view that secular teaching devoid of religious instruction can successfully be maintained, for good secular instruction is . . . essential to the success of the religious mission of the parochial school. I would no more here than in the Rhode Island case substitute presumption for proof that religion is or would be taught in state-financed secular courses or assume that enforcement measures would be so extensive as to border on a free exercise violation. . . .

Ralph E. Reed, Jr.,
"An Agenda for the New Congress:
Speech to the Economic Club of Detroit" (1995)

Editor's Introduction: The Christian Coalition was founded in 1989 by the televangelist Pat Robertson after his failure to win the 1988 Republican presidential nomination. The grassroots politics organization draws its support largely from evangelical and conservative Christians. Ralph Reed, the executive director since the organization's founding, is applauded by many and feared by others for his success in swelling its ranks and pocketbook. The Christian Coalition focuses upon such social and moral issues as abortion and single-parent families, choice in education, and crime. It has considerable political influence, as witnessed in the courting ritual between it and Republican presidential hopefuls.

In the following speech, Reed is greeting the 1994 election of many conservatives to a Congress under Republican leadership with considerable satisfaction. He vows to lobby vigorously for passage of House Speaker Newt Gingrich's "Contract with America." It is interesting to compare Reed's speech with that of Kennedy. Even given the obvious difference that Reed is not running for elective office, he clearly has a very different vision of the relation of religion to politics in America. He affirms the principle of separation of church and state and holds that there should be no religious test for holding office. Yet he also believes that the voices of people of faith should be heard in politics and that they should use all the techniques of influence at their disposal to affect the outcome of elections and to shape the public policy agenda.

* * *

It is an honor for me to be with you today in this, one of the nation's most distinguished forums, as we enter the most historic 100-day period in American politics since Franklin Delano Roosevelt swept into office 62 years ago.

[Text omitted]

This election signaled the largest single transfer of power from a majority party to a minority party in the 20th century. Republicans gained 52 House seats, eight Senate seats, 11 governorships, and 472 state

---

Source: The Christian Coalition, 1995. Reprinted by permission of the Christian Coalition.

legislative seats. . . . But the election was more than a partisan victory. It was a victory for ideas and ideals. It was a landslide for a particular kind of change: pro-life, pro-family, low-tax, and unapologetically committed to restoring traditional values. It was also, sadly, one of the ugliest campaigns in recent memory. For throughout this last election season, some tried to divide the American people based on their religious beliefs. In Massachusetts, a candidate for U.S. Senate was publicly attacked, not because of his stands on the issues, not because of his voting record, but because he was an elder in his church. In South Carolina, a candidate for governor was told that "his only qualifications for office are that he speaks fluently in tongues and handles snakes."

Democratic Party officials attacked churchgoing Americans as "fire-breathing fanatics" and "card-carrying members of the flat earth society." Editorialists warned that Republicans were "in the midst of a blood war for the heart and soul of their party." And "Left unchecked, [religious conservatives] could become . . . the secret weapon for Democrat's re-election." But the exact opposite occurred. They were the key to a conservative tidal wave. Exit polls found that 33 percent of all voters were self-identified born-again evangelicals or pro-family Roman Catholics. It was the largest turnout of religious voters in modern American political history. The results were astonishing. They voted 70 percent Republican and only 26 percent Democrat.

It is my fervent hope that never again will a major political party raise what John F. Kennedy once called "the so-called religion issue." At the Christian Coalition, we believe that there should be no religious test, implicit or explicit, to serve in any office of public trust. We believe anyone should be allowed to run for public office without where they attend church or synagogue ever becoming an issue. And we believe that church and state should remain separate institutions.

In that spirit, today I challenge the new chairman of the Democratic National Committee, Senator Chris Dodd of Connecticut. I call on Senator Dodd to repudiate the religious bigotry employed by his party during the last campaign, and to pledge that as national chairman he will not tolerate it in the future. In exchange, we pledge to work with the Democratic Party wherever and whenever possible to advance our mainstream agenda of lower taxes, limited government, tougher laws against crime and drugs, and a restoration of values.

The 1994 elections were also important because they gave people of faith what we have always sought: a place at the table, a sense of legitimacy, and a voice in the conversation that we call democracy. We have become a permanent fixture on the American political landscape, too large, too significant, and too diverse to be ignored by either major political party.

[Text omitted]

In the coming months we must resist the temptation to respond to the attacks that will surely come with the weapons and the words of our critics. We must remain ever cheerful, always positive, calmly confident that the basic decency and fairness of the American people will be with us in the tough days ahead. And we must do more. We must keep our message on the issues—limiting government, reducing taxes, restoring values—and not engage in the character assassination of our foes or the cult of personality among our friends.

In the words of Martin Luther King, we must also forsake violence of the fist, tongue, or heart. For that reason, it has never been more important for us to denounce violence, especially when it originates from within our own ranks. Let me state unequivocally that we renounce the recent terrorism against abortion clinics with all that we are. When demented and deranged individuals take human life in the name of life itself, they are guilty not only of hypocrisy, but of inflicting more harm to our compassionate cause of peace and non-violence than all our foes put together.

We must also remember, as Bill Clinton forgot, that simply winning an election is not synonymous with victory. Aristotle wrote, "We become brave by doing brave acts." For us this is a time for boldness. We must be brave enough to be daring, but also mature enough to be patient, never forgetting that the wheels of change turn slowly, and the levers of government must be pulled one notch at a time. It took us 60 years to get into this mess, and we will not get out of it overnight.

Ours is a time for compassion rather than cruelty, for innovation, not imitation, and for cooperation, but not compromise or capitulation. It is a time for hard heads and soft hearts. It is a time, as Abraham Lincoln said, when "The dogmas of the quiet past are inadequate to the stormy present. As our case is new, so we must think anew and act anew." Lincoln's opponent in the Civil War, Confederate leader Jefferson Davis, was once asked what it would mean if his side lost the war. "You should," he said, "put on our tombstone: death by a theory." Well, on Nov. 8, the American public chiseled the epitaph "death by a theory" on the tombstone of liberalism.

Policies once judged by the height of their aspirations are now judged by the depth of their failures and the magnitude of their casualties— casualties we read about daily in our newspapers and view nightly on our television screens. Our society—any society—cannot survive when its inner cities resemble Beirut, when children pass through metal detectors into schools that are war zones, when one out of every three children is born out of wedlock, and when an African-American male under the age of 35 in this city has a higher likelihood of being killed than an American soldier in Vietnam.

Our first step in replacing this tired, liberal order has already begun. For the next 86 days, we must simply pass the Contract with America. The Christian Coalition will do its part. We will launch the largest single lobbying effort in our history, beginning tomorrow when all fifty of our state chairmen fly to Washington to personally work for passage of the Balanced Budget Amendment. By combining old-fashioned shoe-leather politics with the technology of the information highway, we will utilize fax networks, satellite television, computerized bulletin boards, talk radio, and direct mail, we will mobilize our network of 1.5 million members and supporters in 1,425 local chapters in support of the Contract. We will spend an estimated $1 million to deluge Capitol Hill with phone calls, faxes and telegrams. Passing the Contract is critical in restoring the trust and confidence of the American people in their government.

But there is much more to be done. What will come after the Contract? Let me suggest four priorities for the new Congress to take up after the first hundred days. First, the government should promote and defend—rather than undermine—the institution of the family. As a society, we simply cannot survive another 30 years of no-fault divorce and no-consequence parenthood. The intact family is the most effective department of health, education and welfare ever conceived. Catholic lay theologian Michael Novak is right when he concludes, "If [the family] fails to teach honesty, courage, desire for excellence and a host of basic skills, it is exceedingly difficult for any other agency to make up for its failures." Our primary task, therefore, is to take power and money away from government bureaucrats in Washington and return it to parents and children. To this end, we must relieve the crushing tax burden on the American family. The average family of four now spends 38 percent of its income on taxes—more than it spends on food, clothing, housing, and recreation combined. To their credit, the Republicans have proposed a $500-per-child tax credit for middle class working families. That is a good downpayment. But we should go further by tripling or quadrupling the standard deduction for children so that no family of four in American making less than $30,000 pays a dime in federal income tax.

The federal government must no longer subsidize those agencies and programs that promote values contrary to those that we teach in our homes. Taxpayer funding for the National Endowment for the Arts, the National Endowment for the Humanities, and the Corporation for Public Broadcasting should be terminated. If we are going to ask single mothers in our inner cities to sacrifice by getting out of the wagon and helping to pull it, it is only fair that we require some sacrifice from all Americans.

We should also eliminate taxpayer subsidies that encourage family break-up and the taking of innocent human life. According to the Gallup organization, 72 percent of the American people are opposed to using tax dollars to pay for abortion. We support tightening the Hyde Amendment and ending federal subsidies that threaten human life. In addition, funding for the Legal Services Corporation, which every year pays for 200,000 divorces—more than one out of every three divorces in America— should be reduced.

I recently met with the pastor of an African-American church in one of the nation's largest cities who told me that his church sponsors ministry outreach centers to poor minority teens who are at risk for falling into a life of crime or drugs. He went into one such center and asked twelve boys, all under the age of fifteen, how many of them had a father. Not a single boy raised his hand. It is tragic enough that one of every two marriages ends in divorce, and that millions of children in our nation have never known a father or may not know anyone who has a father. It is unconscionable for the federal government to pay for family break-up with tax dollars.

Our goal is not to legislate family values, but to see to it that Washington values families. The values of faith and family that we advance are cherished in our hearts, taught in our schools, honored in our homes, and celebrated in our churches and synagogues. They are not so weak or insecure that they require the agency of the government to win their converts. But it is not too much to ask the government to be the friend rather than the foe of families. Our second priority is to radically downsize and re-limit government. The values that we espouse are learned, not mandated. These are the values taught around kitchen tables, and on fathers' knees, during bed-time stories, and at prayer meetings, midnight mass and Sabbath services. They are values that suffer when weighed down by the heavy hand of government. We subscribe to the old-fashioned wisdom that in a conservative society, traditionalist ends can be achieved through libertarian means. Anything that reduces the role of government bureaucracy and regulations out of our lives and homes is a step in the right direction. Ronald Reagan once said, "The closest thing to eternal life on earth is a federal program." For some of these programs, the time has come for a decent burial. A good first step would be to eliminate several Cabinet departments, including Commerce, Energy, Housing and Urban Development, and Education. In my view, education will be the number one social issue for the remainder of this decade, and our top legislative priority at the Christian Coalition is to abolish the Department of Education or downgrade it to agency level. We should de-federalize education policy, other than civil rights enforcement, by block granting federal functions back to states, locally elected school boards, and parents. We should return much of the $33 billion we spend at the federal level—70 percent of which never reaches the classroom—and convert it into scholarships or vouchers so that parents can send their children to the best school in their community, whether private, public or parochial.

Our third priority should be to replace the failed and discredited welfare state with a community- and charity-based opportunity society. For most of our history, welfare was not the function of government, but of homes, churches, synagogues, and civic associations like the Salvation Army. This compassionate society was defined by generosity, not by handouts and pity. In this light, the Great Society plan was not a bold new step, but a failed experiment in social engineering on a massive scale.

Glenn Loury, a brilliant economist from Boston University, who also happens to have grown up in the inner-city, said recently, "[I]n every community there are agencies of moral and cultural development that seek to shape the ways in which individuals conceive of their duties to themselves, of their obligations to each other, and of their responsibilities before God." If these institutions are not restored, through the devoted agency of the people and not their government, [it] threatens the survival of our republic."

We must replace the pity of bureaucrats with the generosity of churches and synagogues; the destructiveness of handouts with the transforming power of responsibility; the centralized approach of the Great Society with the care of responsive communities and local government. The federal government spends over $200 billion on 436 welfare programs spread out over four Cabinet departments. The current system penalizes work, discourages marriage, punishes the family, and consigns millions to hopeless poverty. It has enslaved the very people it promised to protect. We recommend consolidating most federal welfare programs in the form of block grants and returning them to the states with a few common-sense reforms. Reforms that discourage out-of-wedlock births and encourage work. Reforms that allow private and religious institutions to provide help to mothers and children in need. Reforms that reinvigorate rather than atrophy the communities. This block grant scheme should not, however, become just another massive new entitlement. The clear goal should be to eliminate, in the course of the next decade, federal involvement in welfare and shift responsibility to private charities and the faith community.

The fourth and final priority of the new Congress should be to secure religious liberty and freedom of conscience for all of our citizens. Too often, a strange hostility and scowling intolerance greets those who bring their private faith into the public square. Consider the following: In Missouri, a child caught praying silently over lunch was sent to week-long detention. In southern Illinois, a 15-year old girl was handcuffed, threatened with mace, and shoved into the back of a police car. Her crime?

Praying around the flagpole before school hours. And in Texas, a student drew a picture of his church and his family, only to have it torn up by the teacher.

We believe, as the Supreme Court ruled in *Tinker v. Des Moines School District* in 1969, that a child does not shed his right to freedom of speech when he crosses the schoolhouse gate. Earlier this year, our organization honored Bishop Knox, the African-American principal from Wingfield High School in Jackson, Mississippi who was fired for allowing his students to pray. After his dismissal, more than 4,000 people gathered at the state capitol in protest. Thirty years ago, people marched on ballot boxes and state capitols in the old Confederacy to demand the right to vote. Today, they march on those same state capitols for freedom of speech, including speech with a religious content. We are co-laborers in that struggle and we will not rest until their rights are secured.

For us the issue is much broader than voluntary school prayer. We seek to redress three decades of systematic hostility toward religious expression by government agencies, the schools, and the courts. We will propose a religious liberty statute and constitutional amendment, modeled after the Religious Freedom Restoration Act of 1993, to guarantee the right of all Americans to express their faith without fear of discrimination or persecution. These four priorities—ensuring that government is the friend rather than the foe of the family, limiting the size of government, replacing the welfare state with a compassionate society, and securing religious freedom for all—are the embodiment of our legislative agenda.

But in the end—and this is important—we will be judged as a movement not by how many precincts we organize, nor how many bills we pass into law, nor how many people are elected to office. We will be judged by how we act and by who we are. As Emerson said, "What we are speaks louder than what we say." As he began his campaign for the presidency in 1860, Abraham Lincoln addressed the students at Cooper Institute. In that speech, he urged that "all parts of this [country] shall be at peace, and in harmony with one another. Let us each do our part to have it so. Even though provoked, let us do nothing through passion or ill temper." Think about the time in which Lincoln uttered those words. Brother prepared to face brother across dark and bloody battlefields, the Union was being torn asunder, and the survival of our form of government hung in the balance. Yet Lincoln's call was for civility and respect for foes.

As we begin our crusade, may these words be more than an exhortation. They must be our own contract with ourselves, our fellow citizens, and with God, as to how we are to carry out our mission. If Lincoln's challenge becomes our challenge, and if his motto becomes our motto, then we can restore America to greatness again. Thank you and God bless you.

SUGGESTIONS FOR FURTHER READING

Robert S. Alley, ed., *James Madison on Religious Liberty* (Buffalo, NY: Prometheus Books, 1985).

Robert N. Bellah, *The Broken Covenant: American Civil Religion in Time of Trial*, second edition (Chicago: University of Chicago Press, 1992).

Sacvan Bercovitch, *The American Jeremiad* (Madison, WI: University of Wisconsin Press, 1978).

Stephen L. Carter, *The Culture of Disbelief: How American Law and Politics Trivialize Religious Devotion* (New York: Basic Books, 1993).

Roger Finke and Rodney Stark, *The Churching of America 1776–1990: Winners and Losers in Our Religious Economy* (New Brunswick, NJ: Rutgers University Press, 1992).

David J. Garrow, *Bearing the Cross: Martin Luther King and the Southern Christian Leadership Conference* (New York: William Morrow, 1986).

Edwin S. Gaustad, *A Religious History of America*, revised edition (San Francisco: Harper & Row, 1990).

Alan Heimert, *Religion and the American Mind: From the Great Awakening to the Revolution* (Cambridge, MA: Harvard University Press, 1966).

Will Herberg, *Protestant, Catholic, Jew: An Essay in American Religious Sociology*, revised edition (Garden City, NY: Anchor Books, 1960).

Leonard Levy, *The Establishment Clause: Religion and the First Amendment* (New York: Macmillan, 1986).

Perry Miller, *Roger Williams: His Contribution to the American Tradition* (New York: Atheneum, 1962).

John Courtney Murray, *We Hold These Truths: Catholic Reflections on the American Proposition* (New York: Sheed and Ward, 1960).

Reinhold Niebuhr, *Pious and Secular America* (New York: Scribner & Sons, 1958).

Sun Bear, *Buffalo Hearts: A Native American's View of Indian Culture, Religion, and History* (Spokane, WA: Bear Tribe Publishing Co., 1970).

Garry Wills, *Under God: Religion and American Politics* (New York: Simon and Schuster, 1990).

CONCLUDING ESSAY
Richard C. Sinopoli and Teena Gabrielson, Pluralism and Identity Politics Today: Three Case Studies

What does it mean to be an American? If the readings in this volume show one thing, it is that this has been a key question throughout our history. It is a question to which many different answers have been given in politics and in culture—and one that will never be resolved with finality. American identity is as much a subject of dispute today as it ever has been. Whatever the unique features of our contemporary situation, having become better informed about the ways this question has manifested itself historically, we are better equipped to deal with the issues it raises today. In this conclusion, we will explore three current examples of identity politics today, those having to do with sexual orientation and with two immigrant groups with different social characteristics and histories—Chinese- and Mexican-Americans. We will look for continuities and changes in the perceived relations between these groups and the American political community as a whole. First, some summing up is in order.

THREE MODELS OF "BEING AN AMERICAN"

Everyone whose writings are included in this collection has a unique perspective on American politics and society and on how pressing political issues pertain to his or her own life. Nonetheless, it is sometimes useful for observers to draw analytical distinctions and create typologies which enable us to see commonalities and differences more sharply. In that light, we draw a distinction among three models of Americanism derived from the readings. We call them *orthodox*, *pluralist*, and *adversarial* Americanism. Analytical distinctions are helpful tools to promote understanding but must be used with care. It is possible, for example, that a single thinker might exhibit more than one of these views of Americanism in a single work. Indeed, we think this is true in some cases. In such cases, our distinctions help us to see tensions and ambiguities in American political thought that were not visible before.

Orthodox Americanism is the view that to be an American is to be a person with a certain type of character. What this character is varies from author to author, but most commonly it consists of the following elements with variations in balance among them. To be an American is to abandon one's prior cultural attachments and to begin anew. It is, following

Hector St. John de Crevecoeur or Frederick Jackson Turner, to strip off the garments of civilization and to be reshaped by life on the farm and/ or the frontier. There the attributes of self-help, ruggedness, community solidarity, and rough-hewn democracy are fostered by the environment into which the immigrant or migrant from more settled regions is thrown.

The orthodox American is a God-fearing person and a patriot. He sees America as an exceptional nation that has much to teach the world about individual liberty, enterprise, and self-government. Lincoln takes this view of America's unique moral role in human history so far as to describe us as the "last best hope," a hope that free government, of, by, and for the people "shall not perish from the earth." The authors of **The Federalist Papers** also subscribed to a milder version of this view, insofar as Hamilton in the first Federalist Paper argues that the issue at stake in the debates over adopting the Constitution is whether men—not just Americans—can be governed by "reflection and choice" or whether their public affairs must depend upon "accident and force."

Orthodox Americanism holds that American democracy depends on such common cultural attributes or mores as those just discussed. It is not simply that these attributes describe how we are. They also describe in significant measure how we *must be* if our democracy is to work and our liberties are to be valued. Some, like Crevecoeur and Turner, seem to believe that these attributes grow naturally like seeds planted in the earth of American soil.[1] Others, like the Anti-Federalists, the Know-Nothings, and Theodore Roosevelt, take the view that they have to be nurtured by families, schools, churches, and other institutions in civil society as well as in courts of law and legislative assemblies.

It is not surprising that those who adopt the view that Americans are a special—even a chosen—people with a unique national purpose will worry that this distinct American character may be corrupted by external influences. We see this fear of corruption already in the letters of Brutus and Cato, who believe that republican political institutions rest upon a deep moral consensus about the best way to live. This consensus helps to generate high levels of mutual trust, which grows out of face-to-face contact with those not unlike ourselves. Thus, for Brutus and Cato, expansion of the powers of a national government was dangerous mainly because it would break down the commonalities of states and localities that made virtuous self-government possible.

Brutus and Cato were concerned about the political effects of diversity at a time when white Americans were much more like each other in terms of language, religion, and culture than they were later to become. With the influx of massive immigration and with the end of the abhorrent institution of slavery, orthodox Americanism took another turn. We see it expressed in the 1850s in the views of the then quite popular Know-

Nothing Party. Members of this Party and of the nativist societies out of which it grew were motivated not only by economic fears of immigrants but by concerns that foreigners raised in nondemocratic political systems that granted few personal freedoms would endanger American values. This fear extended most fully to Roman Catholics who, the Know-Nothings believed, would hold forever a deeper allegiance to the pope than to any American mayor, congressman, or President. Theodore Roosevelt also fears that a hyphenated Americanism could not be sustained and that our unique experiment in liberty and self-government was doomed if immigrants failed to become Americans "in heart and soul, in spirit and purpose...." To be an American was more than to reside within our borders and abide by our laws. It was, for Roosevelt, a way of life.

Pluralist Americanism is the view that to be an American is to hold that we must be alike in some ways that pertain directly to politics even if we differ significantly in others that pertain to particular cultural and communal attachments. Holders of this model disagree that Americans must be such in heart and soul. For them, America is a framework within which given communities who may differ a great deal in terms of culture agree to tolerate each other and to participate in political institutions that preserve and protect their rights to be themselves. The framework provides for the basic liberties to live where we choose and with whom we choose, to worship or not as we choose, to communicate freely with each other, and even to organize ourselves as interest groups and lobby government for further rights or benefits. Moreover, a government that provides such a framework deserves our allegiance. When it does not protect our freedom, as has been the case for many minorities in our past, particularly African-Americans and Native Americans, the reasons for allegiance to it are weakened.

Pluralist Americanism is expressed by W. E. B. Du Bois in his remarks on the place of the African-American in the United States, where he justifies both racial solidarity and a loyalty to the country as a whole. Blacks are Americans in "political ideals, language and religion." Further than that, he writes, Americanism need not go. The "souls of black folks," to use Du Bois' famous phrase, are their own and need not be surrendered to some homogenized, deracinated ideal of what an American ought to be. Du Bois' wishes "to make it possible for a man to be both a Negro and an American without being cursed and spit upon."[2]

Horace Kallen suggests that Americanism need not even go this far when he likens the country to a chorus or a symphony. "Our spirit," he writes, is "not a voice, but a chorus of many voices singing a different tune." The melody sung by each represents the emotional and spiritual life of each immigrant group. This melody may be harmonized with the rest, but it maintains its unique resonance.

The proponent of pluralist Americanism may believe that the range of voices in the chorus will narrow over time, i.e., that immigrants will become more homogeneous as they live longer in American society. This is an empirical judgment on the capacities of our system to foster assimilation through popular culture, schools, and other means of subjecting diverse people to similar cultural influences. He believes, however, that Americanization is not a good to be forced down the throats of immigrants or other minorities. As Edward Steiner argues in the epigraph heading Part Three, such forced Americanization is both bad policy and bad morals. We can draw an analogy to the proponent of religious freedom who might believe that religious diversity will diminish in time in the United States. If this happens through free choice it is not problematic, but if it occurs through state coercion, it clearly is.

Adversarial Americanism is the rejection of an American ideal in either its orthodox or pluralist forms. It is reducible to the belief that American society is essentially immoral and beyond saving in the liberal democratic form that we know it. Malcolm X expresses this view in claiming not to be an American and in viewing the "American dream" as a nightmare. Marcus Garvey before him adopted a similar view regarding race relations in the United States. Catharine MacKinnon and bell hooks are *adversarial Americans* as well. This is evident in the former's claim that the First Amendment and the Constitution as a whole were built upon the exclusion of women and that this is a flaw that cannot be corrected by later letting women into the system. She, along with bell hooks, and Emma Goldman before them, agree that gender equity and the realization of women's needs require a social and political system that is radically different than ours in terms, economic organization, and family structure. *Adversarial Americanism* is exhibited in a different form by religious groups like the Amish, who do not wish to change American society but do wish to withdraw from it in order to practice and preserve their religious way of life.

AMERICANISM AND POLITICS

These three models of Americanism are pervasive throughout our history, though the adversarial one has had far fewer adherents in either its revolutionary or separatist form. We would argue that most of the tensions regarding American identity—and the fit of particular communal attachments to race, ethnicity, gender, or sexual orientation with it—have occurred between adherents of orthodox and pluralist Americanism, and sometimes within the minds of given individuals who hold to both to varying degrees. We will also suggest, however, that identity politics today offers a new twist where multiculturalism in some of its forms, as well as gay and lesbian politics, adopt simultaneously a wish for inclusion and an adversarial posture. Before making this point, however, we must consider the relation between these models of Americanism and the political ideologies we have discussed throughout this book.

What we have called pluralist Americanism draws largely upon the public philosophy of liberalism as described in the introduction to this volume. Remember that liberalism as a political philosophy has always addressed itself to the problem of pluralism. Its paradigmatic question has been how people with different conceptions of the good life, religious or cultural, can live together in peace despite their disagreements over what gives their lives meaning. A contemporary American political philosopher, John Rawls, has described the goal of liberalism as creating political institutions that are the product of what he calls an "overlapping consensus."[3] The gist of this idea is not unlike the defense of pluralism offered by Horace Kallen or John Dewey.

Essentially, Rawls holds that people in liberal societies must share certain political values such as beliefs in tolerance, individual rights, and majority rule. They must likewise accept the legitimacy of political institutions, such as the judicial system which is charged with deciding cases when the rights of persons and the will of the majority conflict. What liberal citizens need not do, however, is to agree with each other on the full range of issues that concern their conceptions of what gives life meaning. The need for consensus goes only so far. Political institutions provide a framework within which people can agree to disagree. The deepest levels of human aspiration, found in faith, family, and numerous other forms of communal solidarity, are essentially private matters shielded from the power of the state. This explains the sense in which Steiner, Kallen, or Dewey can talk about hyphenated Americans or Du Bois can discuss being an American and a "Negro." My soul is nurtured in communities outside of the state and politics, but it is a *liberal politics* that preserves and protects my right to forge my identity free from the threat of coercion.

Liberalism has deep roots in American politics and society. Remember, we are speaking of liberalism as a political philosophy that has evolved over the past three hundred years, not about the contemporary ideology emerging from the New Deal. But we have never been *only* liberals, nor have we always applied our liberal principles to all peoples.[4] We treated the latter issue in our introduction and will not explore it further here. Rather, we will explore a tension between the liberal commitments most of us espouse—even those who call ourselves conservatives—and orthodox Americanism.

In holding that to be an American is to adopt a certain way of life, replete with the character traits and virtues we have discussed already, the proponent of orthodox Americanism puts himself at odds with a core value of liberalism. This is not intentional or even always observed. It would be wrong, for example, to describe Theodore Roosevelt as an enemy of liberalism. He too values individual rights, private property, and majority rule. What he and others like him may not see—or agree with—however, is that it is just as wrong for the liberal state to dictate an "American lifestyle" as it would be to establish a state religion.

This does not mean that the state must condone any and all lifestyles. Nor does it mean that the state should be indifferent to the moral conduct of its citizens. Far from it. Certain types of virtues like tolerance and a sense of fair play are essential to living together as a free people and the state has a role in inculcating them.[5] It does mean, however, that the state ought not to impose a vision of the good life on those people who merely want to be left alone to live their life as they choose so long as they respect the rights of others to do the same.

If this tolerant disposition has not been found in our history with the frequency we might like, there are reasons for this. Among them is the peculiar faith Americans have long had in their sense of historical mission, their faith in American exceptionalism. An aspect of Americans' self-image is to see ourselves as a "shining city on a hill," or as Lincoln's "last best hope" on earth, or as a nation with a "manifest destiny" to spread across a content, or as the principle defender of democracy throughout the world. While a sense of national pride is or can be praiseworthy, when it devolves into a sense of self-righteousness it makes us vulnerable to intolerance and illiberalism.

If America is seen as representing a way of life that is peculiarly virtuous, even religiously sanctioned, those who do not share that way of life are more easily viewed as impediments or threats. Thus, Native Americans are seen as standing in the way of the creation of a continental empire. Immigrants who fail to assimilate are viewed as not simply ignoring but *rejecting* a virtuous way of life, and ought to be "Americanized." In its ugliest form this moralistic Americanism leads to Congressional investigations which bear curious resemblances to religious inquisitions. The Army–McCarthy hearings of the 1950s spring to mind, as do the hearings held before the interestingly titled "House Un-American Activities Committee" (HUAC), hearings aimed at exposing nonexistent communists in government and in Hollywood.

It is an open question whether we as a people can be loyal, patriotic Americans without lapsing into what John Dewey describes as the dangerous form of nationalism, a form so prominent in the world today, that defines itself in hateful opposition to those unlike itself. There are in American history roots of both the liberal nationalism of Dewey and the intolerant boastful nationalism of the Know-Nothings and their ilk. There are also *adversarial Americans* who would contest the proposition that the United States deserves either loyalty or affection.

THE DOMINANT CULTURE AND MINORITY GROUPS: WHAT KIND OF AMERICAN AM I?

The story of American identity has two main threads: how members of the dominant culture understand themselves; and how members of minorities seeking or rejecting inclusion see their own aspirations fitting with life in the American mainstream. We have explored this story through the readings in this volume and will continue the exploration briefly here by looking at three case histories in identity politics, each with different lessons to teach about the nature of "Americanism" and its impact on individual lives today.

A. Gay and Lesbian Lifestyles: A Mixed Lesson in Identity Politics

At a recent conference of gay and lesbian writers, the playwright Edward Albee (author of *Who's Afraid of Virginia Wolfe?* and other highly acclaimed works) began a keynote address with the following observation:

> I am many things. . . . I am white; I am therefore in a minority. . . . I am a male. Therefore, I am in a minority. . . . I am deeply mired in middle age; there again I am in a minority. . . . I am a writer, which puts me in a minority; and I am gay, which also puts me in a minority. I find all of these minorities very, very interesting. I have found that none of them has gotten in my way or stopped me from saying exactly what I want to say as a writer and as everything else in my life.

Albee went on to say that he was concerned to see the gay civil rights movement tend in the direction of separatism. He did not want to see it "ghettoized." Moreover, he was a writer who was gay, not a *gay writer* if the latter meant that he had to deal only with themes concerning male homosexuals. "My intention is, and I hope that my sensibility is, such that it transcends my gayness and has something to do with the needs and pain of us all."[6]

According to one observer, Albee's remarks set off a storm of controversy at the conference and became the focus of intense debate. An ad hoc caucus of lesbians and gays of African descent found his remarks insensitive to people of color and urged that "people of color be included on every panel, and persons of color serve as moderators."[7] Others no doubt reacted strongly against Albee's rejection of the view that his being gay necessarily represented a deep commonality with other homosexuals.

In contrast to many of the other groups we have examined in this text, homosexuals do not have "ascriptive characteristics," or immediately observable traits such as skin color or gender, which allow others to instantly identify them as part of a group. This offers many gay men and lesbian women the ability to conceal their sexuality from others with whom they do not wish to share this aspect of their lives. As Andrew Sullivan, an editor for the opinion journal, *The New Republic* , states, "gay people are not uniformly discriminated against; *openly* gay people are."[8] Sullivan is not arguing that lesbians and gay men should stay "in the closet" or in any way be ashamed of their sexuality in order to promote their equal treatment. Instead, he offers this point to illustrate how the politics of homosexuality are different from those of race or gender, and to emphasize that these differences have significant consequences.

There have always been homosexuals in American society, though the visibility of gays and lesbians has increased markedly over the past twenty-five years. It was not until 1973 that the American Psychiatric Association removed homosexuality from its list of mental illnesses. This followed by four years an event that was, if not the origin, then certainly a focal point of the gay rights movement. On June 28, 1969, the New York City police raided a gay bar in Greenwich Village (located in lower Manhattan) called the Stonewall Inn. The customers of the Inn resisted and in fact barricaded the police inside the bar. This event was followed by three days of protest in which the chant of "Gay Power" frequently rang out. Stonewall was a significant step in increasing the visibility of homosexuals and has become a rallying cry of parts of the gay rights movement up to this day.[9]

Since that time, a great many more homosexuals have "come out of the closet," thereby becoming visible to the broader public and, at the same time, organizing as a political force.[10] While prejudice and violence against homosexuals are still rife, the fact that so many more homosexuals are openly so indicates the perception at least that the costs of being identified as a gay or lesbian are less than they have been in our past. Living an openly homosexual lifestyle and forging a sense of identity built around it is a more viable choice than before.

Assimilationist versus Adversarial Gay Politics

In gay and lesbian politics there are not only adversarial segments, but also "assimilationist" ones. Individuals who seek to gain social equality through working within the existing political and social institutions and who value integration with the larger society are frequently referred to as assimilationists. "Adversarial" in this context refers to a separatist strain of minimizing contact with straight society beyond what is essential and forging one's most important commitments to others within a relatively autonomous gay or lesbian community. Shane Phelan explains this divide in the context of lesbian political strategies:

> In the lesbian feminist strategy, the priority is on the creation of a community and a history that will offer the lesbian a sense of belonging rather than exclusion, positive identity through membership in a group that has a culture of its own—culture, in fact, superior to that denied them. On the other hand a "reformist" strategy has focused on the elimination of institutional and legal barriers to membership in the larger society and on the development of a sense of pride, not as lesbians per se, but as persons who are lesbian.[11]

One issue confronting gays and lesbians is which of these paths the movement ought to take. Indeed, there is some ambivalence among gays and lesbians as to whether they must represent distinct paths at all. As one writer notes, it "is possible for gay people today to live in a supportive gay community, shop at gay businesses, vacation at gay resorts, participate in gay community and cultural events, but still deny the truth of their lives to families, employers, friends and government." The same author argues, however, that the emergence and growth of such communities threatens to isolate gays in a new "lifestyle closet," where gays and lesbians withdraw from political involvement, thereby leaving important goals such as domestic partners legislation, support for AIDS funding, and antidiscrimination laws, unmet.[12] At the same time, she accepts the view that the "truth" of these people's lives is found in gay communities rather than at work or with family and straight friends. Their sexual orientation, that is, defines what is most essential about them as people.[13]

In any case, there is considerable difference of opinion among gays and lesbians as to what model of intragroup solidarity as well as what relation to heterosexual society they ought to follow. At a philosophical level, the movement is divided between a liberal wing which shares the goals of pluralist Americanism, understood as a desire to maintain a gay identity and communities that are not discriminated against and are tolerated by the broader public. On the other hand there is an adversarial strain that doubts the capacity of straights for tolerance, and in any event seeks something more than tolerance from the general public.

This confusion arises in part from the unique status of homosexuals as neither a visible nor an insular minority. Unlike African-Americans, women, or even first-generation immigrants, homosexuals have had the choice of remaining "in the closet," i.e., invisible to the heterosexual population. There is a high psychic cost in doing so, but it has been a feasible option for many. Moreover, unlike these groups, homosexuals have not been unified by obvious political or economic goals (self-identified gays and lesbians are moderately more wealthy than heterosexuals), as abolition and the franchise were bonds for African-Americans and women in the nineteenth century. Even the battle against AIDS, which has provided a political focus, is unlike these other struggles as it is widely recognized as a major social problem by gays and straights alike, and government is funding research and health benefits, even if not to the degree that activists would like. Given these factors, much of gay and lesbian politics emerges from a desire for recognition or acceptance that cannot be captured in the language of granting or respecting rights. For some, this does not mean simply to be let alone to form whatever consensual bonds one wishes. In the therapeutic language of our day, there is a desire to be "validated." This amounts to the view that I have not found my identity until I get you to accept it as being at least as good as yours. The question that arises is whether this is a demand that citizens in a liberal state can reasonably make of each other.

We can illustrate both possible answers to this question in the words of two prominent writers, one of whom is gay, the other lesbian. Andrew Sullivan rejects both the view that homosexuals should see themselves as victimized minorities needing protective legislation unique to them and that they should seek a separatist path emphasizing their differences from heterosexuals at the expense of their commonalities as human beings. Sullivan describes his politics as liberal and writes:

> This liberal politics affirms a simple and limited criterion: that all public . . . discrimination against homosexuals be ended and that every right and responsibility that heterosexuals enjoy by virtue of the state be extended to those who grow up different. And that is all. No cures or re-educations; no wrenching civil litigation; no political imposition of tolerance; merely a political attempt to enshrine formal civil equality, in the hope that eventually, the private sphere will reflect this public civility.[14]

Homosexuals have the same right to not be discriminated against in the public sphere that all people do. They do not, in Sullivan's view, have a right to be loved, admired, or "validated" by other citizens. Tolerance is as much as we can demand of our fellow citizens.

For a prominent lesbian writer, Angelia R. Wilson, tolerance is not enough.

> Such toleration, a cardinal virtue of western liberal thinking, is both in theory and in practice an accommodating minimum, and can only be seen as a substitute for equality. And while liberal political

theorists may pronounce the social value of toleration, the experience of those tolerated is not, as we learned in the 1980's, that of equality.[15]

Wilson questions whether toleration can provide the necessary foundation for equality among individuals, apparently meaning by equality some right to "equal recognition" or acceptance. She also claims that tolerance itself connotes disapproval, and therefore grants the majority group the power to define the sphere of tolerable actions. She writes,

> So can toleration be a virtue? Perhaps it is a virtue of the privileged. But to the oppressed it is experienced as a hidden untrustworthy vice. Toleration is untrustworthy because it is accompanied by pre-determined limits of what does and does not constitute acceptable action. Once these moral limits are violated, toleration lapses into moral prescription and legal alienation.[16]

Tolerance can have the connotation Wilson suggests. I am willing to tolerate actions and people even when I cannot condone them. For example, I might tolerate my sister listening to heavy metal music even though I think it is horrible. The political question is, what is the alternative to tolerance? Sullivan's view is that there is none. There is no right to equality understood as an equal validation of all lifestyles or orientations. Wilson seems to disagree, though what she would replace tolerance with is less clear.

The political goals of the adversarial strain in gay and lesbian politics are not always easy to identify. It was more common in the late 1960s and early 1970s, when "Gay Liberation" organizations were forming to link homosexuality with a revolutionary politics. In her 1973 book, *Lesbian Nation*, Jill Johnston draws out these themes. She describes a political transition of that period:

> The militant gays had moved very fast from the conservative 60's homophile organizations seeking civil libertarian reform and other appeals for integration into society as "an oppressed minority group." The militant Gay . . . conceived that Gay Liberation was an axis for revolutionary change.[17]

Such change would entail, among other things, a fundamental restructur-ing of the family—an institution described by other gay liberationists as a tool for "heterosexual programming,"—of educational institutions that also participate in "brainwashing," and an end to heterosexual sex.[18] Inter-course between men and women was described as an "invasion" of the woman and the function of a "biological inequity." Moreover, "until all women are lesbians there will be no truly political revolution."[19]

The revolutionary theme has diminished in the gay community as it has in society generally since the early 1970s. Gay radicals today appeal more to the notion of a separate "national" identity than to the political transformation of society as a whole. One such example is the gay male organization founded in the 1980s, Queer Nation. This group appropriates a term used in derision of gays as an act of defiance. They strike a confrontational tone in one of their slogans, "BASH BACK!," an angry response to violence against gays, and in a manifesto in which each subsection begins with the phrase "I hate straights . . ." and then provides a reason. In the words of one sympathetic observer,

> Queer Nation seeks to redefine the community . . . and to take it into what's been claimed as straight and visible space. "QUEERS READ THIS" asks to be read as the accompanying declaration of nationalism. It says: In this culture, being queer means that you've been condemned to death; appreciate our power and our bond; realize that whenever one of us is hurt we all suffer; know that we have to fight for ourselves because no one else will.[20]

Actions consistent with the tactics of Queer Nation are designed to call attention to differences between gays and straights and to heighten the tensions between them as a way of expressing a uniquely, and often quite angry, gay sensibility.

In sum, gay and lesbian identity politics involve two (or more) elements that are in conflict. Albee and Sullivan represent a strain we could describe as assimilationist, liberal, or pluralistic. It entails openness about one's sexual preferences but does not define those preferences as defining the "truth" of one's existence in its totality. They demand nondiscrimination and tolerance of society, but ask little more. In this view, acceptance or affirmation of one's "lifestyle" built around sexual orientation is not a civil right. Nondiscrimination in housing and employment is or should be. The adversarial strain, in contrast, demands more of society even as it expects less. This goal is a recognition that homosexuality as a lifestyle is "affirmatively good."[21] Yet, while seeking this recognition, it confronts the heterosexual society with a sharp critique of the essential institutions of civil society and government.

Another tension demonstrated in the Albee debate seems inherent in much of contemporary identity politics. No sooner is an identity affirmed than it is challenged for failing to recognize diversity within itself. Thus, "gay identity" is challenged by racial minorities as failing to give due weight to their experiences and representing the voice of the "privileged." As there are always numerous ways in which people are different (think of the differences between you and your fellow students), the question becomes which among these are deemed politically and socially significant—and why. The more the recognition of differences becomes an end in itself, the more the risk of fragmentation increases and intragroup solidarity declines.

B. Chinese-Americans: A Model Minority?

Immigrants of color have always faced obstacles to integration into American society that white immigrants have not. In the next two sections we will explore the different histories and identity struggles of two such groups. In this section we focus on Asians in the United States, with a particular attention on Chinese-Americans, who constitute the largest Asian nationality in the United States and the one with the longest history here. The ironies of this history are many, as Chinese-Americans have gone from being viewed by most whites as simply laborers who were not part of society to being a "model minority," one whose paths to success other groups should emulate. This is a different road than any other immigrant group has traveled. Yet the struggle to forge an identity that gives homage both to the customs of one's native land and to one's newfound Americanism bears similarities to the stories of other immigrant groups.

Demographics and History

The lure of the gold rush brought many people to the state of California, including many Chinese who spoke of America as the "Gold Mountain." These new immigrants came to the United States in growing numbers during the nineteenth century, numbering 35,000 in 1860, the first time the U.S. Census marked their presence, and growing to 105,000 by the year 1880.[22] These Chinese immigrants were largely male, the ratio of men to women being 33 to 1 in 1860, 29 to 2 in 1870, and 25 to 1 in both 1880 and 1890.[23] Chinese men considered themselves sojourners in the United States. Their goal was to work, earn, and save in the U.S. for a number of years and then return to their families in China—a hope that for many was never realized. Chinese men labored in manufacturing, mining, agriculture, and railroad construction in the west. Chinese workers were commended by employers for their industry, reliability, and ability to quickly learn new skills, and they were prized for their acceptance of low wages.

By the 1870s, the need for labor in California waned as an economic downturn ensued. The rising economic insecurity among white Americans soon led to an outpouring of anti-Chinese sentiment that resulted in violent attacks, economic boycotts on employers of Chinese, and legal restrictions upon the immigrants' employment. For example, in 1871, 20 Chinese men were shot, burned, or hung in one evening in Los Angeles. In 1876 and 1877 outbreaks of violence against Chinese agricultural workers occurred in the farming areas of Chico, California, by the group the Order of Caucasians. Violence toward the Chinese in the Western states was due in large part to the economic anxiety that resulted from the completion of the transcontinental railroad and the effects of a growing national economy on regional ones. The most brutal massacre took place in Hell's Canyon gorge of Oregon in 1887. Thirty-one Chinese miners were robbed, murdered, and mutilated by a white gang, none of whom were convicted for the crime.[24]

Chinese workers were consistently pushed out of many of the areas in which they had originally labored. Lee Chew writes,

> . . . it was the jealously of labouring men of other nationalities— especially the Irish—that raised all the outcry against the Chinese. No one would hire an Irishman, German, Englishman or Italian when he could get a Chinese, because our countrymen [were] so much more honest, industrious, steady, sober, and painstaking. Chinese were persecuted, not for their vices, but for their virtues. There never was any honesty in the pretended fear of leprosy or in the cheap labor scare, and the persecution continues still, because Americans make a mere [pretense] of loving justice.[25]

After the completion of the railroad and the exodus of Chinese from agricultural and mining jobs, urban residence of Chinese greatly increased. Chinatowns grew within cities and many Chinese turned to laundering and restaurants as their new source of income. These efforts did not take huge amounts of capital to begin and offered a small sense of independence to the owner of a shop or restaurant, even if it entailed endless hours of work.

In response to nativist and economic pressures, the United States Congress passed the Chinese Exclusion Act in 1882. This Act ended Chinese immigration, initially, for a period of ten years. However, it was not lifted until 1944. Immigration of Chinese to the United States did not exceed its level reached during 1871–1880, in which 123,200 arrived, until a century later; from 1971–1980, 124,300 Chinese immigrants arrived.[26] The regrowth of the Chinese population in America began when the Chinese Exclusion Act was lifted, but did not change dramatically until after the 1965 Immigration Act. This act ended the national-origins quota system and allowed 20,000 immigrants from each Eastern country to enter per year and exempted immediate family members of U.S. citizens from the quota.[27] Between 1981 and 1990 the American Chinese population increased by 102 percent.[28]

Model Minority

The post-1965 Chinese immigrants have been described by some as a "model minority," a notion that contrasts greatly with the reception of the first wave of Chinese immigrants to these shores. The "model minority" idea was first articulated by William Petersen in 1966 in reference to Japanese immigrants. Petersen drew upon the experience of the Japanese in America to note that despite discrimination, Japanese-Americans had achieved a socioeconomic status on par with that of white Americans. Petersen attributed the Japanese achievement largely to the values of family, respect for authority, and a dedication to education and hard work.[29]

This idea of a "model minority" gradually gained currency in American culture, particularly among conservatives who cited it to show that race was not an obstacle to success and that government programs to lift minorities were not required. It was soon applied universally to Asian-Americans. The 1970 census indicated that Asians were approaching income parity with native-born non-Hispanic whites. These statistics fueled the fire, and in the mid-1980s Asian success stories became a staple in news and opinion magazines and television programs like *60 Minutes*. As the notion grew, however, so did questions of its validity. Professor Bob Suzuki writes,

> [Asian] scholars analyzed the 1970 census data more closely and reached the conclusion that the model minority characterization of Asian Americans was inaccurate, misleading, and a gross over generalization. They found that while many Asians had, indeed, achieved middle class status, there was still a far larger proportion of people with incomes below the poverty level among Asians than among whites.[30]

Looking back from the 1990s, the educational and income levels of Chinese-Americans (not all Asian-Americans) are roughly on a par with those of non-Hispanic whites. In fact, Chinese-Americans surpass whites in education levels. In 1990, 35% of the Chinese female population had attained a Bachelor's degree or higher, as had 46.7% of the male population. These rates are significantly higher than those of the total population, in which 17.6% and 23.3% of females and males had achieved this level of education.[31] In terms of income, Chinese-Americans surpass whites in per capita terms and even more so in family income, due largely to the fact that more members of immigrant Chinese families are in the work force.[32] There is evidence, however, that Chinese-Americans are paid somewhat less than whites when one controls for level of education.[33] There are three possible explanations for this. First, incomes are explained both by education level and by time in the job. Since so many Chinese immigrants have arrived in the past ten or so years, they have been working for shorter periods of time compared to natives and, over time, their wages should rise. Second, language skills may in some cases prevent rising into managerial positions in firms. Third, there may be a "glass ceiling" reflecting lingering prejudices and the paucity of Chinese-Americans in "old boys networks" that impedes promotion in some firms.[34]

The Chinese-American experience in the United States is a success story when measured in conventional terms of education, income, and wealth. This is not to say that all Chinese-Americans are doing well. Their poverty rates are roughly 50% higher than those of non-Hispanic whites.[35] Nonetheless, insofar as it captures their relative success, the model minority idea has merit. However, it is also a deceptive idea, especially if its purpose is to hold Chinese-Americans up as an example to other immigrant groups.

Many more Chinese people come to America with high levels of educational skills, capital, and entrepreneurial experience than is the case with immigrants from Latin America and from other parts of Asia. Any valid comparison of attainment here would have to take into account the different starting points of different immigrant groups. Second, the "model minority" idea tends to be applied to all Asians indiscriminantly, and this obscures important differences among Asian peoples. Recent immigrants from Southeast Asia—e.g., Laos, Cambodia, and Vietnam— do not fare nearly so well as Chinese- or Japanese-Americans by the measures we have been using and should not suffer from an invidious and unjustified comparison emerging from an Asian stereotype held by non-Asian Americans. In sum, the "model minority" idea can be a polarizing one that heightens interethnic tensions, overemphasizes cultural and even racial determinants of success, and obscures relevant differences that explain the economic and educational performance of various ethnic groups.

Identity

The Chinese were first welcomed into the United States, and though they were thought to be "exotic" and foreign, their general characteristics of industry, responsibility, and perseverance were valued by employers. These stereotypical characteristics of the Chinese began to be perceived more negatively by white workers as the economy worsened and jobs became scarce. Chinese-Americans were also frequently characterized as tricky or sly. An enormously popular poem entitled "The Heathen

Chinee," written by Bret Harte for the *Overland Monthly* in 1870, depicts Chinese men as sneaky and conniving and draws upon the fear that Chinese men will enjoy economic success at the expense of white Americans. This fear is clearly stated in the *Marin Journal* in 1876,

> We have won this glorious land inch by inch from the red man in vain; we have beaten back the legions of George the Third for nothing; we have suppressed rebellion and maintained the integrity of our country for no good purpose whatever, if we are now to surrender it to a horde of Chinese, simply because they are so degraded that they can live on almost nothing, and underbid our own flesh and blood in the labor market. The people of California cannot endure it.[36]

The fear of Chinese labor was accompanied by another common fear of recent immigrants: that they could not be assimilated into American society. In an 1878 California State Senate report on the Chinese, this fear is represented.

> During the entire settlement in California they have never adapted themselves to our habits, modes of dress, or our educational system, have never learned the sanctity of an oath, never desired to become citizens, or to perform the duties of citizenship, never discovered the difference between right and wrong, never ceased the worship of their idol gods, or advanced a step beyond the musty traditions of their native hive. Impregnable to all the influences of our Anglo-Saxon life, they remain the same stolid Asiatics that have floated on the rivers and slaved in the fields of China for thirty centuries of time.[37]

We have witnessed similar complaints addressed to other immigrant groups, especially Roman Catholics from Ireland and Italy. It is made worse in this case, however, by racial bias.

Racist thought in America frequently asserts that similar traits exist across groups judged to be inferior. In the years following the Civil War, many Americans thought of blacks and Chinese in similar terms.

> White workers referred to the Chinese as 'nagurs,' and a magazine cartoon depicted the Chinese as a bloodsucking vampire with slanted eyes, a pigtail, dark skin, and thick lips. Like blacks, the Chinese were described as heathen, morally inferior, savage, childlike, and lustful. Chinese women were condemned as a 'depraved class,' and their depravity was associated with their physical appearance, which

seemed to show 'but a slight removal from the African race.' Chinese men were seen as sensuous creatures, especially interested in white women.[38]

With the closing of immigration from China and other countries in Asia, and with the segregation of many Chinese-Americans in urban neighborhoods, the tension between Asian and white Americans eased toward the end of the nineteenth century. Still, in the years between the Chinese Exclusion Act and the reintroduction of immigration from Asia, most Asian-Americans were faced with the dilemma of understanding themselves as both Asians and Americans and somehow pulling these traditions together into an identity which suited their position. Victor Wong writes, "There was endless discussion about what to do about the dilemma of being *caught in between* . . . being loyal to the parents and their ways and yet trying to assess the good from both sides. We used to call ourselves just a 'marginal man,' caught between two cultures. . . ."[39]

The notion of being caught between two cultures echoes the thoughts of W. E. B. Du Bois in the pieces reprinted in this volume. Just twelve years after Du Bois described the African-American experience in these terms, Jade Snow Wong wrote of the problems of identity for Asian-American women. After working her way through college without the help of her parents, who were committed to the education of their sons, Jade Snow must learn to walk the bridge between her home and her life as an educated American woman. She writes,

> Jade Snow no longer attempted to bring the new Western learning into her Oriental home. When she entered the Wong household, she slipped into her old pattern of withdrawal, and she performed her usual daughterly duties—. . . in the role of an obedient Chinese girl. But now she no longer felt stifled or dissatisfied, for she could return to another life in which she fitted as an individual.[40]

Like many immigrants before them, contemporary Chinese-Americans find themselves in the process of carving out an identity which can be true to their traditions and compatible with those of a multicultural American society. In this they face the same challenges of earlier immigrant groups. The success of the Chinese-Americans in the United States is explained in some part by the traditional norms and virtues we have discussed in the previous section. At the same time, success in America tends to undermine traditionalism. This is even more true today, when businesses are more mobile than ever before in search of opportunities to reduce material and labor costs. Individuals and nuclear families also become more mobile in search of employment and educational opportunities, weakening the bonds of support and the handing down of customs provided by extended families. This is especially so as the country's legal and moral climate quite rightly cease to support segregationist policies, thereby freeing minorities to leave ethnic enclaves. Old immigrants leave ethnic neighborhoods along with the communal supports they provide and integrate into the broader society as new immigrants take their place. Second- and third-generation immigrants adopt the norms and behavior patterns of their peers as much as or more than those of their parents or grandparents. In these ways, success tends to undermine the very traditions that contribute to it. These are challenges of identity that "hyphenated Americans" long have faced. Whatever the unique features of those of Chinese origin in the United States, including their past subjection to racial hatred, there is no reason to believe that Chinese-Americans will be exempt from them.

C. Mexican-Americans: Crossing Borders

History and Demographics: 1848–1930

In 1848 the Treaty of Guadalupe Hidalgo ended the Mexican-American War but firmly established enduring ethnic conflict not only between white Americans and those of Mexican descent but also between Mexicans and Mexican-Americans. The area of land acquired by the United States in the aftermath of the war covered all or parts of what are now California, Arizona, Nevada, Utah, Wyoming, Colorado, Kansas, Oklahoma, and New Mexico. It was populated by an estimated 75,000 to 100,000 Mexicans.[41] The people, trapped within the politics of warring countries and international borders, were offered two choices by United States officials: move to Mexico, or become U.S. citizens automatically in one year. With this decree, the people who had lived on this land for years before white settlers came to America became Mexican-Americans.

Acquisition of the American Southwest presented a difficult problem for many Americans. Mexicans had long been stereotyped as an inferior race in America, and the possibility of annexing Mexican land resulted in a choice between expansionism and fears of an "unassimilable race." An article in the Richmond Whig in 1846 stated, "We have far more to dread from the acquisition of a debased population who have been so summarily manufactured into American citizens than to hope from the extension of our territorial limits. . . ."[42] John C. Calhoun pronounced his displeasure by arguing that Mexicans constituted a melding of "impure races, not [even] as good as the Cherokees or Choctaws," and asked, "Can we incorporate a people so dissimilar to us in every respect—so little qualified for free and popular government—without certain destruction to our political institutions?"[43] Despite these fears, the desire for expansion prevailed.

By the beginning of the twentieth century, the proportion of Mexican-Americans owning significant tracts of land had decreased greatly. Largely due to the growth of irrigation systems in agriculture, the growing national economy provided by the newly established railroad, the high costs of litigation over land disputes, and the unfamiliarity of Mexican-Americans with American customs and procedures, Mexican-Americans found themselves occupying the lower rungs of the socioeconomic ladder and, in most areas, politically powerless.

The arrival of thousands of Mexican immigrants nearly coincided with the barring of Chinese immigrants, and the American Southwest was provided with a continuing source of cheap labor. By the late 1920s, "Mexican labor dominated most sectors of low-wage work in the Southwest" in agriculture, mining, and the railroads.[44] Clearly, Mexican workers had taken many of the menial jobs that the Chinese had been forced out of due to white Americans' fear of their success. This seeming contradiction between anti-Chinese sentiment and filling these positions by another ethnic minority was not lost upon Americans of the time. In 1911, the Dillingham Commission (a congressional panel) stated,

> Mexican immigrants are providing a fairly acceptable supply of labor in a limited territory in which it is difficult to secure others, and their competitive ability is limited because of their more or less temporary residence and their personal qualities, so that their incoming does not involve the same detriment to labor conditions as is involved in the immigration of other races who also work at comparatively low wages. While the Mexicans are not easily assimilated, this is not of very great importance as long as most of them return to their native land after a short time.[45]

The economic depression following the stock market crash of 1929 instilled anxiety and fear in the nation as a whole, and in the Southwest this led to anger over Mexican labor. The *Brawley News* editorial in 1935 ran, "There seems plenty of relief work for the aliens—but for the American pioneer, who battled scorpions, sidewinders, rattlesnakes, the ever boiling sun of the desert . . . there seems to be nothing but the scrap heap. The sooner the slogan 'America for Americans' is adopted, the sooner will Americans be given the preference in all kinds of work—instead of Aliens."[46] This sentiment and the economic turmoil of the Great Depression resulted in the repatriation of an estimated 350,000 to 600,000 persons of Mexican descent between 1929 and 1937.[47]

The repatriation of thousands of Mexican-Americans caused great pain and anxiety among this population. A single Mexican-American family may include members born in the United States, Mexican nationals, and naturalized Mexican-American citizens. This variation makes maintaining family cohesiveness more difficult and fosters tensions between Mexican-Americans settled here and recent immigrants. Given these conditions, it is not surprising that Mexican-American political and cultural elites have devoted considerable attention to the question of what it means to be a Mexican-American. In the years after the Great Depression, this question was intertwined with positions taken on Mexican immigration and on how to combat discrimination in the United States.

On Becoming Mexican-American: 1930–Present

Before the Treaty of Guadalupe Hidalgo and for some time after, Mexicans born in territories gained by the United States in the war identified primarily with their region of origin. They considered themselves to be Nuevomexicanos, Tejanos, or Californios rather than Mexicans. However, as white settlement of these areas rose, Mexican-Americans found themselves to be a smaller and increasingly discriminated against proportion of the population. They then began to identify with one another in a larger sense as people of a similar race or La Raza.[48]

Jose Vasconcelos, a Mexican philosopher who spent time in Texas around the turn of the century, is presumed to be one of the earliest promoters of this term. His philosophy is explained as follows, "*La Raza* identifies Vasconcelos' theory that the mixed races of the world, i.e., the Indian and the Mediterranean, are genetically destined to become a super-race, a *raza cosmica* that would someday inherit the earth. . . ."[49] This theory is more poetic than scientific in inspiration, as Luis Valdez, founder of El Teatro Campesino (The Farmworkers' Theater) and political activist, argues.

> That we Mexicans speak of ourselves as a 'race' is the biggest contradiction of them all. The *conquistadores*, of course, mated with their Indian women with customary abandon, creating a nation of bewildered half-breeds in countless shapes, colors and sizes. Unlike our fathers and mothers, unlike each other, we *mestizos* solved the problem with poetic license and called ourselves *la raza*. A Mexican's first loyalty— when one of us is threatened by strangers from the outside—is to that race. Either we recognize our total unity on the basis of *raza*, or the ghosts of a 100,000 feuding Indian tribes, bloods and mores will come back to haunt us.[50]

The idea of *La Raza* can be seen as a means to foster a sense of unity among Mexican-Americans in the face of white prejudice and internal differences. In this, it was at best a limited success. Tensions between United States citizens, resident aliens, and new arrivals have persisted in the presence of more or less continuous immigration.[51] Three factors appear to be the primary contributors to these tensions between Mexican-American citizens and Mexican immigrants: (1) the perception of Mexican-Americans that Mexican immigrants are an economic threat; (2) internal distinctions among Mexicans in customs and vernacular; and (3) the prejudice of white society.[52] Much of Mexican-American political activity in the United States can be seen as ways to address these tensions.

In the period of the Great Depression leading up to World War II, Mexican-Americans were faced with a window of opportunity amid the crisis. The strong rhetoric against German racism and the glorification of American democracy glaringly pointed to the racial problems within the United States. Mexican-Americans capitalized upon this contradiction, and the positions of many organized groups during this period illuminate the continued ambivalence of Mexican-Americans regarding their relation to new immigrants and to the broader American public.

The League of United Latin American Citizens (LULAC), formed in 1929, organized principally around Americanization. This organization, one of the first Mexican-American political organizations, included only United States citizens of Mexican descent. Therefore, to a certain degree it augmented the rift between Mexican immigrants and Mexican-American citizens.

> LULAC leaders consciously chose to emphasize the American side of their social identity as the primary basis for organization. Consequently, in pursuit of much-needed reforms they developed a political program designed to activate a sense of Americanism among their constituents. Considering themselves part of a progressive and enlightened leadership elite, LULAC's leaders set out to implement general goals and a political strategy that were similar in form and content to those advocated early in the century by W. E. B. DuBois and the National Association for the Advancement of Colored People: for 'an educated elite' 'to provide the masses with appropriate goals and lift them to civilization.'[53]

The goals of LULAC were defined by the need to better conditions for American citizens of Mexican descent and to conform to a model of integration and Americanization in order to reach those goals. LULAC was successful in alleviating the plight of Mexican-American citizens in many arenas, yet the organization's leaning toward Americanism resulted in positions on issues such as immigration and labor policies that emphasized only one side of the Mexican-American equation. In contrast to

LULAC, other political organizations developed to address the other side of the hyphen.

Organized in 1928, the *Confederacion de Uniones Obreras Mexicanas* (CUOM), a Mexican-American labor organization, was established to unite Mexicans residing in the United States and to promote a common ethnic identity. While both LULAC and CUOM favored an end to Mexican immigration, they differed on the political and cultural strategies and goals that Mexican-Americans should pursue in the United States. Gutierrez writes,

> Thus, where LULAC and similar groups called for a program of Americanization, naturalization, political education, and the acquisition of English as a strategy designed to facilitate Mexican-Americans' eventual amalgamation into American society, CUOM sought to conserve among its members a virtually autonomous variant of Mexican culture in the United States.[54]

By the late 1930s and 1940s another perspective on the conditions of Mexican-Americans began to emerge. The problems surrounding Mexican labor and Mexican immigration continued to be a source of discontent. Union organization of Mexican-American workers was extraordinarily difficult, given labor practices of recruiting noncitizen Mexicans to break strikes and provide cheap labor. For years, these conditions provoked animosity between Mexican-Americans and Mexican workers. However, such Mexican-Americans as communist labor leader Emma Tenayuka began to place the blame for these conditions upon American employers and the United States and Mexican governments. Tenayuka also rejected the goal of assimilation and demanded that white Americans respect the culture, work, and history of Mexican-Americans. Though this was certainly a minority perspective at the time, it provided the roots for later Mexican-American thought.

During this same period, George Sanchez, an influential scholar in the field of education and a political activist, stressed the responsibility of the United States government to Mexican-Americans and coined the term "forgotten Americans" in reference to them. Writing in 1940, Sanchez states,

> ... the national government never made due recognition of its responsibilities to the native people of the region it acquired from Mexico. It failed to take note of the fact that those people were, in effect, subject peoples of a culture and a way of life radically different from that into which they were suddenly and unwittingly thrust by a treaty. The government also failed to appreciate the fact that the

territory lacked the economic resources, the leadership, and the administrative devices necessary to launch an effective program of cultural rehabilitation.[55]

Unlike Tenayuka's Marxist views, those of Sanchez lie within a pluralist, multicultural model of democracy. In this he calls to mind Horace Kallen, but Sanchez also claims that the experience of Mexican-Americans is exceptional in that they were a native people and are therefore unlike other immigrants. He writes that the Mexican-American "is not impelled by the driving motive to become an 'American' that drive[s] the immigrants who fled Italy, or Germany, or Greece in comparatively recent years. He is at home and at ease about his culture, his language, his belongingness here."[56]

The themes we have seen expressed in the idea of *La Raza*, in the antiassimilationist views of Tenayuka, and in the multiculturalism of Sanchez were given new form in the 1960s in what has come to be known as the Chicano Movement. This movement grew out of the dislocations of the mid-1960s, the frustration of young Mexican-Americans with levels of inequality and discrimination, and the success of Cesar Chavez in organizing farm workers across California. Like Vasconcelos's notion of "la Raza," proponents of the "Chicano idea" invented a term of art to accentuate Mexican-American unity and pride of heritage. The concept of "Aztlan" grew out of this movement and refers to "the presumed ancestral homeland of the Aztecs and thus, by extension, of the Mexican people. Interpreted as the lost territories that Mexico had surrendered to the United States in 1848 after the Mexican War, to Chicano activists Aztlan represented the symbolic territorial base of the Chicano people. . . ."[57] Social worker and educator Lydia Aguirre sums up the principle ideas of the Chicano Movement as follows:

> Chicano power simply means that in the finding of identity—that is, a right to be as he is, not Mexican, not Spanish, not speaking either a 'pure' English or a 'pure' Spanish, but *as he is*, a product of a Spanish–Mexican–Indian heritage and an Anglo-Saxon (American, or, as Mexico says, Estado Unidense) influence—he will unite with his brothers in heritage. As he has pride and unity, so will he lose his self-consciousness and self-degradation and thereby will gain status and power.[58]

Between Cultures: Mexican-American Identity Politics

Mexico and the United States have been described as two countries divided by a common history. Mexico is the largest trading partner of the United States. It is a country with which we have a two thousand mile border which several hundred thousand legal and illegal immigrants cross each year, many of whom work here for a period and return to their native land. As already noted, much of the American west was acquired from Mexico through conquest. As recent political conflicts over immigration, over the North American Free Trade Agreement, and over the fall of the Mexican peso show, Mexican-American relations will play an important role in both our foreign and domestic policies and politics.

The complexities of the relation between these two great countries is mirrored in the lives of individuals who share some allegiance, however ambivalent, to each. Mexican-American writers have expressed these ambivalences in many different ways. Albert S. Herrera writes of the experience of being between two cultures in a manner which calls to mind the conflicting ideas of Theodore Roosevelt and Horace Kallen on "Americanization":

> Some citizens of Mexican descent regard the label 'Mexican-American' as an effrontery. They say that it is discriminatory and segregating. They point out that naturalized American citizens born in the various European countries are not referred to as English-Americans, German-Americans, French-Americans, or Danish-Americans. . . . The Mexican-American wants to be himself. Why should he apologize to anyone for the color of his face or the shape of his nose? Why should he hesitate to speak Spanish among other members of La Raza, . . . or to take pride in his Indian-Spanish culture? These acts can be of great value to the Mexican-American, and he is a fool to be 'assimilated' or 'acculturated' away from them. . . . And so Mexican-Americans and black Americans and Chinese-Americans and Indian Americans who are seeking a dual culture—their own and that of the European-American—are in pursuit of a wider and fuller life.[59]

Herrera stresses the benefits of identifying oneself as a member of a "dual culture." Others find that the tension between these two cultures can be so intense and extreme that it is nearly paralyzing. Enrique Hank Lopez states,

> During this phase of my childhood the cultural tug of war known as 'Americanization' almost pulled me apart. There were moments when I would identify completely with the gringo world . . . ; then quite suddenly I would feel so acutely Mexican that I would stammer over the simplest English phrase. . . . Can any of us really go home again? I, for one, am convinced that I have no true home, that I must reconcile myself to a schizo-cultural limbo, with a mere hyphen

to provide some slight cohesion between my split selves. This inevitable splitting is a plague and a pleasure.[60]

The pleasures and pains of hyphenated Americanism described by Herrera and Lopez have been experienced many times before in our history. For white ethnics, they were resolved primarily by uncoerced assimilation into middle-class society as, over time, cultural links to the country of origin grew increasingly remote. This seems a likely prospect for Chinese-Americans as well. This remoteness is less likely to be experienced by a considerable portion of the Mexican-American population, given the proximity of Mexico to the United States and the continued influx of immigrants, both of which keep a Mexican cultural option alive in some form in this country. Moreover, the value of assimilation is questioned by key opinion elites as well as by large segments of the population. This attitude, we would suggest, emerges both out of a general resurgence of ethnic pride captured today under the banner of "multiculturalism" and from an understandable frustration with the poor living conditions of many Mexican-Americans in urban and rural America. Mexican-American "identity politics" bears resemblances to the struggles of prior immigrant groups, but it is also different from them for the reasons discussed in this section.

MULTICULTURALISM AND DIVERSITY: SOME FINAL THOUGHTS

We have now explored the themes of unity and diversity, the *unum* and the *pluribus*, in many of its manifestations in American political and social thought. We have also considered in some detail the political, moral, and philosophical positions that have emerged from debates relating to the inclusion of previously excluded groups into the American political mainstream. There is one last issue for us to return to at the end of this volume. Is there too much focus today on the *pluribus* at the cost of the *unum*? Let us look briefly at the source of this concern, particularly as it relates to the politics surrounding multiculturalism.

Multiculturalism as it is commonly understood today has been a movement to introduce through education a greater appreciation of ethnic and racial differences as well, in some instances, as those based on sexual orientation. This in and of itself is a good thing. As we have said repeatedly, American history is largely a history of diversity and how best to respond to it. Recognizing the unique contributions of different types of people to American democracy is healthy and historically valuable. There are two dangers that critics see in a multicultural agenda as presented by many of its advocates in education, however. The first is that the goal of multicultural education often is aimed more at psychological uplift than it is at knowledge. The goal, that is, is not so much to better understand how given minorities have taken part in and contributed to American and world history but to improve the "self-esteem" of given groups by trumpeting their accomplishments and virtues, often at the expense of others. The second danger is that people become so absorbed in exploring and promoting their particular identities that they come to undervalue the importance of the identity they share with other Americans. They overplay differences at the expense of our commonalities as citizens. And without some sense of what we have in common, no society, least of all a democratic one, can long endure.

The potential casualties of the wrong kind of multiculturalism are, critics say, *truth* on the one hand and the ideal of *universal citizenship* on the other. Educator Diane Ravitch sums up the first view this way: "Once ethnic pride and self-esteem become the criterion for teaching history, certain things cannot be taught."[61] History becomes a morality play, as it is in the writings of one advocate of Afrocentrism, Leonard Jeffries, who divides the world into racial categories of cold, materialistic "ice" people versus warm, communalistic "sun" people and places all virtue in one category and all vice in the other. Such a simplistic story of good versus evil cannot do justice to the motivations and beliefs of real human beings. But if multicultural or, in this case, Afrocentric education takes as its aim bucking up self-esteem, there are indeed certain truths, those that reflect positively on the "victimizer" or negatively on the "oppressed," that cannot be taught.[62]

Political theorist Jean Bethke Elshtain highlights the second concern. "If one sees in democratic principles, including the insistence that we are obliged to reach out to one another rather than to entrench in our isolated groups only a cover for hidden privilege," Elshtain writes, "one stalls out as a citizen." Citizenship requires a capacity to see other people in the political community as our *peers*. They are people with whom we share the moral values that make democracy possible, such values as fairness and equal respect. We deemphasize these commonalities, Elshtain argues, at our own peril. She cites approvingly another political theorist, Sheldon Wolin, who adds that "the politics of difference and the ideology of multiculturalism have contributed [to weakening commitments to democracy] by rendering suspect the language and possibilities of . . . common action, and shared purposes."[63]

How do we assess these criticisms? The authors of this chapter have some sympathy with these concerns, even as we have described the case for a pluralist Americanism. American history should be explored with as much honesty and openness as we can muster. This is often a painful process as it is filled with much racism, bloodshed, and intolerance. We must recognize our failings, but this history should not become a simple story of good and evil, of victim and victimizers, however. A cult of victimization limits our capacity to acknowledge the valuable contributions a Thomas Jefferson or James Madison have made to developing vitally important political principles such as freedom of speech and worship. These principles are valuable whatever the moral failings of these particular individuals—who held slaves—might have been. Those who attack the political regime that embodies these principles to a considerable degree because of the moral failings of its founders owe us their best efforts in explaining how a good society could be structured in their absence. A purely adversarial multiculturalism, such as exhibited by the attack on Western culture of Stanford University students in the epigram heading Part 3, does not offer such an alternative. Indeed, it does not offer a morally guided political theory at all.

Multicultural or identity politics that lays too much stress on the victim status of minorities, ironically, undermines the important contributions truly oppressed groups have made to their own liberation. Frederick Douglass, for example, did not see himself merely as a victim in need of a boost in self-esteem. He saw a political system that permitted slavery and was wrong and he dedicated his life to changing it. He then pursued the cause of equality and dignity for all peoples in other ways, as through his support of the suffragist movement. Through it all, he maintained the kind of perspective we see displayed in his piece in this volume, in which he can recognize both the flaws and the virtues of the best white ally the slaves found, Abraham Lincoln. Thus, Douglass was not just a victim, though as a former slave he was that—he was also an active agent of change. Moreover, his tremendous pride and dignity grew not from some largely fictional identity constructed for him by Afrocentric academics, but from his willingness to express his character in morally guided political action.

At its worst, identity politics can foster the very political passivity and isolationism it purportedly seeks to combat. For Douglass, or Du Bois, or King, it was concerted, thoughtful, moral action that contributed to throwing off the negative self-image white society perpetuated among African-Americans. This moral guidance had many points of origins, both religious and humanist. These points made sense, however, only assuming a shared humanity of all peoples and a basic right to be treated justly, to which all persons are entitled. It emphasized not only identity but a capacity to *identify with* others.[64] If, on the other hand, the world is divided simply into oppressors and oppressed, victimizers and victims, the only practical guidance we can learn from this lesson is that it is better to be one rather than the other, a cynical message to be sure.

Despite our criticisms of multiculturalism as it is commonly understood in contemporary debate, we do not see that the alternative to an overemphasis on separate identities needs to be what we have called orthodox Americanism. We *are* different in ways that are worth recognizing and that can enrich us all. As the philosopher Charles Taylor argues, it is a warranted presumption that "all human cultures that have animated whole societies over some considerable period of time have something important to teach all human beings."[65] This is as true of the culture of African-Americans in the United States as it is of the cultures of immigrant groups like those of Mexican or Chinese origin. There is much we can learn from each other and many lessons that would be lost if we felt a need to be all the same. Moreover, multiculturalism properly understood can combat a certain drab uniformity that many observers from Alexis De Tocqueville to James Bryce (in this collection) have seen as a particular danger of the American way of life.

There are other practical reasons for seeing a value to multiculturalism, or what some have called "hyphenated Americanism." As Michael Walzer observed in the piece reproduced here, one vice of American society is its tendency to encourage an excessive form of individualism. Our heroes are often lonely if moralistic outsiders, played in movies by the likes of Clint Eastwood or Charles Bronson, who take on evil-doers by themselves and then leave the communities they save behind. They are celebrated in song by people like Bruce Springsteen whose characters, as in the song "Born to Run," express their rage and alienation by fleeing their homes on a motorcycle and taking to that great symbol of anonymous freedom, the American highway. We see it as well in our politics, where Americans are increasingly demanding more of government for themselves as they grow less willing to pay the taxes to support the services they demand. We see it in our residential patterns, where Americans are among the most mobile people on the earth, constantly tearing away from family and friends to seek opportunity in other parts of the country or the world.

Cultural identity is by definition a common identity, and one can make the case, as Walzer does, that virtually any form of common identity is better than none at all. Cultural identities provide moral guidance. I learn the proper ways to treat children, to interact with the elderly, to work and to pray, from my parents, aunts, and uncles, who have learned it from theirs, and so on. Cultures provide us with a rootedness, with a moral center that "rugged individualists" risk losing—and that the extreme mobility of labor and capital under contemporary economic conditions tends to undermine. This brings us to our last point on this topic.

Before urging the unalloyed good of assimilation, as critics of multiculturalism such as Arthur Schlesinger, Jr., tend to do, we should pay some attention as to what we are asking people to be assimilated. Let us explain. A recent study of Mexican-American high school students in a central California town provides some illuminating results.[66] It divided students for the purposes of the study into three segments: (1) recent Mexican immigrants who were in the United States less than five years; (2) Mexican immigrants here five or more years; and (3) American citizens of Mexican descent. The researchers found that recent immigrants displayed the lowest dropout rates and highest levels of academic achievement. They also tended to dress less "stylishly" than their peers and, according to teachers and school staff, to be more courteous and attend class more regularly than the other groups. The U.S.-born Mexicans, self-described Chicanos, not only dropped out at higher rates and attended class less frequently, but expressed the view that to do well in school was to be a "schoolboy" or a "wannabe," both terms of derision.

We should be careful not to draw hasty conclusions from one study. Nonetheless, it points to a lesson worth stressing, even if cautiously. Many Americans growing up in the poverty and despair of our inner cities, where many immigrants continue to settle, do not judge themselves by the same standards of success as does middle-class society. This is as much or more a function of class as it is of race or ethnicity. In our past, proponents of assimilation like Theodore Roosevelt took for granted that assimilation was to adopt middle-class values and desires. They also took for granted that immigrants through self-discipline, muscle, and sweat could work their way up the economic ladder and have reasonable prospects of getting those things all "right thinking" Americans want, such as a home of their own and a good education for their children.

Today we cannot accept these assumptions so uncritically. Economically, we continue to be a society with much upward mobility. However, opportunities that once existed for workers with high school education or less have declined dramatically as we move from an industrial to a postindustrial knowledge-based society. This makes higher education more vital than ever to economic success and limits the range of opportunities of those who do not have the time or resources to pursue it. As important, assimilation in too many places in our country today means adapting to a crime-ridden, drug-infested, and despairing way of life. This is a national tragedy and one to which we believe our country has grown far too callous. Nonetheless, under such conditions, the last thing we should want to do is to contribute to the weakening of immigrant cultures which can counteract these all too frequent pathologies of contemporary urban America. If anything, our public policy should aim at supporting multiculturalism properly understood and the moral resources traditions imported to our shores continue to offer.

It is up to every reader of this volume to sort out how best to harmonize the demands of universal American citizenship with a particular identification. The readings in this volume show that we are not alone in this struggle of hearts and minds. The theme of dualism, of being an American but also something else, is pervasive in American political and social thought. So is the issue of how best to allow for liberty, and thereby difference, while still maintaining enough in common to foster a society of mutual respect and toleration. This was James Madison's concern in 1787 and, for all its twists and turns since then, it is still ours today.

ENDNOTES

1. Though Turner was pessimistic that these attributes could survive the closing of the frontier. See his piece in Part 1.

2. From *The Souls of Black Folks*, quoted in Peter I. Rose, " 'Of Every Hue and Caste': Race, Immigration, and Perceptions of Pluralism," in *The Annals of the American Academy of Political and Social Science*, Vol. 530 (November 1993): 187–202.

3. John Rawls, "The Idea of an Overlapping Consensus." *Oxford Journal of Legal Studies* 7, (1971): 1–25.

4. See Rogers Smith, "Beyond Tocqueville, Myrdal, and Hartz: The Multiple Traditions in America," *American Political Science Review*, Vol. 87 (September 1993): 549–566, for a useful discussion of the dangers of ignoring illiberalism in American history.

5. William Galston, "Liberal Virtues." *American Political Science Review*, Vol. 82 (December 1988): 1277–1290.

6. Edward Albee, "One 'Minority' Speaks to Another," *Out/look* (Fall 1991), p. 18.

7. "Recommendations from the Ad Hoc Caucus of Lesbians and Gays of African Descent," *Out/look* (Fall 1991), p. 19.

8. Andrew Sullivan, "The Politics of Homosexuality," *New Republic*, (May 10, 1993): 24–37, at p. 34.

9. The 1994 Gay Games in New York City, a series of athletic events modeled on the Olympics in which homosexuals participated, were also promoted as the twenty-fifth anniversary of the Stonewall incident, for example.

10. President Bill Clinton's campaign promise to lift the ban on gays in the military, and the 1995 presidential campaign flap over Senator Robert Dole's initial acceptance and then rejection (then acceptance again) of a contribution from the Log Cabin Republicans, a gay Republican organization, are but two indications of the heightened political activism of homosexuals and some controversies associated with it.

11. Shane Phelan. *Identity Politics, Lesbian Feminism and the Limits of Community* (Philadelphia: Temple University Press, 1989), p.166.

12. Urvashi Vaid, "After Identity." *The New Republic* (May 10, 1993), p. 28.

13. This notion that one's "true," i.e., most deeply personal or spiritual existence, is found in a particular community while one works within a political framework that all such communities share has been seen before in Horace Kallen's and John Dewey's defenses of multiculturalism. The difference here is that sexual orientation, not a common land of origin with all the linguistic and cultural similarities this implies, form the basis for this "truth." The social philosopher Michel Foucault has written interestingly on this theme. Foucault points out that the notion that one's sexual identity is the core of one's being, the most fundamental definition of one's sense of self, is a peculiarly modern construct that has been enhanced in the twentieth century by the influence of Sigmund Freud and his followers. It is a notion that would have been alien to much of human civilization and one, we suspect, we would be better off without. See Michel Foucault, *History of Sexuality*, translated by Robert Hurley (New York: Pantheon Books, 1978).

14. Sullivan, "Politics of Homosexuality," p. 36.

15. Angelia R. Wilson. "Which Equality? Toleration, Difference, or Respect," in *Activating Theory: Lesbian, Gay and Bisexual Politics*, ed. Joseph Bristow and Angelia R. Wilson, (London: Lawrence & Wishart, 1993), p. 173.

16. Ibid., p. 176.

17. Jill Johnston. *Lesbian Nation: The Feminist Solution* (New York: Simon & Schuster, 1973), p. 149.

18. These phrases are from various "gay liberationist" writings discussed in Jean Bethke Elshtain, "Homosexual Politics: The Paradox of Gay Liberation," *Salmagundi* (Fall 1982-Winter 1983), pp. 252–280. On programming, Elshtain, p. 266.

19. Johnston, *Lesbian Nation*, p. 149, 166. Andrea Dworkin develops the same extreme view on the "injustice" of heterosexual sex in her book, *Intercourse* (New York: The Free Press, 1987).

20. Lauren Berlant and Elizabeth Freeman, "Queer Nationality," ed. Michael Warner, *Fear of a Queer Planet: Queer Politics and Social Theory* (Minneapolis: University of Minnesota Press, 1993), p. 198.

21. Phrase of a gay activist quoted in Elshtain, "Homosexual Politics," p. 257.

22. Gale Research Inc. Susan Gall, ed. *The Asian American Almanac* (Detroit: Gale Research Inc., 1995), p. 278.

23. Ibid.

24. Roger Daniels, *Asian America: Chinese and Japanese in the United States Since 1950* (Seattle: University of Washington Press, 1988), pp. 57–66, and Sucheng Chan, *This Bitter-Sweet Soil* (Berkeley: University of California Press, 1986), pp. 110–112, 369–386.

25. "The Life Story of a Chinaman," in *The Life Stories of Undistinguished Americans*, ed. Hamilton Holt (New York: Routledge, 1990), pp. 184–185.

26. *Asian American Almanac*, p. 279–281.

27. Ronald Takaki, *Strangers from a Different Shore* (New York: Penguin Books, 1989), p. 419.

28. *Asian American Almanac*, p. 285.

29. William Petersen. "Success Story, Japanese-American Style," *New York Times Magazine* (January 9, 1966), p. 21.

30. Bob Suzuki. "Asian Americans as the Model Minority," *Change* (November/December 1989), p. 14.

31. U.S. Department of Commerce, Economics and Statistics Administration, *We the American . . . Asians* (Bureau of the Census, Sept. 1993.), p. 4.

32. William O'Hare, "America's Minorities—The Demographics of Diversity," *Population Bulletin* 47, no. 4, (1992), p. 34, and *We the American* . . ., p. 9.

33. Herbert Baringer, Robert Gardner, and Michael Levin, *Asians and Pacific Islanders in the United States* (New York: Russell Sage Foundation, 1993), p. 266.

34. A 1988 study by the U.S. Commission on Civil Rights found that, "U.S.-born Asian American men were between 7 and 11 percent less likely to be in managerial occupations than non-Hispanic white men with the same measured characteristics. "Civil Rights Issues Facing Asian Americans in the 1990's," U.S. Commission on Civil Rights (February 1992), p. 133.

35. *We the American* . . ., p. 7.

36. *Quoted in* Elmer Clarence Sandmeyer. *The Anti-Chinese Movement in California* (Urbana: University of Illinois Press, 1973), p. 38.

37. Ibid., p. 39.

38. Takaki, *Strangers*, p. 101.

39. *Quoted in* Ibid., p. 260.

40. Jade Snow Wong. *Fifth Chinese Daughter* (New York: Harper and Brothers, 1945), p. 168.

41. David Gutierrez, *Walls and Mirrors: Mexican-Americans, Mexican Immigrants, and the Politics of Ethnicity* (Berkeley: University of California Press, 1995), p. 13.

42. Ibid., p. 16.

43. Ibid., p. 16.

44. Ibid., p. 45.

45. Ibid., p. 47.

46. Ibid., p. 72, *Brawley News*, March 15, 1935.

47. Ibid., p. 72.

48. Ibid., p. 30.

49. Ralph Guzman. *The Political Socialization of the Mexican American People* (New York: Arno Press, 1976), p. 87.

50. Luis Valdez. "The Tale of La Raza," ed. Ed Ludwig and James Santibanez, *The Chicanos: Mexican American Voices* (Baltimore: Penguin Books, 1971), pp. 95–96.

51. According to a 1992 Latino National Political Survey, 75% of Mexican-American citizens agreed with the statement that "There are too many immigrants" in the United States. Surprisingly, 84% of noncitizens of Mexican origin agreed with the same statement. A reasonable hypothesis as to why the latter number is larger is that noncitizens are more threatened by a loss of employment due to new immigration than are citizens. Cited in Jesse Laguna, "Latinos Want a Tighter Border Too," *Los Angeles Times*, Op-Ed, September 23, 1994.

52. Gutierrez, p. 59–60.

53. Ibid., p. 77.

54. Ibid., p. 104.

55. George Sanchez. excerpt from *Forgotten People*, ed. Philip Ortego, *We Are Chicanos* (New York: Washington Square Press, 1973), pp. 11–12.

56. Quoted in, Mario Garcia, *Mexican Americans* (New Haven: Yale University Press, 1989), p. 267.

57. Gutierrez, p. 185.

58. Lydia Aguirre, "The Meaning of the Chicano Movement," in *We Are Chicanos*, p. 123.

59. Albert S. Herrera. "The Mexican American in Two Cultures," in *The Chicanos: Mexican American Voices*, pp. 251–254.

60. Enrique Hank Lopez. "Back to Bachimba," in *The Chicanos: Mexican American Voices*, p. 265, 269.

61. Quoted in Arthur Schlesinger, Jr., *The Disuniting of America* (New York: WW Norton, 1992), p. 96.

62. For an excellent, historically rich treatment of the development and function of the idea of Afrocentrism, see Clarence E. Walker, *You Can't Go Home Again: The Problem with Afrocentrism* (New York: Oxford University Press, forthcoming).

63. Jean Bethke Elshtain, *Democracy on Trial* (New York: Basic Books, 1995), p. 75.

64. I borrow this phrase from Henry Louis Gates, chairman of Harvard University's Afro-American Studies Department. See his *New York Times* op/ed piece, "A Liberalism of Heart and Spine," March 27, 1994.

65. Charles Taylor, *Multiculturalism and "The Politics of Recognition": an essay* (Princeton, NJ: Princeton University Press, 1992), p. 66.

66. Results are reported in an article by two sociologists. Alejandro Portes and Min Zhou, "Should Immigrants Assimilate?" *Public Interest* 116 (Summer 1994): 18–33.

APPENDIX

THE CONSTITUTION OF THE UNITED STATES OF AMERICA

We the people of the United States, in order to form a more perfect union, establish justice, insure domestic tranquility, provide for the common defense, promote the general welfare, and secure the blessings of liberty to ourselves and our posterity, do ordain and establish this Constitution for the United States of America.

Article I

SECTION 1. All legislative powers herein granted shall be vested in a Congress of the United States, which shall consist of a Senate and House of Representatives.

SECTION 2. The House of Representatives shall be composed of members chosen every second year by the people of the several states, and the electors in each state shall have the qualifications requisite for electors of the most numerous branch of the state legislature.

No person shall be a Representative who shall not have attained to the age of twenty five years, and been seven years a citizen of the United States, and who shall not, when elected, be an inhabitant of that state in which he shall be chosen.

Representatives and direct taxes shall be apportioned among the several states which may be included within this union, according to their respective numbers, which shall be determined by adding to the whole number of free persons, including those bound to service for a term of years, and excluding Indians not taxed, three fifths of all other Persons. The actual Enumeration shall be made within three years after the first meeting of the Congress of the United States, and within every subsequent term of ten years, in such manner as they shall by law direct. The number of Representatives shall not exceed one for every thirty thousand, but each state shall have at least one Representative; and until such enumeration shall be made, the state of New Hampshire shall be entitled to chuse three, Massachusetts eight, Rhode Island and Providence Plantations one, Connecticut five, New York six, New Jersey four, Pennsylvania eight, Delaware one, Maryland six, Virginia ten, North Carolina five, South Carolina five, and Georgia three.

When vacancies happen in the Representation from any state, the executive authority thereof shall issue writs of election to fill such vacancies.

The House of Representatives shall choose their speaker and other officers; and shall have the sole power of impeachment.

SECTION 3. The Senate of the United States shall be composed of two Senators from each state, chosen by the legislature thereof, for six years; and each Senator shall have one vote.

Immediately after they shall be assembled in consequence of the first election, they shall be divided as equally as may be into three classes. The seats of the Senators of the first class shall be vacated at the expiration of the second year, of the second class at the expiration of the fourth year, and the third class at the expiration of the sixth year, so that one third may be chosen every second year; and if vacancies happen by resignation, or otherwise, during the recess of the legislature of any state, the executive thereof may make temporary appointments until the next meeting of the legislature, which shall then fill such vacancies.

No person shall be a Senator who shall not have attained to the age of thirty years, and been nine years a citizen of the United States and who shall not, when elected, be an inhabitant of that state for which he shall be chosen.

The Vice President of the United States shall be President of the Senate, but shall have no vote, unless they be equally divided.

The Senate shall choose their other officers, and also a President pro tempore, in the absence of the Vice President, or when he shall exercise the office of President of the United States.

The Senate shall have the sole power to try all impeachments. When sitting for that purpose, they shall be on oath or affirmation. When the President of the United States is tried, the Chief Justice shall preside: And no person shall be convicted without the concurrence of two thirds of the members present.

Judgment in cases of impeachment shall not extend further than to removal from office, and disqualification to hold and enjoy any office of honor, trust or profit under the United States: but the party convicted shall nevertheless be liable and subject to indictment, trial, judgment and punishment, according to law.

SECTION 4. The times, places and manner of holding elections for Senators and Representatives, shall be prescribed in each state by the legislature thereof; but the Congress may at any time by law make or alter such regulations, except as to the places of choosing Senators.

The Congress shall assemble at least once in every year, and such meeting shall be on the first Monday in December, unless they shall by law appoint a different day.

SECTION 5. Each House shall be the judge of the elections, returns and qualifications of its own members, and a majority of each shall constitute a quorum to do business; but a smaller number may adjourn from day to day, and may be authorized to compel the attendance of absent members, in such manner, and under such penalties as each House may provide.

Each House may determine the rules of its proceedings, punish its members for disorderly behavior, and, with the concurrence of two thirds, expel a member.

Each House shall keep a journal of its proceedings, and from time to time publish the same, excepting such parts as may in their judgment require secrecy; and the yeas and nays of the members of either House on any question shall, at the desire of one fifth of those present, be entered on the journal.

Neither House, during the session of Congress, shall, without the consent of the other, adjourn for more than three days, nor to any other place than that in which the two Houses shall be sitting.

SECTION 6. The Senators and Representatives shall receive a compensation for their services, to be ascertained by law, and paid out of the treasury of the United States. They shall in all cases, except treason, felony and breach of the peace, be privileged from arrest during their attendance at the session of their respective Houses, and in going to and returning from the same; and for any speech or debate in either House, they shall not be questioned in any other place.

No Senator or Representative shall, during the time for which he was elected, be appointed to any civil office under the authority of the United States, which shall have been created, or the emoluments whereof shall have been increased during such time: and no person holding any office under the United States, shall be a member of either House during his continuance in office.

SECTION 7. All bills for raising revenue shall originate in the House of Representatives; but the Senate may propose or concur with amendments as on other Bills.

Every bill which shall have passed the House of Representatives and the Senate, shall, before it become a law, be presented to the President of the United States; if he approve he shall sign it, but if not he shall return it, with his objections to that House in which it shall have originated, who shall enter the objections at large on their journal, and proceed to reconsider it. If after such reconsideration two thirds of that House shall agree to pass the bill, it shall be sent, together with the objections, to the other House, by which it shall likewise be reconsidered, and if approved by two thirds of that House, it shall become a law. But in all such cases the votes of both Houses shall be determined by yeas and nays, and the names of the persons voting for and against the bill shall be entered on the journal of each House respectively. If any bill shall not be returned by the President within ten days (Sundays excepted) after it shall have been presented to him, the same shall be a law, in like manner as if he had signed it, unless the Congress by their adjournment prevent its return, in which case it shall not be a law.

Every order, resolution, or vote to which the concurrence of the Senate and House of Representatives may be necessary (except on a question of adjournment) shall be presented to the President of the United States; and before the same shall take effect, shall be approved by him, or being disapproved by him, shall be repassed by two thirds of the Senate and House of Representatives, according to the rules and limitations prescribed in the case of a bill.

Section 8. The Congress shall have power to lay and collect taxes, duties, imposts and excises, to pay the debts and provide for the common defense and general welfare of the United States; but all duties, imposts and excises shall be uniform throughout the United States;

To borrow money on the credit of the United States;

To regulate commerce with foreign nations, and among the several states, and with the Indian tribes;

To establish a uniform rule of naturalization, and uniform laws on the subject of bankruptcies throughout the United States;

To coin money, regulate the value thereof, and of foreign coin, and fix the standard of weights and measures;

To provide for the punishment of counterfeiting the securities and current coin of the United States;

To establish post offices and post roads;

To promote the progress of science and useful arts, by securing for limited times to authors and inventors the exclusive right to their respective writings and discoveries;

To constitute tribunals inferior to the Supreme Court;

To define and punish piracies and felonies committed on the high seas, and offenses against the law of nations;

To declare war, grant letters of marque and reprisal, and make rules concerning captures on land and water;

To raise and support armies, but no appropriation of money to that use shall be for a longer term than two years;

To provide and maintain a navy;

To make rules for the government and regulation of the land and naval forces;

To provide for calling forth the militia to execute the laws of the union, suppress insurrections and repel invasions;

To provide for organizing, arming, and disciplining, the militia, and for governing such part of them as may be employed in the service of the United States, reserving to the states respectively, the appointment of the officers, and the authority of training the militia according to the discipline prescribed by Congress;

To exercise exclusive legislation in all cases whatsoever, over such District (not exceeding ten miles square) as may, by cession of particular states, and the acceptance of Congress, become the seat of the government of the United States, and to exercise like authority over all places purchased by the consent of the legislature of the state in which the same shall be, for the erection of forts, magazines, arsenals, dockyards, and other needful buildings;—And

To make all laws which shall be necessary and proper for carrying into execution the foregoing powers, and all other powers vested by this Constitution in the government of the United States, or in any department or officer thereof.

SECTION 9. The migration or importation of such persons as any of the states now existing shall think proper to admit, shall not be prohibited by the Congress prior to the year one thousand eight hundred and eight, but a tax or duty may be imposed on such importation, not exceeding ten dollars for each person.

The privilege of the writ of habeas corpus shall not be suspended, unless when in cases of rebellion or invasion the public safety may require it.

No bill of attainder or ex post facto Law shall be passed.

No capitation, or other direct, tax shall be laid, unless in proportion to the census or enumeration herein before directed to be taken.

No tax or duty shall be laid on articles exported from any state.

No preference shall be given by any regulation of commerce or revenue to the ports of one state over those of another: nor shall vessels bound to, or from, one state, be obliged to enter, clear or pay duties in another.

No money shall be drawn from the treasury, but in consequence of appropriations made by law; and a regular statement and account of receipts and expenditures of all public money shall be published from time to time.

No title of nobility shall be granted by the United States: and no person holding any office of profit or trust under them, shall, without the consent of the Congress, accept of any present, emolument, office, or title, of any kind whatever, from any king, prince, or foreign state.

SECTION 10. No state shall enter into any treaty, alliance, or confederation; grant letters of marque and reprisal; coin money; emit bills of credit; make anything but gold and silver coin a tender in payment of debts; pass any bill of attainder, ex post facto law, or law impairing the obligation of contracts, or grant any title of nobility.

No state shall, without the consent of the Congress, lay any imposts or duties on imports or exports, except what may be absolutely necessary for executing its inspection laws: and the net produce of all duties and imposts, laid by any state on imports or exports, shall be for the use of the treasury of the United States; and all such laws shall be subject to the revision and control of the Congress.

No state shall, without the consent of Congress, lay any duty of tonnage, keep troops, or ships of war in time of peace, enter into any agreement or compact with another state, or with a foreign power, or engage in war, unless actually invaded, or in such imminent danger as will not admit of delay.

Article II

SECTION 1. The executive power shall be vested in a President of the United States of America. He shall hold his office during the term of four years, and, together with the Vice President, chosen for the same term, be elected, as follows:

Each state shall appoint, in such manner as the Legislature thereof may direct, a number of electors, equal to the whole number of Senators and Representatives to which the State may be entitled in the Congress: but no Senator or Representative, or person holding an office of trust or profit under the United States, shall be appointed an elector.

The electors shall meet in their respective states, and vote by ballot for two persons, of whom one at least shall not be an inhabitant of the same state with themselves. And they shall make a list of all the persons voted for, and of the number of votes for each; which list they shall sign and certify, and transmit sealed to the seat of the government of the United States, directed to the President of the Senate. The President of the Senate shall, in the presence of the Senate and House of Representatives, open all the certificates, and the votes shall then be counted. The person having the greatest number of votes shall be the President, if such number be a majority of the whole number of electors appointed; and if there be more than one who have such majority, and have an equal number of votes, then the House of Representatives shall immediately choose by ballot one of them for President; and if no person have a majority, then from the five highest on the list the said House shall in like manner choose the President. But in choosing the President, the votes shall be taken by States, the representation from each state having one vote; A quorum for this purpose shall consist of a member or members from two thirds of the states, and a majority of all the states shall be necessary to a choice. In every case, after the choice of the President, the person having the greatest number of votes of the electors shall be the Vice President. But if there should remain two or more who have equal votes, the Senate shall choose from them by ballot the Vice President.

The Congress may determine the time of choosing the electors, and the day on which they shall give their votes; which day shall be the same throughout the United States.

No person except a natural born citizen, or a citizen of the United States, at the time of the adoption of this Constitution, shall be eligible to the office of President; neither shall any person be eligible to that office who shall not have attained to the age of thirty five years, and been fourteen years a resident within the United States.

In case of the removal of the President from office, or of his death, resignation, or inability to discharge the powers and duties of the said office, the same shall devolve on the Vice President, and the Congress may by law provide for the case of removal, death, resignation or inability, both of the President and Vice President, declaring what officer shall then act as President, and such officer shall act accordingly, until the disability be removed, or a President shall be elected.

The President shall, at stated times, receive for his services, a compensation, which shall neither be increased nor diminished during the period for which he shall have been elected, and he shall not receive within that period any other emolument from the United States, or any of them.

Before he enters on the execution of his office, he shall take the following oath or affirmation:—"I do solemnly swear (or affirm) that I will faithfully execute the office of President of the United States, and will to the best of my ability, preserve, protect and defend the Constitution of the United States."

SECTION 2. The President shall be commander in chief of the Army and Navy of the United States, and of the militia of the several states, when called into the actual service of the United States; he may require the opinion, in writing, of the principal officer in each of the executive departments, upon any subject relating to the duties of their respective offices, and he shall have power to grant reprieves and pardons for offenses against the United States, except in cases of impeachment.

He shall have power, by and with the advice and consent of the Senate, to make treaties, provided two thirds of the Senators present concur; and he shall nominate, and by and with the advice and consent of the Senate, shall appoint ambassadors, other public ministers and consuls, judges of the Supreme Court, and all other officers of the United States, whose appointments are not herein otherwise provided for, and which shall be established by law: but the Congress may by law vest the appointment of such inferior officers, as they think proper, in the President alone, in the courts of law, or in the heads of departments.

The President shall have power to fill up all vacancies that may happen during the recess of the Senate, by granting commissions which shall expire at the end of their next session.

SECTION 3. He shall from time to time give to the Congress information of the state of the union, and recommend to their consideration such measures as he shall judge necessary and expedient; he may, on extraordinary occasions, convene both Houses, or either of them, and in case of disagreement between them, with respect to the time of adjournment, he may adjourn them to such time as he shall think proper; he shall receive ambassadors and other public ministers; he shall take care that the laws be faithfully executed, and shall commission all the officers of the United States.

SECTION 4. The President, Vice President and all civil officers of the United States, shall be removed from office on impeachment for, and conviction of, treason, bribery, or other high crimes and misdemeanors.

Article III

SECTION 1. The judicial power of the United States, shall be vested in one Supreme Court, and in such inferior courts as the Congress may from time to time ordain and establish. The judges, both of the supreme and inferior courts, shall hold their offices during good behaviour, and shall, at stated times, receive for their services, a compensation, which shall not be diminished during their continuance in office.

SECTION 2. The judicial power shall extend to all cases, in law and equity, arising under this Constitution, the laws of the United States, and treaties made, or which shall be made, under their authority;—to all cases affecting ambassadors, other public ministers and consuls;—to all cases of admiralty and maritime jurisdiction;—to controversies to which the United States shall be a party;—to controversies between two or more states;—between a state and citizens of another state;—between citizens of different states;—between citizens of the same state claiming lands under grants of different states, and between a state, or the citizens thereof, and foreign states, citizens or subjects.

In all cases affecting ambassadors, other public ministers and consuls, and those in which a state shall be party, the Supreme Court shall have original jurisdiction. In all the other cases before mentioned, the Supreme Court shall have appellate jurisdiction, both as to law and fact, with such exceptions, and under such regulations as the Congress shall make.

The trial of all crimes, except in cases of impeachment, shall be by jury; and such trial shall be held in the state where the said crimes shall have been committed; but when not committed within any state, the trial shall be at such place or places as the Congress may by law have directed.

SECTION 3. Treason against the United States, shall consist only in levying war against them, or in adhering to their enemies, giving them aid and comfort. No person shall be convicted of treason unless on the testimony of two witnesses to the same overt act, or on confession in open court.

The Congress shall have power to declare the punishment of treason, but no attainder of treason shall work corruption of blood, or forfeiture except during the life of the person attainted.

Article IV

SECTION 1. Full faith and credit shall be given in each state to the public acts, records, and judicial proceedings of every other state. And the Congress may by general laws prescribe the manner in which such acts, records, and proceedings shall be proved, and the effect thereof.

SECTION 2. The citizens of each state shall be entitled to all privileges and immunities of citizens in the several states. A person charged in any state with treason, felony, or other crime, who shall flee from justice, and be found in another state, shall on demand of the executive authority of the state from which he fled, be delivered up, to be removed to the state having jurisdiction of the crime.

No person held to service or labor in one state, under the laws thereof, escaping into another, shall, in consequence of any law or regulation therein, be discharged from such service or labor, but shall be delivered up on claim of the party to whom such service or labor may be due.

SECTION 3. New states may be admitted by the Congress into this union; but no new states shall be formed or erected within the jurisdiction of any other state; nor any state be formed by the junction of two or more states, or parts of states, without the consent of the legislatures of the states concerned as well as of the Congress.

The Congress shall have power to dispose of and make all needful rules and regulations respecting the territory or other property belonging to the United States; and nothing in this Constitution shall be so construed as to prejudice any claims of the United States, or of any particular state.

SECTION 4. The United States shall guarantee to every state in this union a republican form of government, and shall protect each of them against invasion; and on application of the legislature, or of the executive (when the legislature cannot be convened) against domestic violence.

Article V

The Congress, whenever two thirds of both houses shall deem it necessary, shall propose amendments to this Constitution, or, on the application of the legislatures of two thirds of the several states, shall call a convention for proposing amendments, which, in either case, shall be valid to all intents and purposes, as part of this Constitution, when ratified by the legislatures of three fourths of the several states, or by conventions in three fourths thereof, as the one or the other mode of ratification may be proposed by the Congress; provided that no amendment which may be made prior to the year one thousand eight hundred and eight shall in any manner affect the first and fourth clauses in the ninth section of the first article; and that no state, without its consent, shall be deprived of its equal suffrage in the Senate.

Article VI

All debts contracted and engagements entered into, before the adoption of this Constitution, shall be as valid against the United States under this Constitution, as under the Confederation.

This Constitution, and the laws of the United States which shall be made in pursuance thereof; and all treaties made, or which shall be made, under the authority of the United States, shall be the supreme law of the land; and the judges in every state shall be bound thereby, anything in the Constitution or laws of any State to the contrary notwithstanding.

The Senators and Representatives before mentioned, and the members of the several state legislatures, and all executive and judicial officers, both of the United States and of the several states, shall be bound by oath or affirmation, to support this Constitution; but no religious test shall ever be required as a qualification to any office or public trust under the United States.

Article VII

The ratification of the conventions of nine states, shall be sufficient for the establishment of this Constitution between the states so ratifying the same. Done in convention by the unanimous consent of the states present the seventeenth day of September in the year of our Lord one thousand seven hundred and eighty seven and of the independence of the United States of America the twelfth.

In witness whereof We have hereunto subscribed our Names,

G. WASHINGTON
Presidt. and deputy from Virginia

New Hampshire: JOHN LANGDON, NICHOLAS GILMAN
Massachusetts: NATHANIEL GORHAM, RUFUS KING
Connecticut: WM SAML. JOHNSON, ROGER SHERMAN
New York: ALEXANDER HAMILTON
New Jersey: WIL: LIVINGSTON, DAVID BREARLY, WM. PATERSON, JONA: DAYTON
Pennsylvania: B. FRANKLIN, THOMAS MIFFLIN, ROBT. MORRIS, GEO. CLYMER, THOS. FITZSIMONS, JARED INGERSOLL, JAMES WILSON, GOUV MORRIS
Delaware: GEO: READ, GUNNING BEDFORD JUN, JOHN DICKINSON, RICHARD BASSETT, JACO: BROOM

Maryland: JAMES McHENRY, DAN OF ST THOS. JENIFER, DANL CARROLL
Virginia: JOHN BLAIR—, JAMES MADISON JR.
North Carolina: WM BLOUNT, RICHD. DOBBS SPAIGHT, HU WILLIAMSON
South Carolina: J. RUTLEDGE, CHARLES COTESWORTH PINCKNEY, CHARLES
  PINCKNEY, PIERCE BUTLER
Georgia: WILLIAM FEW, ABR BALDWIN

AMENDMENTS TO THE CONSTITUTION OF THE UNITED STATES

Amendment I   (1791)

Congress shall make no law respecting an establishment of religion, or prohibiting the free exercise thereof; or abridging the freedom of speech, or of the press; or the right of the people peaceably to assemble, and to petition the government for a redress of grievances.

Amendment II   (1791)

A well regulated militia, being necessary to the security of a free state, the right of the people to keep and bear arms, shall not be infringed.

Amendment III   (1791)

No soldier shall, in time of peace be quartered in any house, without the consent of the owner, nor in time of war, but in a manner to be prescribed by law.

Amendment IV   (1791)

The right of the people to be secure in their persons, houses, papers, and effects, against unreasonable searches and seizures, shall not be violated, and no warrants shall issue, but upon probable cause, supported by oath or affirmation, and particularly describing the place to be searched, and the persons or things to be seized.

Amendment V   (1791)

No person shall be held to answer for a capital, or otherwise infamous crime, unless on a presentment or indictment of a grand jury, except in cases arising in the land or naval forces, or in the militia, when in actual service in time of war or public danger; nor shall any person be subject for the same offense to be twice put in jeopardy of life or limb; nor shall be compelled in any criminal case to be a witness against himself, nor be deprived of life, liberty, or property, without due process of law; nor shall private property be taken for public use, without just compensation.

Amendment VI   (1791)

In all criminal prosecutions, the accused shall enjoy the right to a speedy and public trial, by an impartial jury of the state and district wherein the crime shall have been committed, which district shall have been previously ascertained by law, and to be informed of the nature and cause of the accusation; to be confronted with the witnesses against him; to have compulsory process for obtaining witnesses in his favor, and to have the assistance of counsel for his defense.

Amendment VII   (1791)

In suits at common law, where the value in controversy shall exceed twenty dollars, the right of trial by jury shall be preserved, and no fact tried by a jury, shall be otherwise reexamined in any court of the United States, than according to the rules of the common law.

Amendment VIII   (1791)

Excessive bail shall not be required, nor excessive fines imposed, nor cruel and unusual punishments inflicted.

Amendment IX   (1791)

The enumeration in the Constitution, of certain rights, shall not be construed to deny or disparage others retained by the people.

Amendment X   (1791)

The powers not delegated to the United States by the Constitution, nor prohibited by it to the states, are reserved to the states respectively, or to the people.

Amendment XI   (1798)

The judicial power of the United States shall not be construed to extend to any suit in law or equity, commenced or prosecuted against one of the United States by citizens of another state, or by citizens or subjects of any foreign state.

Amendment XII   (1804)

The electors shall meet in their respective states and vote by ballot for President and Vice-President, one of whom, at least, shall not be an inhabitant of the same state with themselves; they shall name in their ballots the person voted for as President, and in distinct ballots the person voted for as Vice-President, and they shall make distinct lists of all persons voted for as President, and of all persons voted for as Vice-President, and of the number of votes for each, which lists they shall sign and certify, and transmit sealed to the seat of the government of the United States, directed to the President of the Senate;—The President of the Senate shall, in the presence of the Senate and House of Representatives, open all the certificates and the votes shall then be counted;—the person having the greatest number of votes for President, shall be the President, if such number be a majority of the whole number of electors appointed; and if no person have such majority, then from the persons having the highest numbers not exceeding three on the list of those voted for as President, the House of Representatives shall choose immediately, by ballot, the President. But in choosing the President, the votes shall be taken by states, the representation from each state having one vote; a quorum for this purpose shall consist of a member or members from two-thirds of the states, and a majority of all the states shall be necessary to a choice. And if the House of Representatives shall not choose a President whenever the right of choice shall devolve upon them, before the fourth day of March next following, then the Vice-President shall act as President, as in the case of the death or other constitutional disability of the President. The person having the greatest number of votes as Vice-President, shall be the Vice-President, if such number be a majority of the whole number of electors appointed, and if no person have a majority, then from the two highest numbers on the list, the Senate shall choose the Vice-President; a quorum for the purpose shall consist of two-thirds of the whole number of Senators, and a majority of the whole number shall be necessary to a choice. But no person constitutionally ineligible to the office of President shall be eligible to that of Vice-President of the United States.

Amendment XIII   (1865)

SECTION 1. Neither slavery nor involuntary servitude, except as a punishment for crime whereof the party shall have been duly convicted, shall exist within the United States, or any place subject to their jurisdiction.

SECTION 2. Congress shall have power to enforce this article by appropriate legislation.

Amendment XIV   (1868)

SECTION 1. All persons born or naturalized in the United States, and subject to the jurisdiction thereof, are citizens of the United States and of the state wherein they reside. No state shall make or enforce any law which shall abridge the privileges or immunities of citizens of the United States; nor shall any state deprive any person of life, liberty, or property, without due process of law; nor deny to any person within its jurisdiction the equal protection of the laws.

SECTION 2. Representatives shall be apportioned among the several states according to their respective numbers, counting the whole number of persons in each state, excluding Indians not taxed. But when the right to vote at any election for the choice of electors for President and Vice President of the United States, Representatives in Congress, the executive and judicial officers of a state, or the members of the legislature thereof, is denied to any of the male inhabitants of such state, being twenty-one years of age, and citizens of the United States, or in any way abridged, except for participation in rebellion, or other crime, the basis of representation therein shall be reduced in the proportion which the number of such male citizens shall bear to the whole number of male citizens twenty-one years of age in such state.

SECTION 3. No person shall be a Senator or Representative in Congress, or elector of President and Vice President, or hold any office, civil or military, under the United States, or under any state, who, having previously taken an oath, as a member of Congress, or as an officer of the United States, or as a member of any state legislature, or as an executive or judicial officer of any state, to support the Constitution of the United States, shall have engaged in insurrection or rebellion against the same, or given aid or comfort to the enemies thereof. But Congress may by a vote of two-thirds of each House, remove such disability.

SECTION 4. The validity of the public debt of the United States, authorized by law, including debts incurred for payment of pensions and bounties for services in suppressing insurrection or rebellion, shall not be questioned. But neither the United States nor any state shall assume or pay any debt or obligation incurred in aid of insurrection or rebellion against the United States, or any claim for the loss or emancipation of any slave; but all such debts, obligations and claims shall be held illegal and void.

SECTION 5. The Congress shall have power to enforce, by appropriate legislation, the provisions of this article.

Amendment XV (1870)

SECTION 1. The right of citizens of the United States to vote shall not be denied or abridged by the United States or by any state on account of race, color, or previous condition of servitude.

SECTION 2. The Congress shall have power to enforce this article by appropriate legislation.

Amendment XVI (1913)

The Congress shall have power to lay and collect taxes on incomes, from whatever source derived, without apportionment among the several states, and without regard to any census of enumeration.

Amendment XVII (1913)

The Senate of the United States shall be composed of two Senators from each state, elected by the people thereof, for six years; and each Senator shall have one vote. The electors in each state shall have the qualifications requisite for electors of the most numerous branch of the state legislatures.

When vacancies happen in the representation of any state in the Senate, the executive authority of such state shall issue writs of election to fill such vacancies: Provided, that the legislature of any state may empower the executive thereof to make temporary appointments until the people fill the vacancies by election as the legislature may direct.

This amendment shall not be so construed as to affect the election or term of any Senator chosen before it becomes valid as part of the Constitution.

Amendment XVIII (1919)

SECTION 1. After one year from the ratification of this article the manufacture, sale, or transportation of intoxicating liquors within, the importation thereof into, or the exportation thereof from the United States and all territory subject to the jurisdiction thereof for beverage purposes is hereby prohibited.

SECTION 2. The Congress and the several states shall have concurrent power to enforce this article by appropriate legislation.

SECTION 3. This article shall be inoperative unless it shall have been ratified as an amendment to the Constitution by the legislatures of the several states, as provided in the constitution, within seven years from the date of the submission hereof to the states by the Congress.

Amendment XIX (1920)

The right of citizens of the United States to vote shall not be denied or abridged by the United States or by any state on account of sex. Congress shall have power to enforce this article by appropriate legislation.

Amendment XX (1933)

SECTION 1. The terms of the President and Vice President shall end at noon on the 20th day of January, and the terms of Senators and Representatives at noon on the 3d day of January, of the years in which such terms would have ended if this article had not been ratified; and the terms of their successors shall then begin.

SECTION 2. The Congress shall assemble at least once in every year, and such meeting shall begin at noon on the 3d day of January, unless they shall by law appoint a different day.

SECTION 3. If, at the time fixed for the beginning of the term of the President, the President elect shall have died, the Vice President elect shall become President. If a President shall not have been chosen before the time fixed for the beginning of his term, or if the President elect shall have failed to qualify, then the Vice President elect shall act as President until a President shall have qualified; and the Congress may by law provide for the case wherein neither a President elect nor a Vice President elect shall have qualified, declaring who shall then act as President, or the manner in which one who is to act shall be selected, and such person shall act accordingly until a President or Vice President shall have qualified.

SECTION 4. The Congress may by law provide for the case of the death of any of the persons from whom the House of Representatives may choose a President whenever the right of choice shall have devolved upon them, and for the case of the death of any of the persons from whom the Senate may choose a Vice President whenever the right of choice shall have devolved upon them.

SECTION 5. Sections 1 and 2 shall take effect on the 15th day of October following the ratification of this article.

SECTION 6. This article shall be inoperative unless it shall have been ratified as an amendment to the Constitution by the legislatures of three-fourths of the several states within seven years from the date of its submission.

Amendment XXI   (1933)

SECTION 1. The eighteenth article of amendment to the Constitution of the United States is hereby repealed.

SECTION 2. The transportation or importation into any state, territory, or possession of the United States for delivery or use therein of intoxicating liquors, in violation of the laws thereof, is hereby prohibited.

SECTION 3. This article shall be inoperative unless it shall have been ratified as an amendment to the Constitution by conventions in the several states, as provided in the Constitution, within seven years from the date of the submission hereof to the states by the Congress.

Amendment XXII   (1951)

SECTION 1. No person shall be elected to the office of the President more than twice, and no person who has held the office of President, or acted as President, for more than two years of a term to which some other person was elected President shall be elected to the office of the President more than once.

But this article shall not apply to any person holding the office of President when this article was proposed by the Congress, and shall not prevent any person who may be holding the office of President, or acting as President, during the term within which this article becomes operative from holding the office of President or acting as President during the remainder of such term.

Section 2. This article shall be inoperative unless it shall have been ratified as an amendment to the Constitution by the legislatures of three-fourths of the several states within seven years from the date of its submission to the states by the Congress.

Amendment XXIII (1961)

Section 1. The District constituting the seat of government of the United States shall appoint in such manner as the Congress may direct: A number of electors of President and Vice President equal to the whole number of Senators and Representatives in Congress to which the District would be entitled if it were a state, but in no event more than the least populous state; they shall be in addition to those appointed by the states, but they shall be considered, for the purposes of the election of President and Vice President, to be electors appointed by a state; and they shall meet in the District and perform such duties as provided by the twelfth article of amendment.

Section 2. The Congress shall have power to enforce this article by appropriate legislation.

Amendment XXIV (1964)

Section 1. The right of citizens of the United States to vote in any primary or other election for President or Vice President, for electors for President or Vice President, or for Senator or Representative in Congress, shall not be denied or abridged by the United States or any state by reason of failure to pay any poll tax or other tax.

Section 2. The Congress shall have power to enforce this article by appropriate legislation.

Amendment XXV (1967)

Section 1. In case of the removal of the President from office or of his death or resignation, the Vice President shall become President.

Section 2. Whenever there is a vacancy in the office of the Vice President, the President shall nominate a Vice President who shall take office upon confirmation by a majority vote of both Houses of Congress.

Section 3. Whenever the President transmits to the President pro tempore of the Senate and the Speaker of the House of Representatives his written declaration that he is unable to discharge the powers and duties of his office, and until he transmits to them a written declaration to the contrary, such powers and duties shall be discharged by the Vice President as Acting President.

SECTION 4. Whenever the Vice President and a majority of either the principal officers of the executive departments or of such other body as Congress may by law provide, transmit to the President pro tempore of the Senate and the Speaker of the House of Representatives their written declaration that the President is unable to discharge the powers and duties of his office, the Vice President shall immediately assume the powers and duties of the office as Acting President.

Thereafter, when the President transmits to the President pro tempore of the Senate and the Speaker of the House of Representatives his written declaration that no inability exists, he shall resume the powers and duties of his office unless the Vice President and a majority of either the principal officers of the executive department or of such other body as Congress may by law provide, transmit within four days to the President pro tempore of the Senate and the Speaker of the House of Representatives their written declaration that the President is unable to discharge the powers and duties of his office. Thereupon Congress shall decide the issue, assembling within forty-eight hours for that purpose if not in session. If the Congress, within twenty-one days after receipt of the latter written declaration, or, if Congress is not in session, within twenty-one days after Congress is required to assemble, determines by two-thirds vote of both Houses that the President is unable to discharge the powers and duties of his office, the Vice President shall continue to discharge the same as Acting President; otherwise, the President shall resume the powers and duties of his office.

Amendment XXVI   (1971)

SECTION 1. The right of citizens of the United States, who are 18 years of age or older, to vote, shall not be denied or abridged by the United States or any state on account of age.

SECTION 2. The Congress shall have the power to enforce this article by appropriate legislation.

Amendment XXVII

No law varying the compensation for the services of the Senators and Representatives shall take effect until an election of Representatives shall have intervened.

CPSIA information can be obtained
at www.ICGtesting.com
Printed in the USA
BVHW031325150520
579774BV00001B/1